D0152153

Housing and Racial/Ethnic Minority Status in the United States

Recent Titles in
Bibliographies and Indexes in Sociology

HOUSING AND RACIAL/ETHNIC MINORITY STATUS IN THE UNITED STATES

AN ANNOTATED BIBLIOGRAPHY WITH A REVIEW ESSAY

JAMSHID A. MOMENI

Foreword by Christopher Silver
Preface by Robert D. Bullard

BIBLIOGRAPHIES AND INDEXES IN SOCIOLOGY, NUMBER 8

GREENWOOD PRESS
NEW YORK • WESTPORT, CONNECTICUT • LONDON

Library of Congress Cataloging-in-Publication Data

Momeni, Jamshid A., 1938-
   Housing and racial/ethnic minority status in the
United States.

(Bibliographies and indexes in sociology,
ISSN 0742-6895 ; no. 8)
   Includes indexes.
   1. Minorities—Housing—United States—Bibliography.
I. Title. II. Series.
Z7164.H8M64 1987   016.3635'9   86-27089
[HD7288.72.U5]
ISBN 0-313-24820-6 (lib. bdg. : alk. paper)

Library of Congress Catalog Card Number: 86-27089
ISBN: 0-313-24820-6
ISSN: 0742-6895

First published in 1987

Greenwood Press, Inc.
88 Post Road West, Westport, Connecticut 06881

Printed in the United States of America

The paper used in this book complies with the
Permanent Paper Standard issued by the National
Information Standards Organization (Z39.48-1984).

10 9 8 7 6 5 4 3 2 1

TO
MY FATHER

Who left us forever, but he taught me
something that never leaves me
The least return from trying and failing is to learn
To fail to try is to suffer from the
unestimable loss of what could have been learned

CONTENTS

FIGURE AND TABLES

FOREWORD

Even after nearly twenty years of federally mandated equal opportunity in housing, we have yet to make good on the commitment to safe, decent, and affordable housing for minorities in the United States. This is not to suggest that there has been no change in the status of minorities as measured by the quality of housing since the enactment of Title VIII of the Civil Rights Act of 1968. To the contrary, the past two decades have witnessed more profound changes in housing than any comparable period in the twentieth century. In the process, however, the principal problem for minorities (and low-income Americans in general) of segregation in substandard housing has been compounded and complicated by an array of new problems, flowing directly from sweeping changes in the overall housing market.

Housing affordability and value now constitute two critical factors in assessing the housing status of minorities. Even though substandard housing persists as an impediment to progress in minority communities, the 1980 census substantiates the continued reduction of this traditional measure of housing status. At the same time, shifts in the locus of minority communities from the center city to the periphery of many urban areas underscores the persistence of a filtering process, enabling low income groups to improve the quality of their housing as the overall housing stock increases.

Yet, in the face of these seemingly positive trends in minority housing, a growing body of literature is questioning the traditional measures of progress and posing a new research agenda oriented to the changing face of the housing market and its implications for low-income and minority groups. A number of key questions emerge from this reexamination of minority housing status. For example, to what extent has minority suburbanization been accompanied by resegregation in the face of fair housing initiatives? Has home ownership increased among minorities and provided upward economic mobility through improved housing values, or are minorities still restricted by income and discrimination to the least desirable and least valuable units? Directly related to this is the increasing cost of owner-occupied and rental housing secured by minorities, not only in absolute terms, but also as a proportion of their income. With limited additions to the subsidized housing stock and erosion of the public housing component, especially since 1980, how have the low-income minorities been affected in their search for affordable shelter?

Finally, the relevance of exploring the issue of affordability as a decisive measure of housing quality is particularly germane to the problems faced by a growing elderly population, and by those who, for various reasons directly attributable to housing market dynamics, make up the ranks of the "homeless." It is evident that the recent move toward a market approach in meeting housing needs has brought about a shift in the orientation of housing research to better gauge the impacts of this change on minorities. As of yet, however, no attempt has been made to assemble new findings into a synthetic package.

Professor Momeni's *Housing and Racial/Ethnic Minority Status in the United States* takes an important first step toward a comprehensive understanding of the complexities of the minority housing market over the past two decades. In an extended introductory review essay, Momeni examines the leading indicators of housing differentials by race and ethnicity as revealed in the 1980 census. This is particularly useful since so much of the available literature on minority housing has relied heavily upon the 1970 data. Yet the heart of the work is the more than one thousand detailed bibliographic entries running the gamut of issues related to the housing status of minorities. These carefully constructed summaries of the research literature cover topics such as redlining, fair housing, the impacts of various housing initiatives (including subsidized and public housing), the problems of the elderly and the homeless, and special attention to the policy debates that impact upon housing for minorities.

Momeni's annotated entries not only summarize the latest research but, more importantly, organize that literature in such a way as to shift the focus of housing analysis from the traditional concern for condition to one that incorporates the housing market approach. While it is obvious that researchers will benefit from this succinct and complete collation of the minority housing literature, *Housing and Racial/Ethnic Minority Status in the United States* offers more than a new reference tool. Its unique contribution is to supply an assessment of housing research that can, and should, be used by policy makers at all governmental levels to evaluate the effects of past endeavors in shaping future directions in the housing field.

Christopher Silver
Associate Professor
Urban Studies and Planning
Virginia Commonwealth University
August 1986

PREFACE

The goal of decent, safe, and sanitary housing for all Americans has not been achieved after nearly five decades of federal legislation, Presidential mandates, and government initiatives. Government intervention into the housing industry has not affected all segments of society in the same way. Federal policies, for example, have played a central role in the development of spatially differentiated metropolitan areas in which blacks and other visible ethnic minorities are segregated from whites, and the poor from the more affluent households. Moreover, the nation's racial and ethnic minorities have not benefited from the changing housing opportunity structure to the same extent as their white counterparts.

Home ownership, nevertheless, remains an integral part of the "American Dream." At present, over two-thirds of the nation's households own their homes. The shift after World War II from a nation of renters to one of home owners has not been equally distributed across all segments of society. Moreover, the benefits that accrue to home ownership have by-passed millions of Americans. This is particularly true for the poor, blacks, and other ethnic minorities. For example, the decade of the seventies saw the home ownership rates for whites rise from 65 percent to 68 percent by 1980. Black home ownership rates were 42 percent in 1970 and 44 percent in 1980. The housing options (owning vs. renting) that are available to the nation's racial and ethnic minorities have been shaped largely by individual and institutional discrimination, spatial location and geographic concentration of the minority population, housing construction priorities, and inadequate incomes which may preclude ownership.

Minority housing is inextricably tied to both race and economic conditions. The nation's racial and ethnic minorities as a group pay a higher proportion of their income for housing, are more likely to live in older and/or inadequate residences, and are less likely to own the housing in their neigh-

borhoods. Inability to afford housing, however, is not just limited to minority households. Less than one-fifth of the nation's white families and only
one-tenth of the nation's black families could afford the average price of a
new house (more than $70,000) in 1979. The end result of inadequate
income of minority households has meant reduced housing choices, decreased mobility, overcrowded and segregated housing concentrated in central cities, and limited wealth accumulation from lack of home ownership.

Inadequate housing and the nation's ethnic minorities are disproportionately clustered in central city neighborhoods. Nearly one-third of all
metropolitan housing units and approximately one-half of all inadequate
housing units are located in central cities. Despite the various governmental
efforts over the past several decades, housing inadequacy has been increasing
in the country's large urban areas. The bulk of single-family homes built in
the 1970s and early 1980s were concentrated in suburbia. The primary benefactors of suburban housing expansion were whites, households with above
average income, and former home owners who had accumulated equity
capital to finance the down payment for a suburban home.

The housing literature is rather diverse and no general consensus has been
reached in terms of the action plans or strategies for addressing minority
housing needs. However, there is general agreement that the artificial
barriers to free choice in the housing market and the residuals of the nation's
"apartheid-type" housing policies need be removed. The various forms
of discrimination have contributed to the decline of many central city neighborhoods, have confined many minority residents to segregated and often
overcrowded areas, and have denied a substantial segment of the American
society a basic form of investment: home ownership. The federal government working alone cannot eliminate the institutional barriers to free
choice. Efforts to strengthen federal fair housing laws will need to be coordinated jointly with state and local fair housing efforts and incorporate strong
enforcement provisions.

Recent trends suggest that minority and lower-income households can
expect less from government in terms of housing subsidies and programs to
stimulate ownership and production of new housing. Federally assisted
housing for low and moderate income households has occupied a lower
priority in recent years, and the lack of a coherent national urban policy is a
clear signal to an uncertain future regarding urban centers and housing for
the poor.

Dr. Momeni has assembled in this unique and timely 12-chapter volume
the first and the most comprehensive annotated bibliography of works on
housing and minority status in the United States. The 1,007 citations are
quite extensive and conveniently organized into major topical areas including housing condition, discrimination and redlining, residential segregation,
fair housing and integration, rental housing (and rent control), home
ownership, housing subsidy, public housing, housing regulations and litiga-

tion, elderly housing, housing policies and politics, and homelessness. In short, it is the most exhaustive synthesis of major literature on minority housing ever brought together in one volume. The lead essay, "Minority Housing Differentials: Analyses of Data from 1980 Census," is of particular value. Professor Momeni, utilizing the latest available and comparable data, discusses the main indicators of minority housing differentials among major minority groups in the country—blacks, American Indians, Asian Americans, and Hispanics. The value of the lead essay lies in the author's ability not only to provide his readers with previous research findings, but also to bring them up-to-date on the status of minority housing.

Housing and Racial/Ethnic Minority Status in the United States is an excellent reference book on minority housing issues. For years to come, this book will be of great utility to individuals who are interested in issues which revolve around resource allocation and equity, as well as public officials and private industry representatives who are largely responsible for shaping and reshaping the nation's housing policies. It is an excellent source book for academicians, planners, urban sociologists, and community activists alike, as it provides easy access to the state of research under one cover, organized in the best academic tradition.

Robert D. Bullard
Associate Professor
Texas Southern University
August, 1986

ACKNOWLEDGMENTS

Without the work of the authors who are cited here, this book would not have been possible. I am truly indebted to all the contributors listed in the *Author Index* and their respective publishers.

While working on this volume, I wrote letters to a number of authors requesting copies/reprints of their publications. Their positive responses not only saved me time and expense, but most importantly, provided me with additional incentive to proceed with the completion of this volume. They are: Shirley Better, Robert D. Bullard, Suzanne Bianchi, Donald O. Cowgill, Joe T. Darden, Anthony Downs, John E. Farley, Reynolds Farley, Arnold R. Hirsch, William Hojnacki, Mary Jo Huth, Mary R. Jackman, Robert W. Jackman, John F. Kain, Jill Khadduri, Stanley Lieberson, Douglas S. Massey, John M. Quigley, Juliet Saltman, Christopher Silver, Daphne Spain, David Varady, John M. Weicher, and Anthony Yezer. The notes of encouragement that accompanied the reprints from some of the original authors are particularly appreciated. The support by Dr. Lawrence E. Gary, director of the Institute for Urban Affairs and Research, Howard University, is appreciated.

Special thanks are due to my wife, Mahvash, for her moral and material supports, and for her taking care of various family chores as I worked on this volume. There is no suitable compensation, but I am deeply indebted to my sons, with whom I had hardly any time to spend during the project.

PROLOGUE

This is a companion volume to an earlier work, *Race, Ethnicity, and Minority Housing in the United States* (Greenwood Press, 1986). While the earlier work is an edited collection of 11 articles dealing with housing problems of blacks, American Indians, Asian Americans, and Hispanics in the United States, this volume presents an up-dated article and 1,007 selected annotated references on racial and ethnic minority housing in the country. Each citation is provided with adequate annotation covering the main purpose, data, method, findings, and its conclusion(s). The lead article analyzes the minority housing differentials using the latest census data. The purpose of the lead essay has *not* been to review or repeat what other researches have found previously, but rather aims to assess the qualitative and quantitative aspects of the minority housing conditions as of 1980.

This prologue considers two major topics: (a) the rationale for pursuing this project, and (b) the method and organization of this volume.

(a) *The Rationale*: Every U.S. census taken—particularly since 1940— has revealed significant new developments in the housing conditions of Americans. Prior to the 1980 census, however, comparable data for various minority groups (excepting blacks and American Indians) were not tabulated. Thus, our knowledge regarding the changes in minority housing remain unknown. Now that comparable data for blacks, American Indians, Asian Americans, and Hispanics have been collected and tabulated, there is the opportunity to analyze the changes and trends in minority housing as compared to the majority group.

The rationale for the presentation of this volume is to facilitate and stimulate fresh research on minority housing and its socioeconomic, legal, humanitarian, and political consequences in the society. The volume presents a synthesis of the state-of-research on racial and ethnic minority housing differentials by bringing together the results of more than 1,000 selected studies zeroing in on minority housing in the nation, buried in widely dispersed documents. It provides scholars, researchers, and policy makers with easy access to the main body of literature under one cover. In addition to its obvious value as a major source of information and reference, this book chronicles historical patterns of change in the housing conditions of minorities in the country.

The entries were selected from among many possibilities. The first priority in selecting the articles for citation/annotation was given to those that deal primarily with low-income and/or minority housing. Another consideration in the selection process was to avoid repetition of entries with similar contents. The important point to remember is that the present volume is the first and most complete book on the subject. In order to have a thorough comprehension of the problem, one does not need to review every and all pieces of the literature. A representative sample should suffice. The present volume, with its 1,007 entries, far exceeds this requirement.

(b) *Organization and Method*: This volume is organized under twelve chapters: Chapter 1 includes works primarily dealing with the general conditions, patterns, changes, quality and quantity of minority housing. More specifically, any item that could not clearly be classified under chapters 2 through 12 is cited in chapter 1. Chapter 2 deals with works relative to discrimination in housing and redlining as a form of discrimination (discrimination in mortgage money lending). Chapter 3 deals with the question of residential segregation. Chapter 4 is concerned with the interrelated issues of fair housing, residential integration, and desegregation. Chapter 5 encompasses material on rental housing in general and rent control in particular. Chapter 6 is concerned with minority home ownership and the value of homes owned by minority groups. Chapters 7 through 9 deal with minority housing and federal intervention—housing subsidy, public housing, and regulatory actions (including the housing laws and courts), respectively. Chapter 10 cites the major literature on the elderly housing problems; chapter 11 brings together materials relative to policy and the politics of minority housing in the nation; and finally, chapter 12 deals with the question of homelessness.

Except in a couple of cases, every publication appears only once. However, there is no way of guaranteeing that all references included in a given chapter will not also discuss topics covered in the remaining chapters. This is primarily due to the fact that all entries in a given chapter, in addition to their main focal points, also discuss several related topics.

The lead essay is not intended to provide an overall summary of the 1,007 entries in this volume. Rather, its main purpose is to provide new data and insight regarding minority housing characteristics using the most recent census data.

A conventional annotated bibliography provides a brief and general overview regarding the contents of a given entry. This volume departs from that tradition by providing a compilation of abstracts/summaries and conclusions of the major publications on racial and ethnic minority housng in the country. To achieve this objective, and in view of the fact that some of the authors cited provided an abstract or a summary, whenever possible the original authors' summaries are used. This method is employed because an abstract or summary written by the original author reflects more accurately the original author's contentions and findings than one paraphrased by someone else. Thus, using such summaries/abstracts whenever possible (e.g., if fairly short), would best serve the pivotal aim of the present volume as a research tool. However, for a significant majority of the items cited (more than two-thirds), no such summaries existed. Also, given the limitation of space, in some cases the existing summaries were too long to be included intact. In these instances I have either written the summaries or have shortened the existing long ones. The summaries written by the original authors are marked by a single asterisk (*) at the end of the annotation; the symbol (@) at the end of the annotation indicates that the original author's summary has been modified, primarily shortened. It must also be pointed out that whenever the original author's summary consisted of two or more paragraphs, they have been pulled together to form a single paragraph.

J.A.M.
August 1986

MINORITY HOUSING DIFFERENTIALS: ANALYSES OF DATA FROM 1980 CENSUS

Jamshid A. Momeni, Howard University

The national housing goal has not been achieved for all Americans nor have the benefits of homeownership been made equally available to all. For the nation's poor, decent housing often has been beyond their means. For many of the nation's minority families, the factors of race and ethnic origin have operated devastatingly as economics to deny them the benefits of decent housing or opportunities to exercise housing choice. As of 1970 nearly two out of every three white families owned their own homes, but only two out of every five black families were homeowners. For this group of Americans the national housing goal remains largely a shadowy slogan without substance.

The U.S. Commission on Civil Rights, 1971

Housing is one of the basic necessities of life. Faced with the horrendous housing problems of the 1940s, the United States Congress in 1949 proclaimed the national goal of "a decent home and suitable living environment for every American Family." In the meantime, housing quantity, quality, discrimination, and affordability have been the major areas of concern in the past thirty years for all Americans, and for minorities in particular. As many citations in this volume indicate, since the enunciation of the national housing goal the nation has significantly succeeded in solving the housing problems of the 1940s and the 1950s, eliminating both severe shortages and substandard units. Yet, there is much more to be done, especially with respect to low-income and minority housing. By all standards of measurement, a substantial disparity in housing conditions by race, ethnicity and income persists, pointing at the relative deprivation of these groups. Jackson (1958) wrote: "It is axiomatic that America will attain neither national maturity nor unqualified international respect until minority groups share, in actuality, our cherished and vaunted democratic way of life. Still on the list of problem areas where inequities exist is the field of housing for minority groups." Davis (1967) stated: "Too many people in our country are badly housed. According to the 1960 census, 10.6 million units of the 58.3 million housing units were considered substandard. . . . Except where aided by grants or subsidies, the *poor* [emphasis mine] of the nation are found in substandard housing."

The *purpose* of this study is to assess the qualitative and quantitative aspects of housing differentials by race and ethnicity in the U.S. in 1980. The analysis will include an examination of differentials in adequacy, quality, affordability and homeownership by various racial/ethnic groups. Relative to future trends, expected demographic factors that affect housing shall be examined. The data for this study are primarily drawn from the 1980 census published statistics. The unit of analysis is a household (a group of people, related or unrelated, who live in the same housing unit more than 50 percent of the time) as opposed to a family. There are many racial and ethnic groups in the United States. In this study they are grouped under five major categories: white, black, American Indian, Asian American, and Hispanic. The American Indian category includes Eskimos and Aleuts; the Asian American category includes subgroups such as Chinese, Filipino, Japanese, Asian Indian, Korean, Vietnamese, Hawaiian, Samoan, Guamanian, Bangladeshi, Burmese, Hmong, Cambodian (Kapuchea), Laotian, Malayan, Pakistani, Sri Lankan (Ceylonese), Thai, Polynesian, Micronesian, and Melanesian; in this article, the terms "Hispanic" and "Spanish Origin" are used interchangeably, and refer to all those who identified themselves as belonging to one of the Spanish Origin categories listed in the 1980 Census questionnaire item 7. The major Hispanic subgroups are Mexican American, Puerto Rican, and Cuban. Persons of other Latin American, and South or Central American origins fall in the Hispanic category. For the purposes of literary convenience, hereafter we refer to these racial/ethnic groups as white, black, American Indian, Asian American, and Hispanic or Spanish origin. Unless otherwise specified, the analyses that follow are based on the data from the United States Metropolitan areas. Most minorities, as will be seen later, are concentrated in the metropolitan areas, and thus, the U.S. Bureau of the Census has provided separate tabulation for all of the above mentioned minority groups for the metropolitan United States.

Minority Housing and Location. Housing is always considered in connection with its location. Discussions on metropolitan and non-metropolitan, or central city living relate to a limited choice of location. Dahmann (1985: 511) observed "Conventional wisdom tells us that the quality of residential environment declines with increasing size of settlements and with increasing centrality within settlements. The perception that large settlements and inner-city neighborhoods provide residential environment *that are less than desirable* [emphasis mine] is both long standing and widespread." This contention is supported by popular and scholarly accounts in the past and in recent years. According to Dahmann (1985), during the 1970s, the United States witnessed a restructuring of its settlement pattern (system) towards deconcentration and suburbanization. Central city areas often represent units occupied by persons in service works, laborers, or those who had received no more than elementary education; and most housing units are rented units in old and dilapidated structures. As pointed out by Berry and Kasarda (1977: 221), older cities often bear the stamps of "obsolescence, high density, high industrialization, and aging inhabitants." Gorham and Glazer (1976: 5) point out that "housing is more than shelter. It is fixed in a neighborhood. The place and the neighborhood supplement the shelter of the house by meeting other needs and desires: personal security, information, access to jobs, credit, friends, as well as standard public services. It is infinitely more difficult to improve neighborhoods than it is to improve shelter." The following data (U.S. Bureau of the Census, 1983a: Table 38) show the pattern of residence by location, race and Spanish origin.

Location	U.S. Total	White	Black	Amer. Indian	Asian Amer.	Hispanic
U.S. Total	100.0	100.0	100.0	100.0	100.0	100.0
Inside SMSA's	74.8	73.3	81.1	49.0	91.4	87.6
Central Cities	29.9	24.9	57.7	20.9	46.3	50.3
Outside SMSA's	25.2	26.7	18.9	51.0	8.6	12.4

As the above data indicate, 57.7 percent of blacks, 46.3 percent of Asian Americans, and more than 50 percent of Hispanics, as compared to only 26.7 percent of whites, are concentrated in the central city component of the SMSA's. The high concentration of blacks, Asian-Americans, and Hispanics in the metropolitan areas on the one hand, and in central cities on the other hand, is regarded as having an adverse impact on their housing conditions. Many observers have alluded to the fact that city-to-suburban migration is closely related to the personal income of the residents. Those with higher income have a much greater flexibility in choice of residential location than those with limited income, who are socially and economically forced to be confined to the central city location (Berry and Kasarda, 1977: 221). If central-city location is any indicator of housing quality, it certainly points to the plight of minority households, a large proportion of whom are confined to the inner city location.

Aside from the metropolitan-nonmetropolitan or central city/suburban location, structure type is an important variable, for there is a wide majority-minority differential in the socioeconomic, demographics, and housing condition of those residing in various structure types (Momeni and Brown, 1986). According to the 1980 census, about two-thirds of all year-round housing units in the United States are single family homes (54 million one family, detached units, and 3.5 million one-family, attached units). This indicates the desirability of single-family structures (detached or attached) as having the most demand, and thus, by implication, as the most preferred form of housing. The proportion of minorities living in owner-occupied single-family-housing (SFH) units, is far less than that of whites.

Table 1 displays data on the majority/minority pattern of residence in 1980 by structure type. These data reveal that minority owners of 1-unit housing is 1.8 to 6.1 percent lower than white owners of 1-unit detached or attached housing. Among renters, 43.8 percent of American Indians, as opposed to 30.9 percent of whites, reside in 1-unit housing. However, the corresponding proportions for the remaining three minority groups (black, Asian American, and Hispanic) are lower than that for whites, pointing to the fact that whites occupy more than their own share of the single-family units in the nation.

Table 1: Pattern of Residency by Structure Type, Race, and Spanish
         Origin, 1980

Units in Structure	All Groups	White	Black	Amer. Indian	Asian Amer.	Hispanic
OWNERS						
U.S. Metropolitan Areas	100.0	100.0	100.0	100.0	100.0	100.0
1 Unit detached or attached	87.1	87.4	85.6	81.3	84.9	83.6
2 or more units	6.9	6.4	10.9	6.8	13.9	12.0
Mobile home or trailer, etc.	6.0	6.2	3.5	11.9	1.2	4.4
RENTERS						
U.S. Metropolitan Areas	100.0	100.0	100.0	100.0	100.0	100.0
1 unit detached or attached	30.5	30.9	30.1	43.8	19.9	27.7
2 or more units	66.8	65.9	68.8	50.9	79.4	70.6
Mobile home or trailer, etc.	2.7	3.2	1.1	5.3	0.7	1.7

Source: Computed by the author from statistics in Tables A-7, A-20, A-32, A-42, A-53, and A-64 in the U.S. Bureau of the Census (1984).

As the data in Table 1 show, among homeowners, 87.4 percent whites as compared to 85.6 percent blacks, 81.3 percent American Indians, 84.9 percent Asian Americans, and 83.6 percent Hispanics, lived in 1-unit detached or attached housing. Also, among renters, with the exception of the American Indians, a smaller proportion of minorities than whites lived in 1-family (1-unit) housing. The disparity is especially evident among Asians and Hispanics as compared to whites.

Mobile Homes. As pointed out by several researchers cited in this volume (Bair, 1967; Cohen, 1976; French and Hadden, 1968; Trippett, 1972), mobile homes, trailers, etc. (hereafter simply referred to as mobile homes) are among the least expensive and least desirable housing. Shiefman, Werba, and Associates (1972) indicated that the total cost of owning an average mobile home is somewhat less than the lowest-rent new-apartment, and significantly less than the lowest-cost new housing available today without subsidy. They further pointed out that in many areas, however, homes and apartments in the lowest cost bracket are not available even if one is desired, and thus, low-income minorities are forced to use mobile homes. Trippett (1972) states: "The first report of the 'mobile home revolution,' were romanticized, telling of the return of the spirit of the covered wagon. But now the phenomenon may be seen as a new form of ghettoization, and as an indictment of America's failure to provide decent homes for low-income groups."

At the national level, there were 17 mobile homes for every 1000 population in the United States in 1980. The corresponding figures for whites, blacks, and hispanics were 19, 26, and 78 per 1000 population, respectively, pointing to the fact that a higher proportion of minorities have resorted to mobile homes as a place to live than have whites. The data in Table 1 do not support this contention, for they relate to metropolitan areas only. As shown earlier, a large proportion of minorities are concentrated in the central cities which are not zoned for mobile homes (Donabed, 1981).

SOCIOECONOMIC AND DEMOGRAPHIC CHARACTERISTICS

It is often contended that most minority householders do not have the economic power necessary to enable them to secure adequate housing (Bender and Green, 1972; Newman and Struyk, 1983; Phillips, 1972). Thus, it is important to examine the socioeconomic and demographic factors which may act as strong predictors of housing conditions and tenure.

Economic Status. As indicated earlier, the inner city residence of most minorities is associated with their economic condition. Several citations in this volume have asserted that housing conditions can be determined or easily predicted from the economic conditions of the household. Table 2 contains data on median income and poverty status of minorities in U.S. metropolitan areas by tenure and location.

As may be noted from Table 2, with the exception of Asian-Americans, minority householders have significantly lower median income than whites. Among owners, the median income for blacks in the total U.S. metropolitan areas was $15.5K as compared to $20.9K for white householders—that is, blacks' median income was about 74 percent that of whites in 1980. Blacks, the largest of all minorities, have the lowest median income as compared to all other groups. As to the proportion of owners with income below the poverty line, again Table 2 reveals that there is a

Table 2: Median[a] Income and Poverty Status by Race and Spanish
          Origin, 1980.

	Median Income			Percent Below Poverty		
Race/Ethnicity	Metro Areas	Inside SMSA's	Cntr. City	Metro Areas	Inside SMSA's	Cntr. City
OWNERS						
Total	20.5	22.3	20.6	7.8	6.1	7.4
White	20.9	22.7	21.2	6.7	5.2	5.8
Black	15.5	17.4	16.9	19.1	15.3	15.4
American Indian	15.5	19.4	19.6	20.5	11.9	10.3
Asian American	27.5	28.0	26.3	4.9	4.6	5.2
Hispanic	19.1	20.1	18.7	12.7	11.0	12.4
RENTERS						
Total	11.3	11.7	10.6	21.8	20.5	24.3
White	12.0	12.5	11.6	17.7	16.2	18.4
Black	8.2	8.6	8.1	38.1	36.2	38.1
American Indian	9.9	10.4	9.6	31.3	27.8	30.5
Asian American	12.6	12.8	12.0	22.5	22.1	23.5
Hispanic	10.2	10.4	9.7	31.1	30.1	33.5

a: Median is chosen over mean because in dealing with positively
    skewed distributions such as income, median is a better measure
    of central tendency than mean. Figures are rounded to the
    nearest $1000.

Source: Computed by the author from statistics in Tables A-3, A-4,
        A-16, A-17, A-28, A-29, A-38, A-39, A-49, A50, A60, and A-61
        in the U.S. Bureau of the Census (1984).

significant minority-majority disparity. While 5.2 percent of white owners
inside SMSA's (Standard Metropolitan Statistical Areas) and 5.8 percent in
the central city component had income below the poverty line, the parallel
figures for blacks were 15.3 and 15.4 percent respectively, followed by Hispanics and American Indians, with a significantly higher proportion below
the poverty line than whites.

In general, the median income of renters is significantly lower than that of
home owners in every category in Table 2. And, among renters, the
economic disparity is even more dramatic. For example, 38.1 percent of
blacks, 30.5 percent of American Indians, 23.5 percent of Asian Americans,
and 33.5 percent of Hispanic renters in central cities fell below the poverty
line, as compared to only 18.4 percent of whites. These data underscore the

fact that minorities in general, and minority renters in particular, are at the bottom of income stratum.

As a rule, the total mortgage one can secure today is about 2 to 2.5 times the family's annual income. Most minorities with annual incomes below $15,000 can hardly qualify for enough mortgage to purchase a decent home. Income, labor force participation (LFP), and occupational status are often used as *objective* criteria for determining economic status and social class. It is a truism that income, LFP and occupational status are also highly interrelated. Based on data not shown here, the lower annual income of minorities is associated with their lower rates of employment (or higher unemployment rates) and lower occupational status. That is, the minority housing problems stem from their high rate of unemployment and lower occupational status.

Household Type, Age, and Marital Status. Household type, age, and marital status are important predictors of housing status. For example, age is positively associated with income, occupational status and tenure since older individuals have had more time than younger people to purchase their own home. As may be noted from the data in Table 3, generally speaking, the median age of renter-occupied householders, regardless of race and household type, is lower than the median age of owners.

Marital status is often associated with a person's status as a householder. One-person householders, for example, are often individuals who are separated, divorced, or widowed. That is, household structure may be used as an indicator of tenure and housing conditions. For this reason, Table 3 displays data on household type and householders' age, by tenure and location. The data on household type also depict information on the marital status. Statistics on separation, divorce, and widowhood (Sep + D + W) are often used as a measure (or index) of family disorganization. According to Momeni (1984: 41), for the white population of the nation as a whole in 1980, 21.4 percent of the female population age 15 and older were either separated, divorced, or widowed; the corresponding figure for blacks was 30.5 percent.

The following observations can be made from the data presented in Table 3: (1) home owners, irrespective of race and place of residence, are significantly older than renters; (2) minority home owners are somewhat younger than their majority counterparts; (3) the median age of home owners in central cities is slightly (less than 1 year) higher than the median age of owners in the entire metropolitan areas; (4) nearly 30 percent of black female householders and 22 percent of American Indian female householders were homeowners in the metropolitan United States in 1980, as compared to 17 percent of white female householders; (5) home ownership among Asian American and Hispanic female householders is markedly lower as compared to other groups in the table, both in the metropolitan and central city locations; (6) irrespective of minority group membership

Table 3:   Household Type and Median Age, by Tenure, Race,
           and Spanish Origin, 1980

Tenure and Race/Ethnicity	Household Type				Household Type			
	MC*	MHH*	FHH*	Mdn Age*	MC*	MHH*	FHH*	Mdn. Age*
OWNERS								
Total	75.1	7.1	17.8	49.7	69.5	8.4	22.1	51.8
White	76.3	6.7	17.0	49.9	71.1	8.1	20.8	52.4
Black	60.0	10.4	29.6	50.2	58.5	10.7	30.8	50.4
American Indian	68.2	9.9	21.9	44.9	68.7	9.2	22.1	44.5
Asian American	81.4	6.5	12.1	44.2	78.8	7.2	14.0	46.7
Hispanic	78.4	6.8	14.8	44.7	76.2	7.1	16.7	45.5
RENTERS								
Total	36.5	23.7	39.8	35.4	31.1	25.2	43.7	36.7
White	37.8	24.2	38.0	35.3	32.2	26.6	41.2	36.8
Black	26.2	21.9	51.9	36.9	23.6	22.2	53.2	37.6
American Indian	41.2	21.9	36.9	33.5	38.0	23.7	38.3	33.0
Asian American	49.6	24.9	25.5	34.9	47.5	25.6	26.9	36.1
Hispanic	48.5	19.6	31.9	34.0	44.7	19.8	35.5	34.6

*:   MC, married couple;   MHH, male householder;   FHH, female householder;
     Mdn., median.

Source: Computed by the author from statistics in Tables A-1, A-2, A-14,
     A-15, A-25, A-26, A-36, A-37, A-47, A-48, A-58, and A-59 in the U.S.
     Bureau of the Census (1984).

and location (metro vs. central city), home ownership among male householders is substantially lower than among female householders. The latter
observation is of particular interest in view of the fact that the median
income of female householders is lower than their male counterparts, and
the proportion of female householders with income below the poverty line
is significantly greater than male householders.

Regarding renters, the most important observations are: (1) while
married couples constitute the significant majority of home owners, irrespective of race and Spanish origin, they constitute the minority among
renters; nearly 38 percent of white, 26 percent of black and 41 percent of
American Indian renters are married couples; (2) the proportion of married
couple renters are much larger among Asians (49.6 percent) and Hispanics
(48.5 percent) than other groups, but they still constitute less than 50
percent of the renters.

HOUSING QUALITY AND QUANTITY

Every housing unit has a quantitative and qualitative dimension. Indexes of quality deal with some aspects of the dwelling unit structures, and micro-neighborhoods. Housing quality is difficult to measure; yet, it may be defined as the total of some bundles of structural characteristics and services consumed by the urban households. Kain and Quigley (1970: 532) concluded that "the quality of the bundle of residential services has about as much effect on the prices of housing as such objective aspects as the number of rooms, number of bathrooms, and lot size."

Home Value. Value is usually measured by the respondent's estimate of how much the property (house plus lot plus neighborhood) would sell for if it were for sale on the day census questionnaires were completed. As just alluded to, in buying housing, "families jointly purchase a wide variety of services at a particular location. These include a certain number of square feet of living space, different kinds of rooms, a particular structure type, [interior design], an address, accessiblity to employment, a neighborhood environment, a set of neighbors, and a diverse collection of public and quasipublic services including schools, garbage collection, and police protection" (Kain and Quigley, 1970: 532). Many researchers have attempted to devise statistical estimates of the contribution of these individual attributes to the total payment (rent or purchase price), but the complexity of the subject matter has prevented researchers from devising any viable estimate. "Difficulty in measuring the physical and environmental quality of the dwelling unit and surrounding residential environment is perhaps the most vexing problem encountered in evaluating the several attributes of bundles of residential services. These problems are so serious that the U.S. Bureau of the Census omitted all measures of dwelling quality from the 1970 housing census." (Kain and Quigley, 1970: 532). However, the actual "market value" of a unit provides an *overall* estimate of houisng quality (e.g., neighborhood and microenvironment) and quantity (e.g., lot size, number of rooms, etc.).

Data in Table 4 show the median and mean values of minority homes in the United States total and the U.S. metropolitan areas. A cursory examination of these data reveal that, with the exception of Asians, the median/mean minority home values are significantly lower than the value of homes owned by whites. For instance, in the nation as a whole, the median value of homes owned by blacks was $27,000, as compared to $48,600 for whites—that is, the median value of homes owned by blacks was only 56 percent of the value of homes owned by whites. There is considerable variation in the value of homes owned by minority groups. The median/mean home valued owned by Asians is highest in the nation, even in comparison to home owned by whites. Despite this, however, as will be seen later in the article, there is a twist of irony relative to Asian housing conditions in the country, becaue based on some other indicators of housing

Table 4: Median/Mean Values of Owner-Occupied Housing Units, by Race
         and Spanish Origin, 1980

Place of Residence	U.S.	Metro Area* Median	Mean	Inside SMSA's Median	Mean	Central City Median	Mean	Percent With no Mortgage
Total	47.2	47.2	55.8	51.5	61.0	43.3	53.2	35.4
White	48.6	48.8	57.3	52.9	62.7	46.3	56.4	35.8
Black	27.2	27.1	33.8	30.2	36.4	26.9	33.3	33.2
Amer. Indian	34.3	35.4	43.3	46.1	53.8	43.3	51.2	39.7
Asian American	83.9	82.9	94.6	84.8	96.6	79.6	92.7	16.8
Hispanic	44.7	44.9	52.0	48.7	55.6	39.1	46.8	27.8

*: Metro Area, a short form for metropolitan area.

Source: Computed by the author from statistics in Tables A-1, A-14, A-25,
   A-36, A-47, A-58, and the corresponding B- and C-Tables for inside SMSA's
   and Central Cities of SMSA's, respectively, in the U.S. Bureau of the
   Census (1984). For the U.S. figures see U.S. Bureau of the Census
   (1983b: 1-9).

quality/quantity, the Asian minority housing conditions do not measure up
to whites' housing conditions. If market value, argued earlier, is a reflection
of housing services consumed by different groups, the data in Table 4 do
show that minorities are at a great disadvantage. The last column in Table 4
shows the proportion of homeowners with no mortgage commitments. As
these data demonstrate, with the exception of the American Indian category, a higher proportion of homes owned by whites, than those owned by
minorities, were free from mortgage obligations.

There is another dimension to the home value (and also monthly contract
rent) that has had serious impact on minority housing in the nation. The
following figures (U.S. Bureau of the Census, 1983b: 1-9) show the pattern
of change in *median* home value (see also figure 1) and *median* monthly
contract rent in the country since 1940.

Year	Value	Dollar Change	Percent Change	Rent	Dollar Change	Percent Change
1940	2,400	—	—	18	—	—
1950	7,400	5,000	208	36	18	100
1960	11,900	4,500	61	58	22	61
1970	17,000	5,100	43	89	31	53
1980	47,200	30,200	178	198	109	122

According to these figures, the median value of owner-occupied single
family homes increased between $4,500 and $5,100 per decade between

FIGURE 1: **Median Value of Owner-Occupied Housing Units: 1940-1980**

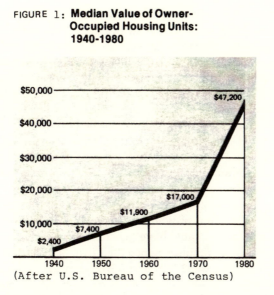

(After U.S. Bureau of the Census)

1940 and 1970, and $30,200 between 1970 and 1980, or an increase of 178 percent during the 1970s. The increase was 43 percent during the 1960s, 61 percent during the 1950s, and 208 percent during the 1940s.

Median Contract Rent. As the above data demonstrate, *median* monthly contract rent has also increased steadily over the past four decades, but at a somewhat slower rate than the median value of owner-occupied homes. It may be noted that the increase in median contract rent was 100 percent in the 1940s, 61 percent in the 1950s, 53 percent in the 1960s, and 122 percent in the 1970s. The analyses of changes in home values and contract rents are important, for they reveal the fact that minorities are priced out of the housing market. The increases in the minority households' incomes have not kept up with the rapid changes in home values and contract rents. Thus, minorities are forced by the market to settle for less than adequate housing or for the cheapest units they can find. The following figures (U.S. Bureau of the Census, 1983b: 1-9) reflect the monthly median rent paid by various racial/ethnic minorities.

Minority Group	1980 Monthly Contract Rent in $
White	208
Black	156
American Indian	172
Asian American	237
Hispanic	188

Generally, better quality housing requires higher rents. It may be noted that the general pattern of contract rent paid by different groups follows the same pattern as their respective median home values. Asians with the highest median home value also paid the highest monthly contract rent, followed by whites, Hispanics, American Indians, and blacks with the lowest median home value and the lowest monthly contract rent. One possible interpretation of these figures is that even in the rental market, blacks are least adequately housed. Again, this is based on the assumption that low rent means low housing services.

Home Ownership. A housing unit is regarded as "owner-occupied" if the owner(or co-owner) lives in the unit, regardless of the mortgage status. Any unit not classified as "owner-occupied" is classified as "renter-occupied," regardless of the method of payment of rent (in cash or in kind). Manning Marable (1985), a black sociologist, wrote: "The heart of the great American Dream has for generations been the ownership of a home." He emphasizes that while 67 percent of whites were home owners by the late 1970s, the "black Americans' dreams have generally been deferred in this area. Barely one in five black families owned their own homes from 1890 through World War II. During the 1960s and 1970s, however, the percentage of black home owners doubled up to 44 percent in 1975." Social scientists interested in the relationship between social status and race have looked at some variables indicative of social class position. In such studies, however, the use of annual income and occupational status have overshadowed the use of financial holding and home equity, which should play a major role in determining the economic power and the social standing of the families. Some studies (Lampman, 1959; Kolko, 1962), however, have emphasized the need and the importance of wealth accumulation through home ownership and home equity as a significant factor in determining one's social and economic position. Henretta and Campbell (1978), Parcel (1982), and Jackman and Jackman (1980) discuss various benefits of home ownership and argue that asset accumulation is an important aspect of social and economic status, and that the differentials in home investment by race significantly contribute to the differences in wealth, and thus, social class. The following data (U.S. Bureau of the Census, 1983b: 1-7) show the pattern of minority home ownership in 1980.

Majority/Minority Groups	Percent Home Owner in 1980
U.S. Total	64.4
White	67.8
Black	44.4
American Indian	53.4
Asian American	52.5
Hispanic	43.4

Prior to the 1980 census, the U.S. Bureau of the Census did not publish separate statistics for all of these groups. Thus, it is not possible to assess the changes in the rate of minority home ownership over time. However, for the U.S. as a whole, home ownership has risen steadily since 1940. It rose from 43.6 in 1940 to 55 percent in 1960; between 1950 and 1960, it rose from 55 to 61.9 percent; during the following decade it rose from 61.9 to 62.9 percent, and during the 1970-80 period it increased to 64.4 percent (U.S. Bureau of the Census, 1983b: 1-7).

Overcrowding. Overcrowding is generally measured by the number of "persons per room," which is calculated by dividing the number of persons in each occupied housing unit by the number of rooms in the unit. Overcrowding is a serious problem for some groups, and it generally means lowering the quality of housing and life. It happens among groups who cannot afford adequate space for their household size. Units with 1.01 or more persons per room is defined as "overcrowded." Data in Table 5 show housing units with 1.01 or more persons per room by minority group membership, tenure, location, and lack of complete plumbing facilities for exclusive use. These data reveal that: (1) irrespective of tenure, location, and the availability of complete plumbing facilities in the housing unit, overcrowding is a much more serious problem among all minorities, including Asians with the highest median home value, than it is among whites; (2) for all groups including whites, overcrowding is substantially higher in housing units which lack complete plumbing for exclusive use than in those with complete plumbing facilities; (3) overcrowding is much more serious among renters than among owners irrespective of location (inside SMSA's and Central cities); and (4) it may be recalled that the median home value of Asians is the highest in the nation, but overcrowding is also more acute among this group than among blacks with lowest median home value. The data in Table 5 show that as a whole, overcrowding is also a more serious problem among American Indians and Hispanics than among blacks.

Minority Housing and Structural Characteristics. The data in Table 6 summarize the 1980 Census results regarding six selected structural characteristics of minority housing.

1. *Year Structure Built (Age).* The age of a housing unit is an indicator of the quality of housing. Age is a factor causing decay and dilapidation. In addition, older structures often don't have the kind of equipment (e.g., gas line, dishwasher, garbage disposal, etc.) that are placed in newer buildings as standard equipment. The data in Table 6 show the racial occupancy of housing units built in 1949 or earlier (i.e., 30 years or more old). As these data show, both among owners and renters, a significantly higher proportion of units owned or rented by blacks than those owned or rented by whites were 30 or more years old. However, a substantially smaller proportion of homes owned/rented by the Asian American group were 30 or more years old, perhaps reflecting the higher median value of homes owned or rented by this minority group.

2. *Number of Rooms.* "Rooms" refer to the number of whole rooms used

Table 5: Overcrowding: Percent Units with 1.01 or More Persons
          per Room by Location, Race, Spanish Origin, and
          Plumbing Facilities, 1980.

Location and Race/Ethnicity	Owners		Renters	
	Metro Areas	Lack CPFEU*	Metro Areas	Lack CPFEU*

U.S. Metropolitan Areas

Total	2.7	15.9	6.6	15.4
White	1.8	11.4	4.0	9.7
Black	8.2	17.3	11.8	21.0
American Indian	15.4	59.1	15.5	38.3
Asian American	11.6	26.8	25.0	34.2
Hispanic	15.2	39.5	24.0	14.2

Inside SMSA's

Total	2.5	14.3	6.5	13.6
White	1.7	11.5	3.9	14.8
Black	7.2	15.8	11.0	16.7
American Indian	7.4	44.7	11.3	20.5
Asian American	11.3	35.8	25.4	35.7
Hispanic	15.1	43.4	24.0	32.4

Central Cities Inside SMSA's

Total	3.0	14.6	7.4	13.2
White	1.8	12.3	4.1	8.3
Black	6.7	13.1	11.0	14.4
American Indian	5.6	18.6	11.5	16.0
Asian American	12.7	37.2	26.6	35.4
Hispanic	15.3	34.9	23.3	29.8

*: CPFEU, Complete Plumbing Facilities for Exclusive Use.

Source: Computed by the author from statistics in Tables A-1,
    A-2, A-14, A-15, A-25, A-26, A-36, A-37, A-47, A-48, A-58,
    A-59, and the corresponding B- and C-Tables for Inside
    SMSA's and Central Cities, respectively, in the in the U.S.
    Bureau of the Census (1984).

Table 6:   Six Selected Structural Characteristics of Minority Housing
           by Tenure, Race, and Spanish Origin, 1980.

Structural Characteristics	Total	White	Black	Amer. Indian	Asian Amer.	Hispanic
OWNERS						
. Percent structures 30 or more years old (%)	34.3	33.9	42.6	28.8	20.7	31.1
. Median No. of rooms	6.0	6.0	5.8	5.3	6.0	5.5
. Percent Units with 4 or more bedrooms	21.1	21.3	18.7	16.8	31.3	18.6
. Lack complete plumbing facilities	8.2	6.0	2.9	10.9	0.2	1.5
. Percent with central heating system	86.6	88.3	70.8	66.5	76.6	72.5
. Percent with central air conditioning	31.4	32.4	20.3	21.8	30.3	27.7
RENTERS						
. Percent structures 30 or more years old (%)	40.2	39.1	44.7	36.4	34.2	45.5
. Median No. of rooms	4.0	4.0	4.0	4.0	3.3	3.8
. Percent Units with 4 or more bedrooms	3.6	3.4	4.5	4.9	2.8	3.0
. Lack complete plumbing facilities (%)	3.1	2.4	5.8	6.6	4.7	4.5
. Percent with central heating system	8.8	84.1	74.4	71.7	73.4	72.7
. Percent with central air conditioning	22.1	24.0	15.8	16.0	17.4	14.7

Source: Computed by the author from statistics in Tables A-1, A-2, A-14,
   A-15, A-25, A-26, A-36, A-37, A-47, A-48, A-58, and A-59 in the U.S.
   Bureau of the Census (1984).

for living purposes only (U.S. Bureau of the Census, 1984: A-6). Number of
rooms in a housing unit is a *quantitative* measure of space available to the
household. Generally speaking, units with more rooms are preferred over
units with fewer rooms which provide little space for the occupants. As the
data in Table 6 reveal, the median number of rooms in homes owned by
blacks (5.8 rooms), American Indians (5.3 rooms), and Hispanics (5.5
rooms) was smaller than the median number of rooms in units owned either
by whites (6.0 rooms) or by Asian Americans (6.0 rooms). On the whole,
renters in 1980 had much smaller housing space available to them than
owners. The median number of rooms in units rented by Asian Americans
and Hispanics was 3.3 and 3.8, respectively, as opposed to 4.0 rooms in
homes rented by whites, blacks, and American Indians.

3. *Bedrooms.* "Bedrooms" refer to the number of rooms designated mainly for sleeping purposes. A living room with a sofabed, while able to be used for sleeping, is not considered a "bedroom." On the other hand, a room used as a guest room, though not used frequently, is regarded as a "bedroom" (U.S. Bureau of the Census, 1984: A-6). The number of bedrooms in a housing unit is another *quantitative* measure of space available to the household. A typical home in the U.S. has three bedrooms. Any housing unit with 4 or more bedrooms may be considered medium or large in size. The data in Table 6 also show units with 4 or more bedrooms by tenure, race and Spanish origin. As may be noted, (with the exception of Asian American owners) a smaller proportion of minority owned units had 4 or more bedrooms. This shows another dimension of minority housing in the country. The data in Table 6 also demonstrate that regardless of race or Spanish origin, significantly less housing space was available to renters in 1980 than to owners. The disparity between groups was also wider. For instance, 24.0 percent of white renters, as opposed to only 14.7 percent of Hispanic renters, had 4 or more bedrooms in their units.

4. *Plumbing Facilities for Exclusive Use.* As defined by the U.S. Bureau of the Census (1984: B-6) housing units with "complete plumbing facilities for exclusive use" consist of those units which have cold and hot piped water, a flush toilet, and a bathtub or shower inside the housing unit for the exclusive use of the household. "Lacking complete plumbing for exclusive use" refers to those units in which (a) all three specified plumbing facilities are present inside the unit, but are also shared by another household, and (b) some or none of the specified facilities is available. The degree of completeness of plumbing facilities is another indicator of housing quality. Table 6 also provides data on plumbing facilities by tenure, race, and Spanish origin. As may be noted from these data, among owners, with the exception of American Indians, all minorities fare better than white owners. This is perhaps due to the fact that a large proportion of minorities, as shown earlier, reside in the central cities inside SMSA's, where plumbing is usually available. As for the renters, however, the same pattern did not hold true. All units rented by minorities had higher plumbing problems than those rented by whites. But, on the whole, there are significantly less plumbing problems among home owners than among renters.

5. *Central Heating System.* The availability of central heating systems —a central warm-air furnace or electric heat pump—in a housing unit greatly enhance housing quality, for these constitute the most desirable home heating equipment today. Based on the 1980 census data presented in Table 6, both among owners and renters, a significantly higher proportion of units occupied by whites were equipped with central heating system than units occupied by minority households. Among owners, 88.3 percent of homes owned by whites were equipped with central heating systems, as opposed to 70.8 percent of homes owned by blacks, 66.5 percent of homes

owned by American Indians, 76.6 percent of homes owned by Asian Americans, and 72.5 percent of homes owned by Hispanics.

6. *Central Air Conditioning.* Similarly, the availability of a central air system (CAS) is a structural feature that greatly enhances the quality of housing. On this score, the data in Table 6 also demonstrate the disadvantages suffered by the minority groups. A significantly smaller proportion of homes owned by minorities, especially those owned by blacks and American Indians, were equipped with a CAS than those owned by the white majority group. A similar pattern prevailed among renters, where a smaller proportion of units rented by minority groups than by whites were equipped with a CAS.

Minority Housing and 1-Person Householder. One of the surprising findings of this analysis relates to housing conditions of 1-person householders. In view of the much discussed discrimination against women in employment, promotion and equal pay, and in view of the fact that more women than men are on the poverty roll, it makes sense to think that 1-person female householders are in the worst possible shape regarding housing. The data presented in Table 7, however, cast serious doubts on this contention. Irrespective of race and Spanish origin, a substantially larger proportion of units occupied by 1-person male householders lack complete plumbing facilities for exclusive use than do the units of female householders. For example, 8.5 percent of the units occupied by black males lacked complete plumbing facilities, as opposed to 6.0 percent of the units occupied by black females. The corresponding figures for American Indians are 21.4 and 11.2 percent, respectively. Similarly, a higher percentage of 1-person male householders lived in mobile homes than did their female counterparts.

In sum, the foregoing analyses show a relatively significant gap in the majority-minority housing conditions in 1980. The major factors responsible for the differential seems to stem from the wide income differences between various groups. It is concluded that most minorities with low incomes cannot afford the housing adequate for their needs. These disparities in the majority-minority housing conditions are expected to continue as long as the income gaps among racial/ethnic groups persist.

Table 7: Selected Housing Conditions of 1-Person Male and Female
Householders, by Tenure, Race, and Spanish Origin, 1980

Characteristic	Owners			Renters		
	Total	MHH*	FHH*	Total	MHH*	FHH*

Lack Complete Plumbing Facilities for Exclusive Use

Total	2.7	4.1	2.1	4.2	6.0	2.8
White	2.3	3.6	1.8	3.5	5.1	2.4
Black	7.0	8.5	6.0	7.6	11.0	5.5
American Indian	15.7	21.4	11.2	9.4	12.5	6.2
Asian American	1.4	1.7	1.2	6.1	7.2	4.8
Hispanic	4.2	5.3	3.3	6.7	8.9	4.1

Percent Living in 1-Unit Detached or Attached Housing

Total	78.9	75.8	80.3	17.9	19.8	16.5
White	78.6	75.4	80.1	17.3	19.5	15.8
Black	83.4	80.9	84.9	21.8	22.2	21.5
American Indian	77.5	74.2	80.0	27.4	27.8	26.9
Asian American	70.4	68.8	71.6	11.7	11.6	11.8
Hispanic	75.8	72.4	78.3	17.0	17.0	17.0

Percent Below Poverty Level

Total	19.8	12.7	23.3	29.0	24.6	32.5
White	18.2	11.4	21.5	28.8	24.1	32.2
Black	38.2	25.1	46.3	38.0	29.2	46.0
American Indian	35.8	30.2	40.2	31.7	25.3	38.5
Asian American	14.8	8.3	19.2	23.2	20.7	26.1
Hispanic	29.9	18.3	38.6	31.8	24.4	40.2

Percent Living in Mobile Homes

Total	9.0	11.7	7.6	2.2	2.9	1.7
White	9.4	12.4	8.0	2.5	3.2	1.9
Black	3.5	5.3	2.3	0.9	1.2	0.6
American Indian	14.4	17.0	12.5	4.1	4.5	3.6
Asian American	4.0	3.6	4.2	0.8	0.8	0.8
Hispanic	7.7	9.9	6.0	1.7	2.1	2.1

Source: Computed by the author from statistics in Tables A-11,
    A-24, A-35, A-46, A-57, and A-68 in the U.S. Bureau of the Census
    (1984).

REFERENCES

Bair, Frederick, Jr. 1967. Mobile Homes: A New Challenge. *Law and Contemporary, Planning* 42 (6): 12-14.

Bender, Lloyd, and Bernal L. Green. 1973. Ghettos and Poverty in the Ozarks. *Planning* 39 (7): 13-15.

Berry, Brian J. L., and John D. Kasarda. 1977. *Contemporary Urban Ecology*. New York: Macmillan Publishing Co., Inc., 497 pp.

Cohen, Matthew. 1976. Mobile Home Subdivisions: The No Frills Home is Here. *Planning* 42 (6): 12-14.

Dahmann, Donald C. 1985. Assessments of Neighborhood Quality in Metropolitan America. *Urban Affairs Quarterly* 20 (4): 511-535.

Davis, Tom L. 1967. Cooperative Self-help Housing. *Law and Contemporary Problems* 32 (2): 409-415.

Donabed, Joseph E. 1981. Zoning: Mobile Home Options and Opportunities. *Western City* 57 (7): 6-7.

French, Robert Mills, and Jeffrey K. Hadden. 1968. Mobile Homes: Instant Suburbia or Transportable Slums? *Social Problems* 16 (Fall): 219-26.

Gorham, William, and Nathan Glazer, eds. 1976. *The Urban Predicament*. Washington, D.C.: The Urban Institute.

Henretta, John C., and Richard T. Campbell. 1978. Net Worth as an Aspect of Status. *American Journal of Sociology* 83 (March): 1204-1223.

Jackman, M., and R. Jackman. 1980. Racial Inequalities in Home Ownership. *Social Forces* 58: 1221-1234.

Jackson, Hubert, M. 1958. Public Housing and Minority Groups. *Phylon* 19 (1): 21-30.

Kain, John F., and John M. Quigley. 1970. Measuring the Value of Housing Quality. *Journal of the American Statistical Association* 65 (330): 532-548.

Kolko, Gabriel. 1962. *Wealth and Power in America*. New York: Praeger.

Lampman, Robert J. 1959. Changes in the Share of Wealth Held by Top Wealth-holders, 1922-1956. *Review of Economics and Statistics* 41 (Nov.): 379-392.

Marable, Manning. 1985. The Housing Crisis. *Washington Afro-American* (Newspaper), March 30, 1985, p. 4.

Momeni, Jamshid A. 1984. Demography of Racial and Ethnic Minorities in the United States: A Political and Sociodemographic Review. In: *Demography of Racial and Ethnic Minorities in the United States*. Jamshid A. Momeni. Westport, Connecticut: Greenwood Press. Pp. 3-44.

Momeni, Jamshid A., and Diane R. Brown. 1986. *Housing Characteristics of Black Female Householders: An Analysis of Data from the 1970 and 1980 Censuses*. Washington, D.C.: Institute for Urban Affairs and Research, Howard University. Occasional Paper No. 25. 68 pp.

Newman, Sandra J., and Raymond Struyk. 1983. Housing and Poverty. *Review of Economics and Statistics* 65 (2): 243-53.

Parcel, Toby L. 1982. Wealth Accumulation of Black and White Men: The Case of Housing Equity. *Social Problems* 30 (2): 199-211.

Phillips, Kenneth E. 1972. The Poor and the Housing Issue. *Urban Lawyer* 4 (2): 242-47.

Shiefman, Werba, and Associates. 1972. The Mobile Home Market. *Appraisal Journal* 40 (3): 391-411.

Trippett, Frank. 1972. Mobile Homes: The New Ghettos. *Saturday Review* 55 (39): 51-55.

U.S. Bureau of the Census. 1983a. *General Population Characteristics: United States Summary.* 1980 Census of Population, PC80-1-B1. Washington, D.C.: GPO.

———. 1983b. *General Housing Characteristics: United States Summary.* 1980 Census of Housing, HC80-1-A1. Washington, D.C.: GPO.

———. 1984. *Metropolitan Housing Characteristics: United States Summary.* 1980 Census of Housing, HC80-2-1. Washington, D.C.: GPO.

U.S. Commission on Civil Rights. 1971. *Home Ownership for Lower Income Families: A Report on the Racial and Ethnic Impact of Section 235 Program.* Washington, D.C.: GPO.

Housing and Racial/Ethnic Minority Status in the United States

1
MINORITY STATUS AND GENERAL HOUSING CONDITIONS AND CORRELATES

0001.   Abrams, Charles.   1963.   The Housing Order   and Its Limits.   **Commentary** 35
        (1): 10-14.

On November 20, 1962, "President Kennedy read a prepared statement
announcing that he had signed an Executive Order banning discrimination in
federally aided housing.   Thus, more than two years after attacking his
Republican predecessor of failing to end housing discrimination 'with the
stroke of a pen,' Mr. Kennedy finally made good on his own promise to do so."
This article attempts to find out what were the forces that had caused
President Kennedy to wait so long before taking action, and what would this
Executive Order is expected to accomplish.   The author concludes that "the
President's delay in signing the Order only exemplified the deep roots
racial discrimination had won in America.   Much still remains to be done if
these roots are ever to be destroyed."

0002.   Abrams, Charles.   1966.   The Housing Problem and the Negro.   **Daedalus** 95
        (Winter): 64-76.

This article examines the 1965 riots of Watts area in Los Angeles, and
attempts to link these disturbances to segregation, poverty and black
housing condition in the area.   It is concluded that "if the Los Angeles
rioting reveals the underlying weaknesses of the current federal approach to
segregation, poverty, and housing, and if it stimulates some fresh thinking
on these problems, it may compensate at least in part for the terrible havoc
it wreaked."

0003.   Aldrich,   Howard.   1975.   Ecological   Succession   in   Racially   Changing
        Neighborhoods: A Review of the Literature.   Urban Affairs Quarterly 10 (3):
        327-48.

"This paper reports on a review of the literature on ecological succession in
racially   changing   neighborhoods."   The   review   is   divided   into   three

phases: (1) the causes and the initial conditions of succession; (2) the process of racial change; and (3) the social and economic consequences of racial change. The author also discusses the policy implications that can be drawn from racial succession.

0004. Alexander, Robert C. 1972. Fifteen State Finance Agencies in Review. Journal of Housing 29 (1): 9-17.

Since the private housing market has failed to meet the need of low- and moderate-income families, housing finance agencies (HFAs) have been created to provide low income families with decent housing at below-market rents, by acting as mortgage bankers. This fundamental role is complemented by administration and coordination of related housing programs. This article consists of a detailed discussion of these roles in the operation of 15 HFAs.

0005. Anderson, Martin. 1964. The Federal Bulldozer: A Critical Analysis of Urban Renewal, 1949-1962. Cambridge, Mass.: M.I.T. Press. 272 pp.

This book is a detailed analysis of what the federal urban renewal program is, why it was started, how it has worked, and what it has accomplished. The author uses a variety of data—e.g., interview data, extensive literature review, and existing statistics. The analysis includes an examination of the impact of the program on the black residential neighborhoods. The main thesis of this book is that the national urban renewal program has failed to produce its intended results, and the chances that it will ever accomplish its goal is very remote at best.

0006. Anonymous. 1972. Growing Issue: Communities Vs. Low-Income Housing. Congressional Quarterly 30 (2): 51-55.

This article looks at problems of the exodus to the suburbs by middle-class white and business, and migration to cities by rural poor in regard to federal policies for dispersal of lower income housing in the suburbs. The article discusses the roles and solutions offered by the courts, HUD, and Congress.

0007. Anonymous. 1974. Home Free: New Vistas in Regional Housing. Washington, D.C.: National Committee Against Discrimination, Inc. 64 pp.

This study details the experimental programs tested over five-year period designed to utilize housing laws, community organizations, governmental units, business and labor groups to increase housing opportunities for all minorities in the metropolitan region. The analysis is based on experimental results from the nine-county San Francisco Bay Area. Points of special interest may be the documentation of a white ghetto in San Leandro, California, discriminatory practices in the lending arena, and the impact of regionalism on racial and ethnic minority housing.

0008. Anonymous. 1979. Displacement Due to Condominium Conversion: Some Evidence. Washington, D.C.: National Association of Realtors. 43 pp.

The main objective of this study is to determine the extent to which lower income minorities are displaced by condominium conversion. This report is based on three studies: Washington, D.C.; Evanston, Illinois; and San

Francisco, California, where condominium conversion has become a political issue. This report focuses on the examination of the socioeconomic characteristics of those households affected by the conversion. The findings indicate that about 25 percent of the displaced households were in the lower-income category, and about 15 to 20 percent of the households had at least one elderly member. For these households, displacement can be a financial and psychological burden. But, results show that the problem of displacement is not as severe as generally believed for those in the middle- and upper income groups. In Washington, D.C., the average cost of finding alternative housing was found to be 14.3 percent greater than the former residence, while in San Francisco it was 5.8 percent less.

0009.   Anonymous. 1980. Factory Built Housing: City Concerns. **Western City** 56 (8): 10-11.

The growing demand for factory built housing for lower and middle income households has the League of California Cities concerned about construction and installation standards. As a result of a 1979 Annual Conference Resolution, the League proposed a Forum on Factory Built Housing Issues. This article relates the issues generated by the representatives of various factory-built housing interests. Among the topics discussed are problems with warranty, various manufacturing problems such as water leaks from rainfall, financing, and standards imposed upon manufacturers.

0010.   Atkinson, Reilly. 1975. Housing Deprivation. **Integrated Education** 13 (3): 85-86.

In this study, housing deprivation is defined in terms of three criteria: (1) physical adequacy; (2) overcrowding; and (3) high rent burden (when the renter pays more than 25 percent of his/her gross income for rent). In 1970, about 13 million households suffered housing deprivation. Over half of these were physically inadequate units (6.9 million), 700,000 were overcrowded, and 5.5 million had a high rent burden. Among black Americans, 1.6 million lived in physically inadequate housing units; 200,000 lived under overcrowded conditions; and, about 900,000 had a high rent burden. That is, 54 percent of all black households had at least one form of housing deprivation as compared to 21 percent of all households in the nation.

0011.   Babcock, Richard, and Fred P. Bosselman. 1967. Citizen Participation: A Suburban Suggestion for the Central City. **Law and Contemporary Problems** 32 (2): 220-231.

The municipal building, zoning, and housing codes currently in effect may be consistent with the goals of residents of small and homogeneous suburbs. "Within our large cities, however, these same characteristics explain much of the failure of such codes to come to grips with the problems of lower income residents of blighted neighborhoods. It is the purpose of this paper to propose a line of examination that will question the relevance of these orthodox rules to current urban conditions and to suggest the testing of a system of code administration and enforcement in our big cities that is not bottomed on those two ancient premises."

0012.   Bair, Frederick, Jr. 1967. Mobile Homes: A New Challenge. **Law and Contemporary Problems** 32 (2): 286-304.

"There is a growing need for good mobile home [low-cost housing] parks and subdivisions, appropriately located in residential environments. Local regulations (backed by state controls) can assure acceptable quality, location, and design. And equitable devices for taxation and other revenue production can assure that the mobile home pays its fair share of governmental costs. Unless local prejudice can be overcome by reason, it seems probable that mounting pressures for areas suitable for mobile home living will lead to increasing activity in the courts."

0013. Ball, William B. 1968. Housing and the Negro: New Life for the Thirteenth Amendment. **America** 119 (July 6): 11-13.

Mr. Joseph Lee Jones and his wife Barbara Jo had attempted to buy a house in St. Louis's suburban Paddock Woods development, a private housing project. The developer refuses to sell the house to the Joneses because they were blacks. The discrimination suit filed by the Joneses reaches the U.S. Supreme Court. Invoking the equal-rights clauses in the Thirteen and Fourteenth Amendments, the Supreme Court rules in favor of the Joneses. This article examines the Court's interpretations of these Amendments as they were applied to this case and to equal opportunity in housing.

0014. Banfield, Edward C., and Morton Grodzins. 1958. **Government and Housing in Metropolitan Areas.** New York: McGraw-Hill. 177 pp.

This book analyzes the role and effect of federal government in the growth (quantity), quality, and the price of housing. It describes the changes needed in the federal structure to improve housing; furthermore, it explains the problems and obstacles, and offers proposals for improving the role that government plays in housing field. As solution, the authors suggest greater collaboration between existing federal units, assignment of specific plan and service task to metropolitan-sized units of the government, and adoption of standard practices in metropolitan areas. They also point out that development is closely linked to government, and that only federal units can afford to spend the large sum of money needed to improve the metropolitan housing conditions.

0015. Banks, Jerry, and Robert F. Clark. 1976. A Venture into Meta-Evaluation: OEO Region IV's Housing Study. **Policy Studies Journal** 4 (3): 249-54.

In 1969 the Office of Economic Opportunity (OEO) Region IV, which includes eight southeastern states, undertook a study of lower income housing conditions in the region. Among other things, the study intended to assess the role in housing of OEO-funded Community Action and Limited Purpose Agencies. The Plans, Budget, and Evaluation Division proposed an evaluation of two contrasting models for providing low-income housing. None of the major recommendations of the evaluation team were included in the official policy statement or the pattern of grant awards in the region. The author suggests that the reason for the lack of impact may have been due to the failure of the evaluation team to consider the political and administrative consequences for the Region IV's management.

0016. Bauman, Gus, Ann Reines Kahn, and Serena Williams. 1983. Inclusionary Housing Programs in Practice. **Urban Land** 42 (11): 14-19.

Inclusionary housing programs are means to encourage developers or force them to provide a share of low-cost homes in areas which are usually considered upper class. The promotion of affordable housing in some wealthier communities where land and housing prices have largely excluded low- and moderate-income housing construction through the implementation of inclusionary programs has been the subject of heated debates in recent years. Part of the public's interest in the problem is wrapped up in concerns over the negative impact of such projects on house and land values in their respective area. This article discusses case studies of inclusionary housing programs in five counties: Montgomery County, Maryland; Orange, Palo Alto, and Davis Counties, California; and, Boulder County, Colorado. The study reveals the strengths and weaknesses in these laws as applied in these five counties.

0017. Beagle, Danny, Al Haber, and David Wellman. 1971. Creative Capitalism and Urban Redevelopment. In: Problems in Political Economy: An Urban Perspective. David M. Gordon (ed.). Lexington, Mass.: D. C. Heath and Company. Pp. 400-04.

The purpose of this article is to illustrate the real objective of urban renewal as it has manifested itself in different localities. The article shows that rather than aiming at providing housing for the poor, as people were originally led to believe it was intending, the urban renewal program in San Francisco explicitly aimed at serving the interests of corporate and large commercial property owners in the city.

0018. Bell, Earl J., and Dianne Kelso. 1986. The Demolition of Downtown Low-Income Residential Buildings: A Discriminant Analysis. Socio-Economic Planning Sciences 20 (1): 17-23.

The research undertaken in this study was concerned with identifying a set of reliable criteria that will indicate those low-income residential buildings in downtown Seattle which are particularly vulnerable to demolition. These criteria could then be used as an early warning system for city staff and housing advocates to anticipate the imminent demolition of low-income housing. Discriminant analysis, a multivariate statistical technique, was used to establish the credibility of these criteria as indicators of demolition as well as their relative contribution to the classification process. The results indicate that discriminant analysis is useful in differentiating between demolished and standing buildings and that the resulting discriminant function can be used for the purpose of classifying and thus prioritizing other buildings not in the sample.*

0019. Bender, Lloyd, and Bernal L. Green. 1973. Ghettos of Poverty in the Ozarks. Planning 39 (7): 13-15.

This article asserts the proposition that "once economic poverty becomes concentrated in a region, our whole national system operates to further intensify that poverty, rather than provide for automatic self-correcting. If further poverty is generated, then surely the national interest is served by identifying the root causes and adjusting them, even at the risk of parting with some deeply held values and institutional arrangements." This study of poverty status and its link to living conditions is based on a sample of 1,413 households in villages with less than 2,500 population and in the open country of the Ozarks Region—125 counties in eastern Oklahoma, northern Alaska, and southern Missouri.

0020.   Berger, Curtis, Eli Goldston, and Guido A. Rothrauff, Jr.   1969.   Slum Area Rehabilitation by Private Enterprise.   Columbia Law Review 69 (5): 739-69.

Some political leaders and federal officials have called for participation by large private corporations in the problems of low and moderate income housing.   The President's Committee on Urban Housing in its report at the end of 1968 recommended private enterprise participation in the production and rehabilitation of needed housing units.   And a fair number of major industrial organizations and trade associations have emphasized the public relations value of housing rehabilitation for the lower income families. In some cities private organizations have banded together to establish private rehabilitation companies.   The author asserts that "a strategy of slum dispersal will be less costly and more consistent with American societal goals than will a plan of a massive ghetto gilding.   Realistically, people will be living in ghetto housing for a good many years. Rehabilitation of the ghetto would, therefore, seem to be both necessary and not inconsistent with long range dispersal strategy."   The purpose of this article, however, is to provide a word of advise to the attorneys handling rehabilitation cases.   "Our purpose in preparing his article will be sufficiently served if some corporate lawyers will note and warn their clients about the terribly complicated and time consuming problems that can arise from a well intentioned venture into social responsibility.   The rehabilitation of occupied housing is comparable to surgery on a live patient without anesthesia.   The business firm which starts rehabilitating low and moderate income housing without employing a capable urban affairs officer or a team of experienced urban consultants will prove to be about as effective as a well intentioned barber undertaking an appendectomy."   The author further emphasizes that the rehabilitation of low and moderate income housing as a problem-solving management job, if handled properly, can help meet an important national need and also can produce tangible profits and benefits to the participating business firm.

0021.   Berry, Brian J. L.   1976.   Ghetto Expansion and Single-Family Housing: Chicago, 1968-1972.   Journal of Urban Economics 3 (4): 397-423.

Analysis of selling prices of single-family homes in the City of Chicago during the period 1968-1972 confirms that, controlling for structure and other characteristics, price levels and rates of price increase were lower in black than in white neighborhoods, and that blacks were willing to pay more to move into white neighborhoods but whites showed an aversion to living in changing neighborhoods or those contiguous to black areas.   Differences in price changes at the white-Latino interface indicate that the most general influence on levels and changes in neighborhood filtering among submarkets segmented by income, race, and other characteristics, but that arbitrage mechanisms must be invoked in the case of the white-black interface.*

0022.   Better, Shirley.   1974.   The Urban Housing Crisis: Opportunity and Challenge.   Black Scholar 6 (4): 2-8.

Based on the 1970 Census data, more than 30 percent of all blacks living in central cities reside in substandard, deteriorating housing units with serious code violations. The aim of the 1974 Housing and Community Development Act is the development of viable urban communities by providing decent housing and suitable living environment for all American families by expanding economic opportunities, principally for persons of low and moderate income. The author asserts that blacks now have a great opportunity to revitalize their communities. More emphasis must be put on rehabilitation of existing units rather than new constructions. It is pointed out that black residents should insist that local governments set aside funds to create programs to train and counsel residents of federally subsidized housing to take more responsibility for maintenance and management of their buildings.

0023.   Beyer, Glenn H. 1965. Housing Problems of Our Central Cities. In: **Housing and Society**, by Glenn H. Beyer. New York: Macmillan.   Chapter 10.

It is generally known that the greatest "proportion of poor-quality housing in the United States is in the central cities of our metropolitan areas. This has resulted from the fact that throughout our history many of the families who have lacked adequate means to afford a decent standard of living have congregated there. Workers in many of these families have always held lower-paying jobs and have wanted to be near their places of work." This article primarily deals with discussing the historical pattern of migration of poor families into the central cities, and a description of housing conditions in these areas.

0024.   Bloom, Howard S. 1981. Household Participation in the Section 8 Existing Housing Program: Evaluating a Multistage Selection Process. **Evaluation Review** 5 (3): 325-40.

This article examines household participation in the national Section 8 Existing Housing Program funded by the U.S. Department of Housing and Urban Development. It develops a prototype for evaluating a multistage selection process which requires potential recipients to pass through several discrete stages before becoming program participants. By comparing the relative success rates of various target groups at each stage of the selection process, local, state, and federal evaluations can provide policy makers and program managers with important information for modifying programs to improve their performance.*

0025.   Blumenthal,   Ralph. 1974.   The   Suburban   Poor. In: **Suburbia   in Transition.** Louis H. Masotti, and Jeffrey K. Hadden (eds.).   New York: New Viewpoints.   Pp. 212-16.

This article describes the conditions of the suburban poor. "They are the suburban poor, and they number 800,000.   They face many of the same problems faced by the urban poor."   The article points out that the suburban poor are particularly helpless, because they lack the population concentration to form a political power base, and they are victimized "by a lack of low-cost housing, isolated by inadequate transportation, and often scorned by their unsympathetic and more affluent neighbors."

0026. Boyer, Brian D. 1973. The $70 Billion Slum. In: **Cities Destroyed for Cash: The FHA Scandal at HUD.** Chicago, Illinois: Follett. Pp. 3-23.

This article attempts to show that the FHA scandal was a deliberate profit motivated program of urban ruin, under the cover of government housing law and with an unlimited financial support from the federal government. The author contends that as a whole, the pattern and evidence in nearly every city pointed to conspiracy between mortgage and real estate interests, supported by government officials. HUD' ownership of about 390,000 housing units was likely, at a price of about $5 billion. The decision to end FHA mortgage for the inner city further compounded the problem. For instance, by September 1972, HUD's offices in New York, Chicago, Detroit, and Los Angeles had effectively red-lined the core cities. The termination of subsidized housing in 1973 for all practical purposes ended the FHA's resale of its repossessed houses. This forced the owners who could not sell their houses to abandon them if they wanted to move, thus adding to the FHA inventory.

0027. Bratt, Rachel G. 1983. The Housing Payments Program: Its Possible Effects on Minorities, Poor. **Journal of Housing** 40 (4): 108-10.

Should federal government housing policy be aimed at producing new subsidized housing or provide low-income people with more buying power? This is a long debated question. The Reagan administration seems to favor a cash payment plan, that based on the recommendations of the President's Commission on Housing, will tighten the eligibility criteria as compared to Section 8 program, targeting only those families with incomes no more than 50 percent of the area's median income. This proposal, if implemented, will essentially eliminate more than 6 million lower income households, mostly blacks, who were previously eligible for federal housing aid. This article discusses the views of the opponents and proponents of the current administration's policy. The author also highlights the irony of the Commission's continued allowance of mortgage interest and property taxes as tax deductible items, a subsidy enjoyed mainly by households with an annual income of $30,000 or higher.

0028. Bratt, Rachel G. 1985. Housing for Low Income People: A Preliminary Comparison of Existing and Potential Supply Strategies. **Journal of Urban Affairs** 7 (3): 1-18.

Although there is a general agreement among housing analysts that affordability has gotten worse and that overall quality has gotten better, there is some debate whether the supply of low cost housing is adequate. Based upon available data, this paper takes the view that many local markets have severe shortages of decent, low cost rental housing. After concluding that cash vouchers would not stimulate housing production, and that the unaided private market is not capable of meeting the demand, a preliminary comparison is made between the two previously tried housing supply strategies for low income people: private market with public incentives and direct production and ownership by the public sector. While a lack of systematic data hampers the analysis, the public housing program emerges in a stronger position than the publicly subsidized multi-family programs that depend on for-profit developers. However, low rent housing production by community and tenant groups presents a compelling and exciting new strategy that warrants further exploration and support. The paper concludes that a national program should be launched to promote community-based housing initiatives.*

0029.   Bratt, Rachel, Chester Hartman, and Ann Meyerson (eds.). 1986. **Critical Perspectives on Housing.** Philadelphia, PA: Temple University Press. 600 pp.

This book consists of a collection of 33 articles, 17 of which are previously published and the remaining 16 are published here for the first time. The book details the nation's housing problems and provides several proposals for change. A wide range of topics are discussed. They include: housing construction industry, homelessness, abandonment, the market's ability to serve women and minorities, rural housing problems, suburbanization, as well as Reagan administration's housing agenda and policy.

0030.   Bressler, Marvin. 1960. The Myers' Case: An Instance of Successful Racial Invasion. **Social Problems** 8 (2): 126-42.

Many studies bear witness to the "fact that efforts by Negroes in the urban North to alter status quo in housing has often met with resistance which has begun in anger and ended in bloodshed. Of late there have been an increasing number of such incidents in the 'new suburbs' which have emerged since World War II. As a consequence such communities as Levittown, Pennsylvania, have become prominent symbols of social racial violence. The success or failure of Negro invasion in such communities may well determine whether all housing in the United States will exist on an integrated or segregated basis." This paper examines the events that transpired, when William Myers, Jr. and his family became the first black family to attempt to get housing in Levittown, Pennsylvania.

0031.   Brooks, Mary E., and Paul Davidoff. 1976. More Cities Looking at Suburban Housing Plans. **Practicing Planner** 6 (3): 6-9.

Hartford, Connecticut, in 1975 challenged the legality of HUD's funding the Community Development Act entitlement grants to 7 of its suburbs on the grounds that they refused to accept minority and lower income households. Hartford City contains nearly 24 percent of th region's population, but about 86 percent of its minorities. The court ruled in favor of the City of Hartford for HUD had failed to undertake an adequate review. The article examines this ruling and points out that it is not at all clear how fully HUD will implement the Act to give maximum priority to lower income families and minorities. But, the author points out that the Hartford's success has caused many central cities to watchdog applications from their regions more carefully.

0032.   Brooks, Mary E., et al. 1982. **More Places to Live: A Study of Interjurisdictional Housing Mobility Programs.** New York: Metropolitan Action Institute. 107 pp.

This monograph describes and evaluates interjurisdictional housing mobility programs (agreements among jurisdictions to allow the exchange or transfer of housing subsidy certificates when a family moves from one jurisdiction to another) designed to increase access to housing across jurisdictional lines for minorities and lower income households. The outcome of this study indicates that mobility programs have encountered many obstacles, but they have responded by designing structures to circumvent such problems rather than trying to remove them. It also finds out that in general, a program's success depends more on a particular administrator's attitude and interest than a specific structure. The study concludes with a set of nine guidelines for the design of equitable interjurisdictional programs .

0033.   Brown, William H., Jr. 1972. Access to Housing: The Role of the Real Estate Industry. **Economic Geography** 48 (1): 66-78.

This article examines the role played by the real estate industry in providing minority access to housing in certain areas. It tries to determine the basis for racial discrimination behavior in housing in an attempt to make some progress in deciding how to intervene most effectively. According to the author, an examination of the "racial practices of real estate brokers offer one such point of intervention." It is concluded that the firm controls that the National Association of Real Estate Brokers "has historically exerted over racial policies and practices of the real estate industry could never have remained so effective had these policies not found a sympathetic response in the racial attitudes of the vast majority of workaday white real estate agents."

0034.   Builders Consortium for Affordable Housing. 1983. Affordable Housing is Possible. **Western City** 59 (6): 10-12.

An eight year effort by Orange County, California, and its builders "demonstrate that, with cooperation, housing can be built that is both affordable and profitable." This article explains that the county participated in the project to test the cost reduction potential of cutting processing time, from site selection through the issuance of building permits, and of certain modifications in development standards in a $6.6 million, 124-unit Bench Mark Villas development. This demonstration shows that quality houses can be built at affordable prices.

0035.   Bullard, Robert D. 1978. Does Section 8 Promote an Ethnic and Economic Mix? **Journal of Housing** 35 (7): 364-365.

Houston, Texas, is a good example of the new prosperity and fast growing city in the United States. The major objective of this study is to "assess the extent to which the Section 8 program in Houston has promoted an ethnic and economic mix of housing for low-income residents." The analysis is based on personal interviews of 200 randomly selected recipients of Houston's housing assistance payment program, that uses Section 8. The author concludes that "the Houston housing Allowance program has had little success in reversing the pattern of racially segregated housing."

0036.   Bullard, Robert D. 1979. Housing and the Quality of Life in the Urban Community: A Focus on the Dynamic Factors Affecting Blacks in the Housing Market. Journal of Social and Behavioral Science 25 (2): 46-52.

In recent years numerous discussions have been centered around the quality of housing in the black community. This study critically examines several conceptual and substantive areas which affect blacks in the housing market. To illustrate the fundamental problems of blacks in the housing market, six specific topics—governmental policies, homeownership, segregation, discrimination, migration and renewed interest in the inner city—were selected for intensive analysis. Market factors, in addition to discriminatory housing practice, continue to deny blacks a basic form of investment: namely, homeownership.*

0037. Bullard, Robert D. 1980. Black Housing in the Golden Buckle of the Sunbelt. **Free Inquiry in Creative Sociology** 8 (2):

For the urban dwellers in the nation, housing continues to be a major problem, despite the private and public efforts over the past few decades. The problem is more serious among blacks and minorities as compared to the general population. This article considers the status of black housing in Houston, Texas, known as the "golden buckle of the sunbelt."

0038. Bullard, Robert D. 1983. Persistent Barriers in Housing Black Americans. **Journal of Applied Social Sciences** 7 (1); 19-31.

This paper examines the quality of housing among the nation's Blacks. While many barriers to decent and affordable housing for Black Americans have been overcome, blacks still do not enjoy complete freedom in the housing market. Over forty years of federal housing policies and programs have achieved mixed results. Black families along with millions of other families must contend with spiraling costs associated with decent housing. In addition, the problems of individual and institutionalized housing discrimination continue to deny a significant segment of our society savings and investment through homeownership. The re-discovery of central city neighborhoods and the reclaiming of closed-in residential areas have intensified the competition between the poor and the affluent in once deteriorating neighborhoods and have accelerated the rate of displacement among the elderly, renters, and minority households.*

0039. Bullard, Robert D. 1984. The Black Family Housing Alternatives in the 1980s. **Journal of Black Studies** 14 (3): 341-51.

This article explains family life cycle—household formation, prechild, child-bearing and rearing, child-launching, postchild, and widowhood or family dissolution—and discusses the problems minorities with children (with an average larger families size) encounter in obtaining decent and affordable housing nationwide. "If a family is a member of an ethnic minority, female-headed, or a large household, the chances of being poorly housed is increased substantially." The author asserts that many black families who are forced into renter market later "discover restricted and limited housing choices because they have children."

0040. Bullard, Robert D., and Odessa L. Pierce. 1979. Black Housing Patterns in a Southern Metropolis: Competition for Housing in a Shrinking Market. **Black Scholar** 11 (2): 60-67.

The focus of this paper is on residential housing patterns of blacks in a sunbelt city, Houston. The migration of individuals to the city has intensified the competition for decent housing. The rapid population growth has also accelerated the competition between lower and middle income residents for close-in neighborhoods of the central city. Spiraling housing costs have limited the single-family home market to a select few. While the overall housing condition in Houston is booming, 'poverty pockets' continue to exist amidst affluence. Black families are less likely to be homeowners than their white counterparts. The need for public housing far exceeds the supply; residency in public housing reflects the segregated patterns of the city: blacks in black neighborhoods and whites in white areas. Blacks' moving to Houston's suburbs lagged behind that of whites; the percentage of blacks in the city's suburbs actually decreased between 1960 and 1970. Overall, the economic prosperity that Houston is experiencing has had little impact in reversing the housing segregation level.*

0041.   Bunce, Harold. 1986. Race, Moving Status, and Urban Services in Central Cities. Social Science Research 15 (1): 82-96.

The influences of race and moving status on the likelihood of receiving unsatisfactory or inadequate urban services are investigated using logistic probability models. The analysis bears upon the perennial issue of felt injustice and the charge that white America has a policy of sustaining separate and unequal societies for minorities in cities. The results also speak to the limits on market adjustments to correct undesirable public outcomes. Statistically significant racial distinctions are isolated in the assessment of five urban services; in three cases these are unambiguously consequential. The extent to which moving costs and limited housing opportunities inhibit housing market adjustments to uneven service provision is measured by a decomposition of essential probabilities for minorities and whites. The evidence generated supports containing policies that expand minority housing opportunities and reduce impediments to the mobility of minorities in urban areas.*

0042.   Caplan, Eleanor K., et. al. 1960. Factors Affecting Racial Change in Two Middle Income Housing Areas. Phylon 21(3): 225-33.

The racial invasion-succession in urban neighborhoods has attracted considerable interest in urban sociology and race relations. This article analyzes the rate of racial transition or invasion-succession sequence in two neighborhoods: Russel Woods in Detroit, Michigan, and Ludlow in Cleveland, Ohio, two areas with black entry at the same time. The focus of this study is on the factors that influence the rate of racial transition. Differences in the rate of racial transition in Russel Woods and Ludlow are fully explored.

0043.   Case, Fred E. 1971. Housing the Underhoused in the Inner City. Journal of Finance 26 (2): 427-44.

Since the beginning of the federally assisted housing program in 1934, about 10 million units have been provided under various federal programs. "However, the Douglas Commission has estimated that at least 600,000 units are needed annually in the decade of the 70's for families who will not be able to afford decent, safe, sanitary housing without some form of assistance." This article makes a cost-benefit analysis of the problem of providing housing for the underhoused and concludes that "housing is a part of a cycle which is involved with the kind of education and training that inner-city residents receive, the kind of business or employment opportunities they have, the amount of family income which can be earned, the ability of the family to obtain housing and the kind of neighborhood and housing which the families can afford or which they get. A careful cost-benefit analysis of inner cities and the housing which is provided there might show that the extent to which any element of the cycle is neglected is the extent to which the public sector pays an increasingly greater cost for ignoring the total problems of inner-city families." That is, the author proposes a wholistic approach to the problem of housing the underhoused.

0044.   Clayton, Glenn A. 1974. Housing Problems of Minorities: Policy Considerations. In: The Urban Science in the Seventies. James F. Blumstein, and Eddie J. Martic (eds.). Nashville, TN: Vanderbelt University Press. Pp. 175-91.

The differences in black-white housing, as measured by a disparity index, is uniformly high in all geographic subdivisions in the U.S. In order to solve these disparities, there is a need for an entirely new legislative approach and a federal land use and urban growth policy that will effectively organize and implement the policy. It must also be recognized that families have the right to live wherever they want. The author also discusses the use of Family Housing Allowance, accentuating the positive by providing an effective means of free choice in housing location.

0045.   Cobb, James W. 1972. The Black Lawyer and Housing. Urban Lawyer 4 (2): 225-32.

This article discusses the problems facing black lawyers in the United States today in the field of housing and urban development. It also discusses the methods of encouraging more black lawyers to be stimulated to qualify to represent black clients in the field of housing. The author, president-elect of a predominantly black bar association, answers some questions regarding the housing ambitions of blacks.

0046.   Cobb, Mary. 1977. West Virginia Tackles Low-Income Housing Needs Via State Coordinated Production, Delivery Program. Journal of Housing 34 (1): 12-17.

Asserting that in 1973 West Virginia's low-income housing situation was a microcosm of the national housing dilemma, this article explains how Governor Moore charged the state Economic Opportunity Office to find a workable answer to the basic housing needs of low income families in the state. The success of the program, its achievements and interrelationships are also discussed.

0047.   Cohen, Matthew. 1976. Mobile Home Subdivisions: The No-Frills Home is Here. Planning 42 (6): 12-14.

Some twenty years ago the demand for low cost single family homes inspired the ingenious land use innovation—the mobile home subdivision. But this subdivision concept never got off the ground, because of the high cost of financing, the exploitation of owners by developers, the lack of municipal regulations, and the lack of FHA mortgage insurance programs. Section 235, a subsidy program for low-income home buyers, was reactivated to include moderate income families and amendments introduced in Congress to include the double-width mobile homes on private lots as beneficiaries of federal subsidies. One of the major conclusions of this essay is that high cost of credit derailed the mobile home subdivision movement, and the low-income families suffered for their poor credit ratings and lack of federal support.

0048. Connolly, Edward. 1981. Refugee Influx Highlights Emergency Housing Problem. **Journal of Housing** 38 (1): 21-24.

The recent migrations of Cuban, Haitian, and Indochinese refugees to the U.S. have exacerbated an already critical housing situation in communities with large concentration of poor and lower income persons. This article examines the housing plight of millions of refugees annually on an international level, with special emphasis on the situation in the United States as a receiver of a large number of refugees. Among other things, this article calls for cooperation in solving the housing problems of this group of disadvantaged people. With regards to the United States the author points out that "the recent refugee crises serve to remind us that there is a housing emergency for many sections of the population that must be addressed."

0049. Connolly, Harold X. 1973. Black Movement into the Suburbs: Suburbs Doubling Their Black Populations During the 1960s. **Urban Affairs Quarterly** 9 (1): 91-111.

This paper studies selected suburban communities in the U.S. that more than doubled the number of their black inhabitants during the 1960s such that blacks constituted at least 10 percent of the total population in 1970. Areas examined are the suburban communities of Hartford, NY City, Newark, Washington, D.C., Detroit, Chicago, St. Louis, Las Vagas, and Los Angeles. The study concludes that "in most instances these suburban blacks clearly surpassed central city blacks in income, education, job status, and home ownership. Less common, except for home ownership, was black socioeconomic parity with white suburbanites. Within this study's scope, it appears that since 1960 the socioeconomic status of Negroes living in the suburbs has improved to a point where city-suburban socioeconomic differences among blacks resemble those observed among whites." The author calls for further research in this area.

0050. Cook, Christine C., and Nancy M. Rudd. 1984. Factors Influencing Residential Location of Female Householders. **Urban Affairs Quarterly** 20 (1): 78-96.

Currently, 25 % of all households are headed by females. Although 75 % of all female householders are urban dwellers, few investigations have examined factors contributing to their centralization. This study focused on the dynamics of residential location among female householders living in one-person, two-or-more person family, and nonfamily configurations. A path model was designed and evaluated that examined the relationships among such variables as tract distance from the central business district (CBD), proportion of structures in the tract built before 1950, tract density, urban/suburban tract designation, median rent per tract, proportion of elderly householders and black householders per tract for each of the female householder groups. The results suggest that female-headed households live close to the CBD, in urban and densely populated tracts, in pre-1950 buildings, and in lower rent units and that socioeconomic and spatial organization factors impact differently on the residential location of each of the household configurations considered.*

0051.   Cooper, James R. 1975. Housing Needs of the Urban Poor: The Problems and Alternatives. American Real Estate and Urban Economic Association Journal 3 (1): 33-47.

"It is the purpose of this article to consider the predicted cost to tax payer of subsidizing the occupants of Section 235 (Sales) and Section 236 (Multi-family Rental) housing programs and some problems of alternative subsidies." The author uses a simulation model of production and occupancy to arrive at cost estimates. The wide discrepancy between costs estimates generated through this simulation model and the subsidy cost estimate of HUD, and the reasons for the discrepancies are discussed.

0052.   Cooper, Mark N., et al. 1983. Equity and Energy: Rising Energy Prices and the Living Standards of Lower-Income Americans. Boulder, Colorado: Westview Press. 302 pp.

The primary purpose of this book is to examine the direct and indirect impacts of rising energy prices on the economic well-being of low and middle income households (about 23 million) in the United States. This evaluation is made from three perspectives: (1) it analyzes the effects of rising energy prices on the purchasing power (including housing services) of different income groups, and shows that there is significant erosion in the disposable income of the low and moderate income groups to the extent they cannot keep up with utility costs increases; (2) the book examines the effects of rising energy prices on the lower income rental housing market. According to the authors, increased utility costs have been a major cause of landlords' disinvestment and increase in abandonment at the low end of the housing market, with obvious impact on the general housing conditions of the poor; and, (3) the last part of the book analyzes the importance of energy costs in the local government budget, posing a severe financial burden on the local governments which in turn reduce the government's ability to deliver services (such as housing) to lower income population.

0053.   Cowger, Bob. 1981. Focus on the Indian in Oklahoma. HUD Challenge 12 (1): 16-20.

The author, a native born Oklahoma Cherokee, looks at the Indian "way of life" with a special interest in housing from the Native American's conception of home and community. Among topics discussed are American Indians' conception of "house versus home," HUD's original entry into Indian housing, HUD's second initiative, and variances in land law in Oklahoma.

0054.   Coyne, Deirdre C., and Carr Kunze. 1978. Section 11(b) Financing Used by Reston, Virginia, to Get Section 8 Cooperative Units Built. Journal of Housing 35 (9): 464-68.

Construction of a cooperative housing development for low and moderate income families located in Reston, Virginia, is near completion. This FHA-insured project is reportedly the first of its kind of newly constructed cooperative housing for low income families to receive 100 percent Section 8 housing assistance payments and Section 11(b) financing. This 102 unit, 7.5 acre cooperative housing was designed to provide as much open space as possible to overcome neighborhood objections about overcrowding. This project for low and moderate income families is surrounded by multi-family housing developments, with an area of single-family homes nearby.

0055. Cressey, Paul Frederick. 1938. Population Succession in Chicago: 1898-1930. American Journal of Sociology 44 (July): 59-69.

The various groups composing Chicago's population have followed definite patterns of [residential] succession in their moving through the city. Back of these changes there has been a common process at work, involving successive stages of invasion, conflict, recession, and reorganization. Measurement of the distribution and movement of the chief groups show that their location is related to their length of residence and to their assimilation into the general life of the city.*

0056. Cuomo, Mario Matthew. 1974. Forest Hill Diary: The Crisis of Low Income Housing. New York: Random House. 209 pp.

During the winter of 1971 and spring of 1972, the controversy over proposed construction of a low income housing project in Forest Hill, Queens, New York, reached its highest pitch. The controversy was interpreted as a fight between blacks and whites, as a critical test of the nation's low income housing policy, and as a defiance of the voice of the middle class who were against the project. The scattered-site project was designed to move a large number of poor blacks into middle income white communities by building low income units in their neighborhoods. The author was then the mediator assigned by Mayor Lindsay's office to settle the Forest Hills' dispute. The author describes that the compromise he made was adopted by the Board of Estimate: there would be three 12-story buildings, as opposed to 24-story towers originally proposed. This did not solve all the problems, however. But, the mayoral election placed a new and safer emphasis on rehabilitating the ghettoes.

0057. Dahmann, Donald C. 1982. Housing Opportunities for Black and White Households. Washington, D.C.: GPO. 18 pp.

With skyrocketing cost of housing, concerns about housing opportunities have increasingly come to focus on affordability. Housing opportunity or affordability depend upon a wide variety of factors such as income, race, stage of life cycle, and personal preferences. This publication investigates the impact of some of these factors on black and white housing opportunities using census data. Some of the topics discussed are the supply of housing, factors contributing to the removal of units from the housing inventory, the newly constructed housing and black access to these units.

0058. Dahmann, Donald C. 1985. Assessments of Neighborhood Quality in Metropolitan America. Urban Affairs Quarterly 20 (4): 511-35.

This investigation utilizes national survey data to show which elements of neighborhoods affect overall levels of satisfaction with local residential environments, how often these elements are perceived as existing, and how often they are evaluated as bothersome. These questions are answered in a geographical framework that disaggregates the nation's metropolitan settlement system by two macrolevel components--size of settlement and centrality within settlements--and one microlevel component--the neighborhood itself. Global assessments of neighborhood quality are shown to be a function of centrality and (secondarily) of size, and the mix of conditions perceived as existing in the local residential environment. Evidence for a geographical basis for policies concerning the quality of residential environments is found to be considerable.@

0059.   Darden, Joe T. 1974. The Quality of Life in a Black Ghetto: A Geographic Review. Pennsylvania Geographer 12 (3): 3-8.

An analysis of a Pittsburgh ghetto has revealed that the quality of life is not the same throughout the ghetto, but increases with distance from the CBD [Central Business District]. Thus, the ghetto is a microcosm of the city as a whole. That is, as distance from the CBD increases, the quality of life within the city as a whole increases. Therefore, the conclusions of E. Franklin Frazier [that the social and spatial pattern described for the City of Chicago as a whole, existed within subcommunities including the Black ghetto] on Blacks in Chicago during the thirties and the conclusions of Donald Deskins [that the Negro sub- community is a microcosm of the city as a whole] on Blacks in Detroit during the sixties, hold true for Blacks in Pittsburgh during the seventies.@

0060.   Davis, Tom L. 1967. Cooperative Self-Help Housing. Law and Contemporary Problems 32 (3): 409-15.

This article examines the concept of self-help cooperative and concludes that "the use of self-help in the construction of cooperative and condominium housing should be explored as one of the methods of achieving home ownership for the low income group in the United States. Self-help has been successfully used in undeveloped countries and is receiving additional interest in the United States."

0061.   Davis, Otto A., Charles M. Eastman, and Chang-I Huan. 1974. The Shrinkage in the Stock of Low-Quality Housing in the Central City: An Empirical Study of the U.S. Experience Over the Last Ten Years. Urban Studies 11 (1): 13-24.

The main purpose of this study centers upon the "change in the stock of low-quality housing in the 50 largest U.S. cities." This study shows that the total stock of housing has increased over the past ten years. There has also been a decline in the stock of low-quality housing. Thus, there is an overall improvement in the quality of housing in the United States during the study period, because the ratio of low-quality units to the total number of units has declined significantly. This study examines the magnitude of the shrinkage in the stock of low-income housing and attempts to explore the measurable factors that may help to explain the decline. The implications of the decline in low-quality housing units are also discussed.

0062.   Darvish,   Rokneddin. 1983. An   Ecological   Investigation   of   the

Relationship Between the Quality of Housing and Selected Structural Characteristics of 180 Cities in the United States. Unpublished Ph.D. Dissertation. North Texas State University. 211 pp.

This is an investigation of the relationships between selected structural characteristics (treated as independent variables) of the community and the quality of housing (dependent variable). The independent variables are city size, sex-age composition, socioeconomic status, racial-ethnic composition, age of the city, regional location, form of government, city type, and occupancy status. The findings indicate "a strong positive relationship between socioeconomic status variables and the quality of housing. The relationship between the percent nonwhites and substandard housing was positive." The author tests several other hypotheses not enumerated here.

0063.   Delaney, Paul. 1974. Negroes Find Few Tangible Gains. In: Suburbia in Transition. Louis H. Masotti, and Jeffrey K. Hadden (eds.). New York: New Viewpoints. Pp. 278-82.

"A small, growing number of black families is increasingly able to penetrate the new outer cities of America, the swelling bands of suburbs that ring the stagnating inner cities. But for most of the 800,000 blacks who fled, technically, to the 'suburbs' in the last decade, the move has been to municipalities like East Cleveland, just a political dividing line away from Cleveland's ghetto." This article indicates that despite so much talk about recent black suburbanization, the actual gain in the improvement of black housing conditions, among other things, is not enough.

0064.   DeLeeuw, Frank, Ann B. Shnare, and Raymond Struyk. 1976. Housing. In: The Urban Predicament. William Gorham, and Nathan Glazer (eds.). Washington, D.C.: The Urban Institute. Chapter 3, pp. 119-78.

This chapter is a comprehensive discussion of housing problem in the United States as a whole. However, within the context of the general housing problem, the authors discuss white American attitudes toward race and housing, race and residential segregation, policies toward residential segregation, slums and the inner city, and the necessity of improving the housing conditions of the poor.

0065.   Deskins, Donald R. 1972. Race, Residence, and Workplace in Detroit, 1880 to 1965. Economic Geography 48 (1): 79-94.

The journey-to-work accounts for one-third to one half of all trips originating at residence. It consumes much worker time and energy. The intent of this article is "to examine the journey-to-work patterns of Detroit's Negro and white populations over time, from 1880 to 1965, in order to determine: (1) if historical continuity is evident in those forces which tend to minimize home-work separation; and (2) what effects, if any, residential segregation has had on Negro worktrip patterns during the time span considered." The study concludes that residential segregation appears to be the factor determining the differentials in journey-to-work-patterns. This has been burdensome and costly to Detroit's Negro workers. It is suggested that the problem can be remedied by eliminating residential segregation, accompanied with equal opportunities in employment.

0066.   Dockson, R. R., et al.   1980. Cooperative Housing: Three Perspectives on
        Ways to Make Housing More Affordable. **Journal of Housing** 37 (2): 90-91.

        Participants in a November 1979 meeting in San Francisco agreed that
        cooperative housing will occupy an increasingly important part of the
        housing picture in the future. The cooperative form of ownership was seen
        as particularly important to low- and moderate-income persons because of its
        relatively affordable initial and continuing costs." This article
        primarily consists of excerpts from the speeches given by three of the
        conference participants.

0067.   Dodson, Jack E.   1960.   Minority Group Housing in Two Texas Cities.   In:
        Studies in Housing and Minority Groups.   Nathan Glazer, and Davis McEntire
        (eds.). Berkeley: University of California Press. Pp. 84-109.

        The aim of this paper is "to describe and analyze the housing situation of
        Mexican and Negroes in San Antonio and Negroes in Houston, Texas." The
        analyses are based on official figures and reports and from interviews in
        both cities with all relevant parties. The main conclusions of this
        investigation are that "members of minority groups in both San Antonio and
        Houston face special problems in obtaining housing; that the quality of
        their housing is markedly inferior to that of nonminority population; that
        up until recent years prejudice and lack of interest in minority group
        housing on the part of builders and mortgage lenders played an important role
        in restricting the supply of housing for minority groups." This study
        reveals that the main cause of inferior minority housing in both cities is
        their poverty. The author suggests that greater subsidy to the poor
        families is a reasonable way for immediate resolution of the problem.

0068.   Dolbeare, Cushing N.   1983.   The Low Income Housing Crisis.   In: **America's
        Housing Crisis.**   Chester Hartman (ed.).   Boston, Mass.: Routledge and
        Kegan Paul. Chapter 2, pp. 29-57.

        This article focuses on the problems of low-income families, pointing out
        that "even though others have growing housing difficulties, for most of the
        last three decades housing problems have generally been confined to low-
        income and minority people." Topics discussed include an overview of the
        housing situation of low-income people, a highlight of accomplishments of
        low-income housing programs, the cost of federal low-income housing
        programs, a discussion of elements of a comprehensive low-income housing
        policy, the need for entitlement programs, and the causes of the present
        housing crisis.

0069.   Donabed, Joseph E.   1981.   Zoning: Mobile Home Options and Opportunities.
        Werstern City 57 (7): 6-7.

        This article explains the myth "that mobile homes are a panacea for the
        housing shortage for low and very low income families remain in doubt, even
        based upon today's cost."

0070.   Drury, Margaret Josephine.   1972.   The Family High-Rise: A Comparative
        Study by Apartment Location Within High-Rise Buildings of the Perception of
        Housing Services and Behavior of Low Income Residents. Unpublished Ph.D.

Dissertation. Cornell University. 202 pp.

In 1968, Congress enacted an amendment to the Housing Act that placed limitation on approval of new high-rise structures in low-income public housing projects. In view of the fact that research on the impact of high-rise building on tenant is scarce, this study attempts to examine whether the location of an apartment within a high-rise building makes any difference in the way "a family relates to its neighbors and the community around it, whether the location affects a resident's perception of or satisfaction with housing services provided, and how the relationships and services differ for residents at different levels of a high-rise building. Results and implications are discussed.

0071.   Duncan, Beverly, and Philip M. Hauser. 1961. **Housing a Metropolis:** Chicago. Glencoe, Ill.: Free Press. 278 pp.

This book is the result of a cooperative research program by the Chicago Community Inventory, University of Chicago, and the governmental agencies of the City of Chicago. It is a general work on housing problem in the Chicago metropolis, but a chapter is devoted to a discussion of "White-Nonwhite Differential in Housing." The characteristics of lower-income families and housing is also discussed in this book.

0072.   Edwards, Ozzie. 1972. Family Composition as a Variable in Residential Succession. **American Journal of Sociology** 77 (4): 731-41.

This paper investigates the extent to which family composition affects black residential succession. From the study of census tracts in Chicago, it appears that younger black families and those with children lead the way in black penetration, while white older families and those with children lead the white exodus. This study also provides evidence of some stability "of family-type composition in areas undergoing racial transition. The latter may be traced to the characteristics of housing in these areas."

0073.   Erskine, Hazel. 1967. The Polls: Negro Housing. **Public Opinion Quarterly** 31 (Fall): 482-98.

This is a summary of a public opinion poll on black housing as a part of a greater investigation of civil rights and race relations. Results are presented in tabular form.

0074.   Fairchild, Halford H., and M. Belinda Tucker. 1982. Black Residential Mobility: Trends and Characteristics. **Journal of Social Issues** 38 (3): 51-74.

This analysis of trends in Black residential mobility uses a multi-disciplinary approach that incorporates contributions from sociology, psychology, economics, demography, and social geography, among others. Contemporary patterns of segregated urban environments are viewed from the perspective of external constraints on Black residential mobility opportunities. These constraints, operating at both individual and institutional levels, include the actions of individual homeowners, realtors, local and federal legislators, and lending institutions. The attitudes of Blacks are viewed as "internal factors" which also serve to maintain segregated living arrangements. The process and consequences associated with urban ghettoization are identified. Recent trends of Black suburbanization, "gentrification," and Latino/Black residential integration, are identified and discussed. The article concludes with an examination of potential future scenarios, provides suggestions for future research, and addresses a number of policy and practical issues.θ

0075. Falk, David, and Herbert M. Franklin. 1976. Equal Housing Opportunity: The Unfinished Federal Agenda. Washington, D.C.: The Potomac Institute. 168 pp.

This is a comprehensive examination of the federal government's role in dealing with equal housing opportunity, in the past and at the present time. It includes a set of recommendations for federal programs and policies that could promote a greater equality in housing opportunities in the future.

0076. Fielding, Byron. 1972. Low-Income, Single-Person Housing. Journal of Housing 29 (3): 133-36.

Legal challenges of skid row residents can prevent urban renewal projects which do not provide decent housing for the single, nonelderly poor. The article describes the NAHRO's support for construction of congregate housing, and congregate housing provisions of the Housing and Urban Development Act of 1970 and HUD-FHA implementing regulations. Local efforts to construct or renew congregate housing are also noted.

0077. Fishman, Joshua A. 1961. Some Social and Psychological Determinants of Intergroup Relations in Changing Neighborhoods: An Introduction to the Bridgeview Study. Social Forces 40 (1): 42-51.

The entry of minority groups into "new" neighborhoods is disruptive of the status needs and aspirations of earlier residents--particularly in the suburbs--as well as of their images of these neighborhoods. The drift toward increased Negro occupancy of such neighborhoods is related not only to the growing Negro pressure for better housing but also to interminority problems, the views and activities of realtors and clergymen, and to the activities of "neighborhood associations."*

0078. Foard, Ashley A., and Hilbert Fefferman. 1960. Federal Urban Renewal Legislation. Law and Contemporray Problems 25 (4): 635-84.

This paper outlines "the early origins, the struggle for enactment, and the development of federal urban renewal legislation. It also discusses separately two of several major issues which recurringly give rise to changes in that legislation. One concerns restrictions in the federal law which direct federal urban renewal aids toward the betterment of housing, as distinguished from the betterment of cities and urban life in general. The other concerns the statutory formula for apportioning the cost of the long program between the federal government and local governments."

0079. Foley, Donald L. 1973. Institutional and Contextual Factors Affecting the Housing Choices of Minority Residents. In: Segregation in Residential Areas: Papers on Racial and Socioeconomic Factors in Choice of Housing. Amos H. Hawley, and Vincent P. Rock (eds.). Washington, D.C.: National

Academy of Sciences. Pp. 85-147.

Institutional barriers to freedom of choice in the housing market may be grouped into three classes: (a) private institutional practices in the rental, sale, and financing of housing; (b) public institutional practices in urban planning and land use controls for urban renewal and the financing, development, and managing of housing; (c) the array of activities that form the community context for housing choices. Within this last class are the distribution of employment, welfare policies, the school system, transportation, and such intangibles as community leadership. This paper focuses on opening up housing choices for minorities and the prospects of this choice being extended by "dispersal" beyond the main inner city communities.@

0080.   Ford, Larry, and Ernst Griffin. 1979. Geographical Review 69 (2): 140-58.

The word "ghetto" evokes the image of rotting tenements, abandoned cars, garbage-strewn vacant lots, congestion, pollution, poverty, crime and so forth. This article first examines the definition and meaning of the word "ghetto", and then proceeds to "examine recent changes in newly developing ghetto communities. Changing residential patterns and landscape features of San Diego's black neighborhoods" are used to exemplify the continuum that is evolving in the ghetto sector.

0081.   Form, William H. 1951. Stratification in Low and Middle Income Housing Areas. Journal of Social Issues 7 (1 & 2): 109-31.

The research on the relationship between housing and social life are very limited and have been dealt with only tangentially. The main focus of this article is to examine the relation of stratification to housing. The author suggests several areas for further investigation of the topic.

0082.   Freidberg, Sidney. 1972. A Rewarding Role for Lawyers in Low and Moderate Income Housing. Urban Lawyer 4 (): 250-258.

Inadequate housing is said to be the root cause of much misery, frustration, bitterness, and breeds a host of other problems--crime, drug, racial polarization, and so on. It has also "been said that housing for low and moderate income families is built by lawyers, not builders. It is certainly true that the services of trained counsel are essential at every stage of planning and development. This burgeoning field affords the legal profession a rewarding opportunity--rewarding financially as well as spiritually--to help achieve the goal set by Congress in the National Act of 1949: 'A decent home and a suitable living environment for every American family regardless of race, creed or color.'"

0083.   French, Robert Mills, and Jeffrey K. Hadden. 1968. Mobile Homes: Instant Suburbia or Transportable Slums? Social Problems 16 (Fall): 219-26.

Mobile homes have grown phenomenally in number--from approximately 170,000 in 1940 to more than one and three quarter million units in 1967--with even greater growth predicted. In 1961 they comprised seven percent of all new housing. By 1966 this figure doubled to 14 percent and represented more than 75 percent of all new homes valued at less than $12,500. The predominant location of mobile home parks on the periphery of cities, combined with the fact that mobile home residents are on the average considerably younger than the general population, lends credence to the speculation that mobile homes are providing "instant suburbia" for young, upwardly mobile, married couples. Other factors raise questions with this interpretation, however, e.g., only 13 percent of mobile home residents compared with 41 percent of the nation's residents are employed in white collar occupations. The relatively short life span and rapid decline in value of mobile homes raises the spectre of a new type of transportable slum which could elude housing reforms by moving beyond the jurisdiction of urban government.*

0084.   Fried, Marc, and Peggy Gleicher. 1961. Some Sources of Residential Satisfaction in an Urban Slum. Journal of the American Institute of Planners 27 (4): 305-15.

Urban renewal planning has assumed that social benefits would accrue the former residents of slums. But the meanings that the slum areas have for their residents and the consequent effects that relocation would have for them have not been adequately understood. Prior to being located from Boston's West End redevelopment area, most residents experienced profound satisfaction from living in the area. Their satisfaction derived, in large part, from the close associations maintained among the local people and from their strong sense of identity to the local places. In turn, people and places provided a framework for personal and social integration.*

0085.   Friedman, Gilbert B. 1968. Uninsurables in the Ghetto. New Republic 159 (11): 19-21.

This article explains the problems ghetto residents and home owners face in obtaining insurance. Implications for ghetto residents are discussed. It also describes the views of some insurance companies on the problem.

0086.   Friedman, Lawrence M. 1967. Government and Slum Housing: Some General Considerations. Law and Contemporary Problems 32 (2): 357-370.

This article reviews the federal effort to eliminate the slums and "provide decent homes for the poorest of the poor, in terms of the social forces that have made the job so far so hard. Clearly the slums have not been eliminated. Clearly many of the poor remain locked in their ghettos, in dark, overcrowded rooms. Clearly, the situation is unhappy. Can we shed any light on the causes and cures?"

0087.   Fuerst, J. S., and Daniel Fuerst. 1979. The Promise of Co-op Housing. Planning 45 (6): 20-24.

Cooperative housing programs may provide a viable housing option for moderate and lower income households. This study, based on observations of about 5,000 co-cop units in the Chicago area, finds that while individual co-ops may vary in the degree to which they adhere to the traditional Rochdale principles (including open membership, one member-one vote, limited return on investment, and education), cooperatives do have a positive effect on their members. Cooperatives can aid in neighborhood integration as well as providing positive role models for both whites and blacks. Successful cooperative housing that employs both sound professional management and careful tenant selection may represent one way of combating increased profiteering and displacement associated with condo-conversions.

0088. Fuerst, J. S., and Roy Petty. 1978. Bleak Housing in Chicago. Public Interest (52): 103-10.

Initially known as Gautreaux v. Chicago Housing Authority (CHA) the now famous Gautreaux suit was brought in 1966. It intended to end segregation in site and tenant selection of public housing projects. The case was fought in Federal Courts for ten years with the plaintiffs winning the case but losing the war; as a result of the Supreme Court's ruling, the opportunities for public housing and the prospects for new projects in Chicago are virtually none existent. The reasons can largely be attributed to the remedies and administration of the decision—CHA was forbidden to build any new public housing in areas where there were more than 30 percent black families, until at least 700 units of new public housing had been built in mostly white areas. Under this restriction, CHA did nothing, and the plaintiffs lost the war. Housing for blacks in Chicago deteriorates daily, and many more vacant sites are available for construction in all black areas, but until the barriers to new housing caused by the Gautreaux decision are broken, the original intentions and desires of the plaintiffs—decent and unsegregated housing—will never be realized.

0089. Gans, Herbert J. 1965. The Failure of Urban Renewal. Commentary 39(4): 29-37.

Since 1949, urban renewal program has provided "local renewal agencies with federal funds and the power of eminent domain to condemn slum neighborhoods, tear down the buildings, and resell the cleared land to private developers at a reduced price. In addition to relocating the slum dwellers in 'decent, safe, and sanitary' housing, the program was intended to stimulate large-scale private rebuilding, add new tax revenues to the dwindling coffers of the cities, revitalize their downtown areas, and halt the exodus of middle-class whites to the suburbs." This article examines the urban renewal program and describes how the program was not achieving its general goals.

0090. Gans, Herbert J. 1968. The Ghetto Rebellions and Urban Class Conflict. Academy of Political Science Proceedings 29 (1): 42-51.

This article deals with the question of the relation between ghetto living condition, housing included, and the spontaneous anger or rebellion exhibited by the ghetto residents.

0091. Gardner, Edward. 1980. Innovative Indian Programs in the Denver Region. HUD Challenge 12 (6): 7-10.

Due to its remote location, thin and widely dispersed population, and limited economic resources, the problem of providing Indians with housing services are unusual and difficult. "The project management concept and the construction of subterranean homes are two innovative methods of meeting some of the problems associated with the development of Indian housing."

0092. Garza, Jose, Richard Martinez, and Perfecto Villarreal. 1977. Hispanics
       and Housing. Journal of Housing 34 (9): 451-53.

       This article reviews what has been done and what is yet to be done in the
       Hispanic housing. More specifically, the article examines HUD's
       activities, the need for more to be done, Hispanic involvement in NAHRO,
       Hispanic Coalition, and a proposed Hispanic housing conference. The goals
       of the Coalition and the proposed conference are also discussed.

0093. Glazer, Nathan, and Davis McEntire (eds.). 1960. Studies in Housing and
       Minority Groups. Berkeley: University of California Press. 228 pp.

       "Brought together in the present volume are the findings of seven local
       studies prepared for the Commission on Race and Housing in connection with a
       broader investigation of housing problems involving minority racial and
       ethnic groups." The studies in this book are: (1) a comparative study of
       black housing in Atlanta and Birmingham; (2) minority group housing
       problems of Mexicans and blacks in San Antonio, and blacks in Houston, Texas;
       (3) blacks in New Orleans; (4) new housing for blacks in Dade County,
       Florida; (5) the housing problem of Puerto Ricans in New York City; (6)
       housing problems of Japanese-Americans in the San Francisco Bay area; and
       (7) a study of racial transition in Russel Woods neighborhood in Detroit.
       Some of the chapters of this book are summarized separately under their
       respective author name.

0094. Goetz, Rolf, and Ken W. Colton. 1980. The Dynamics of Neighborhoods: A
       Fresh Approach to Understanding Housing and Neighborhood Change. AIP
       Journal 46 (April): 184-94.

       In 1978 President Carter announced a national urban policy. The policy
       focused on a number of goals, such as preserving the heritage of our older
       cities, maintaining urban investment, and assisting new cities in
       "confronting the challenges of growth." A large number of those suggested
       policies will be administered or monitored by HUD. Most of our past
       government housing programs have focused on increasing the supply of housing
       and rebuilding the downtown facilities, but they have failed in many areas to
       reverse the decline of cities. In fact, a number of government programs
       have proven counter-productive in their influence. The future could be
       different as changing market forces and population demographics for the next
       fifteen years offer a unique opportunity for neighborhoods, cities, and
       financial institutions to develop a partnership to stimulate
       revitalization. However, new problems will emerge, and a national urban
       policy can succeed only if public and private sectors can work together and
       if policies can be sensitive to the market dynamics of cities. This paper
       outlines a fresh approach to designing housing strategies, based on an
       understanding of these market dynamics.@

0095. Goering, John M. 1978. Neighborhood Tipping and Racial Transition: A
       Review of Social Science Evidence. Journal of the American Institute of
       Planners 44 (1): 68-78.

       The focus of this article is the question of whether there is any social
       science evidence that demonstrates the existence of a racial tipping point.
       Do neighborhoods tip, for example, when they become 30 percent nonwhite?

There is some evidence that neighborhoods undergo a relatively continuous process of change in which racial proportions are only one element in determining population turnover. Though tipping points may well exist in certain areas and under particular conditions, neighborhoods are too variable historically, demographically, and socially to be able to formulate on an a priori basis an iron law of demographic transition.*

0096.   Gove, Walter R., Michael Hughes, and Omer R. Galle. 1979. Overcrowding in the Home: An Empirical Investigation of Its Possible Pathological Consequences. **American Sociological Review** 44 (February): 59-80.

Several recent studies have suggested that, contrary to investigators' initial expectations, household crowding typically has little impact on human. Using a sample collected in Chicago which minimized the colinearity between crowding and socioeconomic variables, we find that both objective crowding (as measured by persons per room) and subjective crowding as indicated by (1) excessive social demands and (2) a lack of privacy are strongly related to poor mental health, poor social relationships in the home and poor child care; and are less strongly, but significantly related to poor physical health, and to poor social relationships outside the home. Furthermore, these three crowding variables taken together, on the average, uniquely explain as much (and with many indicators, more) variance in our dependent variables as is uniquely explained by the combined effects of sex, race, education, income, age and marital status.@

0097.   Grebler, Leo, et. al. 1970. [Mexican-American] Housing Conditions. In: The Mexican-American People: The Nation's Second Largest Minority. By Leo Grebler, et al. New York: Free Press. Pp. 248-70.

Utilizing primarily data collected by the U.S. Bureau of Census and U.S. Bureau of Labor Statistics, this study provides empirical analysis of Mexican-American housing conditions. Factors examined are overcrowding, number of rooms per housing unit, percent units with less than 5 rooms, incidents of substandard housing, neglect of public services, home ownership, factors bearing on poor housing conditions, house value or rent by income, and substandard housing by income and rent. The author also offers an interpretation for inferior housing of the Mexican American community. It is asserted that poverty among Mexican-Americans is a strategic determinant of their housing conditions.

0098.   Green, R. Jeffery, and George M. Von Furstenberg. 1975. The Effects of Race and Age of Housing on Mortgage Delinquency Risk. **Urban Studies** 12: 85 (February): 85-89.

The withdrawal of home mortgage lending from a neighborhood that is perceived to have reached a racial and socioeconomic "tipping point," is considered as a major factor contributing to housing deterioration in an area. "This paper examines the extent to which a high and rising percentage of blacks in 160 wards of Allegheny County, including and surrounding the city of Pittsburgh, are associated with an increase in mortgage delinquency risk on single-family homes." The authors also compare the racial effects model with an alternative which uses the age of the housing units instead of racial factors. Both racial composition and age of homes are found to be significant factors.

0099. Grier, Eunice and George. 1957. Market Characteristics in Interracial Housing. Journal of Social Issues 13 (4): 50-59.

This paper attempts to answer questions such as: "Who are the Negroes who are now moving into housing types and locations previously available only to whites? And, perhaps of more interest, who are the whites who have chosen to live beside Negroes in new private housing open to both groups, in an era when segregation in such housing is the norm?" The authors point out that the marketing to whites of interracial private housing is not determined by the same economic factors exerted in the case of public housing. The findings of this paper suggest that "there is today a white market for interracial housing--and that it is perhaps much broader than many had thought. It does not appear to be made up of ardent integrationists. But freedom from--or lack of susceptibility to--social pressures toward the norm of segregation may be a predominant characteristic."

0100. Grigsby, William G. 1964. Housing and Slum Clearance: Elusive Goals. Annals of the American Academy of Political and Social Science 352 (March): 107-18.

One of the purposes of urban renewal program in the U.S. was to improve the residential living environment for low-income families. But, housing and slum-clearance goals have lost their priority. "The shift away from residential objectives in renewal appears to stem from the fact that the goals are not uniformly held, are interpreted in various ways, are frequently in conflict with one another and with nonresidential goals, and apparently cannot all be achieved via means consistent with prevailing political and social attitudes. Housing goals for the low-income population lack politically acceptable programs of implementation; middle income housing programs lack clear purpose; in the larger urbanized areas, renewal efforts are based in part on a conception of the metropolis which is at odds with the residential preferences of most families." The author asserts that the most serious barrier to the realization of low-income housing goal is the conflict between central city and suburbs. He suggests that if the low-income housing problem is to be solved, the federal government must insert itself in this conflict in a way to re-establish the residential objectives of the slum-clearance program.

0101. Grigsby, William G., and Thomas C. Corl. 1983. Declining Neighborhoods: Problem or Opportunity. Annals of the American Academy of Political and Social Science 465 (January): 86-97.

This study briefly explores the spreading deterioration of urban neighborhoods and the inability of federal housing programs to improve residential conditions in the inner city, which "stand in dramatic contrast to the large, comfortable, and attractive residences in suburbs. The disparity in living environment is not easily explainable in terms of differences in households incomes, since real incomes in many of our older and now unsightly central city neighborhoods have been generally increasing, not falling." The author points out that there are a variety of explanations for the disparity but none is quite convincing. And, the remedies tried over years have not succeeded either. According to this article, the only strategy left to overcome various obstacles and reverse the process of decay lies in altering the expectations of those who live and work in the affected areas.

0102. Gruen, Claude. 1963. Urban Renewal's Role in the Genesis of Tomorrow's
       Slums. Land Economics 39 (3): 285-303.

       The Housing Act of 1949 provided the legislation enabling the American
       cities to embark upon slum clearance project. "Slum clearance is hailed as
       a step toward the goal of the 1949 Housing Act, 'a decent home and suitable
       living environment for every American family.' But as old slums are leveled
       other urban neighborhoods begin to breed new slums." This article examines
       the slum clearance project and the forces that generate new slums outside the
       clearance areas. It concludes that "while the strength of exogenous forces
       can improve the quality of houses, the efficient attainment of this goal
       requires a program that will beneficially utilize the basic determinants of
       housing quality. The current urban renewal policies followed by American
       cities do not constitute such a program. Slum clearance adds to the factors
       that cause new slums to develop, while the conservation programs of urban
       renewal do not offset these factors."

0103. Gruen, Nina J. 1973. Man and His Neighbors Examine. Planning 39 (1) 18-
       21.

       This article deals with the imposition of programs calling for neighborhoods
       to provide housing for all classes, races, and ethnic groups, and the
       reaction to these programs. The author indicates that to provide low income
       housing in the middle income suburbs requires a set of strategies to
       supplement the enforcement of open housing legislation.

0104. Haar, Charles M., and Demetrius S. Iatridis. 1974. Housing the Poor in
       Suburbia: Public Policy at the Grass Roots. Cambridge, Mass.: Ballinger
       Publishing Company. 430 pp.

       This book is based on the conviction that "racial integration of the nation's
       residential patterns, most particularly through the location of low-income
       housing in suburbia and the deep-rooted community conflict it has generated,
       is the most crucial domestic issue facing America in the 70s." The authors
       explore the nature and the extent of this crucial problem in five suburban
       communities in the Boston metropolitan region: Newton, Concord, Canton,
       East Providence, and Stoughton. The book is divided into three parts.
       Part I, "Policy Perspectives on the Controversy," provides a broad public
       policy perspective for the analysis of the said five case studies presented
       in Part II.   Part III, "A Discussion Framework: Policies, Programs and
       Dilemmas," focus on the conceptual issues underlying the cases examined in
       Part II.   The authors have chosen the five cases because each of these cases
       presents certain unique features: collectively, they have made attempts to
       provide low-income housing, and yet they exhibit a wide diversity in
       approaching the problem, and as a whole, they combine to show the intricate
       nature of public policy issues.

0105. Ham,   Andrew   M.   1978.   Hampton   Rehabilitation   Program   Stresses
       Public/Private Cooperation in Upgrading One-Fourth of the City. Journal of
       Housing 35 (9): 472-73.

       The city of Hampton, Virginia, attempts to preserve its housing stock in an

effort to reach low-income, aged, and large families, using loans and
rehabilitation grant money.   The article describes that the Hampton's
department of community development makes loans available to low income
families and individuals.   Grants are made to low-income, aged, and large
families.   The ceiling level of loans range from $15,200 to $27,400;
grants reach the maximum of $8,000 per applicant depending on the total cost
of rehabilitation and the applicant's income.

0106.   Hanna, Sherman, and Suzanne Lindamood. 1979. Housing Preferences of
Blacks and Whites in Montgomery, Alabama. **Housing and Society** 6 (1): 39-47.

Black households tend to have lower quality housing than white households.
The differences may be produced by differences in resources, preferences, or
by discrimination. A 1976 survey of 1,010 households in Montgomery,
Alabama showed the usual pattern of inferior housing for black households.
Regression analyses revealed that controlling for resources and family
composition substantially reduced the differences between blacks and
whites, but significant differences remained. There were, however, no
significant differences in ownership and structure preferences between
blacks and whites. In a regression with satisfaction with the dwelling as
the dependent variable, and race, housing conditions, family composition,
and resource variables as independent variables, the race coefficient was
not significantly different from zero. This provides indirect evidence
that housing preferences of whites and   blacks are similar, and that some of
the differences in housing are due to discrimination.*

0107.   Hansen, Julia L. 1986. Housing Problems of Asian Americans. In: **Race,
Ethnicity, and Minority Housing in the United States.** Jamshid A. Momeni
(ed.). Westport, Connecticut: Greenwood Press. Chapter X.

An examination of the Asian American housing has revealed that although
conditions are improving, this group continues to face significant
problems. Housing of Asian Americans is generally inferior to that of
whites, particularly in terms of overcrowding, but also in terms of home
ownership and plumbing. The problem of overcrowding is most prevalent in
the Western region of the country;   the rate of home ownership is lowest and
the incidence of units lacking complete plumbing is highest in the
Northeast. Housing of Asian Americans is not comparable to that of whites
in spite of the fact that all Asian ethnic subgroups, except, Vietnamese,
exceed whites in income, education, and occupational status. Japanese
American housing is inferior to that of whites despite the fact that median
household income for Japanese is over 25 percent higher than median
household income for whites. In terms of overcrowding, housing of Asians is
less comparable to white housing than black housing is to that of whites.
Resolution of the issue why Asian/white housing inequalities exist requires
further research on the extent of current housing market discrimination
faced by the Asian American subgroups.@

0108.   Hartman, Chester (ed.). 1983. **America's Housing Crisis--What is to be
Done?** Boston, Mass.: Routledge and Kegan Paul. 249 pp.

This book provides a complete picture of housing conditions in the U.S., a
political and economic examination of the causes of the conditions, and a
number of proposals for addressing the problems in the short run, and

restructuring the housing delivery system in the long run. The basic theme and the contents of this book is summarized in the statement that "decent, affordable housing is a right, an entitlement (not merely a goal), and that the country unquestionably has the resources to make this available to all its people" [including racial and ethnic minorities].

0109. Hawkins, Homer C. 1976. Urban Housing and the Black Family. Phylon 37(1): 73-84.

Family size, size of housing unit, and housing availability are major factors that contribute to the process of black overcrowding. In 1970, over 15 percent of dwellings for blacks in urban areas were substandard, compared to 4.3 percent for whites. The urban poverty can be viewed as a containment area, an island of poverty amid an Ocean of plenty. The author asserts that changes must occur at the national level if improved housing for the poor is to become a reality. The article suggests a three-pronged attack on the housing problem: each homebuyer should receive a family housing allowance based upon income; an Urban Expansion Agency should be established to purchase land in blocks and in individual plots for housing construction; and, a mechanism should be devised whereby families would be able to receive direct low-interest loans from the government. The implementation of these measures may alleviate the housing problem of the poor.

0110. Hays, Charles, and John Kimbrough. 1978. Decent Housing--The Unmet Agenda. HUD Challenge 9 (8): 24-28.

"Twenty-one years after the adoption of the housing goal in the National Housing Act of 1949, some 38 percent of all the households in central Appalachia were still living in substandard housing. This article examines the factors that went wrong which in turn prevented the realization of the national goal of providing a decent home for all Americans.

0111. Hill, Herbert. 1966. Demographic Change and Racial Ghettos: The Crisis of American Cities. Journal of Urban Law (Winter): 231-85.

The significant migration of black population to urban areas in the north has resulted in an increase in the rigidity of residential segregation. This has been accompanied by an extension of the ghetto pattern in major cities, coupled with vast urban blight and deteriorating inner-city areas. The federal government has not instituted any program to provide funds for the building of low-income housing in the nonslum nonsegregated areas of the large cities; nor there have been any programs to provide for the integration of lower and middle income families in new housing units. Integrated housing could become a reality only when the ghettos are destroyed and projects are developed to eliminate the overcrowded and substandard units which compose the bulk of city housing for American blacks. Solving this problem is necessary not only to ensure racial equality, but preserve the health of the cities themselves. The cities' lack of financial resources to handle these problems is the result of not only social irresponsibility, but most importantly of the unrealistic taxation relationship between municipalities and the federal power. The author suggests that disbursing power of the federal government be reduced by not less than $50 billion in stages over a five-year period, that this sum be returned to the people in the form of taxing power at the community level, and that these newly available local funds be used for the elimination of racial ghettos.

0112.   Hojnacki, William P.   1981.   The Delivery of Housing Services: Determining Need and Providing for Equity Within a Local Political Framework.   Journal of Urban Affairs 3 (4): 15-28.

This article reports on a survey research project undertaken in South Bend, Indiana that attempted to determine if housing services provided by the city were delivered to those who needed them and if they were distributed equitably. With the implementation of the Housing and Community Development Act of 1974, decisions affecting the delivery of housing services shifted from a federal to a local political framework. The study showed that South Bend was able to successfully satisfy both federal program requirements and demands generated by important political constituencies, but it was not able to ensure that the housing services were delivered equitably to all residents.*

0113.   Holleb, Doris B.   1979.   A Decent Home and Suitable Living Environment. Ekistics 46 (275): 106-09.

In the past three decades, the transformation of residential settlement patterns and a massive increase in new housing constructions and support systems have combined to substantially alter the quality and quantity of housing and community life in the United States. In this article, Holleb examines these trends and the way in which they have been reported in Social Indicators, 1976. The author criticizes the omissions made by this publication. The article concludes that a decent home and suitable living environment for every American family is still an elusive goal.

0114.   Huth, Mary Jo. 1982. The Relationship Between Selected Household Characteristics and Housing in the United States.   Journal of Urban Affairs 4 (1): 33-47.

This article examines the influence of changes in American households (i.e., the phenomenal increase in single-parent families and one-person households, race/ethnicity, household income, family size and structure) on the housing market. Survey research data indicate that many families with children, especially large minority and female-headed families which are disproportionately represented among the poor, suffer severe housing problems. After discussing future housing needs in the United States based upon alternative Census Bureau projections of household formation, several suggestions are made for increasing the supply of inexpensive family rental housing, for reducing restrictive rental practices against families with children, and for facilitating homeownership among lower-income families.*

0115.   Jones, Malcolm. 1958. The Workable Program of a Southern Metropolis, Atlanta, Georgia. Phylon 19 (1): 60-63.

This article discusses three urban renewal projects in Atlanta, the role of government, and how these renewal projects have affected black housing conditions in the city. The City's increased tax revenues in the renewal project areas is also examined.

0116.   Kristof, Frank S. 1976. Housing and People in New York City. **City Almanac** 10 (5): 1-18.

This article examines the City's housing programs from 1946 to 1970. It points out that in spite of major improvement in living conditions of most households from 1950 to 1970, there has been a continuous deterioration in major portions of the city's existing housing stock as a result of rent control and the in-migration of lower income minority families unable to maintain older housing units in good conditions. The author suggests that given the City's population loss during the first half of 1970s, the city must take advantage of reduced pressure to remove rent control without causing a violent disruption of tenants. Failure to decontrol rent means a continued high rate of real estate tax delinquencies, mortgage defaults, and rental housing abandonment.

0117.   Lachman, M. Leanne, and J. Denis Gathman. 1976. Housers of Last Resort: The American Ghetto Today. **Real Estate Review** 6 (1): 60-66.

Who provides housing for the poor? The authors point out that about 80 percent is provided in the private market, most of which are crumbling, and moving toward total collapse. This article explores the extent and potential consequences of low-income housing problems. The study is based on a survey data collected in Cleveland, Ohio. It concludes that "as the private market for low-income housing moves toward collapse, difficult choices will confront government and taxpayers."

0118.   Lamont, Edward M. 1980. Housing Problems for New York City's Low-Income Population. **Journal of Property Management** 45 (1): 35-38.

This article examines rent control and other policies for New York City's lower income renters. "Although this article primarily discusses the situation in New York City, many of the proposed solutions apply to other cities and towns as well."

0119.   Lansing, John B., et al. 1969. **New Homes and Poor People: A Study of Chains of Moves.** Ann Arbor, MI: Institute of Social Research.

This publication examines, among other things, the effects of new housing construction on the poor people in general, and on blacks in particular.

0120.   Lebergott, Stanley. 1970. Slum Housing: A Proposal. **Journal of Political Economy** 78 (Nov./Dec.): 1362-66.

Slowing down the rate at which the stock of low-rent housing depreciates would do more to end slums than any politically conceivable building program. The author suggests a proposal to do just that. If half the 10 million housing units in which officially "poor" families live now depreciate at 5 percent, then we are busy creating 250,000 slum units (or worse) each year. If we could manage to slow that depreciation rate to 3 percent, we would add 100,000 units to the stock of acceptable housing—that is, add twice as many units as the total number of public housing units built last year. The author describes an experiment to be tried in half a dozen public housing projects. It is no panacea, but then there seem to be few around.@

0121.   Leigh, W. A. 1982. The Housing Situation: Shelter Affordability and Blacks. **Urban League Review** 6 (2): 62-65.

The limited ability of blacks, especially black elderly, to adjust to spiraling cost of housing is unparalleled in the United States history. This article reviews and analyzes the pattern for both renters and home owners and concludes that "both the elderly and nonelderly blacks are at a considerable disadvantage relative to other racial groups in their ability to afford and obtain 'decent, safe, and sanitary housing.' This disadvantage is directly related to their disproportionately low-income levels."

0122.   Lieberson, Stanley. 1962. Suburbs and Ethnic Residential Patterns. **American Journal of Sociology** 67 (6): 673-81.

Residential distribution of foreign-born and second-generation groups in the suburbs of several large metropolitan areas are compared with their compatriots' segregation patterns within the central cities of these metropolises. Differences between specific first- and second- generation groups in the magnitude of their dispersion in suburbs are associated with variations in segregation between the same nationalities in the central cities. The changes in ethnic distributions between suburbs during a twenty-year period are similar to those occurring within the central cities for comparable populations. These results suggest that differences in the population composition of suburbs and central cities may obscure the existence of similar behavioral patterns for comparable groups in the two parts of a metropolis.*

0123.   Lincoln, Sherly J. 1980. Single Room Residential Hotels Must be Preserved as Low-Income Housing Alternative. **Journal of Housing** 37 (7): 383-86.

Single room occupancy (SRO) housing has traditionally been regarded by HUD as substandard because it lacks private kitchens and bathrooms. But, as the housing crunch for low- to middle-income singles and elderly population continue to grow, Congress and HUD are beginning to change their views. Efforts are being made to change regulations so that federal funds will be more readily available for SRO programs. A current amendment before Congress would permit SRO housing to be eligible for Section 312. "This amendment would be the first recognition of the need to provide federal assistance for SROs." Many cities are now rehabilitating residential hotels to provide single room occupancy housing. These cities are receiving federal funds through the HUD secretary's fund for innovative grants. The Seattle, Washington, Housing Authority received a grant to revitalize the Atlas Hotel in its International District; the city of Pittsburgh, Pennsylvania, received the kind of grant for its "residential club" program which allows moderate income elderly persons to remain in their neighborhood; in Portland, Oregon, the Burnside Consortium, a neighborhood organization, received a self help development grant from HUD to renovate the Rich Hotel. Other cities involved with SRO housing project are Denver, Colorado, and Los Angeles, California.

0124.   Louis, Francis Gros. 1974. Main's Indian Housing. **HUD Challenge** 5 (8):

14-15.

This article describes the construction of a federally subsidized housing and approval of Federal Grants for neighborhood facilities and water and sewer projects for the Passamaquoddy Indians in Main. The units are developed under the Turnkey III homeownership opportunity project.

0125.   Loury, Glenn C. 1978. The Minimum Border Length Hypothesis Does Not Explain the Shape of Black Ghettos. Journal of Urban Economics 5 (2): 147-53.

In attempting to model the process of residential segregation in urban areas, some researchers have advanced the hypothesis that "spatial allocation of households will emerge which provides the white majority with the least exposure to blacks." This proposition is called "minimum border length" hypothesis. This study shows that "the full implication of the minimum border length hypothesis to be counter to empirical observation. This needn't imply that the hypothesis is without value, as it might still be used to explain the historical evolution of the shapes of certain black ghettos. One rather suspects however that considerable effort will be required to rehabilitate the hypothesis via this route. It is perhaps a bit too crude a notion to successfully explain such a complex social phenomenon."

0126.   MacAllister, Ronald J., Edward J. Kaiser, and Edgar W. Butler. 1971. Residential Mobility of Blacks and Whites: A National Longitudinal Survey. American Journal of Sociology 77 (3): 445-56.

A national survey of 1,500 households reveals that greater black residential mobility is largely explained by tendency among blacks to be renters. This study also shows that blacks are more likely to move only within their neighborhoods and much less likely to move elsewhere in the metro area or to migrate out of it. Possible reasons for this pattern of differential movement by race is discussed.

0127.   MacCahill, Ed. 1975. In Mount Laurel, Issues are not Black and White. Planning 41 (4): 12-13.

The New Jersey Supreme Court concurred with the lower court's interpretation of Southern Burlington County NAACP v. Township of Mount Laurel. The Court ruled that Mount Laurel had in fact unlawfully zoned its land so that poor and moderate-income families could be kept out.

0128.   MacRae, Duncan C., and Raymond Struyk. 1977. The Federal Housing Administration (FHA), Tenure Choice, and Residential Land Use. Journal of Urban Economics 4 (3): 360-78.

This paper extends the standard, urban, residential land-use model to analyze the effects of FHA mortgage insurance. On the demand side, households are differentiated by income and tenure; on the supply side, the cost of housing is related to the asset prices of land and structure and the cost of capital. Hypothesizing that capital cost is a function of household tenure and income [emphasis mine], tenure is chosen to minimizes this cost. The effect of FHA, then is to expand the housing consumption of moderate income households, by reducing their capital cost, while displacing those whose cost is not reduced.@

0129.   Maruda, Thomas N. 1974. Baltimore City's Vacant House Program. Baltimore: The Johns Hopkins University Center for Metropolitan Planning and Research. 69 pp.

The Vacant House Program in Baltimore began in 1969 as an experiment to provide housing for low-income families. It has also become a way of arresting the spread of vacant buildings while revitalizing neighborhoods. On the whole the program has shown that major gut rehabilitation is not only cheaper and quicker than comparable new construction, but also that it is equal to and sometimes better than new construction. On the social front, the project has had the effect of decentralizing social problems that are manifest in and aggravated by the densities of conventional public housing.

0130.   Massel, Benton F. 1972. Maintenance of Slum Housing: Optimal Policy Subject to a Political Constraint. **Journal of Political Economy** 80: 1060-66.

In an article (cited above), Stanley Lebergott (1970) proposed a program to reduce the rate of depreciation of low-rent housing stock. The present article critically examines that proposal. The author shows that the Lebergott proposal is not self-financing, outlines a problem overlooked by Lebergott, regarding the "economics of damage," and indicates how, with modification, the Lebergott proposal can become self-financing.

0131.   Mattox, Joe L. 1976. Inner City Management: There is a Difference. **Journal of Property Management** 41 (5): 205-09.

Any property manager who manages inner city properties is aware that due to a host of causes, multifamily housing operation incomes are generally lower and expenses are usually higher than developments that are privately owned. The different reasons are discussed. They include: lifestyles, attitudes, and tenants' values; the family folkways of black people; the welfare agencies; bad management; and economic and social inequalities imposed on the entire central city. The article concludes that the "suburban managers need clubhouses and social directors; inner city managers need day care centers and community service specialists."

0132.   Mayer, Albert J. 1957. Race and Private Housing: A Social Problem and a Challenge to Understanding Human Behavior. **Journal of Social Issues** 8 (4): 3-6.

This article examines the questions of racially changing neighborhoods and the relationship between housing and social class. It concludes that the subject of race and housing can be viewed as a testing ground for a number of ideas which are actually broader than the subject matter as it first appears.

0133.   Mayo, Mary Lou. 1974. Residential Patterns and Their Socioeconomic Correlates: A Study of Blacks in Westchester County, New York. Unpublished Ph.D. Dissertation. Fordham University. 380 pp.

This dissertation examines the extent to which patterns of residential segregation by race are being established in Westchester County, a suburb of New York, as a result of increased black suburbanization. The patterns of residential succession, the socioeconomic concomitants of racial change in Westchester and the degree to which the County fulfills functions traditional to suburbs for the black population are also explored. The analyses are based on published census data between 1950 and 1970.

0134.   Mays, James. 1982. Housing for the Poor: The New Bootstrap Advocacy. Urban League Review 6 (2): 41-42.

This article examines the concept of "self-help" in relation to housing for the poor. The question of what is the goal is still with us. Should we continue to subsidize housing for the poor? If not, who is to carry the burden? Are we asking the poor to do it by themselves? We know that they don't have the resources to do it. "Self-help initiatives in the housing sector for the low-income will require the investment of capital and resources. Such initiatives will also require clearly stated goals. Shifting the burden is not a solution, and housing block grants of vouchers are merely new 'systems' that promise futures that will be little different from the past."

0135.   McCormick, Joseph P., II. 1984. In Search of Low-Income Housing: The Crisis Continues. Urban League Review 8 (2): 44-56.

"This article examines the continuing assault by the Reagan administration on one set of domestic programs directed toward lower-income households in the United States—the Section 8 rental assistance program and the Public Housing program." The author pays specific attention to the "spending levels proposed for these programs by the Reagan administration in the fiscal year (FY) 1984 HUD budget and how these proposals compared with both actual as well as planned spending for previous years." This article also describes some of the programmatic changes in low-income housing proposed in the FY 84 budget and some of the methods through which the administration seeks to accomplish its budget cutting goals. The article concludes with a discussion of how this budgetary strategy is seen as contributing to the continued rental housing crisis in general, and for the nation's low-income families in particular.

0136.   McFarlin, Emma D., and Vicki Elmer. 1981. A Critical State Strategy for Housing in California. Western City 57 (7): 13-15, 24, 30.

This article examines the extent and the nature of low-income housing and federal involvement in California and concludes that "the problems which affect housing for poor people in California are varied, complex, and highly interrelated."

0137.   McGhee, Milton L., and Ann Fagan Ginger. 1961. The House I Live In: A Study of Housing for Minorities. Cornel Law Quarterly 46 (Winter): 194-257.

The theme and the contents of this article is epitomized in the statement that "judged by its housing, America is a country where the color of your skin matters more than the color of your money, for today one out of every six Americans is unable to live where he wishes to live because of racial or religious discrimination." This study analyzes the existing legislations, and assesses the effects of executive actions and inactions, in order to provide a guide to federal, state and private approaches to the problem of minority housing.

0138. McKee, James B. 1963. Changing Patterns of Race and Housing: A Toledo Study. **Social Forces** 41 (3): 253-60.

A study of Negro housing in Toledo, Ohio tested some common assumptions about race and housing and discovered a post-war transition from renter to owner status for the Negro. The study explored the means by which Negro families had financed purchase of homes, the quality of the homes, comparative prices, and the economic status of the Negro families concerned. Some implications of these findings are noted.*

0139. McMullin, James H. 1973. Notions About the Housing Problem. **Journal of Property Management** 38 (3): 115-17.

The author points out that the "misplaced or over-emphasis on housing production with a current lack or distribution and utilization of housing is one of the sources of today's housing problems." The article advocates a more flexible "system in which governmental assistance be in the form of purchasing power to the individual, instead of his being relegated to 'public housing.'"

0140. Meyer, David R. 1973. Blacks in Slum Housing. **Journal of Black Studies** 4 (2): 139-52.

The subject of black slum housing dates back to early 1900s. The theme is prevalent in the literature. Two approaches to causal factors are apparent: (1) housing discrimination; (2) low-income and discriminatory housing market. This article suggests that a comprehensive approach to black housing, needs to include a simultaneous examination of discrimination and the regularities in black demand for housing quality, and that a more appropriate approach may involve an attack on discrimination in education and employment which reduce the overall access of blacks to income resources, which in turn reduce blacks' ability to consume quality housing. That is, for housing quality to significantly improve, a multi-faceted strategy is needed.

0141. Miller, Alexander F. 1958. Levittown U.S.A. **Phylon** 19 (1): 108-12.

Levittown, Pennsylvania is a low-medium priced housing development typical of many that "mashroomed in the suburbs of large cities since World War II." It is located between Philadelphia, Pennsylvania and Trenton, New Jersey. This article examines the fearful reactions of residents in Levittown when black families began to move in, and concludes that "the problem of changing patterns in housing for minority groups will offer an important challenge to American communities during the years immediately ahead. Whether these problems will be met successfully will depend on how much individual communities have learned from the experiences of Levittown and other cities. The techniques and strategies are known. All that remains is for organizations and people of good will to put them to effective use."

0142. Mills, C. P. 1979. Effective Management Puts an Indian Housing Authority on the Road to Sound Practices. **Journal of Housing** 36 (6): 310-13.

Relative to Public Housing Authorities (PHA), the Indian Housing Authorities are late bloomers. The eligibility of Indian tribes to participate in public housing project does not have any history prior to 1960s. Only in 1961, as opposed to 1936 for public housing, an administrative decision was made allowing Indian participation in public housing. This article reviews the background, problem identification, and the management problems related to the implementation of Indian public housing, and points out that the success achieved by "the Cherokee housing authority is testimony to the validity of the integrated approach," as a useful management tool.

0143.   Mills, Edwin S., and Richard Price. 1974. Suburbanization and Central City Problems. **Journal of Urban Economics** 15 (1): 1-17.

This paper is an empirical study of effects of central city problems on population and employment suburbanization. It is widely believed that high crime, high taxes, and large minority groups in central cities are important causes of rapid suburbanization of U.S. metropolitan areas. A large set of density functions is estimated for population and employment in U.S. metropolitan areas in 1960 and 1970. Thus, relative to central city and suburban measures of crime, taxes, etc., are used in an interactive model to explain population and employment suburbanization. It is found that only racial minorities have an effect on suburbanization.*

0144.   Momeni, Jamshid A. 1986. The Housing Conditions of Black Female-Headed Households: A Comparative Analysis. In: **Race, Ethnicity, and Minority Housing in the United States.** Jamshid A. Momeni (ed.). Westport, Connecticut: Greenwood Press. Chapter VI.

Using 1970 and 1980 census data, this study attempts to examine the housing characteristics of black female-headed households, and to assess trends and changes in their conditions between the two censuses. The paper begins with an introduction providing a background context for the analysis; it is followed by an examination of selected socioeconomic and demographic variables regarded as strong predictors of housing conditions; the analysis concludes with an assessment of black-white differences in selected structural characteristics of units occupied by these groups. Overall, this is a qualitative and quantitative examination of housing units occupied by the black female householders. The causes of poor housing condition of black female householders is also discussed.

0145.   Moncrief, Ed. 1985. Providing Better Jobs, Better Homes: How Salinas Organization Stimulates Economic Development, Pride in Low-Income Neighborhoods. **Western City** 61 (9): 8-10, 12, 20-22.

CHISPA, which means "spark" in Spanish, is a nonprofit housing and development corporation. Projects by this organization are designed to assist Monterey County's lower income population, the Mexican-American framework families of the Salinas Valley. In February 1983, CHISPA established a property management company, CHISPA Housing Management, INC. (CHMI). To date, CHMI has signed management contracts with three housing cooperatives and one rental project totalling 198 units and will oversee the maintenance, resident and tenant selection, and operation of other projects developed by CHISPA. This article explains the successes of CHISPA in turning Mexican-American farmworkers from a migratory pattern of work to settle permanently in decent housing units in regions like Salinas Valley.

0146. Morgan, D. J. 1980. Residential Housing Abandonment in the United States: The Effects on Those Who Remain. Environment and Planning A. 12 (12): 1343-56.

The presence of abandoned housing reduces the quality of life of residents who remain in an area. Respondents in a national survey of the United States who report abandoned housing problems in their neighborhood also report lower levels of neighborhood satisfaction. In areas where abandoned housing is found, community services and neighborhood conditions also tend to be rated low. The effects of abandonment, which is found in bigger cities and in areas of lower social standing, do not carry through to cause individuals to say they desire to move out of the neighborhood. The idea of demolishing abandoned housing to reduce the problem is ratified, but abandonment is only one problem which must be addressed to improve the quality of life.*

0147. Morrill, Richard L. 1965. The Negro Ghetto Problems and Alternatives. Geographical Review 55 (3): 339-61.

The purpose of this article is to trace the origins of the ghetto and the forces that perpetuate it. This study also evaluates different proposals for controlling black ghettos. The author uses the black ghetto in Seattle, Washington to illustrate a model of ghetto expansion as a diffusion process into the surrounding white areas.

0148. Murray, Thomas J. 1976. New Boom in Mobile Homes. DUN's Review 108 (4): 53-55.

After a disastrous slump, the mobile home industry is humming again. "This time the resurgent industry is out to capture the mass-housing market." It is aiming for a huge share of the market primarily those low-income families priced out of the conventional, single family housing market. Factors fueling the resurgence of the industry include the rapid economic recovery, a substantial rise in total employment of low-income workers, a renewed confidence among lending institutions in the viability of mobile homes as an investment, and a sharp improvement in size and quality of the new breed of mobile homes.

0149. National Advisory Commission on Civil Disorder. 1971. Housing Problems in Central Cities. In: Problems in Political Economy: An Urban Prespective. Lexington, Mass.: D. C. Heath and Company. pp. 367-70.

This article is an excerpt from a larger report by the Riot Commission published in 1968. It provides a series of figures on the intensity and the range of housing problems in central cities, particularly in black ghettos. The figures are presented in support of the conclusion that for most of the central city dwellers, "the goal of a decent home and suitable [living] environment is as far distant as ever."

0150.   National Hispanic Housing Coalition. 1982. Housing Research and the
        Hispanic Community. **Urban League Review** 6 (2): 72-75.

        The government needs data to use as basis for decision making on Hispanic
        housing. Unfortunately, the government has paid "little attention to the
        study of the overall housing problems troubling Hispanics, and, as a result,
        has no reliable documentary sources which reveal the housing needs in poor
        Hispanic communities." This article examines this deficiency, calls on the
        government to collect the needed information, points at some sources of
        data, and describes the role and the need for the National Hispanic Housing
        Coalition to fill this gap--to collect and analyze data on Hispanic housing
        and community development needs.

0151.   Nenno, Mary K., et. al. 1982. **Housing and Local Government.** Washington,
        D. C.: International City Management Association. 250 pp.

        This book is a comprehensive treatment of direct housing functions of local
        government, which are still evolving from the leads provided by the federal
        programs initiated in early 1930s. It consists of six chapters and seven
        appendixes packed with information. The chapters discuss topics such as
        evolution of local housing involvement, conservation and rehabilitation of
        existing housing and neighborhoods, local implementation, managing housing
        for the unmet needs, innovative housing finance, the impact of changing
        housing markets, Community Development Block Grants, and local housing
        administration. The book also chronicles legislative developments in the
        housing field.

0152.   Nesbitt, George B. 1956. Dispersion of Nonwhite Residence in Washington,
        D.C.: Some of Its Implications. **Land Economics** 32 (3): 201- 12.

        Recent studies have indicated the increasing peaceful movement of nonwhites
        into better quality existing neighborhoods without mass exodus on the part
        of whites in some neighborhoods. This article "examines the extensive
        racial transition in residence since 1940 in Washington, D.C., where it has
        taken place in dispersed or scattered section and generally without either
        panic and flight on the part of white residents or organized efforts to
        discourage flight and achieve neighborhood readjustment." The purpose of
        this study is to determine the characteristics of housing market demand and
        supply factors that appear to have advanced the type of racial transition
        observed in Washington. It also discusses some of the resultant
        implications of this racial residential transition for a freer housing
        market in the context of housing development and urban renewal programs
        currently underway in such localities.

0153.   Newman, Sandra J., and Ann B. Schnare. 1986. HUD and HHS Shelter
        Assistance: America's Two Approaches to Housing the Poor. **Journal of
        Housing** 43 (1): 22-32.

        In fiscal year 1984, the federal government spent $18.9 billion for housing
        assistance for low income households--$9.9 billion by HUD, and $9 billion by
        the Department of Health and Human Services through welfare programs.
        Contenting that the way these programs operate are fragmented at best, the
        authors examine the efforts of these two federal agencies that provide
        shelter assistance to the poor.

0154. Newman, Sandra J., and Raymond J. Struyk. 1983. Housing and Poverty.
Review of Economics and Statistics 65 (2): 243-53.

This paper provides preliminary evidence on several important issues that
are highly relevant to allocation decisions for housing assistance. The
first concerns short-term versus long-term economic hardship. This
analysis indicates that there are substantial differences in both the
demographic composition of single-year versus permanent poor and in the size
of the population; likely to be permanently versus temporarily in need of
aid. It also suggests that targeting housing assistance to permanently
poor makes sense because these households are the least able to compete or
fend themselves in the market. An additional insight concerns the
convergence of persistent poverty and housing deprivation. Since it is the
permanently poor who live in housing units with higher rates of physical
deficiencies than other poor, it is this group that has the greatest need for
scarce housing assistance dollar; it is also among this group that greater
housing improvement could be realized.@

0155. Nolon, John R. 1979. Coordinating HUD and HEW Programs Would Improve
Housing Conditions. Journal of Housing 36 (9): 447-52.

HUD and HEW [now replaced by HHS, Health and Human Services] are two federal
departments charged with the responsibility of ensuring that all Americans
have a "decent home." Yet, despite their common goal, these two departments
operate completely in different manners. The purpose of this essay is to
point out these differences in operation and to suggest ways in which these
departments could better perform their duties and achieve better housing for
the poor and disadvantaged.

0156. Onderdonk, Dudley. 1979. Overcoming the Dual Housing Market Through
Affirmative Marketing. HUD Challenge 10 (4): 6-9.

Historically, the American housing market has been characterized by unequal
competition between the white majority and black and other minorities. As a
minority group has begun to move into an area, whites have either withdrawn
or have stopped competing for housing. The result is the "dual housing
market," an evil whose causes and treatment through affirmative marketing
are the subject of this article.*

0157. Pendleton, William W. 1973. Blacks in Suburbia. In: The Urbanization of
the Suburbs. Louis H. Masotti, and Jeffrey K. Hadden (eds.). Beverly
Hills, California/London: Sage Publications. Pp. 171-84.

The process of suburbanization is accompanied with the redistribution of
residential patterns in the United States. This article examines the
political and social consequences of this phenomenon in the U.S. in the
fifties and the sixties and concludes that "suburbanization has both
demographic and social dimensions. Blacks appear to participate in the
demographic dimensions, but not in the social dimensions. Black
suburbanization is not unequivocally an indicator of social integration.
Though some blacks in cities are engaged in upward mobility, as indicated
by moves to the suburbs, large parts of the suburbanization of blacks are
probably due to growth in traditionally black areas such as East St. Louis

and Decatur, Georgia."

0158.   Pettigrew, Thomas F. 1973. Attitudes on Race and Housing: A Social Psychological View. In: **Segregation in Residential Areas.** Amos H. Hawley, and Vincent P. Rock (eds.). Washington, D. C.: National Academy of Sciences. Pp. 21-84.

While attitudes toward open housing have become increasingly more favorable over the past generation. However, the trend appears to be the result of factors largely outside the housing realm. Black attitudes favoring open housing have remained stable, perhaps even strengthening in recent years. The attitudes of both whites and blacks are more derivative than causal in the total process of how access to housing is distributed in the United States.@

0159.   Phillips, Kenneth E. 1972. The Poor and Housing Issues. **Urban Lawyey** 4 (2): 242-47.

This article examines the relationship between economic status and housing. It argues that the problem is not housing, or housing shortages. Rather, it is poverty. "A slum is a place where poor people live. If you tear that slum down and move people someplace else and the poverty still exists, there is going to be another slum." Thus, solving poverty must occupy top priority.

0160.   Phillips, K. F., and M. Agelasto. 1975. Housing and Central Cities: The Conservation Approach. **Ecology Law Quarterly** 4 (4): 797-880.

"The thesis of this Article is that the time has come for a sober rethinking of government housing policies and programs and for a new approach giving primary emphasis to the rebuilding of inner city neighborhood and the rehabilitation and conservation of existing housing stock." This 83-page long article examines this thesis in details and concludes that "if the deterioration patterns of central city hardcore poverty areas are to be preserved and marginal neighborhoods restored and conserved, realistic, cost-effective, broad scale, job creating, participatory program approaches must be found. Downtown renewal projects, benign neglect, and suburban by pass strategies have not met theses criteria. The criticism and suggestions put forth in the Article are offered in the hope that a pro-cities commitment will be made and that coordinated and feasible programs will be developed to restore urban communities."

0161.   Pomeranz, William. 1980. How to Tell if Low-Income Housing Rehabs Make Sense. Real Estate Review 9 (4): 87-90.

This article presents a formula called the Inner-City Value Estimation Model (IVEM) developed to help Community Development Corporations to determine the ability of their targeted population to afford the rehabilitated housing. The model uses an eight-step calculation, analyzing such factors as primary and supplementary income, debt obligations, and estimates of monthly shelter expenses to compute the maximum price of a house that a typical family can afford. The article also discusses the advantages and disadvantages of using this model.

0162. President's Committee on Urban Housing. 1971. American Housing Needs.
       In: **Problems in Political Economy: An Urban Perspective.** David M. Gordon
       (ed.). Lexington, Mass.: D. C. Heath & Company. Pp. 371-75.

       This article, an excerpt from the report of President's Committee on urban
       housing, A Decent Home, published in 1968, provides data and evidence on the
       magnitude of housing problem in the nation. Given the avowed goal of
       providing a decent home for everyone, the article highlights the enormity of
       fulfilling that objective.

0163. President's Committee on Urban Housing. 1971. Federal Housing Programs.
       In: **Problems in Political Economy: An Urban Perspective.** David M. Gordon
       (e.). Lexington, Mass.: D. C. Heath and Company. Pp. 375-79.

       This article, an excerpt form the same source indicated in the preceding
       item, outlines the basic features of the major federal housing programs
       designed to provide housing for the poor. The article makes it very clear
       that policy is tending more and more toward subsidy to private industry for
       low-income housing construction. And, that the most recent subsidy
       programs have failed to induce housing for the truly poor.

0164. Price, Richard, and Edwin Mills. 1985. Race and Residence in Earning
       Determination. Journal of Urban Economics 17 (1): 1-18.

       Black Americans have been discriminated against in many forms—in housing,
       employment, education, and income. This paper "is a contribution to the
       classification and measurement of effects of discrimination on earning."

0165. Rafter, David O. 1985. Implementing Urban Housing Rehabilitation
       Programs: A Comparison of the Federal and States Experience. **Journal of
       Urban Affairs** 7 (2): 47-64.

       Federal urban housing rehabilitation is in a state of transition. This
       paper explores the federal shift using data on the recent Wisconsin
       experience with Section 312 and Community Development Block Grant
       rehabilitation loan programs. The article compares these federal programs
       with the Wisconsin home improvement loan program. It concludes that "this
       comparison study does not support the federal withdrawal from providing
       direct single-family rehabilitation loans because it can supplement the
       bond-market orientation of the state approach with a social targeting
       function."

0166. Rainwater, Lee. 1967. The Lessons of Pruitt-Igoe. Public Interest
       (8): 116-26.

       "The Pruitt-Igoe Housing Project is in St. Louis. Built in 1954, the
       project was the first high-rise public housing in the city. It consists of
       33 eleven-story slab-shaped buildings designed to provide housing for about
       2800 families. At present, it houses about 10,000 Negroes in 2,000
       households. What started out as a precedent-breaking project to improve
       the lives of the poor in St. Louis, a project hailed not only by local
       newspapers but by Architectural Forum, has become an embarrassment to all
       concerned." This article consists of a detailed description of Pruitt-Igoe
       project and the implications drawn. The description and analyses are based

on a three year study of the project. For more studies on this project the reader of the present volume may wish to examine several reference to this St. Louis project in the Chapter on public housing.

0167.   Ravetz, Alison. 1975. Housing for the Poor. New Society 32 (653): 71-73.

This article examines the concepts of urban renewal and slum clearance. It also explores the varying effects of urban renewal on existing and emerging racial patterns in the large metropolitan areas.

0168.   Rent, George S., and Clyda S. Rent. 1978. Low-Income Housing: Factors Related to Residential Satisfaction. Environment and Behavior 10 (4): 459-88.

This article examines residential satisfaction among low-income households in an attempt to find the relationship between man's housing values and his housing environments. The analysis is based on a survey of occupants of low income housing projects in selected areas of South Carolina, which found a high degree of satisfaction with both neighborhoods and housing, and that satisfaction was related to social factors such as home ownership, relationship with neighbors, and general life satisfaction.

0169.   Richey, Elinor. 1963. Kenwood Foils the Block-buster. Harper's 227 (1359): 42-47.

This article describes how the women, white and black alike, of Kenwood neighborhood in Chicago got together to save their homes. The article concludes with these remarks: "Much remains to be done. But Kenwood has clearly shown how block-busters can be stopped and how interracial living can be made to work. Because it is a suburban sort of neighborhood, yet one located in the center of a metropolis, Kenwood can perhaps be of help to both city and country communities trying to achieve similar residential blends of Negroes and whites—blends so solid that color is the last thing you notice."

0170.   Rose, Arnold M. 1961. Inconsistencies in Attitudes Toward Negro Housing. Social Problems 8 (4): 286-92.

Many studies on attitudes have produced inconsistent results in the sense that a given individual may hold a number of attitudes toward the same object, perhaps applicable in different setting. This paper examines attitudes toward black housing problems among white residents of a Minneapolis area and shows "a mixture of ignorance and knowledge concerning Negro housing problems and what can be done about them, as well as a mixture of tolerance and prejudice toward having Negroes as neighbors. The most significant finding that emerged from the study was that most of the expressed attitudes were contradicted by other expressed attitudes or by reports of behavior."

0171.   Rose-Ackerman, Susan. 1975. Racism and Urban Structure. Journal of Urban Economics 2 (1): 85-103.

This paper begins the task of integrating models of racist behavior into general theories of urban land use. The paper derives equilibrium prices for a racist city and demonstrates that the city is less dense at the core,

more dense in the suburbs, and covers a larger area than an unprejudiced
city. A more complex theory of housing supply is then developed, and it is
shown that racism's impact on the ghetto depends upon the ease with which
maintenance can be reduced, the cost of replacing abandoned housing, and the
nature of legal controls on housing quality.*

0172.   Rumney, Jay. 1951. The Social Costs of Slums.   **Journal of Social Issues** 7
(1 & 2): 9-85.

This discussion of the social costs of slums—beyond just a balance sheet
of gains and losses of eliminating slums—includes an analysis of the
profitability of slums, definition and meaning of slums, people in slums,
symptoms of slums and blighted areas, types of slums, the formation of slums,
the measurement of slums and blighted areas, the financial cost of slums, and
the housing Act of 1949.

0173.   Sanchez, Jose Ramon. 1986. Residual Work and Residential Shelter:
Housing Puerto Rican Labor in New York City from World War II to 1983. In:
Critical Perspectives on Housing. Rachel G. Bratt, Chester Hartman, and
Ann Meyerson (eds.). Philadelphia: Temple University Press. 202-20.

Puerto Ricans in New York City are one of the most oppressed groups in terms
of housing conditions and housing affordability. This situation does not
stem simply from discrimination by housing providers or the high levels of
poverty experienced by Puerto Ricans. The critical analysis presented here
attributes the housing situation of Puerto Ricans primarily to their class
position as an increasingly idle part of the reserve army of labor. This
status affects their ability to secure decent housing, but their housing
status also, in turn, affects their position as workers in the labor market,
by limiting and constraining their economic and political behavior.*

0174.   Sarno, Dominic R. 1979. Energy Costs Threaten the Poor and Community
Development. **Journal of Housing** 36 (11): 576-581.

This article examines the impacts of spiraling energy costs on low-income
housing. Asserting that people who do not have the means should not be
allowed to freeze, the article concludes that "the abandonment of private
low- and moderate-income units because of increased fuel costs would further
the depletion of the city's lower-cost rental housing stocks."

0175.   Schulman, Marc S. 1982. The Certified Historic Structure: An Aid to
Neighborhood Conservation and Low-Income Housing. **Urban Lawyer** 14(4):
765-69.

The reductions in funding for federal housing programs have stripped away
many of the traditional tools of America's low-income housing producers.
In order to continue to prosper, developers must fully explore the
opportunities available under the tax laws. If a project can combine the
interests of low-income housing with historic preservation, it will satisfy
two important needs of society and contribute to the revitalization of urban
neighborhoods.*

0176.   Shiefman, Werba & Associates. 1972. The Mobile Home Market. **Appraisal
Journal** 40 (3): 391-411.

The total cost of owning an average mobile home is somewhat less than the lowest-rent new apartment, and significantly less than the lowest-cost new house available today without subsidy. In many areas homes and apartments in the lowest-price bracket are not available even if one was desired. This article examines the advantages and disadvantages of mobile homes for low income families.

0177.   Siegan, Bernad H. 1974. Best Housing Hope. **Freeman** 24 (4): 221-23.

The 1968 Housing Act called for the construction or rehabilitation of six million housing units for low and moderate income families over the succeeding decade. It also established a subsidy program to accomplish that goal. If properly calculated, the average cost of these units will end up to be similar to the cost of housing in Beverly Hills, California, but with hardly the same resale value. This article concludes that if builders were able or allowed to produce more private housing, the less affluent will benefit as much as more affluent through the filtering process.

0178.   Silver, Christopher. 1984. The Black Housing Crisis and an Emerging Planning Function. In: **Twentieth-Century Richmond: Planning, Politics, and Race.** By Christopher Silver. Knoxville: University of Tennessee Press. Chapter 3, pp. 97-129.

"Though lacking any formal plan to guide housing and neighborhood improvements, the onset of the Great Depression and the consequent New Deal afforded an opportunity to experiment with both private and public initiatives in low-cost housing. The housing and neighborhood problem of Richmond's blacks continued to be studied and lamented. What distinguished the 1930s and 1940s from previous decades was that tentative steps were taken toward resolution of what many saw as the city's most pressing concern."

0179.   Silver, Christopher. 1986. Housing Policy and Suburbanization: An Analysis of the Changing Quality and Quantity of Black Housing in Suburbia Since 1950. In: **Race, Ethnicity, and Minority Housing in the United States.** Jamshid A. Momeni (ed.). Westport, Connecticut: Greenwood Press. Chapter V.

The process of black suburbanization since the 1950s has brought about a discernible demographic redistribution of blacks in most major metropolitan areas by opening up the moderate and middle income neighborhoods to black occupancy. The gap between black and white communities persist, however. Federal housing policy since the 1960s has played a role in fostering race and class dispersion in the suburbs, although available evidence suggest that the full potential of Fair Housing Act of 1968 and various housing subsidy programs have not been realized. It is clear that segregated racial residential patterns continue to characterize the suburbs even as large numbers of more affluent blacks join the center city exodus. It is also clear that the dynamics of the local housing market dictate the variations in the pace and scope of black entry into white suburban communities across the country. Yet as this analysis has suggested, the suburban opportunities in both publicly assisted and private housing have fostered social changes that have redounded to the benefit of blacks, particularly since 1970. Assuming that the trends of the past decade persist, there is a basis for cautious optimism that black suburbanization will continue to reduce urban racial disparities. Pursuing housing and neighborhood improvements rather than residential integration appears to be a more realistic objective of the suburbanization process over the next decade. This article also makes a qualitative and quantitative assessment of black housing in suburbia.   The study concludes with a discussion of future housing policy as it relates to racial and ethnic minorities.@

0180.   Simms, Margaret C.   1980.   Families and Housing Markets: Obstacles to Locating Suitable Housing.   Washington, D. C.: Urban Institute.   70 pp.

The significance of housing in America is affirmed by numerous acts of Congress providing federal support for housing industry, equal access to housing markets, and providing housing subsidies for the lower income families. However, the evidence indicates that racial and minority groups are still denied equal access to some housing markets, and are disproportionately located in inadequate housing. Data from the Annual Housing Survey (AHS) show that minorities, female householders, or large households are more likely to be poorly housed. Blacks, Hispanics, and female householders are less likely to own homes than the total population. Blacks and Hispanics are twice as likely to live in flawed housing. Discrimination is another problem. Despite the Fair Housing and Equal Opportunity Acts, mortgage lenders and real estate agents continue to discriminate against minorities and women. The author concludes with the suggestion that the formulation of appropriate policies to deal with the current housing problems of minorities cannot be completed without additional research.

0181.   Smith, Wallace F.   (ed.).   1983.   Housing America.   Beverly Hills, California: Sage Publications.   224 pp.

This book is a collection of articles written by well known experts in the housing field. Although it deals with the entire housing issue in the country, it covers many aspects of minority housing problems--federal programs, rehabilitation, public housing, drop in private and publicly subsidized housing construction and its impact on rental housing, abandonment, and so forth. One major conclusion of this book is that despite the many existing housing problems, there has been a significant improvement in the overall housing situation in the U.S. in recent decades, and Americans are one of the best housed nations in the world.

0182.   Snipp, C. Matthew, and Alan L. Sorkin.   1986.   American Indian Housing: An Overview of Conditions and Public Policy. In: Race, Ethnicity, and Minority Housing in the United States.   Jamshid A. Momeni (ed.).   Westport, Connecticut: Greenwood Press.   Chapter IX.

Utilizing the 1970 and 1980 census data and other available statistics, this study attempts to examine the trends/changes in the quality and the quantity of American Indian housing conditions in recent years. Based on the data presented in this study, Indian housing has improved since 1970. The American Indian-occupied units in 1980 were newer, less crowded, and better equipped than they were in 1970. These improvements are accompanied by higher rents and increased housing values. Indian home ownership also increased slightly during the 1970s, except on a number of large reservations where it declined dramatically. The author compares the American Indian housing with black housing; federal involvement in the American Indians housing and the future direction it should take are also discussed.

0183. Spengler, Joseph J. 1967. Population Pressure, Housing, and Habitat. **Law and Contemporary Problems** 32 (2): 191–208.

This is a general treatment of the relation between population pressure and housing crisis. However, the housing problems of nonwhites is also discussed. In this connection, the author states that "it may be noted parenthetically that economic as well as social factors have to be taken into account if the current housing shortage confronting nonwhites is to be greatly reduced. For, while housing values in nonwhite areas tend to lie below those for comparable housing in nearby white areas, and while block-busting can enlarge nonwhite housing areas, urban renewal programs tend to raise the price of affected urban land above the level at which it is economically attractive to most nonwhites. Emphasis upon residential desegregation, it is said, is retarding the construction of low income housing."

0184. Spiegel, Allen David. 1969. Housing and Related Patterns of Middle Income **Negroes**. Unpublished Ph.D. Dissertation. Brandeis University. 285 pp.

A study conducted during 1962–63 collected data on 250 middle-income Negro families living in Boston's Roxbury area when faced with an imminent urban renewal project. Data included information on mobility patterns, militancy attitudes, opinions about Negro and white leaders, opinions about organizations having the best interests of Roxbury at heart and about organizational memberships of the husband and/or wife. Data on age, education, income and other socio-economic variables were also included. Now five years later and after considerable turmoil and undiminished crises in our cities, a follow-up study of the same 250 families was undertaken to determine changes in attitudes and behavior. Generally, the data led to the conclusion that the middle income Negro living in the white suburbs is quite different from his ghetto counterpart. Non-ghetto people appear to be moving more rapidly toward accepting the style and mores of white people and that they live among. Ghetto people appear to be caught between conflicting ideologies of black nationalism and integration. Even though ghetto people appear to be in limbo, the tendency is to lean toward the white dominant society.@

0185. Stanfield, Rochelle L. 1978. Searching for Solutions to Low Income Housing Woes. **National** Journal 10 (20): 797–801.

Most experts agree that there is a shortage of decent housing for lower income families. But there is no consensus as how to overcome the problem: should it be overcome by building more housing? Or by providing more money to the poor to find decent housing. The Carter administration remains undecided and divided on the question of availability versus affordability options. The author points out that until this indecision is resolved, Congress is unlikely to do much about the problem of low-cost housing for minorities.

0186. Sternlieb, George. 1967. Slum Housing: A Functional Analysis. **Law and Contemporary Problems** 32 (2): 349-56.

"The self-help capacity of the poor is limited. Some resident landlords are elderly, others are uneducated, and some lack an appropriate aspiration level. The fact remains, however, that as a group, they are presently the best landlords in the slums, and provide probably the major hope for better maintenance in the future. It will require a talented and understanding guidance operation to help generate landlord enthusiasm, while restraining over-expenditure. The problems here should not be underestimated. It is essential if this operation is to be truly successful, particularly from a morale standpoint, and also from the standpoint of securing long-run improvement, that the advisory service be a guide and an inspiration, not a directorate." This article concludes with a set of suggestions as key to improving the slum housing conditions.

0187. Sternlieb, George. 1972. Abandoned Housing: What Is To Be Done? **Urban Land** 31 (3): 3-17.

The abandoned housing is symbolic of the decay of lower income private housing market. It represents a change in function in the central city. It marks the end of the function of providing a staging ground for new immigrants. The abandoned structures act as a core of neighborhood decay, and they illustrate private disinvestment in inner cities. To deal with the problem, the author emphasizes the need for a resale methodology to permit structures to move into the hands of interested and strong ownership. But, minorities may not have the financial resources to purchase money mortgages from intermediary speculators. The author concludes by suggesting that necessary steps must be taken to restore confidence in the market, confidence in the neighborhood, and confidence in the neighborhood's life style.

0188. Sternlieb, George. 1972. Death of the American Dream House. **Society** 9 (4): 39-42.

The federal subsidy money is running out. Economic and racial factors are keeping low-income families out of the suburbs, and service industries are growing and goods have to compete in the wider global market. All of these variables have significant effects on the American labor force and on housing availability, cost, and quality. The private home, the goal of the blue-collar worker, is rapidly becoming out of reach.

0189. Sternlieb, George, and James W. Hughes. 1983. Housing the Poor in a Postshelter Society. **Annals of the American Academy of Political and Social Science** 465 (March): 109-22.

Housing in the U.S. has come a long way since Franklin Rossevelt's realistic description of "America as a nation: one third ill housed." The authors indicate that "while a relatively small proportion of record [housing] production levels was targeted directly to America's poverty population, the latter's housing condition improved markedly as a result of much-maligned filtering process. But this success will face very serious inhibitors in the future. The breakdown of the traditional housing alliance, the stagnation of real median family incomes, the growing number

of persons under poverty level, and a housing finance system subject to full
market forces and credit competition--for the first time since the New Deal-
-characterize the early 1980s. Within this context, housing for the middle
class is an issue of much more political potency than the housing needs of the
poor. But without the reformation of a broad-based housing constituency,
one of the great achievements of the last generation--the improvement in the
shelter provisions of the poor--must quickly fall."

0190. Stokes, Charles J. 1962. A Theory of Slums. Land Economics 38 (3): 187-
95.

The paradox of slums is that it thrives in both rich and less developed
societies. More importantly, slums persist in the U.S. despite the more
than three decades of attempts to eliminate them. Many explanations for the
prevalence of slums in the developed as well as less developed nations
exist. In this article the author reviews different theories (views)
attempting to explain the persistence of slums, and he adds an explanation
of his own. "Some types of slums exist because they are an index of a paradox.
Rising standards of living are accompanied by rising standards of ability
and competence. In the United States poverty has become a term which
describes the condition of a class more and more composed of the 'incapable.'
These are the people who because of society's standards for entrance into job
opportunities have not been integrated into full participation in the
economic life of the community. How to provide for these unfortunate lest
their presence yield a costly dividend of crime and disease remains the
problem of highly developed societies." The author continues to assert
that the nature of slums in the developed societies is different from the
problem of earlier and less developed days and countries, when and where
slums were and are an index of growth and of unabsorbed immigration to
cities.

0191. Sumka, Howard J., and Anthony J. Blackburn. 1982. Multifamily Urban
Homesteading: A Key Approach to Low-Income Housing. Journal of Housing 39
(4): 104-07.

Multifamily urban homesteading is defined as the cooperative renovation,
ownership, and management of a multifamily residential building.
Asserting that "there has never been a national demonstration of multifamily
homesteading to serve as a readily replicable model for cities across the
country," this article attempts to show that the multifamily homesteading
"holds out the possibility of being an important mechanism for bringing a
substantial number of decaying dwelling units back into useful service" for
low-income families. This article suggests that the federal government can
play a major supporting role in such efforts.

0192. Sussman, Marvin B. 1957. The Role of Neighborhood Associations in Private
Housing for Racial Minorities. Journal of Social Issues 13 (4): 31-37.

Non-whites, today and in the future, will move into all-white middle class
housing areas at accelerated rates. Improved social and economic
conditions of non-whites, limited supply of decent housing in all-Negro
areas, and an improving social climate for biracial housing are the
principal factors affecting this change. Because non-white movement into
middle class housing areas is a relatively recent phenomenon, research on

the effects of this movement upon the stability of biracial communities is scant. Neighborhood associations, as part of an overall community design, abound in our communities. Their structures, functions, and activities vary widely. In middle class housing areas the associations may act to debar non-white in-migration, facilitate the adjustment of Negro newcomers to the majority white population; maintain a biracial population with a social, educational, and physical rehabilitation program; slow down the process of transition from an all-white to an all-Negro community; or maintain, and if possible, improve the physical standards of the neighborhood.@

0193.   Taeuber, Karl E. 1969. Negro Population and Housing: Demographic Aspects of a Social Accounting Scheme. In: Race and the Social Sciences. Irvin Katz and Patricia Gurin (eds.). New York: Basic Books. Pp. 145-89.

This is a study of the relationships between demographic variables and housing among blacks. Many studies have provided measures of housing segregation, crowding, and quality with which to measure black-white differences. However, the author contends that "these are useful, but we must also attempt to determine how the entire process of provision of shelter is affected by race and racism. What role is played by racial residential segregation and changes in racial occupancy? Are there strategic points at which planned intervention might be particularly feasible or effective?" This paper is an empirical study addressing these and similar questions.

0194.   Thomas, Robert H. 1984. Black Suburbanization and Housing Quality in Atlanta, Journal of Urban Affairs 6 (1): 17-38.

During the 1970s, several researchers presented evidence that black suburbanization was increasing in many U.S. metropolitan areas. There was also evidence that blacks were not significantly improving their housing quality through suburbanization. This paper examines 1980 census data to determine whether black population movement in Atlanta is a suburbanization phenomenon leading to better quality housing. Several dozen census tracts are defined as composing Atlanta's black housing space. For each tract's black households, three measures of housing quality are treated as dependent variables. Regression analysis is used to show that a tract's change in black population during the 1970s is associated with all three dependent variables. The addition of suburbanism (population density) as a second independent variable further elaborates the relationship between black population change and two of the housing quality indicators. Thus, black suburbanization in the Atlanta area is leading to better quality housing for black residents.*

0195.   Tolles, Robert. 1973. Housing and Foundations: A Continuing Partnership. Foundation News 14 (3): 21-29.

"Housing is a most crucial need of the urban poor and foundations (along with the government) must continually strive to meet it."

0196.   Travis, Dempsey J. 1979. The 1980 Homestead Act. Black Scholar 11 (2): 57-59.

This article asserts that blacks were not allowed to buy land and were not beneficiaries to the 18th century land "auction" at 8 or 9 cents an acre. Not only that, there are many recorded instances when blacks "had to leave land, home, and personal effects in the middle of the night, simply to escape with their lives." Thus, blacks are still suffering from past wrongs. The author suggests that "if black America is to get off the welfare treadmill, the Congress must enact a 1980 Homestead Act that would be solely applicable to the disenfranchised black Americans, in light of the fact that blacks did not participate when the federal government handed out to homesteaders 250 million acres of land, granted the railroads some 90 million acres of land and sold, at subsidy prices some 430 million acres of land, and these figures do not include the 225 million acres that were granted to the states for public purposes." The author concludes: "The funding of the 1980 Homestead Act would enable black and white America to close the books on past wrongs and stamp them: 'Account closed...paid in full!'"

0197.   Trippett, Frank. 1972. Mobile Homes: The New Ghettos. **Saturday Review** 55 (39): 51-55.

"The first reports of the 'mobile home revolution,' were romanticized, telling of the return of the spirit of the covered wagon. But now the phenomenon may be seen as a new form of ghettoization and as an indictment of America's failure to provide decent homes for low-income groups."

0198.   U.S. Bureau of the Census. 1973. **Housing Characteristics by Household Composition.** 1970 Census of Housing, Subject Reports HC(7)-1. Washington, D.C.: GPO. 624 pp. Appendixes.

This report presents cross-tabulations of housing and household characteristics from the 1970 Census of Population and Housing for the United States, by inside and outside SMSAs. Data are presented separately for all races combined, blacks, and the Spanish origin population.

0199.   U.S. Bureau of the Census. 1984. **Structural Characteristics of the Housing Inventory.** 1980 Census of Housing. Volume 3, Subject Reports. Chapter 4. HC80-3-4. Washington, D.C.: GPO. 617 pp. Appendixes.

This report presents cross-tabulation of sample data on housing and housing characteristics from the 1980 Census of Population and Housing. Data are shown separately for the United States, whites, blacks, and Spanish origin population. Limited data on units in structure also are shown for regions, divisions, and states.

0200.   U.S. Bureau of the Census. 1984. **Metropolitan Housing Characteristics: United States Summary HC80-2-1.** 1980 Census of Housing, Volume 2. Washington, D.C.: GPO. 1005 pp. Appendixes.

This report presents a set of tables for the United States inside SMSAs, and in central cities; and for the four census regions, inside SMSAs, and in central cities. The report is organized to provide a set of 68 tables for each geographic area. There are 11 tables showing data for all households in the area, 2 tables showing data for vacant units, 11 tables for householders of four separate race [white, black, American Indian, and Asian] groups, and 11 tables for householders of Spanish origin.*

0201.   Vogelsang, Frederic. 1972. Low-Income Families in Miami Get Chance at Ownership of Modular Townhouses in New Scattered Site Public Housing Project. **Journal of Housing** 29 (5): 223-28.

"The newest addition to Miami's low-income housing supply combines a rich variety of modern approaches to public housing." The author describes a 373-unit low-income housing project in Miami, Florida, constructed with HUD "in-cities" and Section 207 Low Income Housing Demonstration funds. Site plans and the modular system of construction used by Housing Corporation of America, two home ownership plans used for this Turnkey III project, integration of the developments with communities surrounding the sites and company criteria used for selecting families for the project are also discussed.

0202.   Von Eckardt, Wolf. 1963.   Black Neck in the White Noose.   **New Republic** 149 (16): 14-17.

Some fifteen years after the Supreme Court declared racial discrimination unconstitutional and fourteen years after the urban renewal legislation gave the government the power and the money to replace slums with new housing and move large numbers of people around, "there are only a handful of racially integrated new neighborhoods, although a good many old **integrated** [emphasis mine] neighborhoods have been bulldozed. There is, if anything, more rigid housing segregation today in our cities than there was a decade ago." This article describes the reaction of those who initially welcomed urban renewal as a means to improve their housing situation, but have now become disappointed and bitter about the actual outcome of the renewal program.

0203.   Warner, A. E., and Milton S. Goldberg. 1961. Government and Housing: Accessibility of Minority Groups to Living Space. **Land Economics** 37 (4): 369-73.

In recent years a significant amount of debate bears upon the accessibility of minorities to living space. "The subject is fraught with emotional and deep-seated feelings about the rights of certain religious and ethnic groups to select without restriction the place in which they desire to live. This problem ranges from the extreme notion that the problem does not exist to the other that it threatens to destroy the democratic character of our way of life." This article examines the role of those who are instrumental in providing places to live for all groups residing in urban areas. It also attempts to explore the legal and economic environments in which the controversy exists and tries to evaluate the position of those involved. Among other things, the article concludes that "recent experience in urban real estate markets casts doubt on the widely held notion that property values and rents fall when entry of non-conforming individuals occurs."

0204.   Watanabe, Mark. 1974.   Chinatown Hit by Housing Shortage.   **Race Relation Reporter** 5 (18):1-2.

A report by the San Francisco City Planning Department based on the analysis of 1970 census data, found that population of Chinatown increased from 55,091 to 56,013 between 1960 and 1970. While occupying less than 2 percent of the city's acreage, Chinatown accommodates nearly 8 percent of the city's population with a density more than seven times greater than the city's average. As population increased, the housing stock declined by some 5 percent, with about more than 13 percent regarded as overcrowded. In March 1972, City's Board of Supervisors approved a redevelopment plan for Chinatown. This plan called for the construction of a 180-unit high rise apartment, geared mostly for elderly and low-income households. Unlike other communities, the plan enjoyed a solid support by the residents.

0205.   Watson, Norman V. 1973. Our Gravest Problem is Bad Management. Real Estate Review 3 (1): 65-69.

In view of the fact that the management of federally controlled housing has become a major problem, this article explains how "HUD is taking a closer look at how to ensure better management of federal housing projects."

0206.   Weaver, Robert C. 1976. The Impact of Housing on Jobs and Education. Integrated Education 14 (10: 21-23.

In the U.S., race and housing are two controversial issues that involve an area where the nation's pronouncements and practices have long been at variance. Equal access to housing so permeates the economic, social, and political life of the society that it will not fade away; nor it can be treated with benign neglect. This article examines the relationship between opening up the housing market to minorities and its impacts on their jobs and education

0207.   White, Michelle J. 1978. Job Suburbanization, Zoning and the Welfare of Urban Minority Groups. Journal of Urban Economics 5 (2): 219-40.

This paper poses a model of the effects of job suburbanization and suburban exclusionary zoning on the welfare of blacks and other urban minority groups. It explores the circumstances under which blacks take suburban jobs and whether they are made better off if they do so. The possibilities that blacks outcommute from central area ghettos and that they relocate to suburban housing near the jobs are each considered. A hypothetical governmental project to subsidize the creation of 10,000 suburban jobs for blacks is explored in a cost-benefit framework, stressing the effects of suburban exclusionary zoning on the project's feasibility.*

0208.   Whitson, Edmund R., and Paul A. Brinker. 1958. The Housing of Negroes in Oklahoma. Phylon 19 (1): 106-108.

This article first reviews the poor housing conditions of Negroes in Oklahoma. It then points out that although Negroes have been successfully integrated into the grade and high schools in Oklahoma, the question of housing segregation still remains. "The urban renewal program, however, does not include many Negro homes, and it is highly doubtful that Negroes will be admitted to any of the new structures constructed. Housing is one more front on which emphasis will have to be placed so that equal rights, rather than separate but equal rights, may be obtained not only in education but in all phases of life."

0209.   Williams, Roger M. 1980. Savannah: Restoration Without Gentrification.

Atlantic 246 (5): 4, 8, 12, 16.

Displacing the urban poor has been a vexing problem created by the resurgence of city living as the return of the more affluent, mostly white home buyers and renters has meant the displacement of low-income largely black population. This article explains how "using private initiative backed by federal loans, Savannah is reviving its beautiful Victorian District—without displacing the poor."

0210. Wilson, Jim. 1973. Housing Supply and Demand: Achieving Affordable Housing. **Western City** 55 (4): 15, 23.

In California, the supply of available housing lags behind demand. According to this article, one in every ten existing housing units needs replacement and/or rehabilitation. Skyrocketing costs and shortages of available housing lead to ineffective demand which means that low income families cannot afford adequate housing. In trying to meet the demand, the housing industry impacts land use planning and the need for energy conservation. The author suggests that city officials must take a leadership role in order to increase the supply of new housing units, and promote the maintenance of the existing units to help ensure affordable housing.

0211. Winston, Wyman. 1982. Closing the Black Housing Gap: A Black Cooperative Housing Network. **Urban League Review** 6 (2): 44-49.

"Existing political and economic policies have failed miserably to solve basic housing problems for blacks, the elderly, and other low- and moderate-income minorities. Since the 1940's black communities have been under a relentless stage of siege. The early urban renewal programs began the process by disrupting the social and physical fabric of black communities under the guise of eliminating slum housing. Whole sections of these communities were uprooted, businesses disappeared, families and friends separated. This policy benefited existing political and private business at the expense of the black community. The response to early urban renewal program by blacks was rebellions in cities and towns across the country. Residents interviewed after the disturbances indicated that poor housing was a primary dissatisfaction. Black communities segregated from mainstream America were exposed and susceptible to urban blight—blight brought on by redlining, municipal inaptitude, disinvestment, and slums for profit investment incentives. The same public and private institutions that charged with saving black housing were ultimately responsible for the black housing demise." In this article the author describes the current black housing gap, and calls for the creation of a black cooperative housing network if they were to meet their critical housing needs.

212. Yankauer, Marian P., and Milo B. Sunderhauf. 1963. Housing: Equal Opportunity to Choose Where One Shall Live. **Journal of Negro Education** 32 (4): 402-14.

"Any discussion of 'gains' or 'improvements' in the housing situation of Negros in America must deal both with the physical quality of the housing occupied by Negroes at points in time and also with the quality of the neighborhood in which that housing is situated." This article is precisely that: a discussion of the physical quality of the housing units and the neighborhoods where Negroes live. The problem of residential segregation and its link to physical quality of the units and neighborhood is also discussed.

0213. Yezer, Anthony. 1978. **How Well Are We Housed? 2. Female-Headed Households.** Washington, D. C.: HUD, Office of Policy Development and Research. 19 pp.

This is a study of the housing conditions of black female householders showing that race, ethnic background, household size, and income are among the powerful factors that determine how well the female householder are housed. This research confirms that female householders live in less adequate housing both in qualitative and quantitative terms than the nation as a whole.

0214. Zelder, Raymond E. 1972. Poverty, Housing, and Market Processes. **Urban Affairs Quarterly** 8 (1): 77-95.

This paper examines the deterioration and abandonment of housing units in the United States. Information on demand and cost factors affecting the housing market are presented with a brief description of a model defining supplier behavior for lower income housing. Five potential approaches of quality housing for lower income households are discussed—new construction, anti-deterioration subsidies, direct income subsidies, development of low-cost construction methods, and demolition.

●●●●●●●●●●

2
MINORITY STATUS, DISCRIMINATION, AND REDLINING

0215. Abrams, Charles. 1955. Forbidden Neighbors: A Study of Prejudice in Housing. New York: Harper. 404 pp.

This book is a comprehensive treatment of housing discrimination and segregation as practiced against racial and ethnic minorities--of Chinese and Japanese descent, blacks and Hispanics. The chapters on the role of realtor, and financial institutions provide a documented and thorough analysis of corporate practices that determine housing choices. It provides historical background on the nature, rise and spread of prejudice in the U.S. This book may be regarded as a crusade for equal opportunity and equal treatment for all Americans by highlighting the discrepancy between the American creed and the American deed. It points out that the number of people and institutions working for equal opportunity in housing is increasing. In his final chapter the author outlines a program of action for individuals and government action and calls for an honest interpretation and enforcement of existing laws.

0216. Abrams, Charles. 1960. Discrimination and the Struggle for Shelter. New York Law Forum 6 (1): 3-12.

This article examines discrimination in housing and calls for the "preservation of American principles against the corrosive influences of prejudice and selfish interest. The threat of poverty amidst plenty is not an idle one. For if economic and social stratification are permitted to take root in America, the new identifiable minority groups may become the first important exception in the American scheme of equal opportunity."

0217. Ahlbrandt, Roger S., Jr. 1977. Exploratory Research on the Redlining Phenomenon. American Real Estate and Urban Economic Association Journal 5 (4): 473-81.

There is a relationship between neighborhood decline and the withdrawal of private capital from a neighborhood. Redlining is defined as selective unavailability or limited supply of private mortgage and home improvement financing for a specified area. Redlining is a term used to describe a discriminatory conspiracy on the part of financial institutions to deny capital to specified neighborhoods for usually racial reasons. This article reports the results of some exploratory research that utilizes a "reduced form of regression equation to explain differences in mortgage lending activity among census tracts in the City of Pittsburgh. The results show lenders are more conservative in extending credit in neighborhoods with greater than 20% black population." This study also points out that racial composition of an area may affect the level of risk a lender is willing to take.

0218.   Anonymous. 1969. Discrimination in Employment and Housing: Private Enforcement Provisions of the Civil Rights Acts of 1964 and 1968. Harvard Law Review 82 (4): 834-63.

Title VII of the Civil Rights Act of 1964 and Title VIII of the Civil Rights Act of 1968 constitute respectively the federal laws prohibiting discrimination in employment and housing. Asserting that discrimination in employment and housing will produce income disparity and ghetto neighborhoods, this essay examines in some "detail the provisions for private enforcement of the rights created by title VII of the 1964 Act and Title VIII of the 1968 Act. The note [this paper] has two purposes: first to suggest how experience under title VII can aid in the interpretation of title VIII; and, second, to suggest where changes seem appropriate in order to make the rights created by the Acts more meaningful."

0219.   Anonymous. 1979. Housing Discrimination. San Francisco: Department of Housing and Urban Development, Office of Program Planning and Evaluation. 20 pp.

This is a bibliography that provides an introduction to the scope and content of literature on housing discrimination in the United States published between 1955 and 1978. This bibliography was originally developed to help HUD evaluate the Section 8 Program in Region IX. There are only 43 annotated citations, however, which include books, journal articles, and research studies. The annotations are relatively detailed. In addition, there are 37 unannotated references. The viewpoints are divided between those who cite socioeconomic or class differences as the primary cause of segregation--that is, minorities cannot afford to live in white neighborhoods--and those who feel that racial attitudes are so important that segregation would persist even if the income levels of minority and white populations were the same. Housing costs, employment patterns, and effects of racial change on property values are also covered by some of the references.

0220.   Anonymous. 1982. Legitimizing Racial Discrimination in the Name of Fair Housing: The Case of Section 8 New Construction. Housing Law Bulletin 12 (1): 1-5.

Some recent studies have shown that nonwhites are substantially underrepresented in Section 8 new projects. The finding is hardly surprising, but its magnitude in some cities is startling. This article examines this problem and concludes that "it cannot go unnoted that the Section 8 new constructions' example of denying benefits to nonwhites is a dreadful word, racist."

0221.   Anonymous. 1982. Increasing the Supply of Low-Income Housing in the Face of Racial Discrimination: Three Recent Decisions. Housing Law Bulletin 12 (4): 1-3.

The main vehicle for redressing racial discrimination in housing is Title VIII of the Civil Rights Act of 1968, known as the Fair Housing Act. The Act has mostly relied upon the expansion of housing opportunities beyond the walls of segregated areas. But, the predicament of the poor and low-income minorities has left many intended beneficiaries with more hope than help. It indicates that supporters of Fair Housing Act recognized early on that the Act will only help to prevent discrimination against those who could otherwise purchase a home. In support of this contention, the article analyzes three cases of violation of the Fair Housing Act, and implies that these violations take place throughout the nation frequently.

0222.   Anonymous. 1983. Denial of Section 8 Benefits for Prior Debt to PHA: A Brief Review of the Law. Housing Law Bulletin 13 (1): 13-16.

In recent years, Section 8 Existing Housing applicants have encountered public housing authority (PHA) policies that deny them benefits because of prior debts to the PHA. This essay examines the existing case law on the issue and recommends different approaches helping the applicants and tenants to encounter discriminatory policies and receive their entitled statutory benefits.

0223.   Avins, Alfred. 1960. Anti-Discrimination Legislation as an Infringement of Freedom of Choice. New York Law Forum 6 (1): 13-37.

The labels of "bigot," "bias," "reactionary," "prejudice," "ignorant," and so forth, so freely bantered about in the race relations area as semantic substitutes for thinking cannot obscure the simple fact that compulsory integration is a program by which some people presume to dictate to others in which type of environment they shall live. In doing so, they arrogate to themselves the right of choice of others which constitutes a fundamental human right inseparable from the dignity of each person as an individual. All the fancy phrases of "democratic living," "fair housing," "open occupancy," and "equality" cannot substitute for the denial of the right of freedom of association. Infringement of this right makes anti-discrimination legislation in housing violative of fundamental liberties.*

0224.   Bowman, Elizabeth. 1975. Neighborhood Decay: Is 'Redlining' a Factor? Congressional Quarterly 33 (20): 1040-42.

Community and civil rights groups are pressing Congress to help them prevent private financial institutions from discriminating against certain areas by labeling them as bad risk neighborhoods. This essay reports on Senate hearings on the subject. More specifically, it examines the testimonies at the hearings of legislation introduced by Senator William Proxmire (D-Wis.) that would require lenders to disclose where their mortgage money is going by zip-code area and the amount of savings deposits taken in from each area.

0225.   Branscomb, Anne W. 1960. An Analysis of Attempts to Prohibit Racial Discrimination in the Sales and Rental of Publicly Assisted Private Housing. George Washington Law Review 28 (4): 758-78.

This essay discusses the extent to which legal curbs can be imposed upon the sale or rental of private housing in order to assure equal access to all citizens. The basic problems in this area are in determining whether constitutional restraints apply to private citizens, and the extent to which federal assistance precludes state regulation.@

0226.   Bullard, Robert D., and Donald L. Tryman. 1980. Competition for Decent Housing: A Focus on Housing Discrimination Complaints in a Sunbelt City. Journal of Ethnic Studies 7 (4): 51-63.

Despite the passage of the federal Fair Housing Act of 1968 prohibiting racial discrimination in housing, the number of complaints on housing discrimination is high and segregation in the nation continues to be a major problem. The focus of this study is on housing discrimination in Houston, Texas, a major growth city in the Sunbelt area.

0227.   Carey, Thomas C., George Matish, and Mary Richman. 1975. An Analysis of Recent Housing Discrimination Cases. Journal of Urban Law 52 (Symposium Issue): 897-911.

The enactment of Title VIII of the 1968 Civil Rights Act and the landmark Jones v. Alfred Mayer Co. decision have had significant effect in combating overt discrimination in the sale and rental of housing to racial and ethnic minorities. But, due to its complexity, some questions still remain unanswered. One significant remaining problem is on the effort of minority group members and associations to develop low- and moderate-income housing in predominantly white neighborhoods and suburban municipalities. This study examines recent cases involving suburban integration through low-income housing development projects. The analysis is divided into those cases where: (1) a municipality has thwarted the efforts of a private developer or nonprofit sponsor to build a specific housing project by methods such as refusing to grant necessary rezoning; (2) the municipality itself is the sponsor. The developer and the project is dropped, or its low-income character is modified due to community pressure; and, (3) attempts are made to open up the suburbs to integration and low-income housing.

0228.   Center for Community Change, and the Center for National Policy Review [both in Washington, D.C.]. 1980. Housing Discrimination Must be Dealt with by HUD. Journal of Housing 37 (6): 315-22.

The idea of equal housing opportunity in Chicago, the most segregated city, has always faced a stiff opposition. Racial conflict in Chicago has been central to the city's housing history. Realtors have played an active role in spurring and manipulating the racial conflict on housing. Blacks in Chicago mostly live in a ghetto, a narrow black belt south of downtown business district. White neighborhoods surround the black belt. Racial conflict, violence, restrictive covenants coupled with manipulation by the real estate and financial institutions have historically set the tone and the condition for a housing situation that continues to plague the city. This article examines this perennial problem focusing on the reaction of Marquette Park's residents to the extension of black belt into their neighborhood. The article discusses the reasons behind the conflict, dual housing market, the role of FHA, HUD's response, and the need for actions to be taken. One of its conclusions is that to break the discriminatory and segregated pattern of housing requires extensive reforms by HUD.

0229. Chandler, Robert. 1979. Minorities and Housing: Are the Doors Really
       Open? **Foundation News** 20 (4): 23-24, 36-37.

       Despite the fact that housing discrimination is illegal, it still prevails
       across the nation. In addition to private and volunteer agencies, several
       government agencies are charged with the responsibility to deal with housing
       discrimination cases. But, discrimination still continues because it is
       difficult to prove and prosecute. In this study the author discusses the
       various forms of discrimination such as racial steering, where blacks are
       directed to neighborhoods apart from whites; blockbusting and stiffer
       mortgage terms for minorities who wish to move into a certain area are also
       examined. It is asserted that although the solution to housing
       discrimination must come from many sources, volunteer and private groups do
       play a major role in assuring that all people are treated equally when
       looking for housing.

0230. Commission on Race and Housing. 1958. **Where Shall We Live?** Berkeley:
       University of California Press.

       This is a report of a 3-year study of segregation and discrimination in
       housing against racial and ethnic minorities. This publication includes a
       bibliography of published and unpublished studies of housing discrimination
       in different parts of the country.

0231. Courant, Paul N. 1977. On Models of Racial Prejudice and Urban
       Residential Structure. **Journal of Urban Economics** 4 (3): 272-91.

       Economists have studied the effects of racial prejudice on urban residential
       structure using a set of models that focus on conditions at the border
       between the black and white areas. This paper is a review of the theoretical
       literature on these border models and an investigation of their
       generality. The main result derived in this paper is that border models are
       logically inconsistent without unrealistic assumptions either about the
       incomes of blacks relative to the incomes of whites or about the extent of
       white prejudice. The paper concludes with several suggestions for more
       satisfactory modeling of prejudice and urban structure.*

0232. Daniel, Edwin C. 1975. Redlining. **Journal of Housing** 32 (9): 441-44.

       Redlining, a form of discrimination in mortgage lending, and a practice that
       contributes to urban decay, is being investigated by local, state and
       federal legislators. Congress is moving towards exposing discriminatory
       practices by lenders. Lenders are opposing redlining legislation not
       because of disclosure proposals, but because they are afraid that the
       legislation may lead into a credit allocation, which may endanger the
       stability of their institutions.

0233. Demkowich, Linda E. 1978. Enforcing the Laws Against Discriminatory
       Credit Practices. **National Journal** 10 (41): 1646-47.

       This article reports on a Congressional subcommittee pressing on the federal
       banking agencies crack down and step up enforcement of two important Credit
       laws—one that bars discrimination based on sex, marital status, race,
       national origin, or age, and one that prohibits lenders to assign credit on

the basis of neighborhood's age, location, or composition.

0234.   Deutsch, Martin, and Mary Evans Collins. 1951.   **Interracial Housing:** A **Psychological Evaluation of a Social Experiment.** Minneapolis: University of Minnesota Press.   173 pp.

This book analyzes comparable interracial housing projects in New York City and Newark.   The study is conducted by the Field Foundation's Research Center for Human Relations.   Its main objective is to investigate the effects of occupancy patterns on prejudice.   As a whole, results show that in those projects where blacks and whites lived side by side, a reduction in prejudice and an increase in harmonious democratic intergroups relations took place;   but where the races occupied separate wings or buildings, the original prejudices were mostly retained.   The study concludes that public policy can make a difference in changing social attitudes.

0235.   Eisenberg, Lawrence D.   1968.   Uncle Tom's Multi-Cabin Subdivision: Constitutional Restrictions on Racial Discrimination by Developers. **Cornell Law Review** 53 (2): 314-24.

The suggestion of possible pegs on which the Supreme Court might hang a "sociologically wise" decision to curtail subdivision discrimination is not meant to be all-inclusive.   Other theories have been proposed.   One writer suggests the use of Section I of the Sherman Antitrust Act [1964] in dealing with the problem. One cannot predict with certainty what theory the court will use to satisfy those who feel that constitutional holdings must be founded in strict legal logic.   The Supreme Court has already indicated that civil rights hold a preferred position over property rights.   The civil rights bulldozer has been so powerful in recent years that one stick—the unrestricted alienation of property—in the bundle of sticks we call ownership probably will be unable to block its path.   It is surprising that the stick has not already been plowed under.*

0236.   Fauman, S. Joseph.   1957.   Housing Discrimination, Changing Neighborhoods, and Public Schools.   **Journal of Social Issues** 13 (4):21-30.

Many studies have documented that the areas of residence of Americans are related to their social class.   Neighborhoods tend to be homogeneous with respect to skin color, religion, name, and income.   The status homogeneity of residential areas is inculcated in the peoples mind through neighborhood public schools, serving a particular area marked by status characteristics in membership, curriculum, extra-curricular activities, and so forth.   It is often difficult to break through the walls segregating these neighborhoods.   This article examines the links between social class, status characteristics, housing discrimination, changing neighborhoods, and the role of public schools in perpetuating segregation.   The author concludes with several suggestions to deal with the problem.

0237.   Foster, Arnold, and Sol Rabkin.   1960.   The Constitutionality of Laws Against Discrimination in Publicly Assisted Housing.   **New York Law Forum** 6 (1); 38-58.

The constitutionality of state laws against discrimination in publicly assisted housing still awaits decision by the highest state courts and the federal courts. The author submits that based on the weight of previous cases, the final decisions will and should be such that laws are proper and constitutional in view of the attitude of the courts on related questions. "While the discussion herein has been confined to the question of the constitutionality of laws against discrimination in publicly assisted housing, it is suggested that the reasoning which led to the conclusion that such laws are constitutional is equally applicable to the question of the constitutionality of laws directed against racial and religious discrimination in housing the creation of which was achieved with no form of public assistance whatsoever."

0238.   Galster, George C. 1977. A Bid-Rent Analysis of Housing Market Discrimination. **American Economic Review** 67 (2): 144-55.

The elimination of discrimination in housing has long been a major American social concern. Some economists have attempted to quantify the impact of such discriminatory practices. This is one such study which employs a new approach to assess not only the magnitude of housing price discrimination, but how its burden is incident upon different types of minority households. It develops a model of urban housing market from the bid-rent theory that allows one to isolate empirically the distinct contributions to interracial housing price differentials made by variations in households' preferences, incomes, and housing packages versus those made by discriminatory actions.

0239.   Helper, Rose. 1969. **Racial Policies and Practices of Real Estate Brokers.** Minneapolis: University of Minnesota Press.

The key words to describe this book are: discrimination, Chicago area, and brokers' practices. This book has grown out of the author's Ph.D. dissertation. Its main objective is to provide an in-depth view of racial policies and practices by the real estate brokers. The study is based on two sets of interviews with real estate brokers in Chicago: (1) the initial set conducted during 1955-56 period for the author's doctoral degree; and (2) a follow-up interview carried out during 1964-65 period. One of the major conclusions reached in this study is that real estate brokers' ideology relative to racial discrimination in housing had not changed between 1955 and 1965. The reasons for the lack of change are discussed.

0240.   Hendon, William S. 1968. Discrimination Against Negro Homeowners in Property Tax Assessment. **American Journal of Economics and Sociology** 27 (2): 125-132.

This study has demonstrated that discrimination exists in the property tax between White and Negro homeowners. The Negro homeowners pay more taxes per dollar of tax base than do their white counterparts. Ratios of assessed value to sales price among Negro properties are demonstratively higher than among properties owned by Whites. In addition, the average deviation measures reveal clearly that Negro-owned properties are assessed at higher levels than are White-owned properties.*

0241.   Holbert, Kenneth. 1976. Redlining: A New Dimension in Fair Housing Policy. **HUD Challenge** 7 (4): 20-22.

This article presents an overview of the action taken by HUD since the passage of Title VIII, the 1968 Civil Rights Act (Section 805), a clear enunciation against redlining--discrimination in mortgage lending. In view of the overall authority for the administration and enforcement of Title VII, HUD has developed a program of data collection that supports evidence that redlining still occurs. Aggrieved individuals and groups are pursuing their rights to obtain residential mortgage through the use of administrative process and litigation.

0242. Hood, Edwin T., and Cynthia M. Weed. 1979. Redlining Revisited: A Neighborhood Development Bank as a Proposed Solution. Urban Lawyer 11 (1): 139-71.

Redlining refers to discriminatory practices against a neighborhood by private lenders. This article focuses on redlining process and offers what it considers as a workable solution to the problem of redlining--the establishment of a neighborhood development bank.

0243. Hutchinson, Peter M., James R. Ostas, and J. David Reed. 1977. A Survey and Comparison of Redlining Influences in Urban Mortgage Lending Market. American Real Estate and Urban Economic Association Journal 5 (4) 463-472.

This paper consists of an empirical study of three forms of redlining carried out in the Toledo Standard Metropolitan Statistical Area (SMSA). Mortgage redlining refers to the refusal of lenders to extend credit to certain urban neighborhoods because of: (1) the racial composition; (2) the annual rate of change in racial composition; and (3): the age of housing units in a residential community regardless of racial composition or credit worthiness of mortgage applicants or the condition of a certain individual property. This study shows that neighborhoods characterized by older units seem to receive fewer mortgage loans, that racial composition of a neighborhood has a significant impact on loan approvals, and that redlining practices stem from risk aversion on the part of the financial institutions.

0244. Kain, John F., and John M. Quigley. 1975. Housing Markets and Racial Discrimination. New York: Columbia University Press. 393 pp.

This book presents an empirical analysis of urban housing markets, employing data from a 1967 household survey conducted as a part of the St. Louis Community Renewal Program. Its main purpose is to examine the factors determining the residential choices of households in large urban areas; it analyzes the effects of racial discrimination on market outcomes; and it explores the effects of factors such as race, income, family size, job stability, and other demographic variables on housing expenditures and home ownership. Some of the findings include: (1) homeowners spend significantly more money on housing than do renters of the same socioeconomic status; (2) the chances of being a homeowner is more strongly affected by family composition than by income; and (3) racial discrimination in housing market imposes even greater economic hardship on blacks than most previous studies have suggested.

0245. Kantor, Amy C., and John D. Nystuen. 1982. De Facto Redlining a Geographic View. Economic Geography 58 (4): 309-328.

Redlining is the practice of withholding mortgage credit from an entire neighborhood with the ultimate result that the neighborhood succumbs to deterioration. Social response to prevent disinvestment in urban neighborhoods has been through legal and legislative efforts. The efficacy of these actions remains in doubt. A theory of redlining is presented which focuses on factors that loan committees of financial institutions use when considering loan applications. These factors operate at different geographical scales and include creditworthiness of the applicant, value of the property for sale, quality and stability of neighborhood, and secondary mortgage market potential of the loan in the national market. De facto redlining is the consequence of a chain of decisions involving the housing market and mortgage institutions which may or may not be apparent to those involved. If creditworthiness and soundness of property are spatially correlated with race, housing age, or other inappropriate variables, a dynamic is created that geographically concentrates approved loans in certain neighborhoods to the detriment of others. The spatial variation of conventional mortgage loans in Ann Arbor and Flint, Michigan are evaluated for evidence of de facto redlining through the use of a path analysis of census tract data.*

0246.   Kaplan, Marshall. 1962. Discrimination in California Housing: The Need for Additional Legislation. **California Law Review** 50 (October): 635-49.

This paper presents empirical study of racial discrimination in California housing market. As its test group, it utilizes a total of 5,417 individual sales prices collected from 20 formerly all-white neighborhoods that underwent some degree of nonwhite entry during the course of the study. This data are compared with 4,495 sale prices gathered from 19 closely comparable neighborhoods that remained all-white during the same period (control group). Two broad conclusions of this study were: "first, price changes which can be connected with the fact of nonwhite entry are not uniform, as often alleged, but diverse. Depending on circumstances, racial change in a neighborhood may be depressing or it may be stimulating to real estate prices and in varying degree. Second, considering all of the evidence, the odds are about four to one that house prices in a neighborhood entered by nonwhite will keep up with or exceed prices in a comparable all-white area." The author suggests there is a need to enact tougher laws against discriminatory practices regarding the sale rental, or leasing of all dwelling units and vacant land.

0247.   Kendig, Dennis. 1973. Discrimination Against Women in Home Mortgage Financing. **Yale Review of Law and Social Action** 3 (2): 166-80.

This article explores the problem of sex discrimination in home loan financing. It is divided into three parts: Part I discusses the extent of discrimination, and concludes that discrimination against women is widespread. Part II examines the lenders' arguments that such practices may be justified for economic reasons, and concludes that there is no economic basis for automatically discriminating against women; and in Part III the author argues that present federal and state remedies are inadequate to prevent various forms of discrimination. It is suggested that states should adopt statutes directed at eliminating all forms of home mortgage financing.

0248.   King, Thomas A., and Peter Mieszkowski. 1973. Racial Discrimination,

Segregation, and the Price of Housing.   **Journal of Political** Economy 81 (3): 590–606.

This article presents empirical estimates of racial discrimination in the New Haven, Connecticut, housing market. The results are based on 200 rental units for which there is comprehensive information on the characteristics of the dwelling. Using multiple-regression techniques, we estimate that blacks and whites do pay different amounts for equivalent units. For black female-headed households the markup relative to white males is 16 percent; for black male-headed households, 7.5 percent. Also the work indicates that rents for whites in boundary integrated areas are about 7 percent lower than for black households in these areas.*

0249. Kolbenschlag, Mike. 1975. Guerrilla War Over Redlining Jars Chicago, Threatens to Spread. House and Home 47 (7): 8–9.

Homeowners in some Chicago's racial and ethnic neighborhoods have banded together to form antiredlining associations like the National Peoples Action on Housing (NPAH) and Citizens Action Program (CAP). These groups, bound up by the issue of redlining, claim to have broadened their battle into a national onslaught. Three Savings and Loan Associations have already signed agreement with CAP to dispense fixed amount of conventional mortgage and home repair financing in specific neighborhoods. The Illinois Housing Development Authority has also embarked on a program to make low-interest loans available to institutions that agree to match the funds and distribute the money in specific areas.

0250. Ladenson, Mark L. 1978. Race and Sex Discrimination in Housing: The Evidence from Probabilities of Homeownership. **Southern Economic Journal** 45 (2): 559–75.

This study estimates probability of home purchase equations for years 1969 through 1974. Findings show that the difference in probability of home purchase due to being black fell in the years after the enactment of the 1968 Fair Housing Act and the Section 235 program, but it rose after the suspension of Section 235 in 1973. Thus, it is inferred that the fall was due to the effects of Section 235 rather than the Fair Housing Act. This study also assesses the effects of differences in assets on the differences in probability of home purchase between black and white households. Results show that perhaps 10–20 percent of variation in the probability of home purchase can be explained by differences in assets.

0251. Lake, Robert W. 1981. The New Suburbanites: Race and Housing in the Suburbs. New Brunswick, N.J.: Center for Urban Policy Research, Rutgers University. 303 pp.

In the first part of this book, the author presents a comprehensive synthesis of recent studies on race and housing through the late 1970s. Lake follows the review section by presentation of data of his own, showing that ten years after the enactment of the 1968 federal Fair Housing Act, racial/ethnic discrimination in housing is very well alive.

0252. Lapham, Victoria. 1971. Do Blacks Pay More for Housing? **Journal of Political Economy** 79 (6): 1244–57.

This paper reports on a study of the prices paid by blacks and whites for housing in Dallas in 1960. The technique used to compare the price of housing with different dimensions of characteristics was to estimate implicit prices of characteristics bought by blacks and whites. Two comparisons were made. The first was based on a unit with the average of all black characteristics. The second was based on a unit with the average of all white characteristics. No statistically significant differences were found.*

0253. Lehman, Warren W. 1959. Discrimination in F.H.A. Guaranteed Home Financing. Chicago Bar Record 40 (8): 375-79.

This article examines court cases in California and New York in an attempt to demonstrate that when builders discriminated against blacks the FHA money kept coming, but abiding by the laws against discrimination in California meant a halt in the FHA money.

0254. Lehman, Warren. 1961. Must I Sell My House to a Negro? Chicago Bar Record 42 (6): 283-288.

"Artificially dividing the cities of the North into exclusive racial neighborhoods has been the Yankee's ingenious substitute for the described social patterns of the South. Separation in space--'you live over there; I'll live here'--seemed to let the Yankee abide with abolitionist conscience without facing the consequences. ...In sum, legislation applicable to housing regardless of government involvement can justly include or exclude the individual home owner or the owner-occupant of a small apartment. The decision would be a matter for the discretion of the legislative body."

0255. Lettenberger, Peter. 1962. Civil Rights: Discrimination in Private Housing. Marquette Law Review 46 (2): 237-41.

According to the Massachusetts statute no owner or manger of a multiple dwelling or contiguously located housing accommodations may refuse to rent or lease to any person on account of his race, creed, national origin or color. A large private apartment building had refused to rent to a black applicant. The applicant files compliant with the Massachusetts Commission Against Discrimination, the agency charged with enforcement responsibility. Determination is made that the respondent (the owner of the apartment) had engaged in unlawful discriminatory practices. This article examines the issues surrounding this case and concludes with these words: "it is one thing to tell an owner of an 120 unit apartment building to refrain from discrimination. But it is altogether different to require a person living in his own home who desires to rent out a room not to discriminate. However, all the statutes enacted so far have considered this social aspect, and have restricted the application of their statute. From a social standpoint such a classification seems desirable."

0256. Lim, Gill C. 1982. Discrimination, Time-Lag, and Assessment Inequality in Black Neighborhoods. Review of Black Political Economy 12 (1): 15-28.

This article examines the issue of assessment inequality in black neighborhoods by analyzing two sets of data on residential properties in the city of Chicago. The primary purpose of this study is to evaluate the relative importance of racial discrimination and time-lag in determining the level of assessment-sales ratios. The most significant observation made in this study is that "racial factors are among the most important sources of inequitable assessment practices." However, this study fails to provide evidence in support of the hypothesis that the time-lag between assessments and market transfers is mainly responsible for over-assessments in black neighborhoods.

0257.   Lucey, John K. 1979. The Redlining Battle Continues: Discriminatory Effect V. Business Necessity Under the Fair Housing Act. **Boston College Environmental Affairs Law Review** 8 (2): 357-95.

Challenging the practice of redlining through judicial actions poses certain practical and conceptual problems. Traditionally, courts have frequently required proof of discriminatory intent. In virtually all cases, proving an intent to discriminate is a practical impossibility. Even if proving intent were simple, it is evident that only a small percentage of the harmful lending practices would be affected. The solution is reached by first expanding the definition of redlining, then using the discriminatory effects test which lets the plaintiff prove discrimination indirectly. Finally, a liberal reading of the discrimination provisions of the Fair Housing Act must be accepted.@

0258.   MacRae, C. Duncan, Margaret Austin Turner, and Anthony M. J. Yezer. 1982. Determinants of FHA Mortgage Insurance in Urban Neighborhoods. **Housing Finance Review** 1 (1): 55-71.

Some recent empirical analysis has concluded that racially mixed urban neighborhoods are redlined by conventional lenders while other studies have reached opposite conclusions. Previous theoretical analysis suggests that the same neighborhoods that are neglected by conventional lenders may receive relatively high levels of mortgage insurance under FHA's section 203(b) program. This paper identifies the determinants of FHA mortgage insurance activity, testing the hypothesis that FHA activity is concentrated in middle-income, racially mixed neighborhoods. Results confirm the hypothesis and call attention to the differences between FHA's service to white households under section 203(b) and its service to black households. We find that neighborhood racial composition plays a more significant role in determining the distribution of section 203(b) activity across neighborhoods for black homebuyers than for white homebuyers.@

0259.   Maddala, G. S., and Robert P. Trost. 1982. On Measuring Discrimination in Loan Market. **Housing Finance Review** 1 (3): 245-68.

This paper remedies some defects in the analysis of others who have attempted to measure discrimination in loan markets. The paper argues that one cannot analyze discrimination properly without first specifying a supply and demand model. Also, these supply and demand models should be estimated with just the sub-sample of observations on loans granted, as is usually done. The paper illustrates the method of estimating the supply and demand model with the entire data set, and shows how this makes a difference in results. When the supply and demand model was estimated by two-stage least squares based on just the data on loans granted, the coefficient of the interest in

the supply equation had the wrong sign. The results were much better when
the supply model was estimated by the maximum-likelihood method based on all
the loan applications--those accepted as well as those denied.*

0260.   Mandelker, Daniel R. 1977. Racial Discrimination and Exclusionary Zoning:
A Perspective on Arlington Heights. Texas Law Review 55 (7): 1217-53.

Whether the Constitution dictates that racial discrimination and
segregation be entirely eliminated in the nation is one of the most difficult
issues facing the federal judiciary. "This article examines the extent to
which the fourteenth amendment's prohibition of racial discrimination
forbids exclusionary municipal zoning practices." It also discusses the
issue of the extent to which local governments should require to "administer
their zoning to permit the construction of housing that serves racial
minorities."

0261.   Marantz, J., K. Case, and H. Leonard. 1975. Discrimination in Rural
Housing: Case Studies and Analysis of Six Selected Markets. Cambridge,
Mass.: Urban Systems Research and Engineering, Inc. 251 pp.

This is a report on economic and institutional analysis conducted in six
rural housing markets to determine the magnitude of discrimination by race
and sex, and the ways it is effected and maintained. Results from four
southern sites show virtually complete black segregation which cannot be
explained by income differences or by self-segregation. Three of the four
sites have a dual or segmented housing market, with blacks usually paying
more than whites for equivalent housing. Minorities, including blacks,
Spanish surnamed, American Indians, and women, are more likely to be
renters. Inequality is maintained by fatalism and fear; discrimination
is prescribed by unchallenged tradition; and, women and minorities are
totally excluded from any decision-making institutions, and are otherwise
powerless.

0262.   Marcuse, Peter. 1979. The Deceptive Consensus on Redlining: Definitions
Do Matter. APA Journal 45 (4): 549-56.

The redlining debate is at a crossroads. Either it can move from the
apparently negative definitions of redlining in terms of discrimination,
undue weight given to location, and "numbers games," to focus on strategies
for reinvestment in older neighborhoods and public-private partnerships to
stimulate mortgage lending; or it can pursue its original thrust to its
logical conclusion, and ask whether even thoroughly rational economic
criteria are an adequate base for determining real estate investment
policies if social needs are to be adequately met. The wide divergence in
definitions of redlining in general use highlight the alternatives. All,
at bottom, permit location to be evaluated economically, in the appraisal
process if not in the loan approval process, except for the as yet rarely used
social needs definitions. A variety of ways are available to implement such
a social needs definition, but all are likely to produce conflicts of
interest much greater than the consensus-oriented reinvestment discussion.
Which road the redlining debate will take remains to be seen.*

0263.   Mayhew, Leon H. 1968. Law and Equal Opportunity: A Study of the
Massachusetts Commission Againstt Discrimination. Cambridge, Mass.:

Harvard University Press.   313 pp.

This book examines the impact of Massachusetts antidiscrimination law through the analysis of the actual complaints and their settlements. The analysis includes an exploration of forces that facilitate, shape, and obstruct the implementation of the antidiscrimination laws.

0264. McEntire, Davis. 1957. Government and Racial Discrimination in Housing. Journal of Social Issues 13 (4): 60-67.

Observers of the racial scene concur in judging racial discrimination more "institutionalized," more stubborn and resistant to change in the field of housing than in any other area. Yet, paradoxically, there is no other field in which the claims of the minorities to equal treatment are more secure. The Supreme Court in 1954 sustained a judicial ban on segregation by public housing authorities. However, the significant form of housing discrimination practiced by or with the support of government appear to be beyond the reach of judicial review, at least for the present. This article attempts to document this contention. This is done by reviewing the impacts of various governmental activities in the field of housing in general, and urban renewal in particular. By removing minorities from renewal areas without opening up compensating areas of residence, the urban renewal program threatens a net reduction of living space available to the minority population. Undoubtedly, the program has contributed to intensifying racial segregation. It is doubtful, too, whether the program has thus far accomplished any net reduction of slums, considering the slum-generating effect of crowding the relocated populations into other near slum-areas.@

0265. Mercer, Norman A. 1962. Discrimination in Rental Housing: A Study of Resistance of Landlords to Non-White Tenants. Phylon 23 (1): 47-54.

Discrimination in housing is one of the leading unresolved problems in the nation. Continuation of discriminatory practices in housing means other rights are also jeopardized. Previous studies in the city of Schenectady have shown that half the Negroes continue to be segregated in "wards containing the most crowded and deteriorated housing in the city." The present study attempts to answer the following questions: "Is good rental housing available to Negroes in Schenectady? To what degree do landlords accept or resist rental to non-white tenants?" Findings indicate that housing is there and so are the prospective tenants, but discrimination in the selection of tenants is a major barrier.

0266. Nelson, Susan Caroline. 1976. Housing Discrimination and Black Employment Opportunities. Unpublished Ph.D. Dissertation. Princeton University. 177 pp.

This study explores the relationship between housing discrimination and blacks employment opportunities, from both theoretical and empirical perspectives. The analysis is based on data from the 1970 Census Public Use Sample with neighborhood characteristics for Boston, Massachusetts. The author concludes that "eradicating housing discrimination would improve employment prospects for a substantial number, though not a majority, of blacks. Therefore, eliminating racial barriers in the housing market should be considered among measures designed to improve economic situation of blacks."

0267.   P. G. A., and M. C. G. [Authors have only given their initials]. 1959.
         Racial Discrimination in Housing. University of Pennsylvania Law Review
         107 (4): 515-50.

Among the problems fostered by racial discrimination in the U.S. is the
inadequate housing available to minorities. Housing shortage is more
intense for minorities because of economic and social restrictions on the
market in which they can buy or rent. The nation's low-income population
contains more than its proportional share of certain minorities; and in
general, they can seek only the least expensive housing units. Then there
is also the added problem that certain people refuse to sell or rent to
certain minority groups. The law makers' approach to alleviate the problem
has been by means of anti-discriminatory housing legislation. This article
analyzes the nature of the laws that have been passed, and whom and how they
regulate. It also considers the validity of these laws to see whether they
meet constitutional requirements. The author also discusses the power and
propriety of municipalities passing anti-bias housing ordinances, and the
question of "benign quota"—the government enforced integration. Among
other things, it concludes that the "benign quota" must fall to the
"constitutional demands that government, except possibly in situations of
dire emergency, may not take race into account as a standard for action.
Furthermore, the adoption of 'benign quota' system should be prohibited
because it requires that some individuals suffer exclusion from housing
because the quota for their ethnic group is filled."

0268.   Peel, Norman D. 1970. Racial Discrimination in Public Housing Site
         Selection. Stanford Law Review 23 (1): 63-147.

The purpose of this essay is to analyze the problem of discrimination in the
selection of sites for public housing. The analysis consists of the
following component parts: (1) a summary of the history of public housing
programs, with an emphasis on various mechanisms employed for site
selection; (2) discussion and evaluation of current HUD's criteria for a
"suitable site" and the process of site approval by HUD; (3) the social,
economic, and political considerations involved in site selection is
surveyed by a detail examination of site-selection procedures and problems
of three local housing authorities; and (4) a discussion of judicial role
in reviewing site-selection procedures. The paper concludes with several
suggestions relative to changes in the powers and priorities of HUD and in
the site-selection procedures of Local Housing Authorities that are
required before a national desegregation in public housing could be
achieved.

0269.   Peroff, Kathleen A., et al. 1979. Gautreaux Housing Demonstration: An
         Evaluation of Its Impact on Participating Households. Washington, D.C.:
         HUD, Office of Policy Development and Research. 218 pp.

Gautreaux Housing Demonstration, the result of a series of court actions, is
a federal effort to explore ways of providing metropolitanwide housing for
low-income families through the use of the Section 8 Housing Assistance
Payments Program. Its origin was a suit brought in 1966 by public housing
tenants in Chicago, Illinois, against the Chicago Housing Authority and HUD.

Tenants charged that these agencies had practiced racially discriminatory policies. This report evaluates the impact of the Gautreaux housing demonstration on participating families (typically low-income, black female householders under age 35, separated or divorced, and who had children). The demonstration makes it possible for a small number of families eligible for public housing to move to neighborhoods around the city with small minority residents. During the first three years of its operation, a total of 455 families have been placed, primarily in suburban areas that had 30 percent or less minority residents. The findings suggest a tightening in the number of housing units available for rents since the early stages of the demonstration and an unwillingness of some participants to move to the suburbs where most of the units were located. However, rating their overall experience with the program, Gautreaux participants expressed satisfaction with their neighborhoods and housing, more so than did eligible nonparticipating Gautreaux families or Section 8 movers. Most of the Gautreaux participants preferred to live in the suburbs and in racially balanced neighborhoods. One-third of them did not want to give up the city's convenience and better transportation for the suburbs's higher socioeconomic characteristics.

0270.   Quigley, John M.   1974.   Racial Discrimination and the Housing Consumption of Black Households. In: **Patterns of Racial Discrimination: Volume I.** George M. von Furstenberg, Bennett Harrison, and Ann R. Horowitz (ed.). Lexington, Mass.: Lexington Books. Pp. 121-37.

Empirical research on the impact of race on urban housing prices have produced incomplete results. But, most researchers seem to concur on two relationships: (1) at any point in time, in most cities "otherwise identical" housing units are more expensive in the black ghetto than in the white submarkets; (2) the transition of a neighborhood from white to black occupancy is not typically accompanied by a reduction in property values. Ample studies in support of these contentions are cited. Among topics discussed are restrictions on housing supply for blacks, racial differences in housing expenditures, and the effect of discrimination on housing consumption. It is concluded that residential segregation arise from systematic discrimination against blacks in the sale or rental of housing.

0271.   Rainwater, Lee. 1967.   The Lessons of Pruitt-Igoe. **Public Interest** (8): 116-26.

Pruitt-Igoe, a high-rise public apartment housing project built in St. Louis in 1954 represents the failure of federal government's approach to solving housing problem. It has become a new slum with the "tangle of pathology" present in all slums. It is exemplary of "service approach" to poverty. This article argues that for the lower class families to adopt middle class values what is needed is income, and a service approach to the problem does not provide a remedy because it emphasizes the stigma of poverty and assumes that the poor can change while they are still poor. It is concluded that the most powerful tool to solve the problems of lower-class adaptation is to change the present income distribution to provide the poor with adequate income.

0272.   Rapkin, Chester. 1966.   Price Discrimination Against Negroes in the

Rental Housing Market. In: **Essays in Urban Land Economics.** Berkeley, Calif.: California University Graduate School of Business Administration. Pp. 333-45.

As of this date, residential segregation and economic inequities are the major barriers to the cultural integration of Negroes in American life. Many explanations for the inferior housing status of the Negroes are offered, and it is suggested that "the poor condition of housing occupied by Negroes is due to the fact that, compared with that of whites, housing occupies an inferior position in the scale of Negro consumer preference." The author hypothesizes that the only thesis which can explain the Negro housing situation is that "the poorer condition of Negro housing arises from discriminatory treatment in the housing market, so that the purchasing power of the dollar spent by nonwhites is less than that of the dollar spent by whites." The author discusses the mechanism by which social discrimination leads to distortions in housing market, which in turn results in inferior housing for Negroes. This article concludes that the "Negro who achieves middle-class status is rewarded in housing market by an increasing burden of price and locational discrimination."

0273.   Rich, Jonathan M. 1984. Municipal Boundaries in a Discriminatory Housing Market: An Example of Racial Leapfrogging. **Urban Studies** 21 (1): 31-40.

Racial 'leapfrogging' occurs when some blacks settle farther from the urban core and inner city ghettos than some whites. Previously, this phenomenon has only been discussed as a theoretical possibility by Courant and Rose-Akerman. This article gives evidence of leapfrogging across a municipal boundary under circumstances somewhat similar to those of the Rose-Akerman model. However, the cause of the leapfrogging is less organized than that posited by Rose-Akerman. Blacks jumped over more affluent whites in the inner city to a nearby suburbs because they were discouraged by racial prejudice from locating in white neighborhoods in the central city and because the neighboring community has better schools and less crime.*

0274.   Rubin, Morton. 1959. The Negro Wish to Move: The Boston Case. **Journal of Social Issues** 15 (4): 4-13.

This research investigates the correlates of the wish to move among Negroes living in central city areas of Boston. The data were gathered to help understand some of the factors governing Negro mobility in Boston and its environs. This is part of a larger survey on the migration and adjustment of the Negro to Boston. In this report, demographic, ecological, and social relationships are examined with respect to the wish to move. The findings indicate that discrimination in most suburbs inhibit Negroes from moving into these areas.@

0275.   Saks, J. Harold, and Sol Rabkin. 1960. Racial and Religious Discrimination in Housing: A Report of Legal Progress. **Iowa Law Review** 45 (Spring): 488-524.

This examination of legislation and court actions concerned with housing discrimination reveals an almost complete turn-about in the role played by the law. It shows the law responding in the way Holmes and Cardozo have defined its responses—an equitable adjustment to the pressures of history, custom, past rulings, and morals. It has responded to the pressures of history which make racial discrimination in the U.S. a detrimental factor in our international relations. It has been cognizant of the heightened moral pressures that look upon such discrimination as a negation of American ideals. Equality of opportunity in housing remains an unqualified American ideal but in little than a decade the law has swung about from enforcing racial restrictive agreements to a point where such discriminatory housing practices are not only denied the assistance of the state, but are in a number of states, even banned by statute.@

0276.   Saltman, Juliet.   1979.   Housing Discrimination: Policy Research, Methods and Results. Annals of the American Academy of Political and Social Science 441 (January): 186-95.

Ten years ago some scholars believed that it was impossible to measure the magnitude of racial discrimination in housing directly. Drawing on the experience of local audits, HUD contracted the Fair Housing Contact Services to audit the extent of housing discrimination through successive visits of black and white homeseekers to real estate agents and apartment buildings. The audit showed widespread discrimination effected through various methods such as steering, price differentials, availability, and discourtesy. This paper reports on the study and discusses the possible approaches to strengthen enforcement of federal fair housing laws on national and local levels.

0277.   Saltman, Juliet, and Leslie G. Carr.   1980.   Action Research on Redlining: Methodological Weaknesses, Socio-Political Strength. Urban Affairs Papers 2 (4): 20-35.

A chronological review and methodological critique of action research on redlining in 15 communities is presented. Redlining studies have been conducted or sponsored by three types of researchers: 1) non-profit neighborhood organizations, 2) academic or governmental institutions, and 3) lending institutions. Their findings vary according to the methods employed, and these methods vary according to the sponsors. Despite the methodological difficulties and inadequacies of this type of research, the findings have been used by local neighborhood organizations as a strategy to achieve constructive change in neighborhood reinvestment and revitalization.*

0278.   Schafer, Robert.   1979.   Racial Discrimination in the Boston Housing Market. Journal of Urban Economics 6 (2): 176-96.

Recent studies suggest that price differentials between what whites and blacks pay for housing are largely a function of changes in supply and demand in the two submarkets. These studies, however, estimate models that assume a unified housing market. As a result, imputed prices of housing attributes cannot vary with location, and the analyses obscure important racial price differentials. Based on a more realistic and complex housing market theory, the model described in this paper indicates that housing prices are substantially higher in the ghetto and transition areas than in white areas, and that within the same area blacks must pay more than whites for equivalent housing.*

0279. Schafer, Robert, and Helen F. Ladd. 1981. Discrimination in Mortgage Lending. Cambridge, Massachusetts: The MIT Press. 407 pp.

It is illegal for financial institutions to discriminate against borrowers on the basis of race, sex, marital status, national origin, or age and location of buildings. Nevertheless, minority groups, women, and community leaders continue to complain, often without the ability to prove, that financial institutions violate the laws. This study analyzes mortgage lending data for the Savings Banks Association of New York and HUD in an attempt to identify the actual extent of alleged discriminatory practices, and find out who the real victims of these practice are. The findings suggest that in many cases examined the evidence supports allegation that lenders discriminate illegally. It also provides evidence in support of the allegation that lenders redline older residential areas or largely minority neighborhoods.

0280. Segala, John P. 1980. Redlining: An Economic Analysis. Federal Reserve Bank of Richmond Economic Review 66 (6): 3-13.

The role of redlining in the quality decline of neighborhoods in urban areas has been the subject of heated debate in recent years. This study tries to determine the economic reasons behind redlining behavior on the part of lenders, and evaluates the impact of antiredlining legislation on the mortgage market. The article contends that there are sound economic reasons behind the so-called redlining behavior; and that laws which assume that geographic location is not a valid risk factor and restricts its use are counterproductive. It suggests that: "A better way to increase the availability of urban mortgage credit would be to eliminate usury ceilings and rigid portfolio regulations that reduce the availability of funds to high risk borrowers. Also a reevaluation of FHA loan policies and procedures is in order. The present system encourages unsound lending and costly foreclosures." Relative to unjustified discrimination on the basis of race, the author calls for more vigorous enforcement of current antidiscrimination laws.

0281. Shear, William B., and Anthony M. Yezer. 1985. Discrimination in Urban Housing Finance: An Empirical Study Across Cities. Land Economics 61 (3): 292-302.

The Equal Credit Opportunity Act and the Community Reinvestment Act were enacted to regulate possible discriminatory practices in the supply of credit based on race, sex, and age of borrower and based on property location, respectively. This paper analyzes several approaches to test for the presence of or rationale for different treatment by age, sex, race, or location of the property. It finds all of them inadequate. The authors present an approach of their own based on a labor market model. The model is explained using across cities data.

0282. Silverman, Jane A. 1972. Chicago's "Gautreaux" Cases: Do They Portend a New Role for the Courts in Public Housing or a New Form of Public Housing? Journr ⊥ of Housing 29 (5): 236-40.

This article examines the implications of the Gautreaux suits against the Chicago's Public Housing Authority and HUD alleging discriminatory site selection and tenant assignment procedures. The topics discussed include:

the Gautreaux chronology, the positions of the interested parties, remedies provided by the court to date, the appropriateness of the court's actions and the effectiveness of its role.

0283. Smith, Barton A., and Peter Mieszkowski. 1980. **Study of Racial Discrimination in Housing.** Washington, D.C.: HUD, Office of Policy Development and Research. 144 pp.

This study attempts to clarify some basic facts concerning housing and minorities for a better understanding of the differences in minority-nonminority patterns of housing consumptions. More specifically, it examines the basic issues surrounding discrimination in housing markets, including the question of house price differentials between blacks and whites, the apparent underconsumption of housing by blacks, and the relationship between tenure choice (owner/renter) and race. The analysis is based on data collected in Houston, Texas, Chicago, Illinois, and the national data obtained from the National Longitudinal Survey. The findings provide strong evidence in support of the notion that blacks actually pay less for housing in both the Houston and Chicago housing markets. However, when the researchers control for the neighborhood characteristics, the study reveals that blacks are more likely to underconsume housing, but the magnitude of this effect is sensitive to income specifications used in the analysis.

0284. Smith, Ralph Lee. 1959. Racial Discrimination in Metropolitan Housing. **New Leader** 42 (7): 9-11.

Seven years after the Supreme Court had ruled restrictive covenants unenforceable, the following clause appeared in a property deed signed in Washington, D.C. in 1955: "'No part of the land hereby conveyed shall ever be used, or occupied by, or sold, demised, transferred, convey unto, or in trust for, leased, or rented, or given to Negroes or any person or persons of Negro blood or extraction, or to any person of the Semitic race, blood or origin; which racial description shall be deemed to include Armenians, Jews, Hebrews, Persians and Syrians, except that this paragraph shall not be held to exclude partial occupancy of the premises by domestic servants of the occupants thereof.'" The author argues that the persistence in the language of this deed and the fact that it was given official recognition is at the heart of housing discrimination in the U.S., and it constitutes barrier that hinders progress toward equal housing opportunities in America.

0285. Stewart, John I. 1974. Racial Discrimination in Public Housing: Rights and Remedies. **University of Chicago Law Review** 41 (3): 582-603.

Open discrimination in site selection and tenant assignment has largely been abandoned, and the overt practices that remain are substantially more difficult to prove. Although proof of covert discrimination must be indirect, with a necessarily tenuous link of culpability in a moral sense, a finding of such discrimination is appropriate where statistical evidence plus evidence as to the current and historical operation of explicit policies strongly indicates the systematic use of the criterion of race.@

0286. Straszheim, Nahlon R. 1974. Housing Market Discrimination and Black

Housing Consumption. **Quarterly Journal of Economics** 88 (1): 19-43.

In its introductory section the author examines competing hypotheses that seek to explain black segregation, and black's occupancy of older and lower quality housing; in Part II, a model of black housing consumption is presented; Part III deals with improving black housing conditions; and the final section contains the author's concluding remarks. As a whole, the author presents a strong argument in favor of open housing.

0287. Taggart, Harriett Tee, and Kevin W. Smith. 1981. Redlining: An Assessment of the Evidence of Disinvestment in Metropolitan Boston. **Urban Affairs Quarterly** 17 (1): 91-107.

This study analyzes the residential mortgage activity of financial institutions in metropolitan Boston, and assesses patterns of disinvestment in the area. The analysis is based on data obtained from the state-charted institutions and banks. Interviews are conducted to obtain additional data on home sales, housing characteristics, and home ownership. Three measures of disinvestments are employed. The findings indicate that: (1) the mortgage dollars invested relative to the savings dollars deposited by residents were disproportionately low in most urban areas; (2) the proportion of bank-financed home sales was substantially higher in suburban than in urban areas; and (3) bank home mortgage lending is disproportionately lower in minority and racially changing neighborhoods. These analytical techniques and results are compared with those of major redlining studies in other metropolitan areas.@

0288. Taggart, Tee. 1974. Red-Lining: How the Bankers Starve the Cities to Feed the Suburbs. **Planning** 40 (11): 14-16.

Private lending institutions providing home mortgages have apparently withdrawn their support from many urban areas in the past decade. The National People's Action on Housing was organized in 1972 on the premise that private institutions are not only writing off the inner city areas, but that they continue to encourage suburban growth through their lending practices. This practice known as red-lining, means delineating an area as being too risky to deal with. Some examples of red-lining and efforts to combat it are presented.

0289. Van Alstyne, William W. 1960. Discrimination in State University Housing Programs: Policy and Constitutional Consideration. **Stanford Law Review** 13 (December): 60-79.

In nearly all major university towns a number of students have to live off campus. The universities' off-campus housing office provide a list of registered landlords who have promised not to discriminate against any student. However, some students are often faced with discriminatory practices by the registered landlords. This article discusses the issues of policy and law relative to the existence of racial discrimination in registered, off-campus housing.

0290. Vitarello, James. 1975. The Redlining Route to Urban Decay. **Focus** 3 (10): 4-5.

What seems to distinguish areas that are victims of redlining is that minorities have started to move in or there is the potential that they will. Since the early 1970s, several community organizations have tried to combat redlining by filing complaints of home finance discrimination and have tried to document redlining. Other communities have led "greenlining" campaigns, which involves collecting pledges from individuals and institutions to deposit their savings only in those institutions that agree to plow money back into their neighborhoods. Political pressure on local and state government has proved to be successful. For example, in Chicago, all banks and savings and loan associations bidding for deposits of city funds must sign anti-redlining pledges and disclose all consumer, commercial, and residential loans by zip code.

0291.   Vose, Clement E. 1959. Caucasians Only: The Supreme Court, the NAACP, and the Restrictive Covenant Cases. Berkeley: University of California Press. 296 pp.

This book's focus is on an examination of both state and federal court cases in which the legality of restrictive covenants are tested. More specifically, it analyzes four cases in 1948 in which the Supreme Court ruled that covenants restricting sale and occupancy of property to non-Caucasians were not enforceable; it also deals with the 1953 decision holding that money damages could not be collected from a seller who violated restrictive covenant. Furthermore, the political events leading to these decisions and the practical implications of the Supreme Court's decisions are described.

0292.   Weaver, Robert C. 1955. The Effect of Anti-Discrimination Legislation Upon the FHA- and VA-Insured Housing Market in New York State. Land Economics 31 (4): 303-13.

New York State has passed the Metcalf-Baker Law prohibiting racial discrimination in FHA- and VA-insured loans for the construction of multiple dwelling units, or buildings that involve 10 or more units. Similar bills have either passed or are in the process of passing in some other states. Asserting that the extension of the this non-discriminatory legislation, which is significant on both regional and national levels, has aroused serious forebodings on the part of builders and real estate industry, this article inquires into the dimensions and nature of the problem which the Metcalf-Baker Law has created in New York State.

0293.   Weinberg, Daniel H. 1978. Further Evidence on Racial Discrimination in Home Purchase. Land Economics 54 (4): 505-13.

This article provides empirical evidence on the determinants of home purchase. The author supplies evidence in support of conclusions reached by previous studies. In addition, it comes up with some new findings: (1) female householders appear about 14 percentage points less likely to purchase given a move than otherwise male householder, but only 7 percentage when already owning; (2) in the San Francisco Bay Area during 1957-1964 period, representative renters among black male householders were found to be about 28 percentage points less likely to purchase given a move, Spanish male householders 22 percentage points, and Oriental male householders appeared at least 11 percentage points less likely to purchase than their white counterparts. It is pointed out that these results are not direct

evidence of the presence of discrimination, but alternative explanations
fail to account for the large differences.

0294. Werner, Frances, William M. Frej, and David M. Madway. 1976. Redlining
and Disinvestment: Causes, Consequences, and Proposed Remedies.
Clearinghouse Review 10 (7): 501-42.

As its title indicates, "this paper describes redlining and its consequences
and suggests a variety of remedial actions, all of which could be immediately
implemented by the executive branch without further congressional action.
The phenomenon and consequences of redlining are discussed in some detail in
order to provide the federal agencies with a conceptual framework within
which to fashion the most effective remedies."

••

3
MINORITY STATUS AND
RESIDENTIAL SEGREGATION

0295. Aleinkoff, A. 1976. Racial Steering: The Real Estate Broker and Title
VIII. Yale Law Journal 85 (6): 808-25.

Citing a report by the National Advisory Commission on Civil Disorders,
this article asserts that residential segregation, as documented by the
Commission eight years ago, continues to be nearly universal in the U.S. It
contends that the segregated housing patterns currently observed cannot be
entirely explained by the economic disparities between blacks and whites, or
by individual choices. Rather, to a significant degree such housing
patterns are the result of racial steering practices by the real estate
brokers. This article examines racial steering practices, and concludes
"that virtually all are unlawful under Title VIII [of the Civil Rights Act of
1968]. It argues that Title VIII's most far reaching prohibition against
steering is its 'colorblind' standard, which forbids real estate brokers
from steering customers on the basis of race."

0296. Bahr, Howard M., and Jack P. Gibbs. 1967. Racial Differentiation in
American Metropolitan Areas. Social Forces 45 (4): 521-32.

A theory on the relations among four forms of racial differentiation is
formulated and tested, using data from the 1960 United States Census from a
random sample of 33 Standard Metropolitan Statistical Areas. The findings
generally support the theory with respect to interrelations among
educational, occupational and income differentiation. The relation of
residential differentiation to the other three forms of Negro-white
differentiation is not close, which indicates that residential
differentiation may not be as "basic" to other forms of racial
differentiation as commonly believed.*

0297. Blalock, Hubert M., Jr. 1982. Segregation and Intergroup Interactions.
In: Race and Ethnic Relations, by Hubert M. Blalock, Jr. Englewood Cliffs,
N.J.: Prentice-Hall. Chapter 6, pp. 86-100.

As defined by Blalock, segregation refers to spatial separation, whereas
integration refers to interaction patterns between racial/ethnic groups.
This article analyzes segregation and integration patterns and their

relationships as they relate to American minorities. Topics discussed are: residential segregation in American cities, voluntary segregation, what dominant groups gain from segregation, and the regulation of integration or intergroup contacts. It concludes: "Either the minority is on its way to becoming 'integrated' into the larger social system, or the level of conflict between the two groups is likely to increase."

0298.   Blumberg, Leonard. 1964. Segregated Housing, Marginal Location, and the Crisis of Confidence. Phylon 25 (4): 321-30.

The author offers three propositions and case materials to illustrate residential patterns and discrimination in the United States: (1) the process of racial discrimination is linked to a political process; (2) blacks who have been negatively valued people in the society and political process, tend to live on the marginal residential location; and (3) the current racial relationships point to a crisis of confidence on the part of blacks in the American political process.

0299.   Boal, F. W. 1978. Ethnic Residential Segregation. In: Social Areas in Cities: Processes, Patterns, and Problems. T. D. Herbert, and R. J. Johnson (eds.). Chichester . New York . Brisbane . Toronto: John Wiley & Sons. Pp. 57-95, Chapter 2.

Ethnic residential segregation is a very common characteristic of cities. Many authors take such segregation to be an indicator of the relationship between a particular ethnic group and some other segment of the urban population. This chapter explores the relationships between three elements: ethnic groups, degree of assimilation, and degree and spatial form of residential segregation. It also attempts to examine the factors underlying those situations where ethnic residential segregation is marked.@

0300.   Bohland, James R. 1982. Indian Residential Segregation in the Urban Southwest: 1970 and 1980. Social Science Quarterly 63 (4): 749-761.

The study analyzes Indian segregation in 11 cities in the Southwest in 1970 and 1980. Indian segregation was less than the segregation of either blacks or Spanish Americans, but comparable to the levels reported for other ethnic minorities in the United States. Indian segregation declined between 1970 and 1980, but the decline was least in cities experiencing the greatest growth in Indian population.*

0301.   Branfman, Eric J., Benjamin I. Cohen, and David M. Turbeck. 1973. Measuring the Invisible Wall: Land Use Control and the Residential Patterns of the Poor. Yale Law Journal 82 (3): 483-508.

Low-income families are not randomly distributed throughout American metropolitan areas. Some areas, usually the inner cities, have greater than average concentration of poor people than the suburbs. This may be called income group clustering. Public controls of land use and zoning laws do affect the degree of income group clustering, and these controls may be, at least partly, racially motivated. This article reports and explains the results of a recent study of income clustering in a survey of American

metropolitan areas. Results indicate that income clustering is aggravated
by the imposition of public land use controls, such as zoning in the suburbs.

0302. Cortese, Charles F., R. Frank Falk, and Jack K. Cohen. 1976. Further
Consideration on the Methodological Analysis of Segregation Indices.
American Sociological Review 41 (4): 630-37.

The process of developing an adequate measure of segregation occupied the
literature for over a decade and culminated in the widespread use of the
index of Dissimilarity. The inadequacies of this index...remain with us
and largely have come to be ignored. This research further explores the
difficulties pertaining to limitations in the use and interpretation of the
index of Dissimilarity, demonstrates some of the systematic biases
resulting from these inadequacies and provides a mathematical refinement
which overcomes some of the major problems inherent in the use of this
index.*

0303. Cowgill, Donald O. 1956. Trends in Residential Segregation of Nonwhites
in American Cities, 1940-1950. American Sociological Review 21 (1): 43-47.

This article analyzes trends in residential segregation of nonwhites from
1940 to 1950, and attempts to show that combined indexes for the whole
metropolitan area are more meaningful than indexes for separate
municipalities. It calculates residential segregation indexes for 209
cities in 1950, and comparable scores for 185 of these cities for 1940.
"Comparison of these scores for the two years indicate conclusively that
residential segregation increased during the decade. The composite score
for all 185 cities went up 0.033, and 129 cities increased, while only 52
decreased and 4 remained the same."

0304. Cowgill, Donald O. 1962. Segregation Scores for Metropolitan Areas.
American Sociological Review 27 (3): 400-402.

Combined indexes of segregation for whole metropolitan areas are more
meaningful than the separate indexes for each municipality. This article
presents combined segregation scores for 21 metropolitan areas. Results
show that while combined scores are not greatly different from the separate
indexes of the central cities, they manifest a strong tendency to be higher.
This may be interpreted to mean that the "inclusion of suburbs in the
combined scores gives a fuller and truer measure of the actual degree of
segregation in these metropolitan areas."

0305. Cowgill, Donald O., and Mary S. Cowgill. 1951. An Index of Segregation
Based on Block Statistics. American Sociological Review 16 (6): 825-31.

Arguing that measures of segregation using census tract statistics are not
accurate, this paper presents a segregation index based on block statistics.
Using this index, the author calculates the segregation scores for 187
cities, and concludes that cities with highest scores tend to be resort
cities in Florida, new industrial cities of the South, and borderline cities
between North and South, and industrial cities of the Great Lake area. Low
segregation scores are shown by small cities of New England, cities of the
Mountain and Pacific regions, and some residential suburbs; and that large
cities reflect more segregation than small cities; results also show that

"segregation of nonwhites increases with the proportion of nonwhite dwellings up to about 5 percent, but decreases beyond that point."

0306.   Daniels, Charles B.   1975.   The Influence of Racial Segregation on Housing Prices.   Journal of Urban Economics 2 (2): 105-12.

Census tract data were used to investigate the influence of racial segregation on housing prices in the Oakland, California housing market. White renters were found to pay premium to live in segregated neighborhoods. Racial differences in the implicit prices of specific housing characteristics were also observed in the rental market: a unit of housing space was more expensive in the black rental submarket, while a unit of housing quality cost more in the white rental submarket. No significant differences were found in the prices paid by black and white homeowners, although for methodological reasons these results were less reliable than those for rental housing.*

0307.   Danielson, Michael N.   1976.   The Politics of Exclusionary Zoning in Suburbia.   Political Science Quarterly 91 (1): 1-18.

The poor and minority families who could benefit from relaxed suburban barriers are effectively kept out by high cost of housing and exclusionary zoning policies.   The poor who are the victim of exclusionary practices do not have sufficient political strength to secure influence on local councils and planning boards.   This failure has resulted mainly from the desire of suburbanites to maintain the existing local housing and land use policies.

0308.   Darden, Joe T.   1976.   The Residential Segregation of Blacks in Detroit, 1960-1970.   International Journal of Comparative Sociology 17 (1 & 2): 84-91.

This study attempts to determine the amount of racial residential segregation in Detroit in 1960, to assess the magnitude of changes that occurred from 1960 to 1970, and to find out how much of the segregation could be explained by housing cost inequality between blacks and whites.   Results show that a "high level of black residential segregation existed in Detroit's central city, suburbs, and SMSA in 1960."   Findings also indicate that from 1960 to 1970 level of black residential segregation declined in the central city and the SMSA, but increased in the suburbs, and that while housing cost inequality "explained much more of the black residential segregation in 1970 than in 1960, the bulk of the black residential segregation remained unexplained.   The implication of this study is that low cost housing (although a social necessity throughout the Detroit SMSA) is not the answer to reducing the bulk of the black residential segregation that exists.   Such an answer logically lies in reducing racial discrimination in housing."

0309.   Darden, Joe T.   1976.   Residential Segregation of Blacks in the Suburbs: The Michigan Example.   Geographical Survey 5 (3): 7-16.

Few studies have dealt with the problem of black residential segregation in the suburbs.   The few such studies did not use a measure of black residential segregation which may be applied uniformly to various suburban areas at different time periods.   This article attempts to use such a measure in examining black residential segregation outside central cities of 10 Standard Metropolitan Statistical Areas (SMSAs) of Michigan.

0310.   Darden, Joe T.   1977.   Blacks in the Suburbs: Their Number is Rising, but Patterns of Segregation Persist.   What Are the Causes?   Vital Issues 27 (4): 1-4.

Utilizing data from the 1960 and 1970 censuses, this study shows that during 1960-1970 period, black migration to the suburbs increased in every region of the country except the South.   However, the proportion of the suburban population that was black remained small.   Despite such small population size, blacks were very unevenly distributed, resulting in high levels of residential segregation--a pattern not different from that in central cities.   The author, thus, concludes that ghettoization of blacks in the suburbs is occurring.   That is, the same mechanism that has caused segregation in central cities is expanding to suburbs.   According to Darden, racial steering and the exclusion of black real estate brokers from membership in a predominantly white association are two of the techniques used   to   perpetuate   racial   segregation   in   the   suburbs.   Racial discrimination and steering can be prevented only if laws are enforced.

0311.   Darden, Joe T.   1982.   Black Residential Segregation: Impact of State Licensing Laws.   Journal of Black Studies 12 (4): 415-26.

This study demonstrates that black residential segregation was uniformly high in all states in 1970, and that changes in the state real estate licensing laws have had no impact on lowering such segregation.   Thus, the question is: "Do real estate licensing laws containing explicit fair housing or antidiscrimination provisions have an impact on the lower of black residential segregation?"   Based on the findings of this study the answer is in the negative.   The author discusses the implications of his findings, and concludes that the problem seems to be not the licensing laws themselves, but the lack of enforcement by the real estate license commissioner.   That is, without adequate enforcement of the laws it is likely that racial discrimination will continue.

0312.   Darden, Joe T.   1983.   The Residential Segregation of Hispanics in Cities and Suburbs of Michigan.   The East Lakes Geographer 18: 25-37.

This paper attempts to determine the extent of Hispanic residential segregation in central cities and selected suburbs of Michigan and assesses the extent to which the spatial distribution of Hispanics between census tracts is related to the spatial variation in the cost of housing.   The findings are: (1) residential segregation between Hispanics and whites in Michigan's 12 central cities averaged 35.4 percent in 1980--a level lower than that recorded for 1970;   (2) Hispanics are generally more segregated from blacks than from whites in central cities and suburbs, a pattern consistent with what was recorded in 1970;   (3) segregation between Hispanics and whites in the suburbs is generally less than the levels observed in the central cities;   and (4)   the spatial distribution pattern of Hispanics in owner-occupied housing   is more related to the cost of housing than to the spatial distribution pattern of Hispanics in renter-occupied units, and the segregated distribution pattern of Hispanics in central cities has a strong relationship to the cost of housing.@

0313. Darden, Joe T. 1984. The Residential Segregation of American Indians in Metropolitan Areas of Michigan. **Journal of Urban Affairs** 6 (1): 29-38.

American Indians or Native American residential segregation is viewed within the general framework of ecological theory. According to theorists of human ecology, variations in segregation between groups relates directly to measurable differences on social and economic variables. This study uses 1980 census data and the index of dissimilarity to measure the extent of residential segregation in Michigan's 12 Standard Metropolitan Statistical Areas. Correlation coefficients were computed to assess whether a strong relationship exists between the residential segregation of American Indians and the spatial distribution of housing value and rent. The findings revealed that Indian-white residential segregation is lower than black-white segregation and that American Indians are more segregated from blacks than from whites. The segregated distribution pattern of American Indians is not strongly related to the cost of housing.*

0314. Darden, Joe T. 1986. Accessibility to Housing: Differential Residential Segregation for Blacks, Hispanics, American Indians, and Asians. In: **Race, Ethnicity, and Minority Housing in the United States.** Jamshid A. Momeni (ed.). Westport, Connecticut: Greenwood Press. Chapter VII.

This chapter has revealed that blacks, Hispanics, American Indians and Asian-Americans have differential accessibility to non-segregated housing. Asians have the greatest accessibility and blacks have the least. The differential degree of accessibility is manifest in the differential levels of residential segregation. Asians are the least segregated racial/ethnic minority group and blacks are the most segregated. Asians are also the most suburbanized minority group and blacks are the least. The analyses are based on census data from 12 metropolitan areas of Michigan.@

0315. Darden, Joe T., and J. B. Haney. 1978. Measuring Adaptation: Migration Status and Residential Segregation Among Anglos, Blacks, and Chicanos. **The East Lake Geographer** 13 (June): 20-33.

This study attempts to demonstrate that migration status does influence the level of segregation between racial and ethnic groups, and thus, must be considered in any research on residential segregation. The study is based on data from cities of Lansing and Flint, Michigan. Groups examined are Anglos, Blacks, and Chicanos. This study concludes that "two different patterns of adaptation to multi-ethnic urban settings have been developed among the three racial and ethnic groups compared. For Chicanos, length of time in the city appears to decrease their segregation from the Anglo majority. However, Blacks find that increasing time in the urban environment does not reduce their level of residential segregation."

0316. Duncan, Otis Dudley, and Beverly Duncan. 1955. Residential Distribution and Occupational Stratification. **American Journal of Sociology** 60 (50): 493-503.

Ecological analysis is a promising approach to the study of urban social stratification, for differences in the residential distributions of occupation groups are found to parallel the differences among them in socioeconomic status and recruitment. The occupation groups at the extremes of the socioeconomic scale are the most segregated. Residential concentration in low-rent areas and residential centralization are inversely related to socioeconomic status. Inconsistencies in the ranking of occupation groups according to residential patterns occur at points where there is evidence of status disequilibrium.*

0317.   Duncan, Otis Dudley, and Beverly Duncan. 1955. A Methodological Analysis of Segregation Indexes. **American Sociological Review** 20 (2): 210-17.

Several indexes measuring racial residential segregation have been developed. In this paper, the authors attempt to show that all of these indexes can be regarded as functions of a single geometric construct, the "segregation curve." This article presents a summary of the mathematical analysis made of segregation indexes, and concludes that the proponents of a segregation index formula have to face the difficult problem of validation. "The concept of 'segregation' in the literature of human ecology is complex and somewhat fuzzy, i.e., that concept involves a number of analytically distinguished elements, none of which is yet capable of completely operational description."

0318.   Duncan, Otis Dudley, and Stanley Lieberson. 1959. Ethnic Segregation and Assimilation. **American Journal of Sociology** 64 (4): 364-74.

An ecological conceptualization of the processes of immigrant adjustment permits a demonstration of close correlation of residential segregation and centralization with selected indicators of assimilation, socio-economic status, and social distance ranking of ethnic groups. Changes in residential patterns in Chicago between 1930 and 1950 were in the direction expected on the basis of a positive relationship between assimilation and length of residence; but such changes did not disrupt a pattern of differential segregation and spatial separation of ethnic colonies, this pattern exhibiting remarkable stability over the twenty-year period.*

0319.   Edwards, Ozzie. 1970. Patterns of Residential Segregation Within a Metropolitan Ghetto. **Demography** 7 (2): 185-93.

The residential segregation of families by income and by stage of the family life cycle within Milwaukee's black community resembles in both pattern and degree that in the white community. The greater the difference in income, the more dissimilar are the distributions by census tract. Dissimilarity is greater between younger couples without children and older couples with children than between any other pair of family types defined by husband's age and presence of children. However, segregation by income was substantially greater than by family type in 1960. The bases of selectivity of blacks in "changing" areas of the city, where the proportion black is still relatively low, and of whites in the "suburban" areas adjoining the city are similar. Families in the higher income groups and couples with children are over-represented in these areas. It would appear that given the pressure of limited housing space in the inner core of the black community, given the fact that certain amenities are not available in that area, and given the economic and social barriers which restrict the movement of blacks into the suburbs, the changing areas must function as "suburbs" for the black community.*

320. Farley, John E. 1982. Black Male Unemployment in U.S. Metropolitan Areas:
      The Role of Black Central City Segregation and Job Decentralization.
      Journal of Urban Affairs 4 (3): 19-34.

      Housing segregation has been suggested as an important cause of high
      unemployment among black Americans, because segregation restricts the black
      population to living in those central city areas which are losing jobs.
      Previous studies have not offered a conclusive test of this hypothesis, as
      they present conflicting findings and have a number of methodological
      difficulties. Using regression analyses on data from U.S. SMSAs, it is
      shown that the differential in unemployment rates between blacks and whites
      in U.S. SMSAs (and particularly SMSAs outside the South) is substantially
      influenced both by segregation patterns restricting blacks to the central
      city and by job decentralization. This black/white unemployment
      differential and the overall unemployment rate in an area determine the
      level of black unemployment in the area. Thus, central city segregation and
      job decentralization have important indirect effects on the black
      unemployment rates of U.S. metropolitan areas.*

321. Farley, John E. 1983. Metropolitan Housing Segregation in 1980: The St.
      Louis Case. **Urban Affairs Quarterly** 18 (3): 347-59.

      Metropolitan patterns of black/white housing segregation are analyzed
      through the 1980 census data for the St. Louis Metropolitan area. Using the
      index of dissimilarity as an indicator of segregation, it was found that
      there was no change in central city segregation, and only a modest decline in
      suburban segregation. Analysis of segregation within incorporated places
      revealed that most of the area's population lived in racially homogeneous or
      internally segregated communities, and that virtually all racially mixed
      suburbs away from the major sector of black population were highly
      segregated. It was found that most of the suburbs that did have low
      segregation indices were experiencing rapid black population growth, and
      thus may have been experiencing racial turnover. It is concluded that
      patterns of segregation which have historically existed in the central city
      are now being repeated in the suburbs.*

322. Farley, John E. 1984. P* Segregation Indices: What Can They Tell Us about
      Housing Segregation in 1980? **Urban Studies** 21: 331-36.

      An alternative measure of segregation, the P* index, is explained. This
      measure is computed separately for each racial/ethnic group and, in a diadic
      situation, indicates each group's potential for neighborhood contact with
      the other. The usefulness of this index, as well as the different
      information it provides from that provided by other indices, is discussed.
      P* indices are computed for blacks and whites for the St. Louis metropolitan
      area in 1970 and 1980. The results indicate that neither group experienced
      a sizable increase in residential contact with the other between 1970 and
      1980. The significance of this finding in a context of increasing black
      suburbanization is discussed.*

323. Farley, John E. 1984. Housing Segregation in the School Age Population
      and the Link Between Housing and School Segregation: A St. Louis Case Study.
      Journal of Urban Affairs 6 (4): 65-80.

The age distributions of the black and white populations vary, as do the ways
in which blacks and whites of differing ages are distributed geographically
in metropolitan areas. The nature of these differences is such that, in
racially mixed neighborhoods, black families with children are often mixed
with childless or elderly white adults. For this reason, it is hypothesized
that the school-age (5 to 17 years of age) population is more residentially
segregated by race than is the total population. To test this hypothesis,
segregation indices based on census tract data were compared for the St.
Louis SMSA for 1980, for the total population and the school-age population.
This analysis confirmed that the school-age population was somewhat more
segregated than the total population. The implications of this finding for
the problem of school segregation are discussed, as is the interrelationship
between housing segregation and school segregation.*

0324.   Farley, Reynolds. 1970. The Changing Distribution of Negroes within
Metropolitan Areas: The Emergence of Black Suburbs. **American Journal of
Sociology** 75 (January): 512-29.

Several studies have indicated that central cities and their suburban rings
are coming to have similar racial composition. A closer examination of the
data reveals that suburban rings do not have an exclusively white
population. City-suburban differences in the proportion of black
population are increasing, and patterns of residential segregation by race
within suburbs are emerging which are similar to those found within central
cities.@

0325.   Farley, Reynolds. 1980. Racial Residential Segregation: Is It Caused by
Misinformation about Housing Costs? **Social Science Quarterly** 61 (3 & 4):
623-37.

A number of studies have shown that economic differences between blacks and
whites do not account for high levels of racial residential segregation in
the United States. This study tests the hypothesis that segregation results
from misperceptions about the cost of housing. This study concludes that
this view (hypothesis) cannot be supported. That is both blacks and whites
were equally knowledgeable about housing prices in white neighborhoods and
blacks do not underestimate their own financial abilities. Given that
residential integration is not currently given a high national priority, the
author forecasts that segregation patterns are likely to continue.

0326.   Farley, Reynolds, Howard Schuman, and Suzanne Bianchi. 1971. Black and
White Preferences about Residential Segregation. **Economic Outlook USA** 6
(4): 83-87.

The Kerner Commission warned that this country was moving toward two
societies--one white and one black. Studies on racial segregation in the
metropolitan areas do confirm this assertion. Authors present data showing
the increased level of segregation in Detroit. This article attempts to
investigate the nature and causes of residential segregation in Detroit.
Topics discussed are: some explanations of residential segregation
including the residential preferences of blacks and whites, economic
factors and knowledge of the housing market, integration preferences of
blacks, tipping points and neighborhood transition, and the prospects for

residential integration. It is concluded that until we know more about the sources of these [neighborhood] preferences for whites and blacks, it is difficult to specify what kinds of changes are likely to occur in the distribution of neighborhood preferences."

0327.   Farley, Reynolds, and Karl E. Taeuber. 1968. Population Trends and Residential Segregation Since 1960. **Science** 159 (3818): 953-55.

This article examines special census data for 13 cities and assesses trends in population, migration, and residential segregation from 1960 to mid-decade. Results reveal increasing concentrations of highly segregated blacks in the central cities, while whites tended to concentrate in the suburbs.

0328.   Fly, Jerry W., and George R. Reinhart. 1980. Racial Separation During the 1970s: The Case of Birmingham. **Social Forces** 58(4): 1255-62.

The decade of the 1970s has been one of the considerable racial change in city neighborhoods. Advances were made in reducing social segregation between races, but the residential segregation between blacks and whites has increased. In this study of racial residential segregation in Birmingham, Alabama, more all-white and all-black neighborhoods were discovered in 1977 than in 1970. Birmingham's total population decreased where the prospect of having black neighbors was low and the number of housing units was increasing, primarily due to new construction. The black population tended to increase in neighborhoods that decreased in number of housing units, and many of those neighborhoods were predominantly white not long ago. The most significant result was that blacks and whites were more residentially segregated in 1977 than in 1970.*

0329.   Friedrichs, Robert W. 1959. Christian and Residential Exclusion: An Empirical Study of a Northern Dilemma. **Journal of Social Issues** 15 (4): 14-23.

The main thesis of Gunnar Myrdal's book, **An American Dilemma** (1944) was that a sizable gap exists between the "American Creed" and the prevailing attitude toward blacks. This paper attempts to test this hypothesis and entertains the degree to which Myrdal's thesis is correct. The study is based on interviews with 112 residents in twenty representative neighborhoods of a residential suburb within the New York metropolitan area. It is concluded that the central theme of Myrdal's hypothesis "may be more applicable to the North than to the South."

0330.   Gabriel, Stuart A. 1984. Spillover Effects of Human Service Facilities in a Racially Segmented Housing Market. **Journal of Urban Economics** 16 (3): 339-50.

Previous studies of human service facility spillovers on residential property values have been inconclusive, and have failed to take into account the effects of racial segmentation of housing markets. Likewise, studies of racial discrimination in urban housing markets and price differentials between white and nonwhite areas of the city have failed to consider the impacts of service facilities on prices. This study develops an hedonic price model of housing services in a racially segmented housing market, which considers a variety of human service facilities significantly affect housing prices both positively and negatively, and that these effects vary by racial submarkets. Implications of these findings for the interpretation of past discrimination studies, facility impact studies, and social policy are considered.*

0331.   Goering, John M. 1986. Minority Housing Needs and Civil Rights Enforcements. In: Race, Ethnicity, and Minority Housing in the United States. Jamshid A. Momeni (ed.). Westport, Connecticut: Greenwood Press. Chapter XI.

Minority households continue to experience substantial levels of housing deprivation, segregation, and discrimination. Their housing conditions, although gradually improving in physical condition and the extent of crowding, are increasingly affected by the higher cost of renting or purchasing a home. Minorities in search of decent housing will have to pay more, as well as risk experiencing either subtle or direct forms of discrimination, in order to find a home comparable to that of whites. All too often the act of discrimination will remain unfelt and undetected. Different or fewer apartments and homes are shown to minorities but not to whites. There is a growing divergence in strategies for addressing minority social and civil rights issues. Some voices within the minority community, aware of the diminished popular support for civil rights issues, now argue for increased emphasis on internal or class-based strategies for reform. At the same time, traditional civil rights organizations continue to press for more federal housing subsidies for minorities as well as strong fair housing laws. To federalize or not the solution to minority housing problems is not an ideological contest to be won by any side. External events, outside the control of the leadership of the minority communities, appear likely to overwhelm most federal domestic policy options. Civil rights and the housing conditions of blacks and Hispanics are concerns which only influence the margins of current Congressional and Executive Branch planning. Only a substantial increase in organized support and lobbying for a broad-range of civil rights protections is likely to achieve any credibility and impact. Such an agenda will, in the short run, probably only hold its own against forces aimed at reducing civil rights guarantees. It seems wiser, however, to pursue a more offensive rather than a defensive policy in order to secure as much leverage and credibility for future battles.@

0332.   Goodman, John L. 1983. Explaining Racial Differences: A Study of City-to-Suburb Residential Mobility. Urban Affairs Quarterly 18 (3): 301-25.

City-to suburb residential mobility increased markedly during the 1970s; but, the rate of outmovement by whites was higher than the rate for blacks. This article examines empirically three explanations for this continuing racial difference in suburbanization: (1) socio-economic differences between the white and black central city populations, (2) racially motivated outmovement by whites (white flight), and (3) abnormally low outmovement by blacks (black retention). The study is based on Annual Housing survey data from 35 large SMSAs. It is concluded that "black retention, attributable to actual or anticipated racial discrimination against blacks, is responsible for most of the white-black gap in rates of city-to-suburb movement. The other two explanations play only secondary roles."

0333. Grier, Eunice and George. 1966. Equality and Beyond: Housing Segregation in the Great Society. In: **The Negro American.** Talcott Parsons, and Kenneth B. Clark (eds.). Boston, Mass.: Houghton Mifflin Company. Pp. 524-54.

This article examines the links between riots, racial protest and rising waves of crimes to segregated and poor housing conditions of blacks. The authors call for a quick and decisive action to remedy the problem. "If not dealt with decisively and soon, [the problem] can wreak wholesale destruction upon the objectives of the 'Great society.' The point at issue is the increasing dominance of Negro ghettos, with all their human problems, at the heart of the nation's metropolitan areas. While racial segregation is by no means new to this country, in recent years it has assumed new dimensions." Among topics discussed are the growth of residential segregation, causes and consequences of segregation, the costs of segregation, and the upsurge of civic concerns.

0334. Grodzins, Morton. 1957. Metropolitan Segregation. **Scientific American** 197 (4): 33-41.

As Negroes move in from the South and whites move out to the suburbs a new pattern of segregation emerges in the big cities of the U.S., bringing with it significant economic, social and political problems.*

0335. Hennelly, J. 1972. Urban Housing Needs: Some Thoughts on Dispersal. St. Louis University Law Journal 17 (2): 169-220.

To solve the problem of racial segregation and poverty, some researchers have suggested that ghettos must first be dismantled and low-income housing units be scattered throughout metropolitan areas. The logic given for this proposal is that dispersal will help break the cycle of poverty by bringing them closer to equal employment and educational opportunities, that it will achieve racial integration, and that it will improve the quality of low-income housing. This article argues that dispersing the poor throughout the suburbs will not achieve what its advocates suggest. Actually, dispersal of low-income housing will impede the progress of racial integration. The author suggests that the alternative method, which may achieve what dispersal of low-income groups fails to accomplish, is to disperse working and low-middle-class families. This can be done by an enabling federal legislation, a proposed model of which is presented in this article.   Hennelly asserts that the implementation of his proposal will solve the dual problem of racism and poverty.

0336. Hirsch, Arnold R. 1983. **Making the Second Ghetto: Race and Housing in Chicago, 1940-1960.** Cambridge, England: Cambridge University Press. 362 pp.

Focusing on Chicago, this book attempts to show how private and governmental (federal and local governments) decision making processes, purportedly aimed at improving the public good, has actually acted to maintain a racially segregated society in Chicago.

0337. Hwang, Sean-Shong, and Steve H. Murdock. 1982. Residential Segregation in Texas in 1980. Social Science Quarterly 63 (4): 737-48.

Levels of racial and ethnic segregation for major Texas cities in 1980 are compared to those for 1970. Significant declines in segregation from 1970 to 1980 occurred for all groups, but declines were small between Anglo and Spanish groups. Segregation is unaffected by variation in size of city, percent of population that is Spanish or black, or central city status.*

0338. Hwang, Sean-Shong, Steven H. Murdock, and Rita R. Hamm. 1985. The Effects of Race and Socioeconomic Status on Residential Segregation in Texas, 1970-1980. Social Forces 63 (3): 732-46.

This study uses longitudinal data from 27 central cities in Texas to examine the effects of 1970, 1980, and 1970-80 changes in socioeconomic status on Black-White, Anglo-Spanish, and Black-Spanish segregation. The findings indicate that socioeconomic factors are not significant determinants of racial/ethnic segregation in these periods. Rather, age of city, population growth, and percent of the population of minority status appear to explain patterns of residential segregation.@

0339. Jahn, Julius, Calvin Schmid, and Clarence Schrag. 1947. The Measurement of Ecological Segregation. American Sociological Review 12 (3): 293-303.

The main aim of this paper is to develop an objective measure for the ecological concept "segregation." The presentation is based on data from a series of census tract bulletins on Population and Housing prepared by the U.S. Bureau of the Census.

0340. Jiobu, Robert M., and Harvey H. Marshall, Jr. 1971. Urban Structure and the Differentiation Between Blacks and Whites. American Sociological Review 36 (4): 638-49.

This study examines some of the determinants of black assimilation into large United States cities. The approach is structural, in the sense that independent variables are regarded as attribute of organized populations. The principal independent variables used are levels of residential segregation, industrial structure, percent black, rate of black population increase, and region. It is concluded that "surprisingly, ghettoization is not very important causally when compared with other variables in the system, a significant negative finding in view of current emphasis upon this factor. This analysis suggests that greater attention be paid to organizational dimensions of urban populations as a means of specifying the processes underlying the assimilation of blacks."

0341. Kain, John F. 1968. Housing Segregation, Negro Employment, and Metropolitan Decentralization. Quarterly Journal of Economics 82 (2): 175-97.

This study investigates the relationship between metropolitan housing market segregation and the distribution of nonwhite employment rate, using data from Chicago and Detroit. It concludes that housing market segregation clearly affects the distribution of black employment. That is, results suggest that housing market segregation may reduce the level of black employment and thus contribute to the high unemployment rates of blacks.

0342.   Kain, John F. 1969. **Theories of Residential Location and Realities of Race.** Cambridge, Mass.: Program on Regional and Urban Economics, Harvard University.

This is a detailed analysis of the effects of black segregation on housing markets; it also examines the impact of segregation on broad patterns of urban development.

0343.   Kantrowitz, Nathan. 1973. Ethnic and Racial Segregation in the New York Metropolis, 1960. **American Journal of Sociology** 74 (6): 685-95.

A review of previous research leads to the conclusion that there has been only a minimal decline in interethnic segregation (e.g., Irish from Italian immigrant) in U.S cities since 1930. Moreover, an analysis of the New York-Northwestern New Jersey Standard Consolidated Area census tract statistics indicates that interethnic segregation remains relatively high into the second generation. This suggests that white resistance to racial integration may but compound the strong separatism of ethnic population from one another.*

0344.   Kantrowitz, Nathan. 1979. Racial and Residential Segregation in Boston 1930-1970. **Annals of the American Academy of Political and Social Science** 441 (January): 41-54.

Residential segregation in Boston between European ethnic populations has declined little during the 20th century. Racial segregation rose during the 19th and early 20th century, but has remained stable since about 1940, prior to the expansion of the city's Negro Population. These conclusions indicate that racial segregation is but an extension of the pattern of ethnic separation, especially since Asian and Latin ethnics show similar patterns in the contemporary city. Moreover, segregation levels are only slightly lower in the 1970 SMSA suburban ring than they are in the central city.@

0345.   Kern, Clifford R. 1981. Racial Prejudice and Residential Segregation: The Yinger Model Revisited. **Journal of Urban Economics** 10 (2): 164-72.

Yinger's model of racial prejudice in the housing market is the first rigorous alternative to Bailey's early work. It is important both because his specification of racial prejudice is intuitively plausible and because it has been adopted in much empirical work but never before been subjected to rigorous theoretical examination. However, his derivation of equilibrium conditions rests in part on inappropriate analyses that significantly affect his conclusions. This paper derives what I regard as the appropriate equilibrium conditions. Yinger's original finding that the white community has strong incentives to foster seller discrimination against blacks remain strongly supported.*

0346.   Levin, Arthur J. 1976. Government as a Partner in Residential Segregation. **Center Magazine** 9 (2): 71-74.

The 1968 Fair Housing Act constitutes the first federal move against residential segregation. Prior to the Act, government actions had often been supportive of private discrimination practices. This began with the Federal Home Loan Back Board of the 1930s, with lending criteria that favored white neighborhoods over minority black ghettos. Postwar FHA mortgage insurance financed the white flight from center cities to the suburbs; as late as 1959, only about 2 percent of FHA financing had been available to minorities. Like FHA, the VA program also benefited the middle-class white families. It is asserted that neither public housing programs of the 1930s, nor the 1949 and 1954 Housing Acts, which authorized housing subsidy for lower-income families, nor the rent supplement programs of the 1960s prohibited segregation. According to Levin residential segregation is entrenched in American life through a complex of partnership between the government and private housing industry. This partnership is analyzed and it is concluded that urban renewal programs came to be known as minority removal programs.

0347. Lieberson, Stanley. 1961. The Impact of Residential Segregation on Ethnic Assimilation. Social Forces 40 (1): 52-57.

The residential segregation of immigrants in American cities, long a classical problem, is reexamined for specific immigrant groups in each 10 cities in an effort to ascertain the impact of segregation on other aspects of ethnic assimilation. Ability to speak English, citizenship, intermarriage, and occupational composition of 10 immigrant groups in each city are viewed as a function of their residential patterns and other ecological factors. The dynamic significance of spatial distribution for other dimensions of social behavior is stressed.*

0348. Lopez, Manuel Mariano. 1977. Patterns of Residential Segregation: The Mexican American Population in the Urban Southwest, 1970. Unpublished Ph.D. Dissertation. Michigan State University. 217 pp.

This dissertation examines the degree of residential segregation of Mexican Americans from Anglos and blacks using index of dissimilarity for 56 cities in five Southwestern states--Arizona, California, Colorado, New Mexico, and Texas. Findings indicate that residential segregation in the Southwest declined between 1960 and 1970; and that the greatest decline in index values occurred in the Mexican American from Anglo population index while the smallest decline was noted for the Mexican American from black. The author makes some future housing policy recommendations.

0349. Lopez, Manuel Mariano. 1981. Patterns of Interethnic Residential Segregation in the Urban Southwest, 1960 and 1970. Social Science Quarterly 62 (1): 50-63.

The striking similarity of the overall pattern of residential segregation among Mexican Americans, blacks and Anglos for 1960 and 1970 masks some important changes. City characteristics found to be good predictors of segregation for 1960 fail to adequately account for the same type of segregation in 1970.*

0350. Lopez, Manuel Mariano. 1986. Su Casa No Es Mi Casa: Hispanic Housing Conditions in Contemporary America, 1949-1980. In: Race, Ethnicity, and Minority Housing in the United States. Jamshid A. Momeni (ed.). Westport, Connecticut: Greenwood Press. Chapter IX.

Housing continues to be one of the most persistent problems in the American society. While discrimination is illegal **segregation** has been on the decline, the basic mechanisms of our private enterprise system--that is, loan policies of government agencies and private financial institutions-- have reinforced existing trends which emerged in a discriminatory past. Consequently, Hispanics continue to be segregated from non-Hispanic whites and are more likely to be concentrated in central city housing with its presumably inferior older structures and services; and, they are less likely to own their own homes; more likely to live under crowded conditions; more likely to live in aged housing units or units having structural deficiencies; and, more likely to pay a greater price/rent for comparable housing, resulting in deprivation of the attendant economic and psychic benefits associated with better housing enjoyed by the non-Hispanic whites. While the 1970s witnessed some gains for Hispanics in the housing arena, there were also losses. Even in areas where Hispanics made absolute gains there were often relative losses, as in the case of overcrowding where the decline in overcrowding among non-Hispanic whites was twice as large as that for Hispanics. We can summarize the contemporary situation of Hispanic housing quite simply by altering a traditional Spanish extension of courtesy from "mi casa es su casa" to "su casa no es mi casa." Even in 1980, "your house is not my house!"

0351.   Marrett, Cora B. 1973. Social Stratification in Urban Areas. In: Segregation In Residential Areas: Papers on Racial and Socioeconomic Factors in Choice of Housing. Amos H. Hawley, and Vincent P. Rock (eds.). Washington, D.C.: National Academy of Sciences. Pp. 172-88.

In general, the evidence supports the view that urban areas tend to be segregated by socioeconomic status. Income, for example, does tend to increase as one moves toward the urban fringe. At the same time, considerable heterogeneity among suburbs exists. Five different rationales have been advanced in support of action to reduce socioeconomic stratification in urban areas. It cannot be assumed that greater heterogeneity would produce a more tolerant society.

0352.   Marston, Wilfred G., and Thomas L. Van Valey. 1979. The Role of Residential Segregation in the Assimilation Process. Annals of the American Academy of Political and Social Sciences 441 (January): 13-25.

The assimilation process and the fact of residential segregation are both major emphases in the literature on race and ethnic relations. For a variety of reasons, however, the tendency has been to neglect their relation to one another. This paper offers an explicit connection between the two. This article elaborates on the notion of assimilation and suggests that it can be viewed as a sequential process, beginning with the cultural dimension, proceeding with the socio-economic, and ending with the structural. Furthermore, it contends that the residential segregation of racial/ethnic groups has important consequences for the assimilation process at every juncture.@

0353.   Massey, Douglas S. 1978. On the Measurement of Segregation as a Random Variable. American Sociological Review 43 (4): 587-90.

Index of dissimilarity (D) was introduced by Duncan and Duncan in 1955. Since then D has been used very widely as a measure of residential segregation. But, despite its widespread use, some researchers never felt comfortable with D as a measure of segregation. Thus, in 1976 Cortese, et al. introduced a new measure, Z_D. In this paper the author presents "logical and empirical evidence to show that Z_D is an inappropriate measure of residential segregation."

0354.   Massey, Douglas S. 1979. Residential Segregation of Spanish Americans in United States Urban Areas. Demography 16 (4): 553-63.

Residential segregation among Spanish Americans, whites and blacks is measured in the 29 largest U.S. urbanized areas. Results show that Spanish Americans are much less segregated from whites than are blacks and are less concentrated within central cities. Spanish-white segregation also tends to be much lower in suburbs than in central cities, while black-white segregation is maintained at a high level in both areas. Segregation of Spanish Americans from whites is found to decline with generations spent in the United States. Finally, the relative proportion of Spanish who live in a central city and the relative number of Spanish who are foreign stock, are both highly related, across urbanized areas, to variations in the level of Spanish-white segregation.*

0355.   Massey, Douglas S. 1979. Effects of Socioeconomic Factors on the Residential Segregation of Blacks and Spanish Americans in U.S. American Sociological Review 44 (December): 1015-22.

Human ecologists have theorized that differences in the degree of residential segregation between groups is a result of differences in socioeconomic variables such as income, education, and occupation. Some segregation studies have lent credence to this hypothesis, but results are not conclusive. Hypothesizing that there is an inverse relation between socioeconomic class and the degree of Hispanic segregation from whites, this study compares patterns of blacks and Hispanic segregation relative to the effects of socioeconomic variables. Results reveal that a high degree of segregation between blacks and whites cannot be accounted for by socioeconomic variables alone. In contrast, this study shows that patterns of Spanish-white segregation are highly related to socioeconomic variables.

0356.   Massey, Douglas S. 1981. Social Class and Ethnic Segregation: A Reconsideration of Methods and Conclusions. American Sociological Review 46 (October): 641-50.

Previous research on the relationship between social class and ethnic segregation has produced inconsistent results. This paper resolves these inconsistencies by clarifying some theoretical and methodological issues. Ecological theory hypothesizes an inverse relationship between ethnic segregation and socioeconomic status. We demonstrate that this hypothesis cannot be tested using the method of indirect standardization, but is appropriately examined using either direct standardization or cross-sectional correlation. Given these clarifications, previous research generally supports hypotheses derived from ecological theory and lends credence to a social class interpretation of ethnic segregation.*

0357.   Massey, Douglas S.   1981.   Hispanic Residential Segregation: A Comparison
        of Mexicans, Cubans, and Puerto Ricans.   **Sociology and Social Research** 65
        (3): 311-22.

        Residential Segregation of Mexicans, Cubans, and Puerto Ricans was measured
        in eight U.S. urbanized areas.   These Hispanic groups were found to be
        highly segregated from blacks, and less segregated from non-Hispanic
        whites.   An apparent exception to this generalization was Puerto Rican
        population of the northeast, which was less segregated from blacks than from
        whites.   Hispanics also tended to be less concentrated within central
        cities than blacks.   Mexicans, Cubans, and Puerto Ricans also display a high
        degree of segregation between themselves.   Variation in the degree of
        segregation between these ethnic/racial groups was significantly related to
        intergroup differences in socioeconomic status as well as the nativity
        status of the groups involved.*

0358.   Massey, Douglas S.   1983.   A Research Note on Residential Succession: The
        Hispanic Case.   **Social Forces** 61 (3): 825-33.

        This is a study of neighborhood change in seven Southwestern SMSAs.   Results
        reveal a clear contrast between black and Hispanic residential succession
        processes.   "Under conditions of high black and low white population
        growth, areas of black settlement are very likely to undergo rapid
        residential succession to predominantly black neighborhoods.   Invasion of
        any tract by even a small number of blacks is usually followed by a rapid
        decline in Anglo population, initiating a process of residential succession
        that in most cases leads to the creation of predominantly or entirely black
        area."   In contrast, areas of Hispanic settlement are much less likely to
        undergo rapid residential succession.   These results imply that at any
        given time, Hispanics will be much less segregated from Anglos than blacks.

0359.   McGuire, Martin.   1974.   Group Segregation and Optimal Jurisdictions.
        Journal of Political Economy 82 (1): 112-32.

        Even if people are entirely devoid of any feelings toward each other
        (sympathetic or antipathetic) at a personal level, they may find it in their
        interests to set up and join associations which are segregated on the basis
        of income and/or tastes.   This paper constructs a model to show how wealth,
        technology, and preferences can interact to provide common incentives for
        people to form segregated groups for the provision of local collective
        goods--that is, goods which cannot readily be supplied and priced on a
        variable unit-of-services basis, but which are best provided communally at
        the same level to all members of the association, in such a way that
        nonmembers are excluded from enjoying them altogether.*

0360.   Meade, Anthony Carl, Sr.   1971.   The Residential Segregation of Population
        Characteristics in the Atlanta Standard Metropolitan Statistical Area:
        1960.   Unpublished Ph.D. dissertation.   University of Tennessee.   132 pp.

        The Atlanta SMSA in 1960 witnessed rapid population growth, expansion and
        economic dominance.   According to ecological theories, it is under such
        context that a greater residential segregation may take shape.   This
        dissertation attempts to test this hypothesis using seven socioeconomic
        indicators.   Findings strongly support the hypothesis.

0361.   Meyer, David R.   1973.   Blacks in Slum Housing.   Journal of Black Studies 4 (2): 139-52.

The notion that black housing is slum housing dates back to early 1900s. Two apparent reasons for slum housing are housing market discrimination, and low income. A comprehensive examination of black housing study needs to incorporate a simultaneous examination of discrimination and black demand for housing quality. Improvement in black housing may come only after all forms of discrimination are eliminated.

0362.   Mieszkowski, Peter, and Richard Syron. 1979. Economic Explanation for Housing Segregation. **New England Economic Review** (November/December): 33-39.

Contending that most Americans live in segregated neighborhoods, this "article reviews the economic research on the causes and effects of segregation." This study is divided into four parts. Part I reviews trends in black-white income and housing patterns. Part II examines research regarding explanations for segregation; Part III analyzes the economic impacts of segregation; and in part IV the author concludes that differences "in black and white incomes account for only a small portion of segregation; a greater share of segregation seems to be accounted for by whites being willing to pay significantly more to live in all white neighborhoods than blacks are to penetrate them and by overt discrimination against blacks when they do try to enter white neighborhoods."

0363.   Mooney, Joseph D. 1969. Housing Segregation, Negro Employment and Metropolitan Decentralization: An Alternative Perspective.

Various researchers have examined the effects of residential segregation of blacks on socioeconomic variables such as academic performance, family stability, housing quality, and crime rates. This study attempts to measure the impact of housing segregation on the employment opportunities of segregated blacks and concludes that "although the geographic separation of the ghetto Negro from the burgeoning job areas in the fringe areas reduce to some extent his employment opportunities, aggregate demand conditions, characterized by the unemployment rate in a particular SMSA, play a more important role. It was also found that the geographic separation of inner city Negro females from growing job centers in the suburbs had an almost negligible effect on their employment opportunities."

0364.   Offner, Paul, and Daniel H. Saks. 1971. A Note on John Kain's "Housing Segregation, Negro Employment and Metropolitan Decentralization." **Quarterly Journal of Economics** 85 (1): 147-60.

In his article, "Housing Segregation, Negro Employment and Metropolitan Decentralization," cited above, John Kain examined the effect of residential segregation on relative black employment in different neighborhoods of the Chicago and Detroit metropolitan areas. Among other things he concluded that had blacks been "evenly distributed among the residents of Chicago in 1956, they might have had between 22,157 and 24,622 more jobs." In this paper, using Kain's data for Chicago and using "what we take to be a more appropriate specification of the relevant theory, we arrive at opposite empirical results: namely, the removal of residential segregation might have resulted in a relative job loss for Chicago Negroes in 1956." That is, desegregation may impose some frequently "overlooked economic costs on Negroes."

0365. Rice, Roger L. 1968. Residential Segregation by Law, 1910-1917. Journal of Southern History 34 (2): 179-199.

Prior to 1917 municipal residential segregation of blacks was legal. On November 5, 1917, the Supreme Court of the United States ended this practice in American cities and put to rest a movement (legal segregation of blacks) which had gathered momentum for nearly a decade. This article chronicles the legal history of municipal segregation laws. More specifically, the story is about municipal residential segregation from 1914 to 1917 in Louisville, Kentucky, and the involvement of the National Association for the Advancement of Colored People (NAACP) which successfully fought against "segregation by law" behind the scenes, in city councils, and in the courts.

0366. Roof, Wade Clark. 1979. Race and Residence: The Shifting Basis of American Race Relations. Annals of the American Academy of Political and Social Science 441 (January): 1-12.

Racially-segregated ghettos evolved in early 1900s, first in northern cities and later throughout the country. Levels of urban residential segregation for blacks have remained high over the years. Contrary to expectation, segregation levels have not declined as blacks made economic gains. Despite modest declines in segregation in the sixties, metropolitan decline in the seventies and structural shifts in employment conditions for blacks have resulted in growing concern for problems of de facto segregation. Mounting attention to housing discrimination and the residential basis of black-white tensions are discussed.@

0367. Roof, Wade Clark, Thomas L. Van Valey, and Daphne Spain. 1976. Residential Segregation in Southern Cities. Social Forces 55 (1): 59-71.

A regional model of residential segregation in the South is constructed, using demographic and socioeconomic variables. Based on an analysis of the age, size, percent black, and occupational and income differentials in 32 southern cities, the findings show that: (1) age is still the strongest predictor of residential segregation; (2) socioeconomic factors need to be examined in their traditional southern context as indicators of residential segregation; (3) occupation—not income—differences have the greater effect on levels of residential segregation; and (4) changes in socioeconomic status for blacks in the South have not been accompanied by concomitant changes in residential segregation. Problems of developing and testing causal models of segregation are discussed.@

0368. Saltman, Juliet. 1977. Three Strategies for Reduced Involuntary Segregation. Journal of Sociology and Social Welfare 4 (5): 806-21.

This article examines the involuntary aspects of residential segregation, presents a conceptual model, and notes factors of involuntary segregation. Fair-share plans, exclusionary zoning law suits, and community housing audits are analyzed in terms of their potential impacts in reducing involuntary segregation.

0369.   Sanoff, Henry, et al. 1971. Changing Residential Racial Patterns. Urban
and Social Change Review 4 (2): 68-71.

This article examines residential segregation as a factor inhibiting the
development of informal neighborly relations and as a means of ensuring the
segregation of a variety of public and private services. While emphasizing
the seriousness of the problem, the authors conclude that "in the final
analysis it is attitudes that will determine the ultimate racial composition
of an urban area. With increased occupational, social, and economic
equality, perhaps one day neighbors will be chosen on a basis other than the
color of their skins."

0370.   Schnare, Ann B. 1980. Trends in Residential Segregation by Race: 1960-
1970. Journal of Urban Economics 7: 293-301.

[This] study examines trends in the level of residential segregation by race
in U.S. metropolitan areas. It finds that the majority of housing markets
experienced an increase in segregation between 1960 and 1970. Established
racial patterns were typically maintained, with black population growth
accommodated by the peripheral expansion of minority areas. This general
pattern of development occurred in both high- and low-income neighborhoods,
and typically left the average black with few whites as neighbors. Although
the average white was at the same time exposed to a slightly higher
proportion of blacks, the vast majority of urban whites continued to live in
racially segregated neighborhoods.*

0371.   Schnare, Ann B., and Raymond J. Struyk. 1976. Segmentation in Urban
Housing Markets. Journal of Urban Economics 3 (2): 146-66.

"This study tests the hypothesis that urban housing markets are segmented in
the sense of significantly different prices per unit of housing services
existing contemporaneously in spatially or structurally defined
submarkets. Using an unusually rich data set for single-family, suburban
Boston homes, significant differences in the prices of individual housing
attributes are found; but these differences result in negligible
differences in the overall price per unit of services. A main conclusion is
that the market is working fairly efficiently to eliminate price premiums
and discounts, at least in the proportion of the market analyzed." This
study is significant in view of the impact segmentation in housing markets
have on residential segregation.

0372.   Schnore, Leo F., and Philip C. Evenson. 1966. Segregation in Southern
Cities. American Journal of Sociology 72 (1): 58-67.

A review of existing literature on southern cities suggests that the older
cities are less segregated than newer ones. This study tests this
hypothesis. It examines the 1960 levels of residential segregation by
color in 76 southern cities. Results provide evidence in support of the
hypothesis. That is, there is a negative association between age of the
city and level of segregation.

0373.   Simkus, Albert A. 1978. Residential Segregation by Occupation and Race in

Ten Urbanized Areas, 1950-1970. **American Sociological Review** 43 (1); 81-93.

Some earlier studies have examined occupational residential segregation in a total of ten U.S. urbanized areas in 1950. The present study is a partial replication of these previous investigations, aimed at measuring the changes in residential segregation in the same urbanized areas during the 1950-1970 period. Results show significant changes in segregation by occupational categories. These changes are described.

0374. Smith, Bulkeley, Jr. 1959. The Differential Residential Segregation of Working-Class Negroes in New Haven. **American Sociological Review** 24 (4): 529-33.

Previous studies relative to Negro residential distribution generally have been based on the "fact that Negroes are residentially segregated. Not much has been done with the equally true fact that segregation is not complete or absolute, but a condition which involves some Negroes more than others. Previous studies have dealt with the description, methodology, or measurement of differences in the segregation of Negroes, and have stressed the results rather than the causes of differential segregation. In contrast , this study focuses on factors of behavior and attitudes of segregated and unsegregated Negroes which may help to explain differential segregation."

0375. Spain, Daphne. 1979. Race Relations and Residential Segregation in New Orleans: Two Centuries of Paradox. **Annals of the American Academy of Political and Social Science** 441 (January): 82-96.

Because of its origins as one of the oldest slave trading centers in the country, New Orleans has a unique history in both race relations and residential segregation. Slavery required blacks to live in close proximity to their white owners. This created a mixed residential pattern that was characteristic of other southern cities in the nineteenth century. The rigid caste/race system defined social distance when physical distance was lacking. In the twentieth century, the advent of civil rights and equality for blacks has led to less patriarchal race relations but, paradoxically, greater residential segregation. Blacks have become more residentially isolated since the turn of the century. This essay documents the disappearance of the classic "backyard pattern" in New Orleans.*

0376. Spriggs, William. 1984. Measuring Residential Segregation: An Application of Trend Surface Analysis. **Phylon** 45 (4): 249-63.

Studies of racial residential segregation have discovered that segregation "by race does not vary with, and is more extensive than, segregation by income, occupation, or educational attainment. Thus, the study of residential segregation is an important link, both as cause and effect, in an understanding of many urban problems." Contending that the analysis of racial segregation needs an understanding of the historical context, this article "sets forth a measure of segregation which conforms to the traditional attributes of segregation indices, but is also sensitive to spatial location." It points out some of the shortcomings of existing measures of segregation, explains the method used to create a spatially sensitive index, provides an interpretation of the new segregation index, applies the new methodology to late 19th century Norfolk, and presents the results of its application.

0377.   Taeuber, Karl E.   1965.   Residential Segregation.   **Scientific American** 213 (2): 12-19.

An objective index shows that in every American city Negroes live separately from whites.   Of the three principal causes—choice, poverty and discrimination—the third is by far the strongest.*

0378.   Taeuber, Karl E.   1968.   The Effect of Income Redistribution on Racial Residential Segregation.   **Urban Affairs Quarterly** 4 (1): 3-14.

This article attempts to clarify a number of myths that have hampered the formulation of an effective public policy to prevent racial residential segregation.   In 1965 (cited above) the author contended that the net effect of economic factors in explaining residential segregation is smaller than the effect of discrimination.   In this study he attempts to present a model measuring the potential impact of income redistribution policies on residential segregation, using a hypothetical enhancement of economic status of blacks.

0379.   Taeuber, Karl E.   1968.   The Problem of Residential Segregation.   **Academy of Political Science Proceedings** 29 (1): 101-10.

Using the index of dissimilarity, "it can be shown that Southerners espousing the lesser segregation of their cities or civil rights advocates decrying the unusual segregation of their particular city are all spouting nonsense."   This article shows that irrespective of size, location, and city characteristics, and percent black population, black and white residents are very unevenly distributed.   The author asserts that the elimination of residential segregation is not a sufficient remedy for "the disease of white racism, but certainly is an important component of any effective treatment."

0380.   Taeuber, Karl E.   1975.   Racial Segregation: The Persisting Dilemma. **Annals of the American Academy of Political and Social Science** 422 (November): 87-96.

Although moderate to high social and economic heterogeneity are typical of suburbs as well as central cities, the black population has become highly segregated residentially.   This segregation has little economic base, but is based primarily on racial discrimination.   To date, there is no evidence of sharp shifts in the residential isolation of blacks.   Black suburbanization in some metropolitan areas has followed the central city pattern of segregation.   The altered demographic circumstances of the 1970s and 1980s hold out prospects for change, but those prospects depend on the nation's efforts to reduce continuing discrimination in the sale and rental of housing.@

0381.   Taeuber, Karl E., and Alma F. Taeuber.   1964.   The Negro as an Immigrant Group: Recent Trends in Racial and Ethnic Segregation in Chicago.   **American Journal of Sociology** 69 (4): 374-82.

The process of social and economic advancement and residential dispersion of Negroes cannot usefully be regarded as following the earlier processes of assimilation of ethnic groups. Negro residential segregation has remained high, despite their social and economic progress. Puerto Ricans and Mexicans, the most recent in-migrants, are economically less well off than Negroes, but their residential segregation is already less. A simple model demonstrates that only a small proportion of Negro residential segregation can be attributed to their low economic status.*

0382.   Taeuber, Karl E., and Alma F. Taeuber. 1965. Negroes in Cities: Residential Segregation and Neighborhood Change. Chicago: Aldine.

This book is based on the Ph.D. researches of each author. It consists of a detailed analysis and comparison of racial migration in 10 urban neighborhoods. The main theme of this work is to demonstrate empirical inadequacies in the poverty explanation of residential segregation.

0383.   Taylor, D. Garth. 1979. Housing, Neighborhoods, and Race Relations: Recent Survey Evidence. Annals of the American Academy of Political and Social Science 441 (January): 26-40.

This essay looks at the various uses which have been made of public opinion data in explaining and predicting patterns of racial residential segregation. The author fully discusses the complex factors involved in residential segregation and concludes that : "Simple calculations of the future of integrated neighborhoods or the amount of segregation due to preferences are in error unless they take these complexities into account."

0384.   Van Valey, Thomas L., and Wade Clark Roof. 1976. Measuring Residential Segregation in American Cities: Problems of Intercity Comparison. Urban Affairs Quarterly 11 (4): 453-68.

This study attempts to document differences in the measurement of residential segregation as they relate to city characteristics. The Problems of intercity comparability are discussed and show that there are systematic biases reflected in block and tract indexes, depending upon the size and percent nonwhite population of the cities. The findings suggest that at least consideration of percent nonwhite and city size may be beneficial in sampling or controlling procedures. Consideration of factors such as region, density, number of units, etc., render comparison of indexes computed from differing areal units more reliable, and the possibility of cumulative research results more enhanced.

0385.   Weissbourd, Bernard. 1972. Satellite Communities. Urban Land 31 (9): 1-18.

In this essay Weissbourd proposes a program which among other things, focuses on the problem of segregation. It recommends that the federal government in cooperation with the states, should embark upon a land acquisition for new satellite communities, that antidiscrimination laws should be affirmatively enforced, that existing federal subsidies for housing should be redirected toward families earning between $6,000 and $12,00 a year, that an income maintenance program should be devised for low-income families and that the federal government should provide funds to rebuild standard central city areas. Implications of this proposal, including its impacts on desegregation, are discussed.

0386. Wells, Theodore V., Jr. 1975. Curbing Exploitation in Segregated Housing Markets: Clark v. Universal Builders, Inc. Harvard Civil Rights–Civil Liberties Law Review 10(3); 705-38.

In 1968, Jones v. Alfred H. Mayer Co. breathed new life into the thirteenth Amendment by explicitly recognizing that it empowered Congress to enact a broad-based legislation capable of reaching even private discriminatory practices. Six years after Jones v. Alfred H. Mayer Co. case, the Court of Appeals for the Seventh Circuit has provided further indication of even broader scope of the thirteenth Amendment's power to eliminate private discrimination relative to property rights. In Clark v. Universal Builders, Inc., the court held that it was in violation of Section 1982 of the 1866 Civil Rights Act for a seller of new housing to take advantage of a racially discriminatory housing market situation by demanding from blacks "prices and terms unreasonably in excess of prices and terms available to white citizens for comparable housing." Implications of this decision is discussed.

0387. Williams, Norman, and Edward Wacks. 1969. Segregation of Residential Areas Along Economic Lines: Lionshead Lake Revisited. Wisconsin Law Review 1969 (3): 827-47.

This article argues that the "present system of land use controls tends to subsidize antisocial [segregationist] conduct by local governments; [and] it actually puts a premium on kicking the poor around."

0388. Wolf, Eleanor P. 1957. The Invasion–Succession Sequence As a Self-Fulfilling Prophecy. Journal of Social Issues 13 (4): 7-20.

Contending that there is a widespread agreement that "residential segregation is responsible, in the absence of laws requiring the separation of the races, for their de facto separation in many phases of American life," this article argues that discrimination in housing results in the psychological isolation of blacks, places them in restricted market, and exposes them to additional dangers of economic exploitation and substandard housing.

0389. Works, Ernest. 1962. Residence in Integrated and Segregated Housing and Improvement in Self-concepts of Negroes. Sociology and Social Research 46 (April): 294-301.

An attempt was made to investigate the hypothesis that Negroes in integrated housing have more positive self-concepts than do Negroes in segregated housing. While our data did not confirm this hypothesis, it did show that Negroes in integrated housing tend to undergo more improvement in self concept than do Negroes in segregated housing. This suggests that an improvement in the status of the Negro is associated with an improvement in the Negro's self-concept.*

················◆◆◆◆◆◆◆◆◆················

4
MINORITY STATUS, FAIR HOUSING, DESEGREGATION, AND RESIDENTIAL INTEGRATION

0390. Ackerman, Bruce L. 1974. Integration for Subsidized Housing and the Question of Racial Occupancy Control. Stanford Law Review 26 (2): 245-309.

Court decisions in recent years regarding minority housing have been guided by the principle that minority families eligible for federally subsidized housing are "entitled to some opportunity to choose integrated housing." Because of court rulings HUD and the local authorities are selecting a larger percentage of white-and mixed neighborhood sites for housing projects. But the opportunities for low-income, minority families receiving federal benefits to live in integrated housing projects are still limited. This article examines various legal, and socio-political factors that hamper the achievement of integrated housing projects, and why courts have tolerated numerous violations of the personal rights doctrine. The article concludes that "policy arguments and empirical analysis support the case for using benign quotas in federally subsidized projects. However, antipathy toward benign quotas often is strong, and quota opponents may not find this article's combination of survey findings and policy rationales convincing."

0391. Andrews, Judy. 1980. Fair Housing: Eleven Years After the National Fair Housing Law. HUD Challenge 11 (1): 8-9.

This article chronicles the implementation of fair housing law during the eleven years of its existence, emphasizing the early years of the law, voluntary compliance and the program initiatives. It concludes that "the opening up of communities to all persons regardless of race and income—which is one sure way to reduce disadvantage through exposure and related new opportunities in many areas--depends upon neighborly action and civic pressure by concerned citizens."

0392. Anonymous. 1969. The Federal Fair Housing Requirements: Title VIII of the 1968 Civil Rights Act. Duke Law Journal 1969 (August): 733-71.

A combination of economics and racial discrimination has over many years forced Negroes into unequal and inadequate housing and living conditions. The Federal Fair Housing Act of 1968 attempted to contribute to the arsenal of legislation with which the federal government hopes to eliminate the ghetto from the American scene. This comment examines this most controversial of recent civil rights laws in light of the social context from which it arose. Areas of potential difficulty in interpretation and construction of the statute are analyzed and conclusions drawn as to the probable effectiveness of the Act in relieving the social evils to which it is directed.*

0393. Anonymous. 1974. San Leandro Freedom of Choice in Housing Project. Foster City, California: Del Green Associates. 103 pp.

This is a report on a project that demonstrates different approaches to freedom of choice in housing in San Leandro, California, to all minority groups. It describes how an urban management consultant firm worked with the local real estate industry, homeowners, and landlords in an effort to enlist their active cooperation in working toward the goal of opening up local housing to minorities. The outcomes show that although the project did not succeed in opening a large number of rental or for sale housing units to minorities, it did succeed in bringing patterns and practices of discrimination in the city into open for frank community discussions.

0394. Avins, Alfred (ed.). 1963. Open Occupancy vs Forced Housing Under the 14th Amendment: A Symposium on Anti-Discrimination Legislation, Freedom of Choice, and Property Rights in Housing. New York: Bookmailer.

This is a collection of articles by lawyers, social scientists, and real estate dealers from different parts of the country. Overall, these articles cover a wide range of topics relative to minority housing. The book emphasizes "freedom of choice" by all minority groups.

0395. Balk, Alfred. 1965. The Builder Who Makes Integration Pay. Harper's Magazine 231 (1382): 94-99.

The author describes "how a Philadelphian who believes racial justice can be sound business has proved his point in more than a dozen American cities."

0396. Bartell, Jeffrey B., Charles A. Buss, and Edward R. Stege, Jr. 1968. The Mediation of Civil Rights Disputes: Open Housing in Milwaukee. Wisconsin Law Review 1968 (4): 1127-91.

Mediation and arbitration, which involves negotiation and compromise, is a unique mechanism for resolving civil rights disputes because it is a process that tacitly recognizes power and self interest, and thus the equality of opposing forces. This paper attempts to explain how this technique which has been very successful in the area of labor relations, can be extended to

areas of civil rights such as open housing. In conclusion, the authors
believe that a "careful translation of the elements of the mediation model
into the civil rights arena can produce tangible results. The success of
such a process requires at a minimum, however, a good faith commitment by the
power structure to come to grips with the problems facing the black urban
community."

0397.   Berry, B. J. L. 1979. The Open Housing Question: Race and Housing in
Chicago, 1966-1976. Cambridge, Mass.: Ballinger. 517 pp.

The newly created Department of Housing and Urban Development, in late 1960s
experimented with a number of open housing projects, one of which was the
Leadership Council for Metropolitan Open Communities. This program was
established to counter the thriving segregated housing in Chicago. Berry,
appointed to monitor the Council's activities and provide feedback, in this
book "evaluates the efficacy of the Council's activities and, finding them
lacking, explores the Council's inability to achieve their principal
objective." The book is divided into three parts: Part I deals primarily
with program evaluation; Part II discusses a variety of studies regarding
white attitudes and the dynamics of white flight to the suburbs; and in Part
III, the author examines the consequences of this white flight. This last
section also includes an analysis of changing property prices and
differential tax assessment that may be attributed to white flight.

0398.   Blume, Norman. 1972. Open Housing Referenda. Public Opinion Quarterly
35: 563-70.

In this article the author analyzes previous studies on black housing,
particularly with respect to the areas of disagreement on factors associated
with prejudice and characteristics of supporters of the open housing
referenda--one in Toledo, Ohio, and in cities of Birmingham, Flint, Jackson,
and Saginaw, all in Michigan. The findings indicate "that (Negro) race and
high socioeconomic status correlate most strongly with votes favorable to
open housing."

0399.   Boichel, M. R., H. A. Aurbach, T. Bakerman, and D. H. Elliot. 1969.
Exposure, Experience and Attitudes: Realtors and Open Occupancy. Phylon 30
(4): 325-37.

Realtors are regarded as the gatekeepers to open housing in the area they
serve. This article analyzes the sentiments, attitudes and practice of a
sample of 164 members of the Greater Pittsburgh Board of Realtors in 1965
relative to open housing in general, and their experiences in dealing with
black clients in open housing situation, and exposure in one's residential
business to an environment more conducive to open housing, in particular.
"The most noteworthy finding was of the combined effect of exposure and
experience on attitudes, with experience showing a stronger effect than
exposure."

0400.   Bullard, Robert D. 1978. Does Section 8 Promote an Ethnic and Economic
Mix? Journal of Housing 35 (7): 364-65.

Competition for housing between minorities in Houston, Texas, a city
experiencing a new prosperity, is keen. It is providing a perfect

opportunity for racial discrimination. The city's housing authority provides some 1,800 housing units for lower income, the elderly and handicapped families and individuals with rental assistance under Section 8 program. But demands far exceed the supply of low-income housing. In this article the author attempts to assess the extent to which the Section 8 program has promoted a racial/ethnic and economic mix of housing for lower income residents. Outcomes indicate that Section 8 has had little success in reversing the pattern of racially segregated housing. In spite of attempts to change the pattern, racial discrimination is still the main factor determining where minorities live.

0401. Bullough, Bonnie Louise. 1968. **Alienation Among Middle Class Negroes: Socio-Psychological Factors Influencing Housing Desegregation.** Unpublished Ph.D. Dissertation. University of California, Los Angeles. 250 pp.

This study investigates barriers to desegregation. The study is based on interviews with three groups of middle class Negroes in Los Angeles: (1) 104 persons living scattered throughout a predominantly white neighborhood, San Fernando Valley; (2) 106 residents of a relatively affluent Negro neighborhood; and (3) 120 residents of Baldwin Hills, a mixed neighborhood on the fringe of the central city ghetto. The findings indicate that low socio-economic status remains an important barrier to housing desegregation. Skin shade was also related to residence, although the most light-skinned subjects were found in the mixed Baldwin Hills area rather than the predominantly white Valley. Ghetto subjects were the darkest. Past segregation was related to present alienation scores. Alienation could be conceptualized as an intervening variable linking past and present segregation.@

0402. Casstevens, Thomas W. 1968. California's Rumford Act and Proposition 14. In: The Politics of Fair-Housing Legislation. Lynn W. Eley, and Thomas W. Casstevens (eds.). San Francisco, California: Chandler Publishing Company. Pp. 237-84.

California's fair-housing legislation, culminating in the 1963 Rumford Act, was suspended by the electorate's 1964 adoption of Proposition 14, an initiative constitutional amendment precluding state and local fair-housing legislation. After the state supreme court ruled in 1966 that Proposition 14 violated the Constitution of the United States, the Rumford Act was again enforced.*

0403. Casstevens, Thomas W. 1968. The Defeat of Berkeley's Fair-Housing Ordinance. In: The Politics of Fair-Housing Legislation. Lynn W. Eley, and Thomas W. Casstevens (eds.). San Francisco, California: Chandler Publishing Company. Pp. 187-236.

Racial discrimination in housing became an issue in Berkeley politics in the 1950s, and after local liberals captured a majority on the city council, a fair-housing ordinance was enacted in 1963. Local conservatives counterattacked with a referendum, and in a campaign that attracted nationwide attention, the ordinance was defeated before going into effect.*

0404. Cataldo, Everett F., Michael Giles, and Douglas S. Gatlin. 1975.

Metropolitan School Desegregation: Practical Remedy or Impractical Ideal? Annals of the American Academy of Political and Social Science 422 (November): 97-104.

This article examines the incongruence between the school desegregation and housing segregation. While schools have become legally desegregated, "the absence of significant residential desegregation in the suburbs and the concentration of the black population in central cities make effective school desegregation difficult if not impossible, without consolidated planning for the entire metropolitan region."

0405. Clark, Henry. 1965. The Church and Residential Desegregation: A Case Study of an Open Housing Covenant Campaign. New Haven, Connecticut: College & University Press. 254 pp.

This is a study of an open housing campaign conducted in 1961-62 in "Newfield." The study is based on a combination of statistical analyses, personal interviews, and questionnaires. It contains a rich references to the subjects of desegregation, open occupancy, and racial discrimination in housing. The author develops a model for an effective campaign, and discusses its implications for Christian social actions.

0406. Cottingham, Phoebe H. 1975. Black Income and Metropolitan Residential Dispersion. Urban Affairs Quarterly 10 (3): 273-96.

"As more blacks achieve parity with whites in income, education, and occupational status, more blacks are expected to make residential choices outside the central city, resulting in greater geographical dispersion of black families throughout metropolitan areas." Using the 1970 Census data for Philadelphia SMSA, this study shows that the two ways this proposition is generally interpreted cannot be verified empirically. "The analysis presented suggests that neither the income parity model of black residential dispersion nor an upward shift of black suburban selection functions can be empirically substantiated for the Philadelphia area with secondary data." That is, the "low level of black residential movement from the central city to the suburban areas in the Philadelphia SMSA suggests that black residential decisions are relatively insensitive to income, especially when contrasted with the sensitivity of white residential choice to income. Income is not the only constraint on black residential movement."

0407. Craig, Lois. 1972. The Dayton Area 'Fair Share' Housing Plan. City 6 (1): 50-56.

This article discusses the progress and controversies surrounding the Dayton plan to disperse in four years 14,000 units of federally subsidized housing in the metropolitan area on a 'fair share' basis. It concludes that "it is one thing to get suburban officials to approve a distribution formula and another to get suburban residents to accept specific lower-income housing development."

0408. Domenico, Anita Di. 1978. Equalizing Housing Opportunities in Chicago. HUD Challenge 9(1): 12-13.

A racially discriminatory dual housing has prevailed in Chicago for years.

The city's black population is growing rapidly giving rise to increase in demand for black housing. This demand has been met via block-by-block transition from white to black occupancy at the edges of the existing black neighborhoods. The transition has often accompanied hard racial feelings, hostilities and even violence as the first black has moved into a white neighborhood. This essay describes some examples of such incidences in Chicago, provides historical perspective, reports on HUD's investigation of the problem, and discusses a HUD's demonstration program to remedy the problem.

0409.   Downes, Bryan T. 1973. The Politics of Open Housing in Three Cities: Decision Maker Responses to Black Demands for Policy Change. **American Politics Quarterly** 1 (2): 215-43.

This article summarizes the results of a study which examined change in public policy or the actions of government over time. It represents an effort to increase our understanding of urban policy change by intensively examining the process through which local decision makers, in this case city councilmen, respond to demands to alleviate or solve problems (real or perceived) in their communities. The particular policy change process we examined revolved around the consideration and adoption of open housing ordinances by city governments in three middle-sized Michigan cities. [Findings show that policies have changed, but the problem is still there]. Public policy has changed, for open housing ordinances have been passed, but the housing situation for blacks and other minorities remains essentially the same. In effect, this particular policy change, like many others at the local level, has very little impact on the problem(s) it was "designed" to alleviate.*

0410.   Eley, Lynn W. 1968. The Ann Arbor Fair Housing Ordinance. In: **The Politics of Fair-Housing Legislation.** Lynn W. Eley, and Thomas W. Casstevens (eds.). San Francisco, California: Chandler Publishing Company. Pp. 285-51 (Chapter 8).

Although Ann Arbor's Human Relations Commission was rather easily established in 1957, many struggles and setbacks occurred before Ann Arbor adopted a fair-housing ordinance in 1963. When the ordinance did pass, however, it met widespread acceptance in the community—acceptance that has continued and grown, leading to other gains in the field of civil rights.*

0411.   Farley, Reynolds, Suzanne Bianchi, and Diane Colasanto. 1979. Barrier to the Racial Integration of Neighborhoods: The Detroit Case. **Annals of the American Academy of Political and Social Science** 441 (January): 97- 113.

This is a report on a 1976 study of white and black attitudes toward integration in Detroit, Michigan, metropolis. Results suggest that whites perceived their neighborhoods as being less open to integration than they actually are. This is one of the reasons for the persistence of high levels of segregation. "Blacks overwhelmingly prefer mixed neighborhoods but are somewhat reluctant to move into a neighborhood where they would be the only black family because they fear the hostile reactions of whites." The article concludes with a set of policy recommendations and emphasizes the need to make everyone aware of the lessening hostility of whites toward integration and the existence of laws banning discrimination.

0412. Feingold, Eugene, and Robert J. Harris. 1967. The Obstacles to Fair
       Housing. American Federationist 74 (6): 5-8.

       The movement of blacks to the suburbs has been "generally denied to those
       Negroes who have managed to fight their way into the middle class through all
       the burdens our society places upon them." As a result, blacks have
       replaced whites in large cities, and at the same time the suburbs remain
       almost entirely white. This article examines barriers to fair housing and
       concludes that racial discrimination, one of the basic rules of the American
       housing market, is to be blamed for much of the segregated housing. The
       authors remind us that "as the United States Civil Rights Commission has
       pointed out, housing is almost the only commodity on the open market not
       available on equal terms to all who can pay for it. The article ends with a
       set of recommendations .

0413. Fleming, Harold C. 1976. The Social Constraints. Center Magazine 9 (1):
       16-22.

       This article analyzes and challenges several popular attitudes regarding
       housing integration. For instance, it asserts that arguments in favor of
       neighborhood homogeneity do not justify denying low income families and
       minority members the same degree of freedom of residential choice available
       to the white and more affluent. The poor are placed in public housing with a
       stigma attached to it. But no stigma is attached to either the VA and FHA
       subsidies that are available to the rich. The author takes issue with such
       differential treatment of minority groups.

0414. Frey, Donald S. 1959. "Freedom of Residence" in Illinois. Chicago Bar
       Record 41 (1): 9-21.

       Asserting that "the greatest challenge of our time is to perfect the means
       whereby free men may live together in mutual acceptance with respect for
       differences," the author expresses pessimism that the "people in Illinois
       are making any progress at all in meeting this greatest challenge." The
       paper explores what freedom of residence exists for minorities in the state
       of Illinois, and what are the laws that seek to assure this freedom.

0415. Frey, William H. 1978. Black Movement to the Suburbs: Potentials and
       Prospects for Metropolitan-Wide Integration. In: The Demography of Racial
       and Ethnic Minorities. Frank D. Bean, and W. Parker Frisbie (eds.). New
       York: Academic Press. Pp. 79-117.

       The main objective of this paper is to estimate how much metropolitan-wide
       residential integration could be accomplished in the short run if successful
       open housing in the suburbs were to be implemented. The author compares the
       redistribution patterns associated with different sets of destination
       propensity rates and concludes that "changes that occurred in the city-
       suburb propensities of black and white movers between the late 1950s and late
       1960s have not had a marked effect on increasing black representation in the
       suburbs."

0416. Garcia, Robert. 1980. Hispanics Gain Voice in Fair Housing Struggle.
       HUD Challenge 11 (10): 5-7.

Since the 1968 passage of the Civil Rights Act there has been little change in the unfair practices in the sale and rental of housing taking place in the central cities. Obviously, for change to take place, it must come from the city leaders. In this article Representative Garcia (D-New York) while holding to the view that minorities have a long way to go before achieving parity in housing, enumerates some of the positive accomplishments by Hispanics which occurred recently.

0417. Glazer, Nathan. 1974. On "Opening Up" the Suburbs. **Public Interest** (37): 89-111.

Contending that the American society is divided into black and white and poor/non-poor neighborhoods, among other things, this article examines the facts, analyzes trends, explains the effects and discusses race and class issue relative to "opening up" the suburbs. It also considers the legal and political efforts to open up the suburbs to the poor and blacks. It concludes that no heroic measures are necessary to achieve integration. Rather strict enforcement of the existing laws and voluntary action may "do a great deal in bringing us toward a more integrated society."

0418. Goldblatt, Harold, and Florence Cromien. 1962. The Effective Social Reach of the Fair Housing Practices Law of the City of New York. **Social Problems** 9 (4): 365-70.

"Although the language of the Fair Housing Practices Law is universalistic in offering protection to every citizen without regard to ethnic affiliation, this study found that the **effective** social reach of the legislation was much more restricted." The authors suggest that the relevance of the Fair Housing Practice Law to residential desegregation must be evaluated.

0419. Grayson, George W., Jr., and Cindy Long Wedel. 1968. Open Housing: How to Get Around the Law. **New Republic** 158 (25): 15-16.

According to this article, the National Association of Real Estate Boards (NAREB), "has consistently championed housing apartheid." This essay examines the NAREB's attitudes, words, and housing market manipulation practices. It concludes that "ultimate success [in bringing about open housing] will depend upon the changing realtors' attitudes. Not all are yahoos. Some have accepted open housing on ethical grounds; others see in the law increased demand for their products and higher income. Still, many are imprisoned by decades of realty practices." The author notes that in their major reference work, McMichael's Appraisal Manual, NAREB displays a facsimile of the first 12 constitutional amendments only. The authors state: "It's time the organization [NAREB] recognize the 13th, 14th, and 15th amendments which promise freedom, equality before law, and equal citizenship."

0420. Greenfield, Robert W. 1961. Factors Associated with Attitudes Toward Desegregation in a Florida Residential Suburb. **Social Forces** 40 (1): 31-42.

Attitudes of white parents of school children in Winter Park, as measured by a Likert Scale, are widely distributed but predominantly unfavorable. Favorable and unfavorable attitudes are significantly associated with occupational prestige, education, a configuration indicating relative exposure to southern race relations norms, and regional self-identification.*

0421.   Grey, Peg Savage. 1979.   Fair Housing Laws - What's the Story in Miami? HUD **Challenge** 10 (4): 26-27.

"Plans to revitalize downtown Miami are Super-Bowl big - a super sports arena, a super convention center," and so forth. The author asks: does super-big also mean super better? A panelist at a recent Community Housing Resources Board (CHRB) seminar charges that this super plan does not include providing alternative housing for many low-income and poor families living in the center city who will be displaced by the implementation of the plan. This article reports that "the consensus of the CHRB seminar was that it will take more than concrete and steel to revitalize Miami. Lack of enforcement of fair housing laws result in the perpetuation of ghettos, which breed crime and erode the human spirit. In a country which regards its citizens as its most valuable commodity, Miami must ask itself, 'which comes first, the people or the building.'"

0422.   Gunther, Marc. 1980.   Goodbye to Fair Housing. **Progressive** 44 (4): 39-41.

"Manchester, Connecticut, is a pleasant middle-class suburb of 50,000 people, nearly all white, who work in offices and factories in nearby Hartford. Its voters recently refused $1 million in Federal grants rather than obligate the town to provide housing for the poor and nonwhite." The article explains the reasons for the voters rejection of the grant, and points out that civil rights groups are already challenging the community's refusal of federal aid in an attempt to force the town to obey by the fair housing law. The article concludes with the statement that "there are no signs, however, that Manchester is having second thoughts about its revolt. The next target of the anti-Federalist could be the city's schools or social services. In the meantime, bumper stickers around town bear a coiled snake and the message, 'Don't Tread On Me,'"

0423.   Hahn, Harlan. 1968.   Northern Referenda on Fair Housing: The Response of White Voters. **Western Political Quarterly** 21 (3): 483-95.

Arguments against Negro rights seldom have been expressed solely as blatant prejudice. At various times, the doctrines of states' rights or freedom of choice in private associations have been promulgated either as ideological propositions or as guises for genuine bigotry. Except for the referenda on fair housing, however, Northern voters rarely have confronted the specific task of making decisions on the freedom to choose neighbors and associates or other related civil rights questions. While results of the votes furnished little occasion for hope among civil rights advocates, the referenda have provided an unusual opportunity to assess white reaction to important controversies that affect Negro rights. Conclusions drawn from surveys conducted in both Detroit and California indicate that the opponents of other civil rights issues also were strongly inclined to resist fair housing. While the referenda on fair housing might have offered

opportunities for the expression of prejudice, they also probably reflected
the different social experiences that could have provided voters with an
awareness or an appreciation of the fact of discrimination.@

0424. Hale, Myron Q. 1968. The Ohio Fair-Housing Law. In: **The Politics of
Fair-Housing Legislation.** Lynn W. Eley, and Thomas W. Casstevens (eds.).
San Francisco, California: Chandler Publishing Company. Pp. 149-85.

Lacking the support of more than a few urban Democrats, fair-housing bills
died in an Ohio House committee in 1961 and 1963. In 1965, despite
bipartisan endorsements of the principle, fair-housing legislation was
stalled in a Senate committee until the Ohio supreme court's decision
upholding the Oberlin fair-housing ordinance. Events then moved rapidly.
Democratic legislators strongly supported a fair-housing bill, and Governor
James A. Rhodes played a pivotal role, influencing fellow Republicans to go
along with a modest measure and dissuading realtors from mounting a
referendum campaign to defeat the enactment.*

0425. Holmgren, Edward. 1978. NCDH and the Fair Housing Law. HUD Challenge 9
(4): 17-18.

Title VIII of the Civil Right Act, or Federal Fair Housing Law has been in
effect since 1968. But, it was New York City and not the Federal government
which adopted America's first anti-discrimination housing law in 1957.
Since 1968, many cities and suburban neighborhoods have been opened up to
minorities, and housing marketing practices and public attitudes have
improved, but much work remains to be done in reducing inequities which
condemn lower-income and poor families to substandard housing. Holmgren,
an official of the National Committee against discrimination, in this
article assesses America's progress in fair housing during the 1968-78
decade.

0426. Holshouser, William L. 1982. **Interjurisdictional Mobility and Fair
Housing in the Section 8 Existing Housing Program and in a Housing Voucher
program.** Boston, Mass.: Citizen Housing and Planning Association of
Greater Boston. 27 pp.

This study analyzes issues and makes recommendations relative to
interjurisdictional mobility and fair housing. The paper notes that the
Section 8 Existing Housing program and the Experimental Housing Allowance
Program provide the best indicators of how a voucher program might work.
The article examines problems with these programs and offers
recommendations. It points out that at the present time there are many more
participants in Section 8 Existing Housing program who want to move across
jurisdictional lines than are able to make such moves. Discrimination,
fear of discrimination, and other factors make it very hard for minorities,
female householders, and others to use the Section 8 Existing Housing
program. It is inferred that much the same can be expected in a voucher
program. Therefore, active efforts to assure fair housing opportunities
are essential to neighborhood integrity.

0427. Hunt, Chester L. 1959. Negro-White Perceptions of Interracial Housing.
Journal of Social Issues 15 (4): 24-29.

Housing has been a major point of racial friction in northern cities, and perception that clearly impinges on value judgments reveals a major gap between white and Negro responses. This would support the hypothesis that individual needs may distort perception. On the other hand, both Negroes and whites were hesitant to make explicit the implications of actions which had latent relationship to value conflicts; and their perception of such situations did not show a racial differential. The conclusions imply that whites and Negroes from a similar social class background and with equal exposure to the situation do have a common perception of social situations which is only upset as these situations are disturbed by serious and overtly expressed value conflicts.*

0428. Kelley, Joseph B. 1964. Racial Integration Policies of the New York City Housing Authority, 1958-61. Social Service Review 38 (2): 153-62.

Based on the author's doctoral dissertation (1963), this article reviews the integration policies in New York City. It concludes that "the policies developed by the New York City Housing Authority to promote racial integration contain a mixture of status and welfare ends. That is, objectives concerned with racial integration were paralleled by objectives concerned with quantitative and qualitative aspects of housing. There were instances in which status and welfare goals were mutually reinforcing. The Authority avoided racial integration policies that conflicted with welfare goals, and only one direct conflict of this type was identified (holding vacancies)." The article discusses data indicating the influence of the policies directed at promoting racial integration.

0429. Killingsworth, Mark R. 1968. Desegregating Public Housing. New Republic 51 (19): 13-14.

"Sixteen years ago Mrs. Dorothy Gautreaux moved from her home in Chicago's South Side Negro ghetto to Altgeld Gardens, a Public Housing Project on the city's far southern edge, where the median income is $3,775 and monthly rent for a two-bedroom flat is about $65." The tenants at the Altgeld Gardens were 100 percent black. This article describes the law suit that Mrs. Gautreaux and five other black public housing tenants brought to court demanding desegregated public housing. Asserting that Gautreaux' suit explicitly pointed at HUD and Chicago Housing Authority as partners in discrimination this article concludes that Mrs. Gautreaux' suit may have contributed to the tighter HUD site-selection standard announced in April 1967. However, it is stated that "a victory for Mrs. Gautreaux may make HUD more zealous in enforcing its new policy. But ironically, some of Chicago's housing experts are not sure that desegregated site selections alone will foster much integration."

0430. Ladd, William M. 1962. The Effect of Integration on Property Values. American Economic Review 52 (4): 801-08.

The main objective of this study is to examine the reaction of neighborhood housing prices to racial integration. That is, what happens to property values when blacks move into a previously all white neighborhood? Contrary to the common belief that integration lowers property values, Ladd finds that it "does not affect neighborhood property values."

0431. Lake, Robert W. 1981. The Fair Housing Act in a Discriminatory Market.
       APA Journal 47 (1): 48-58.

       The Fair Housing Title of the Civil Rights Act of 1968 provides an important
       remedy   for   the   individual   homeseeker   encountering   overt   racial
       discrimination in the housing market. However, it is insufficient in
       scope, assumption, and ameliorative approach to counter systemic bias in
       housing market information channels. Data from a survey of 1,004 suburban
       New Jersey homebuyers indicate that unequal access to market information
       raises search costs for black homebuyers while reducing equity accumulation
       upon resale. An affirmative policy initiative is required to encourage
       development of an unbiased institutional structure for disseminating market
       information.*

0432. Landye, Thomas M., and James J. Vanecko. 1968. The Politics of Open
       Housing in Chicago and Illinois. In: The Politics of Fair-Housing
       Legislation. Lynn W. Eley, and Thomas W. Casstevens (eds.). San
       Francisco, California: Chandler Publishing Company. Pp. 65-104.

       Chicago's 1963 fair-housing ordinance and governor Otto Kerner's 1966
       executive order prohibit racial discrimination by real-estate brokers.
       The evolution and enactment of these measures illustrate the adaptivity of
       machine politics--Chicago style--as well as the interplay of city, state,
       and national politics. The court suspension of the executive order and the
       defeat of statewide fair-housing legislation dramatize another side to that
       interplay.*

0433. Langendorf,   Richard.   1969.   Residential   Desegregation   Potential.
       Journal of the American Institute of Planners 35 (March): 90-95.

       Assuming that desegregation is a desirable long-range goal, this paper
       examines the potential for reasonable progress toward that goal, using data
       from eleven of the twelve largest metropolitan areas in the United States.
       This study concludes that although present new suburban housing is too
       expensive for most working-class Negroes, neither costs of existing housing
       nor current income levels appear as significant restrictions on Negro
       suburbanization. Furthermore, existing federal housing aids can
       facilitate construction of suburban low and moderate income housing. Given
       commitment to use of existing tools, a substantial amount of desegregation
       can now occur within the existing suburban housing supply.@

0434. Leager, Robert, and Wayne S. Hyatt. 1978. Neighborhood Revival Through
       Community Association. Urban Land 37 (9): 4-11.

       This article discusses methods for adapting mixed-income mandatory owners
       association for existing neighborhoods and the development of this concept
       to date by the Urban Neighborhood Community Association Project.@

0435. Levin, Mark A. 1977. A Comprehensive Approach to the Challenge of
       Integration. Public Management 59 (11): 24-25.

       Cleveland Heights with a population of 60,000 is an older, inner-ring,
       middle-class, residential suburb of Cleveland, Ohio, with blacks
       constituting 2.5 percent of the population in 1970. As a result of racial

steering, in the 1970s, the first signs of financial disinvestments became evident in the area, and residents perceived a changing community moving toward resegregation. In late 1975, the city manager and his staff met with representatives of community and neighborhood organizations and the real estate industry to find a solution. The result of these efforts was the unanimous adoption of the city council of a resolution which defined a comprehensive municipal program to prevent racial resegregation and maintain the integrated character of the city.

0436. Levine, Robert A. 1972. The Silent Majority: Neither Simple Nor Simple-Minded. **Public Opinion Quarterly** 35 (4): 571-77.

Public opinion polls in recent years have consistently shown northern whites willing to live in desegregated neighborhoods; at the same time, open housing referenda have been defeated and stable integrated neighborhoods are hard to find. The explanation, the author contends, is not that people lie to the polltaker, but rather their beliefs get translated into behavior in ways more complex than might be expected. Some implications for public policy are explored.*

0437. Mathias, McC. Charles . 1978. Fair Housing Programs in Maryland. HUD **Challenge** 9 (4): 8-10.

There is a renewed concern in Congress about HUD's ability to enforce equal housing opportunity as mandated by fair housing law. Senator Mathias (R-Maryland) points out that recent Bills introduced in both Senate and the House are designed to strengthen HUD's enforcement power of fair housing laws. Senator Mathias states: "I believe that legislation upgrading HUD's ability to deal with fair housing law violators would yield the additional benefit of encouraging voluntary compliance with the law." The author describes some programs in the state of Maryland, which have as their objective the opening of the housing market through voluntary measures.

0438. McGrew, John M. 1967. How "Open" Are Multiple-Dwelling Units? **Journal of Social Psychology** 72: 223-26.

Although in New York State discrimination in multiple-dwelling units is illegal, there are many reports of violation of the law. This study is an empirical attempt to assess the extent of the problem. The study is based on data collected from 10 multiple-unit apartment buildings in the central and suburban areas of Buffalo, New York. The findings indicate that "statute had not been effective in producing simple compliance, thus supporting the notion that 'stateways cannot change folkways.' Although the data further show that 66 percent of the discriminating landlords claimed no knowledge of the law, it is not discernible whether this is just a 'claim' or suggestive of inadequate channels of communication."

0439. Milgram, Morris. 1977. **Good Neighborhood: The Challenge of Open Housing.** New York: W. W. Morton. 248 pp.

Racially integrated housing neighborhoods are ideal. They are morally justified, and the creation of them is the most desirable and practical way for Americans to pursue the socio-economic goal of the nation. This book describes how to form and maintain an integrated neighborhood; it discounts the myth that integration is associated with a decline in property values; it holds that zoning laws which often acted as barriers to integration should be fought in the courts, for laws are, but slowly, affirming the right to open housing. Overall, the author advocates the use of different approaches such as affirmative marketing technique to combat discrimination, for studies have shown that integrated neighborhoods have a superior way of life as compared to the segregated ones.

0440.   Millen, James S. 1973. Factors Affecting Racial Mixing in Residential Areas. In: Segregation in Residential Areas: Papers on Racial and Socioeconomic Factors in Choice of Housing. Amos H. Hawley, and Vincent P. Rock (eds.). Washington, D.C.: National Academy of Sciences. Pp. 148-71.

What conditions favor continuing movement into a neighborhood by members of different racial categories and what proportions are necessary to retain a neighborhood that is racially mixed? There is considerable evidence that racial mixing in any given neighborhood is most easily achieved when residents are of similar socioeconomic status. In a mobile society, considerable instability is to be expected. However, there is no consistent evidence of a particular ratio or "tipping point" at which whites will move out of a neighborhood or refuse to enter. Stability depends on the total constellation of local circumstances. In some situations, instability may ensue at very low levels of nonwhite occupancy, in others, stability may persist with nonwhite occupancy approaching 50 percent.@

0441.   Miller, Ted R., and Mildred DePallo. 1986. Desegregating Public Housing: Effective Strategy. Journal of Housing 43 (1): 11-18.

Most public housings prior to the 1964 Civil Rights Act were segregated. The problem continues to persist. This article describes how legal barriers have prevented the developing of a workable desegregation plan, and suggests alternative approaches that may result in integrated housing.

0442.   Mills, Edwin S. 1985. Open Housing Laws as Stimulus to Central City Employment. Journal of Urban Economics 17 (2): 184-88.

It is a known fact that employment has suburbanized on a massive scale in recent decades in the U.S. metropolitan areas. But due to discrimination in suburban housing, minorities and the poor have not been able to follow jobs into the suburbs. This paper studies this problem and suggests that enforcement "of one federal law [integration of suburban housing], to which there is a strong national commitment, might have more success in stimulating central city employment than all the direct attempts put together."

0443.   Monahan, William J. 1977. Providing Opportunities for Scattered Site Housing. HUD Challenge 8 (8): 2-4.

During the past decade, scattered site public housing has played a role in integrating lower income families into various communities. Now, Congress's $35 million allotment for the current fiscal year will allow public housing authorities to purchase 12,000 existing housing units. The use of scattered site housing allows tenants to obtain housing closer to their needs, and to blend more readily into the community. This article discusses the advantages of scattered site housing.

444. Northwood, Lawrence K., and Ernest A. T. Barth. 1965. **Urban Desegregation: Negro Pioneers and their White Neighbors.** Seattle: University of Washington Press. 131 pp.

This book examines the experiences of 15 instances of successful migration of black "pioneer" families into previously all-white neighborhoods in Seattle, Washington. The analysis is based on interviews with black families and their next-door white neighbors. Results indicate that the invading black families by-passed obstructive realtors, received assistance from community organizations, and were, at worst, accepted with muted hostility.

445. Palmore, Erdman. 1966. Integration and Property Values in Washington, D.C. **Phylon** 27 (1): 15-19.

Between 1940 and 1960, the proportion of blacks in Washington, D.C. increased from 27 to 54 percent—it doubled. This rapid increase in the city's black population led to widespread fear that property values may fall. This study shows that "on the contrary, property values in the four integrated census tracts increased over the ten years [1954-55 to 1962-63] at rates comparable to the increases in the two all-white tracts."

446. Palmore, Erdman, and John Howe. 1962. Residential Integration and Property Values. **Social Problems** 10 (1): 52-55.

There is a general fear that when blacks move into a neighborhood property values fall. Research results are inconclusive--while some studies have failed others have substantiated the claim. This article examines the effects of black entry on property values in nine neighborhoods in New Haven, Connecticut. The authors also describe the extent of black influx, the rate of turnover, and compare the occupational characteristics of the blacks with that of their white neighbors. The authors conclude that their findings "agree in general with previous studies in other areas and should help to allay the fears of whites about the effects of residential integration."

447. Patrick, Clarence H. 1964. Desegregation in a Southern City: A Descriptive Report. **Phylon** 25 (3): 263-69.

This is a descriptive study of desegregation process in Winston-Salem, North Carolina. It examines the processes of social change and the changing patterns of traditional accommodation between blacks and whites in the city. The belief in justice and the commitments to equality by the city leaders is believed to have attributed to peaceful racial accommodation in Winston-Salem.

448. Perlman, Sharon. 1979. The Costs of Open Housing Policies. **Policy Studies Journal** 8 (2): 288-99.

Can a state re-assertion of power to override local exclusionary zoning practices "open up" the suburbs for low and moderate income households? Such an approach, tried in Massachusetts over the last ten years, has some notable, though limited results. This study finds that the most notable factor limiting the impact of the "Anti-Snob Zoning" law has been persistent resistance to it by suburbanites. While much suburban opposition stems from racial prejudice and fears, some is based upon rational concern over the costs to local communities of providing services to the residents of subsidized housing. The author suggests that federal subsidies to cover these costs could remove a major barrier to the creation of more housing opportunities in suburbs for low and moderate income persons.@

0449.   Peroff, Kathleen A., et al. 1980. **Gautreaux Housing Demonstration: An Evaluation of Its Impact on Participating Households.** Washington, D.C.: GPO. 202 pp.

This is a study initiated by a law suit brought about by Mrs. Gautreaux and five other residents of a segregated, 100 percent black, public housing project in Chicago. As a result in 1976 the U.S. Supreme Court upheld a ruling by the U.S. Court of Appeals ordering a metropolitanwide desegregation of Chicago's public housing. The Supreme Court ruled that the federal courts "have the authority to direct HUD to engage in remedial efforts in the metropolitan area outside the city limits of Chicago." In response to this ruling, HUD agreed to establish a demonstration project for the plaintiffs throughout the Chicago SMSA. According to this agreement, HUD was to implement a modified version of the Section 8 existing program to house 400 families during the first year and 470 families during the second year of the demonstration. This book analyzes and evaluates the impacts of that demonstration project on the program participants.

0450.   Pettigrew, Thomas F., and M. Richard Cramer. 1959. The Demography of Desegregation. **Journal of Social Issues** 15 (4): 61-71.

Many observers of southern race relations are particularly impressed by the importance of conformity pressures on attitudes and behavior of individual Southerners. Yet these pressures vary widely in intensity throughout different parts of the South. This paper has offered demographic variables as a method of measuring these cultural pressures to conform and of studying their intra-regional variance.@

0451.   Piven, Frances Fox, and Richard A. Cloward. 1966. Desegregated Housing: Who Pays for the Reformers' Ideal? **New Republic** 155 (25): 17-22.

"Pattern of ethnic and racial separation in urban settlement are age old, but improving slum housing has nevertheless recently come to be associated with the goal of racial desegregation." This article discusses problems and ideals facing those who deal with desegregation. Among topics discussed are: what would integration require, what if black poverty were eliminated, consequences of good intentions, taking account of white's hostility, and ways to rehabilitate the slums. The authors conclude: "The point, in short, is that if reformers can be persuaded to forfeit for a time the ideal of desegregation, there might be a chance of mustering political support and money for low-income housing. This would be no small achievement."

0452.   Rapkin, Chester, and William Grigsby. 1960. **The Demand for Housing in Racially Mixed Areas: A Study of the Nature of Neighborhood Change.** Berkeley: University of California Press.

This book analyzes factors influencing white and nonwhite demand for housing in several racially mixed neighborhoods in Philadelphia, Pennsylvania.

0453. Reich, Donald R. 1968. The Oberlin Fair-Housing Ordinance. In: **The Politics of Fair-Housing Legislation.** Lynn W. Eley, and Thomas W. Casstevens (eds.). San Francisco, California: Chandler Publishing Company. Pp. 105-47.

Oberlin, a small town with a history of abolitionist activity in the nineteenth century, passed the first constitutional fair housing ordinance in Ohio, in 1961. Despite a prolonged contest in the courts and despite Oberlin's small size, the ordinance provided a major stimulus for the passage of a statewide law.*

0454. Reid, Clifford E. 1977. Measuring Residential Decentralization of Blacks and Whites. **Urban Studies** 14 (3): 353-357.

Post World War II era has witnessed an enormous suburbanization in the U.S. But, it is often assumed that blacks have not suburbanized at the same rate as whites. This paper attempts to examine the presumption that whites are more suburbanized than blacks, and provides evidence on the change in suburbanization of blacks and whites from 1960 to 1970. "The most striking conclusion of this analysis is the difference in density gradients [a measure of population decentralization] for blacks and whites and the extraordinary change in density gradients for whites that took place between 1960 and 1970."

0455. Roshco, Bernard. 1960. The Integration Problem and Public Housing. **New Leader** 43 (27 & 28): 10-13.

This essay, written in a journalistic style, discusses the pros and cons of integration and its relation to public housing which is currently the most important source of decent housing for non-white poor families. The discussion relates to New York City. The author contends that the New York Housing Authority (NYHA) is the country's largest landlord. It is concluded that the NYHA "has obscured the critical problem of how the nation's largest city will have to absorb the enormously expanded non-white population anticipated during the coming decades. Further, it has avoided consideration of what role the Authority, as the city's largest landlord, is best suited to play."

0456. Saltman, Juliet. 1978. **Open Housing: The Dynamics of a Social Movement.** New York: Praeger. 424 pp.

This book is a case study of Akron, Ohio, fair housing movement. The book tests some six hypotheses regarding the processes and consequences of the institutionalization of fair housing movement. Psychological, collective behavior, and sociological approaches to the problem are analyzed. It enumerates advantages and disadvantages of each approach. It prescribes collective approach as the best method of instituting fair housing in a community. The book is based on the author's Ph.D. dissertation.

0457. Schechter, Alan H. 1973. Impact of Open Housing Laws on Suburban

Realtors. **Urban Affairs Quarterly** 8 (4): 439-63.

This article asserts that discrimination in housing, the bitter fruit of centuries of racial oppression and hatred, is a fact of life in America today. Based on this contention and the proposition that "political scientists must begin to accumulate data on the grass-roots consequences of open housing laws, and that the best way to develop generally accepted definitions and procedures," this article examines open housing laws in two suburban Boston communities. It concludes that "the data gathered during the course of this study demonstrates beyond a reasonable doubt that the Massachusetts and Federal open housing laws have had minimum impact on the two Boston suburbs of Wellesley and Framingham."

0458. Sloan, Martin E. 1986. Fair Housing: Law Versus Reality. **Journal of Housing** 43 (2): 63-70.

Fair housing, which has been accurately characterized as the "orphan of the civil rights movement", has been the law of the land for 18 years. "How effective the law has been?" In response to this question the author examines the intent and practical application of fair housing legislation. What does he find? He concludes: "Indeed, the Department of Justice, under Mr. Reynolds, has virtually abdicated its Fair Housing enforcement responsibility."

0459. Smith, Bulkeley, Jr. 1959. The Reshuffling Phenomenon: A Pattern of Residence of Unsegregated Negroes. **American Sociological Review** 24 (1): 77-79.

The ecological shifts in black population in northern cities has attracted the attention of students of sociology for many years. This study first discusses some previous models—invasion and succession, Rose's scattering, and Brussat's saltatory model—traditionally used to describe these ecological shifts. Then, using the 1940 and 1950 Census block data for New Haven, Connecticut, he discovers and describes a new model called the "shuffling" movement model—when less than one percent of residents in a block are black.

0460. Stanfield, Rochelle L. 1976. Suburban Dilemma: Is the Federal Aid 'Carrot' Worth the Open Housing 'Stick'? **National Journal** 8 (23): 788-93.

Since 1970, the federal government has come full circle in its commitment to fair housing. Former HUD's Secretary, George Romney championed the cause in 1970 under the banner of "open communities," but, under political pressure, the Nixon Administration yielded to the status quo. James T. Lynn remained cool to the idea, but his successor, Carla A. Hills, is pressing ahead once again to establish incentives for the dispersal of low-income housing into suburbia. Recent court decisions are fueling Hill's drive. All interests involved see the achievement of equal opportunity in the suburbs as a very slow process.@

0461. Stanfield, Rochelle L. 1979. Fair Housing—Still Doors to Open After 11 Years. **National Journal** 11 (8): 734-38.

Despite the 1968 Fair Housing Act, doors are still closed to blacks, women minorities. Since its enactment thousands of private individuals have won court cases involving fair housing complaints. Now the Carter Administration is seeking legislation that will give the government the power to seek cease-and-desist court orders; the administration is also taking the necessary steps to improve the administration of the 1968 Act.

0462.   Stein, Marshall D. 1984. The Fair Housing Act: The Burden of Proof. Journal of Housing 41 (2): 43-44.

The 1968 Fair Housing Act constitutes the basis for much litigation on housing discrimination against racial/ethnic minorities. This article traces the development of the Act and its implications, and discusses how the problem of "burden of proof" makes it difficult to fully enforce the law.

0463.   Sudman, Seymour, Norman M. Bradburn, and Galen Gockel. 1969. The Extent and Characteristics of Racially Integrated Housing in the United States. Journal of Business 42 (1): 50-92.

This article is based on a study conducted by the National Opinion Research Center during 1966 and 1967. Because of its national scope, it provides estimate of how many white and black Americans live in integrated neighborhoods. The findings indicate that contrary to a widespread belief in the U.S., "integrated neighborhoods are much more common than most Americans think they are." According to this study, as of 1967, 19 percent of Americans resided in integrated neighborhoods.

0464.   Tillman, James A., Jr. 1961. The Quest for Identity and Status: Facets of the Desegregation Process in the Upper Midwest. Phylon 22 (4): 329-39.

Fair housing is a fundamental component of intergroup relations in the U.S. today. Building on the notion that if effective programs of action are to be formulated regarding intergroup relation, this paper attempts to provide a greater understanding of desegregation as an example of race relations in the upper Midwest.

0465.   Walker, Jack L. 1968. Fair Housing in Michigan. In: The Politics of Fair-Housing Legislation: State and Local Studies. Lynn W. Eley, and Thomas W. Casstevens (eds.). San Francisco, California: Chandler Publishing Company. Pp. 383-82.

The normal channels of law making in Michigan state government were clogged by partisanship and legislative-executive conflict by late 1950s. Governmental responses to the mounting pressure for fair-housing policies bypassed the legislative process in the 1960s, with an abortive attempt at administrative regulation and with a sweeping interpretation of the civil-rights provision in the new state constitution.*

0466.   Weaver, Robert C. 1956. Integration in Public and Private Housing. Annals of the American Academy of Political and Social Science 304 (March): 86-97.

Housing integration is complete "when people of minority and majority groups are treated as individuals with no conscious concern for their ethnic background. Had we achieved this state, there would be no occasion for the present" essay. Using data relative to the states of Connecticut and New York, this article attempts to see how much the nation has progressed in integrating its neighborhoods. It concludes: "Although there is no overwhelming body of evidence indicating a break in the color bar in housing, signs of change are appearing. When viewed in the light of general trend away from segregation, it is clear that housing has lagged and is lagging in the development of interracial patterns."

0467.   Weaver, Robert C. 1965. **Dilemmas of Urban America.** Cambridge, Mass.: Harvard University Press. 138 pp.

This is a book written by the Secretary of the Department of Housing and Urban Development at the time of its publication. It deals with an array of topics ranging from metropolitan area planning to urban renewal, to racial integration in housing, to the roles of government versus private sector. Overall, it calls for providing decent housing for those Americans who have been the victims of prejudice and are trapped in the subworld of the nation's slums.

0468.   Weaver, Robert C. 1980. The Fair Housing Amendments: Opportunity to Fulfill a Promise. **HUD Challenge** 11 (4): 4-7.

In this article, the author traces fair housing gains and deficiencies since the 1930s, when the federal government first became involved with housing.

0469.   Weaver, Robert C. 1985. Fair Housing: The Federal Retreat. **Journal of Housing** 42 (3): 85-87.

The federal government has given up the fight for fair housing. This is because of the current policies to leave the battle for adequate low-income housing in the hands of local civil rights agencies. In this article, the author discusses some of the reasons for and consequences of lack of federal commitment (federal retreat) on low-income housing opportunity goals.

0470.   Weinberg, Meyer. 1980. Integrating Neighborhoods: An Examination of Housing and School Desegregation. **Journal of Housing** 37 (11): 630-36.

This article examines the difference and links between housing and school desegregation. It concludes: "The attainment of desegregated housing does not automatically presage desegregation in schools. One reason is the uneven, spatial character of desegregated housing in a community with sizable income differences. School desegregation will develop spottily. A more basic reason is the collective character of schools as opposed to the individual character of housing units, especially single-family dwellings. A community's open housing campaign may succeed while stopping outside the house door, but school desegregation and, ultimately, integration requires a far greater and a far deeper involvement."

0471.   Welfeld, Irving. 1976. The Courts and Desegregated Housing: The Meaning (if Any) of the Gautreaux Case. **Public Interest** (45): 123-35.

"In what has been termed a landmark case, the Supreme Court ruled in Hills vs. Gautreaux that when the federal government has been guilty of racially discriminatory practices with regard to the siting of city public-housing projects, it can be ordered to adopt a housing assistance plan that ignores municipal boundaries." In search for a practical meaning for this court decision, the author concludes: "The Gautreaux decision ...simply adds another burden to an already overburdened housing policy. Its consequences for racial integration are predictable--there won't be many." This article is reprinted in: **Housing Urban America.** Jon Pynoos, Robert Schafer, and Chester Hartman (eds.). New York: Aldine Publishing Company, 1980. Pp. 111-19.

0472. White, William J.   1975.   Mixed-Income Housing in Massachusetts: Bucking a National Trend. **Urban Land** 34 (3): 3-13.

The establishment of the Massachusetts Housing Finance Agency (MHFA) is regarded as the first legislation to create a clear policy of encouraging the socio-economic integration of housing. This article describes the successes of MHFA in establishing mixed income housing developments. The author also discusses the results of an independent study conducted to measure the effectiveness of the MHFA's operation.

0473. Wolfinger, Raymond E., and Fred I. Greenstein. 1968. The Repeal of Fair Housing in California: An Analysis of Referendum Voting. **American Political Science Review** 62 (3): 753-69.

In 1963 the California legislature passed the Rumford Act, making discrimination by realtors and the owners of publicly assisted apartment buildings illegal. On the November 1964 ballot an initiative provision (Proposition 14) was put to vote that would amend the state constitution to repeal the Rumford Act and prevent the state or any locality within the state from adopting any fair housing legislation. About 96 percent of those who voted, voted for Proposition 14. But in May 1967, the Supreme Court declared Proposition 14 unconstitutional. This article "describes various aspects of the voting decision, both for their historical interest and as evidence on more general problems of political behavior, including the role of campaigns in clarifying the choices before voters, the adequacy of 'direct democracy' devices such as referenda, the degree to which whites are willing to support Negro aspirations for equality, and the ways in which civil rights attitudes and voting behavior differ among various population groups."

0474. Wyant, William K., Jr. 1957. A Residential Neighborhood Is Integrated-- and Renewed: Holding Action. **New Leader** 60 (27): 16-19.

"Housing, even more than education, is the strongest bastion of racial discrimination in both the South and the North; local government has been as wary of dealing with it as Congress. Here, then, is a story of community action by private citizens that may well be studied in every city in the nation."

0475. Zelder, Raymond E. 1970. Residential Desegregation: Can Nothing Be Accomplished? **Urban Affairs Quarterly** 5 (3): 265-77.

In a 1968 article (cited in this bibliography in the chapter on segregation), Karl E. Taeuber advanced the view that economic factors are not significant in the racial patterns of housing. Taeuber stated that: "poverty has little to do directly with Negro residential segregation...that if income were the only factor at work in determining where white and Negro families live, there would be very little racial segregation." In present article, Zelder examines the validity of different indexes devised to measure segregation, and develops a measure of his own. But more importantly, he questions Taeuber's thesis including all other studies that have supported it. He concludes that "uncritical acceptance of Taeuber's formulation of the residential segregation issue places one in a most unhopeful position."

0476. Zeul, Carolyn Ruth. 1976. **Neighborhood Racial Composition and the House-Choice Process: Implications for Suburban Integration.** Unpublished Ph.D. Dissertation. Cornell University. 221 pp.

This study explores the potential for suburban neighborhood integration as larger number of blacks are moving to suburbs. It focuses on preference as to neighborhood racial composition as a factor in choosing a suburban house. The study is based on a sample of 287 blacks and whites who had purchased a suburban house since 1972. The outcomes show that whites wanted more neighborhood racial homogeneity than blacks. And, those wishing more homogeneity also were found to be more aware of racial make-up in looking for a house. Overall, the author concludes: "Because the majority of blacks were willing to accept any amount of mixing with whites while the majority of whites were willing to accept a neighborhood mixed half and half, a potential for suburban neighborhood racial integration does exist." It is cautioned, however, that this generalization may not be applicable to all suburban neighborhoods.

••••••••••••••••••••••••••••◆◆◆◆◆◆◆◆◆••••••••••••••••••••••••••••

5
MINORITY STATUS
AND RENTAL HOUSING

0477. Anonymous. 1974. Consolidation of Low Rent Housing Activities. HUD
Challenge 5 (8): 21-22.

Consolidation and regionalization of local housing authority programs in
the smaller communities of Maine, New Hampshire, and Vermont have resulted
in lowering the administrative costs, staffing, maintenance, fiscal
reporting functions and generally more effective and efficient operation.
The Boston Regional Office of HUD is currently developing a demonstration
study for the consolidation of low-rent housing authorities within the
Blackstone Valley of Rhode Island. The article indicates that
consolidation strategy is an economically sound method of managing low-rent
housing authorities.

0478. Appelbaum, Richard P., and John I. Gilderbloom. 1983. Housing Supply and
Regulation: A Study of the Rental Housing Market. Journal of Applied
Behavioral Science 19 (1): 1-18.

This article explores three approaches to the problem of severe crisis in
rental housing. It finds difficulties with each approach: (1) Rent
control, advocated by tenant groups, is at best a stop-gap measure that
eliminates large increases in rents; it fails, however, to provide
additional housing; (2) Public sector program, including both housing
allowances and public housing, are especially costly during inflationary
periods and therefore are being severely curtailed; and (3) the private
sector approach—summed up as "build more housing"—is examined in detail,
in light of data obtained from 115 self-contained U.S. housing markets in
1970. It is found that contrary to the predictions of supply-side

theorists, housing markets characterized by a large amount of new rental housing construction do not have lower rents. Nor is vacancy rate, another indicator of relative supply, found to be associated with rent levels. These findings seriously question the wisdom of housing policies that call for an end to local land-use and building regulations, under the false belief that such regulations are responsible for artificially restricted supply and hence higher prices and rents. The authors conclude with some policy recommendations of their own.@

0479.   Askwig, William James. 1969. A Rent Stamp Program to Increase Standard Rental Housing for Low-Income Households in Metropolitan Areas in the United States. Unpublished D.B.A. Dissertation. Texas Tech University. 196 pp.

The purpose of this dissertation is to propose a combination of rent and food stamp program, called the "rent stamp" program, to raise the housing standard for low-income metropolitan renters. The 1968 Fair Housing Act and its predecessors are considered here as inadequate in attacking the substandard rental housing problem because they do not consider the trade-off problem between "housing and food expenditure and rely too heavily on government supported mortgage interest rates as the form of subsidy. The proposed rent stamp program will require a 58 percent effort (25 percent for rent and 33 percent for food) by all participating low-income families. Effort is defined as a ratio of the dollar amount spent for gross rent and food to households income from all sources. This 58 percent effort entitles eligible households to purchase rent and food stamps at a discount. The amount of the discount will depend upon family income and the price index in each metropolitan area." The author also discusses the eligibility of program participant and the agency responsible to administer the program, and recommends that the test program for the proposal be conducted in a major metropolitan area to measure program's effectiveness in increasing the standard of housing for the low-income families.

0480.   Barnes, Peter. 1974. 25 Million Disadvantaged Tenants Lamenting the Rent. New Republic 170 (15): 15-17.

In 1969, according to the U.S. Census Bureau, most renters were poor, young and nonwhite. The renters' handicap is that they haven't amassed enough savings to lift themselves out of the status of tenancy. The renters not only paid for the cost of housing but also a good-sized portion to make up the profits for the banks, insurance companies, real estate agents and the landlords. Lopsided tax laws enable landlords to refinance buildings increase rents and avoid paying capital gains on the equity tenants have built up for them. Attempts by the government to aid renters including rent control, co-ops, and municipal ownership of land and index loans are also reviewed here.

0481.   Bloomberg, Lawrence N., and Helen H. Lamale. 1975. The Rental Housing Situation in New York City, 1975. New York: Housing and Development Administration. 295 pp.

The New York State legislation in 1962, authorized the continuation of rent controls, and provided for a survey of housing situation every three years. This is one of the several reports prepared in compliance with that

requirement (previous reports are: F. S. Kristof, 1964; C. Rapkin, 1966; P.
L. Niebanck, 1968; and G. Sternlieb, 1973). Like its predecessors, it
attempts to provide empirical data on the housing situation in New York. By
statute this is a "survey" of the existing rental situation as they are. It
gives , for example, vacancy rate below 5 percent for every category of
housing; it spells out tenants' difficulties resulting from rising cost of
housing, restricted choices, crowding, deterioration in quality, and so
forth; overall, it provides the implication, without making any explicit
recommendation, that there is a need for rent control to continue.

0482. Bredemeier, Kenneth. 1985. Washington's Rent Control Battle: Who Wins,
Who Loses? **Urban Land** 44 (6): 34-35.

With the exception of New York City, rent control has been a fixture in
Washington for 14 years, longer than in any American city. With
Washington's rent control law due to expire on April 30, 1985, the D.C. City
Council enacted a new law thought by most observers to signal a victory for
those against rent controls. "The new law exempts single-family housing
from rent controls and promises a four-year phasing out of controls on
apartments, should vacancies exceed 6 percent." This article also
describes the continuing debate and controversies regarding rent controls
and its presumed advantages and disadvantages.

0483. Brenner, Joel F., and Herbert M. Franklin. 1977. **Rent Control in North
America and Four European Countries.** Washington, D.C.: Council for
International Liaison. 78 pp.

This short paperback is a comparative analysis of rent control housing
policy in the United Kingdom, the Federal Republic of Germany, France, the
Netherlands, British Columbia, and the United States. It discusses
similarities and differences. But the discussions on European countries
are more detail and provide more background information than the authors'
treatment of the situation in the United States. This is perhaps justified
due to the fact that the book is aimed at American readers who need more
background information about the European nations than the U.S.

0484. David, Harris, and Michael Callan. 1974. Newark's Public Housing Rent
Strike: The Highrise Ghetto Goes to Court. **Clearinghouse Review** 8:581-87.

In April 1970 a group of concerned public housing tenants residing in Newark,
New Jersey declared city-wide rent strike. The strike commenced to protest
the deplorable living conditions in the Newark public housing. This
article examines the cause and consequences of this rent strike.

0485. Dorsen, Norman, and Stanley Zimmerman. 1967. **Housing for the Poor: Rights
and Remedies.** New York: New York University Law School, Project on Social
Welfare Law, Supplement No. 1. 261 pp.

The volume consists of articles by different authors on landlord-tenant
relations, housing codes, tenant unions, and federal government housing
programs. The main objective of this volume is to expand the understanding
of attorneys representing poor clients seeking decent housing.

0486. Downs, Anthony. 1983. The Coming Crunch in Rental Housing. **Annals of the**

American Academy of Political and Social Science 465 (January): 76-85.

Rental housing still accommodates over one-third of all U.S. households, with eight out of nine rental units provided by private owners. The recent moves of many better-off households to homeownership have shifted the composition of renters toward higher fractions of the poor. The author predicts that rents will soon begin rising rapidly, thus, penalizing the poor. It is pointed out that rent controls will provide short-term relief, but in the long-run it will aggravate shortages. The author proposes that if rents are allowed to rise sufficiently to motivate builders to build new units, while helping the poor through voucher subsidy program, may be a better alternative to rent control.

0487.   Eagleton, Thomas F. 1977. Why Rent Controls Don't Work. **Journal of Property Management** 42 (6): 317-18.

This article is written by Senator Eagleton (D-Missouri). According to Senator's investigation, rent control, enacted with best intentions to help low- and middle-income families, actually works against them. The reasons given are: First, it reduces the supply of new housing, as builders and mortgage lenders are reluctant to provide capital where there is an inadequate return to the investor;   second, it contributes to urban blight as owners become less willing to repair and maintain the property;   third, it creates a demoralizing and costly red-tape for owners;   and fourth, it contributes to city' fiscal problems through administrative costs and loss of property tax revenues because of abandonments and reduced assessments. Senator Eagleton concludes: "Throughout my political career I have worked to promote decent housing for poor and elderly Americans. Opposition to rent controls is consistent with this record."

0488.   Eden, Ernie. 1978. Cooperative Housing--A Viable Alternative to the Rental Market. **HUD Challenge** 9 (3): 26-28.

With more and more people coming to the city and prices continuing to go up, many poor families cannot afford to pay the rents. Cooperative housing exists as an alternative. It can provide a way to stabilize neighborhoods, improve the housing stock, and provide housing at reasonable prices for less privileged people. This article discusses cooperative housing and its benefits; it also examines cooperative programs that exist in Baltimore and Chicago.

0489.   Farb, Warren Edward. 1971. An Estimate of the Relative Supply and Demand for Substandard Rental Housing in Major U.S. Cities. Unpublished Ph.D. Dissertation. Washington University. 130 pp.

"The main objective of this study was to construct relative supply and demand schedules for the substandard rental housing market." The author uses these schedules to analyze past government and private programs which were designed to eliminate substandard housing, and to measure the effectiveness of future policies. The analysis is primarily based on census data mostly collected prior to 1950. The study sample is restricted a cross section of major cities in the U.S. A major conclusion of this study is that "an income subsidy to substandard housing unit households is recommended as a viable alternative to current methods of replacing substandard dwelling units."

0490. Fowler, George. 1978. The Bitter Fruit of Rent Control. **Nation's Business** 66 (8): 63-66.

Adopted in the name of helping the poor and the elderly, rent control is now in effect in over 250 jurisdictions from Washington, D.C. to Alaska. About one-in-eight rental units are regulated. The housing experts disagree over whether rent controls have positive or negative effects. Some experts have suggested that rent controls discourage private investment and encourage landlords to abandon their properties, or try to convert them into non-rental buildings. The author discusses the negative effects of rent control in jurisdictions such as Washington, D.C., New York City, Fort Lee, New Jersey, and California. He concludes: "A growing national phenomenon [rent control] is advocated as a way to help the poor. The evidence shows that it often harms them instead."

0491. Fredland, J. Eric, and C. Duncan MacRae. 1979. FHA Multifamily Financial Failure: A Review of Empirical Studies. **Journal of the American Real Estate and Urban Economics Association** 7 (1): 95-122.

The FHA addresses the rental housing needs of low- and middle-income households through multifamily project mortgage insurance programs. These programs have been hindered, however, by substantial financial losses due to project default, assignments, and foreclosure. A review of existing empirical studies suggests that characteristics of project owners, the quality of project management, the adequacy of HUD screening, project construction, and project location all have an impact on financial viability. The results do not support claims that tenant characteristics are associated with failure. Although financial variables are closely related to failure, they are little used in the studies reviewed.*

0492. Freilich, E. 1980. Rent Control Changes Recommended. **Empire State Report** 6 (2): 1, 20-22.

The Temporary State Commission on Rental Housing has come up with some recommendations to be considered by the 1980 session of the New York State Legislature. This article reviews these recommendations, and the history of rent control in New York and concludes: "Today the state and local governments share responsibility for rent regulation. What is needed, say many landlords, is a phasing out of all controls. What is imperative, say tenants, is a strengthening, as well as simplification, of the rent laws. A shift in power over those controls from the local level to Albany may mean less visibility for downstate tenants, but an integrated body of state housing law could prove to be in the interest of both tenants and landlords."

0493. Friedman, Joseph, and Daniel H. Weinberg. 1981. The Demand for Rental Housing: Evidence from the Housing Allowance Demand Experiment. **Journal of Urban Economics** 9 (2): 311-31.

This paper provides new evidence on the price and income elasticities of demand for rental housing by low income households. Housing expenditures of households participating in the Housing Allowance Demand Experiment and receiving housing allowances in the form of a proportional rent rebate are analyzed. These rent rebates experimentally vary the effective relative price of housing and thus enable estimation of the price elasticities. Natural income variation enables estimation of income elasticities. Analysis is carried out using two functional forms and a variety of models of housing dynamics. The estimated income and price elasticities of demand are 0.36 and -.22, respectively. When the sample is restricted to include only households headed by couples, the elasticity estimates are 0.47 for income and -.36 for price. These estimates are lower (in absolute value) than have been previously estimated and it is suggested that this may be due to the low income nature of the sample.*

0494. Goodwin, Susan Ann. 1975. Rental Housing in Metropolitan Boston: Quality Measurement with Public Policy Applications. Unpublished Ph.D. Dissertation. Tufts University. 246 pp.

This is a cross-sectional study of rental housing quality in the metropolitan Boston area for 1970. The analysis is based on two sets of data: (1) A survey of 20,000 units provides average monthly rental data for 57 cities and towns; (2) Median census tract data provide similar information for the 466 census tracts in the same cities and towns. Regression analysis technique is employed to analyze the data. The author develops a model describing the characteristics of the most advantageous cities for the location of public housing, based on the provision of a "standard" rental housing package.

0495. Gornick, Vivian. 1976. The 60,000 Rent Strikes at Co-Op City. Liberation 19 (8 & 9): 33-37.

This article examines the rent strike by the 60,000 tenants of the New York City's state-financed Co-Op City. Faced with eviction, litigation, and fines against strike leaders, some 80 percent of the tenants continue to solidly support the strike. Why? Because maintenance, security, and services have been reduced; 200 of the 500 employees have been laid off; and hot water, heat, and corridor lighting have been cut back by the city. The state is moving to repeal the law against rent increases as part of a new fiscal austerity program to make the city solvent. The residents are 75 percent white and are mostly lower-middle income working class families; one third, are elderly persons with fixed incomes. And most of them are paying considerably more rent than those at the rent controlled housing they left behind, with a 100 percent rent increase in the 6 year since Co-Op City began operation.

0496. Gulinello, Leo J. 1972. What is the Responsibility of Local Housing Authorities for the Safety and Security of their Residents. Journal of Housing 29 (2): 72-76.

The author traces the legal history of landlord-tenant relationship, citing recent court decisions which impose growing responsibilities on local housing authorities for the safety and security of their residents. It is concluded that "the next few years will bring increasing pressure and demands to make public housing developments safe to live in. Since the ability to provide this degree of adequate protection is already beyond the capability of the average city police force, it is ... reasonable to confess that this necessary protection must come from a source greater than the

modern municipality. Failure to recognize these facts and to plan ahead
will result in vast concrete jungles unfit for human habitation and the
social annihilation of a large segment of the American public who depend upon
public housing for a 'home.'"

0497.   Hancock, Paul Roger. 1982. Urban Housing Markets: A Study of Working
         Class Housing and Capitalist Production in the United States with an
         Econometric Analysis of the Mortgage Market in Allentown, Pennsylvania.
         Unpublished Ph.D. Dissertation. New School for Social Research. 220 pp.

         This study first considers a controversy in the literature regarding rent
         theory and the origins of the urban housing crisis in the U.S. Theories
         discussed include the federal role in promoting suburbanization, and the
         presence of monopoly-property forces and discriminatory lending practices.
         The author argues that "these divergent theories, all centered in the
         circulation sphere of capitalist production, need to be reconciled with the
         requirements of capital accumulation." The second part of this
         dissertation deals with an historical schema "within which questions of
         housing can be related to the 'pace and pattern of capital accumulation.'
         The function, location and tenure of urban housing in the United States is
         then related to four stages of U.S. capitalist production: The commercial
         port period, the factory town period, the industrial city period and the
         corporate or post-industrial city era." With this stage-theoretic schema
         in the background, the author then examines the independence and importance
         of mortgage lending activity and urban redevelopment plans as determinants
         of the structure of housing development in Allentown, Pennsylvania.
         Results fail to support the hypothesis that lenders ratify or directly
         support the decisions of urban planners by not lending in residential
         neighborhoods targeted for redevelopment. Despite this, however, the
         author suggests that his model may prove useful if employed in similar
         investigations.

0498.   Harvey, D. Harvey. 1974. Class-Monopoly Rent, Finance Capital, and the
         Urban Revolution. Regional Studies 8 (3 & 4): 239-55.

         Different financial institutions operate together to relate national
         policies to local conditions, and to create localized structures in which
         class-monopoly rents can be realized. The case of Baltimore where
         speculators-developers via manipulation of zoning laws create such class-
         monopoly rents on the suburban fringe is discussed. Interacting policies
         of governmental and financial institutions structure the city
         geographically. For example, the inner city is dominated by cash and
         private loan transactions with almost no institutional or governmental
         investments in housing; home ownership in white ethnic areas is financed by
         small savings and loan institutions; the black residents depend on "land-
         installment contracts" for housing finance; Urbanization creates
         artificial islands of opportunities for realizing class-monopoly rents.

0499.   Haugen, Robert A., and A. James Heins. 1969. A Market Separation Theory of
         Rent Differentials in Metropolitan Areas. Quarterly Journal of Economics
         83 (4): 660-72.

         "The purpose of this paper is to generate a model designed to explain rent
         differentials between white and nonwhite sections of cities based upon

rather simple notions of market separation." The authors test these
notions using a cross-section regression analysis of 1960 census data for
U.S. metropolitan areas. The most striking finding of this study is "that
policies designed to reduce the rate of white migration out of center cities
to suburbs may have adverse effects." These effects are enumerated.

0500.   Henderson, Juanita. 1978. Rents, Subsidies for AFDC Recipients.
         Journal of Housing 35 (9): 469-70.

         This article analyzes federal policy regarding the Aid to Families with
         Dependent Children (AFDC) Program as it relates to public housing rents and
         Section 8 Subsidies.

0501.   Khadduri, Jill, and Raymond J. Struyk. 1981. Improving Section 8 Rental
         Assistance: Translating Evaluation into Policy. Evaluation Review 5 (2):
         189-206.

         The article reviews the tortuous process of implementing the findings of a
         series of evaluation studies of the Lower Income Housing Assistance Program
         (Section 8) to alter the program's structure. To understand the process,
         the role of the Research Office in HUD' policy process and the pressures for
         program improvement external to the agency are reviewed, as are the
         evaluation findings themselves. The actual "translation" process--
         involving actors from the office administering the program, the Research
         Office, the Secretary's staff, and the Department's principals--is then
         recounted. The article concludes with some notes on the criteria of the
         policy process; inertia that remained even though the conditions for
         change seemed propitious.*

0502.   Koeppel, Barbara. 1981. For Rent, Cheap, No Heat. Progressive 45 (3):
         23-25.

         "In the heart of east Baltimore's Black ghetto, the brick on the six room
         rowhouse is crumbling, the steps sag, and the wooden trim is rotten. But the
         stark signs of decay are no warning for the scene inside." Tenants in lower
         income housing have an extremely difficult time trying to get their
         landlords to maintain their properties. Landlords argue that the low rents
         they receive are inadequate to cover the maintenance costs of their
         buildings and still reap a profit. The cities have to deal with this problem
         because their budgets do not contain a sufficient amount for subsidized
         housing. Also the judicial system is to be blamed for the slow processing
         of claims and the difficulties in protecting tenants' rights. As these
         problems continue, one out of every three renters live is substandard
         housing.

0503.   Kriegsfeld, Irving M. 1977. Rent Control: A Plague on Property. Journal
         of Property Management 42 (5): 229-33.

         The federal rent control ended in 1973. But a recent study reveals that
         about 14 percent of America's total urban population still live in rent-
         control jurisdictions. This article analyzes the rent-control issue and
         comes up with this recommendation: "Rent control, left alone, will not go
         away. Neither will the economic problems which caused rent control.
         Owners of rental housing must abandon their customary low profile and wage an

aggressive affirmative action program. They must vigorously pursue private and public means to move communities from destructive regulatory controls to rental assistance subsidy strategies which can help solve the underlying problems rather than continue the illusion of solution through rent controls."

0504.   Krier, James E. 1967. The Rent Supplement Program of 1965: Out of the Ghetto, Into the...? **Stanford Law Review** 19 (3): 555-78.

The rent supplement provision of the 1965 Housing and Urban Development Act constitutes a major phase of war on the breeding grounds of poverty, namely tenement slums and ghettoes. According to this Act, the government will pay part of the rent for qualified lower income persons living in private housing. This article examines this program and draws some tentative and pessimistic conclusions: "When all is said and done, it is impossible to predict the impact of the rent supplement on the housing scene today or in the years to come. We should probably not, however, expect too much. In many ways the program seems closely related to public housing. Apparently funds will contribute primarily to rent in 'projects' rather than small, widely dispersed dwellings. The housing itself will apparently be no 'better' in quality—in style of living provided—than public housing. Only modest accommodations will be allowed. Not that the accommodations will be substandard, but they will not rise above the level of old-style public housing projects."

0505.   Kristof, Frank S. 1975. Rent Control Within the Rental Housing Parameters of 1975. **American Real Estate and Urban Economic Association Journal** 3 (3): 47-60.

This is a detailed examination of rent control and its politics in New York City in the light of its relevance for other cities in the country. It examines several parameters of rent control. They are: mortgage, debt service, taxes, operating costs, and monthly rent, in both 1970 and 1974. Relative to New York City, the author concludes: "Since the late 1950s and up to the present time, rent control has become so completely a political football between the state legislature and the City of New York, that the original intention of 'moving ahead from a controlled to uncontrolled housing market as fairly and speedily as possible' not only has vanished from sight but has disappeared from the legislation authorizing rent control. Born as a World War II emergency measure, it bids fair to be perpetuated as a permanent institution on legal grounds that appear increasingly dubious and an economic rationale that largely has eroded." This article ends with a set of recommendations for other cities in the nation, the leaders of which may be tempted to indulge in an experiment with rent control.

0506.   Lamont, E. M. 1980. Housing Problems for New York City's Low Income Population. **Journal of Property Management** 45 (1): 35-38.

This article discusses "rent controls and other policies and programs in New York City" in the light of their relevance for other cities in the U.S. The author notes that in New York City property owners abandon some 30,000 apartment units each year. He asks: "What can be done to preserve buildings and improve conditions both for owners and occupants?" He finds that rent control "is an important source of housing troubles in New York." To remedy the problem, the author calls for "a more assured stream of rental income from welfare tenants" in order to give the property owners the confidence and incentive to maintain their building to code.

0507. Lea, Michael. 1982. Rent Control as Income Distribution Policy. Real Estate Review 12 (1): 79-82.

For many years, rent control has been the subject of controversy. It is an issue that has polarized the landlord-tenant relations, because the interest of these two groups are fundamentally at odd. This article examines rent control as a social policy to redistribute income. It concludes that "rent control is an extremely inefficient and inequitable method of income redistribution."

0508. Lett, Monica. 1976. Rent Control: Concepts, Realities, and Mechanisms. New Brunswick, N. J.: Center for Urban Policy Research, Rutgers University. 294 pp.

This is a case study in three states: Massachusetts, New Jersey, and New York. The book begins with sketch of some conceptual questions, provides a list of administrative alternatives, statutory actions and judicial decisions, and a discussion of operating costs. It provides a useful review of U.S. rent control legislations in general, with a focus on legislations enacted after World War II, with full description of cases Fort Lee in New Jersey, New York City, and four communities in Massachusetts. Details of rent control laws in the selected communities are provided—current legislation, dates of passage and amendments, and so on. Overall, Lett's data, analyses, discussions, and interpretations focus on the argument against rent control. For this reason, discussions regarding the plight of the low-income tenants' hardship and the profit motives of landlords are visibly absent.

0509. Marcuse, Peter, Harvey Goldstein, and Moon Wha Lee. 1979. Rental Housing in the City of New York. New York: City of New York Housing Preservation and Development Administration, Office of Rent Control. 350 pp.

After many years of debate on the costs and benefits of rent control in New York City, results are still inconclusive. This report is a descriptive study of the New York rent control situation. It describes the reality of the present situation and examines the ebbs and flows of rent control in the past 20 years.

0510. Mayer, Neil S. 1985. The Impacts of Lending, Race, and Ownership on Rental Housing Rehabilitation. Journal of Urban Economics 17 (3):349-74.

"This paper presents an empirical analysis of landlords' rehabilitation investment decisions in a large sample of buildings in one city—focusing on impacts of lending patterns, race, and ownership. The study finds that availability of loans from major institutional lenders—banks and savings and loans—in a neighborhood has a substantial independent impact on repair decisions, after controlling for multitude of other neighborhood and building variables. For all landlords taken together, loan availability problems rather than owners' discriminatory attitudes seem to discourage some otherwise profitable repairs in black neighborhoods. But significant differences appear between owner-occupied landlords and others. After detailing these findings, the paper summarizes several policy directions they suggest."

0511. McCormick, Delia. 1980. Section 8 Moderate Rehabilitation: A Review of Early Program Experiences. Journal of Housing 37 (11): 623-29.

The existing rental housing are disappearing at an alarming rate--600 to 800 thousand units are lost each year due to the lack of maintenance. This article examines the causes and consequences of this problem and points out that "it would take massive public subsidies to replace this [rental] housing, and that public policies and programs are needed to prevent the lack of maintenance that is leading to an accelerated removal of low-rent housing stock from the market." The Section 8 moderate rehabilitation program enacted during Carter administration to deal with the problem is also reviewed relative to its effectiveness to reclaim deteriorated and abandoned housing. Initial assessments conducted by Public Housing Authorities across the country demonstrate the effectiveness of the program as a vehicle for preserving privately owned, modest rental housing. "With approximately 3,000 units under agreement nationwide, there is sufficient program experience to provide an indication of the program's initial success and effectiveness as a tool to upgrade substandard housing and provide affordable housing for lower-income families."

0512. Nenno, Mary K., and Cecil E. Sears. 1985. Rental Housing: Outlook for the Low-Income. Journal of Housing 42 (5): 174-76.

The economic, demographic, and public policy factors that operated in the 1970s are bound to influence the housing activities in the 1980s. In this article Nenno and Sears explore the outlook for low-rent housing in the 1980s and forecast the direction it will take. "It may be that the rental housing crisis which was debated but did not occur in the late 1970s will finally erupt in the last years of the 1980s. That appears to be the sad fact, but the best hope for serious attention to the low-income housing need."

0513. Olsen, Edgar O. 1972. An Economic Analysis of Rent Control. Journal of Political Economy 80 (Nov./Dec.): 1081-1100.

Rent control affects the allocation of resources and the distribution of well-being. In New York City in 1968, it is estimated that occupants of controlled housing consumed 4.4 percent less housing services and 9.9 percent more nonhousing goods than they would have consumed in the absence of rent control. The resulting increase in their real income was 3.4 percent. Poorer families received larger benefits than richer families. The cost of rent control to landlords was twice its benefit to their tenants. The estimates are produced within the framework of a simple general equilibrium model; the data are on thousands of families and their apartments.*

0514. Olsen, Edgar O., and William J. Reeder. 1981. Does HUD Pay too Much for Section 8 Existing Housing? Land Economics 57 (2): 243-51.

Section 8 provides subsidies to low income families living in privately owned rental housing that meets certain standards. It is the second largest low income rental program in the U.S., surpassed only by public housing. Under this program a 4-person family with an income of less than 80 percent of the area's median is issued a certificate. The certificate holder has two months to rent a unit that meets the specified quality standards at less than the regional fair market rent (FMR) ceiling. This article examines the rent paid by the Section 8 participating families and concludes: "We have shown that FMR ceiling limits potential Section 8 participants to choose from a pool of eligible units, the majority of which are underpriced. Therefore, one could observe an increase in rents for Section 8 units without any subsidized unit renting for more than the mean rent of comparable units prevailing before the rent increase." Overall, this article disputes a 1976 HUD's evaluation of the program which concluded that Section 8 pays rents higher than the mean of comparable subsidized housing.

0515. O'Mara, W. paul. 1976. Airy View Condominiums, Washington, D.C. **Urban Land** 35 (7): 10-13.

This article examines the successful rehabilitation of Airy View Condominiums in the Kalorama Triangle section of Washington, D.C., and concludes that recent Washington legislation on rent control will hinder similar rehabilitation projects in the future.

0516. Palmer, Robert G. 1970. Section 23 Housing: Low-Rent Housing in Private Accommodations. Journal of Urban Law 48 (1): 255-78.

The Congress first authorized low-rent housing (Section 23) in private accommodations in 1965. This article examines the Section 23 statutory framework as interpreted by the HUD regulations, discusses preferred tenants and their eligibility, surveys the quality of leased housing units, and reviews the location of leased units in light of the major goal of Section 23 housing of economic and racial integration. In all, the article attempts to determine what the program is expected to accomplish, and what will it in fact accomplish. The strengths and basic weaknesses of the program are also discussed.

0517. Peavy, John, Jr. 1972. Section 236 and Other Housing Programs. **Urban Lawyer** 4 (2): 312-14.

The 1968 National Housing Act established Section 236 as an assistance program for rental or cooperative multi-family housing for low to moderate income families. This article briefly explains the major features of Section 236 and other housing programs--Section 221(d)(3) of the 1965 Housing Act, Section 235 Home Ownership for Lower Income families, 221(h) and 235(j) Rehabilitation and Sales Program, and Public Housing. The major objective of the article is to provide the legal profession with information about various programs, and the potential for litigation arising from them.

0518. Peirce, Neal R. 1977. The Creeping Cancer of Rent Control. **Nation's Cities** 15 (10): 26-7.

This article examines data on rent control and concludes that rent control, once thought to be the salvation of tenants, may prove to be the worst enemy. He recommends: "So the message for localities is crystal clear. For those with rent control, phase out the program as quickly as possible. For those who haven't yet ventured down the primrose path of control: don't."

0519.   Piven, Frances Fox, and Richard A. Clowara. 1967. Rent Strike: Disrupting
the Slum System. New Republic 157 (23): 11-15.

"For a few feverish months during the winter of 1963-64, rent strikes broke
out in New York's ghettos. Activists of various persuasions moved in to
canvass the tenements, blending the language of the building codes with the
language of direct action." This article describes the causes and
consequences of the strike and recommends that the disruptive strategy
employed by the strikers is always uncertain about bearing any fruits,
because it is not guided by the legal and political conventions laid down by
the powerful groups who make the rules. "Unable to meet these requirements,
they can only lose."

0520.   Prescott, James Russell. 1967. Rental Formation in Federally Supported
Public Housing. Land Economics 43 (3): 341-345.

"The purpose of this article has been to describe more accurately rental
formation in federally-supported public housing projects. Obviously, many
other important issues have not been considered. The isolation and
measurement of external benefits and the use of alternative subsidies such
as flat rate charges or certificates redeemable by landlords are among the
issues. The influence of tenants accepting income reductions or moving
from supra to substandard rental housing in order to become eligible for
public housing" is a possible phenomenon within the context of discussion
but it has been excluded.   This article points out that the traditional
analysis of income and excise subsidies is oversimplified and inaccurate
when applied to housing projects receiving federal support. Furthermore,
it is suggested that the use of variable pricing to influence project vacancy
rates, promote efficiency in project operation.

0521.   Rubenstein, David. 1981. The Neighborhood Movement. Progressive 45
(3): 26-27.

This article argues that rent control can help preserve neighborhoods by
reducing the population mobility, which is a usual occurrence after a large
rent increase. The author also challenges the notion that poor people are
more mobile. Rather, he puts the blame on the rich who are responsible for
moving them around.

0522.   Schoshinski, Robert S. 1966. Remedies of the Indigent Tenant: Proposal
for Change. Georgetown Law Journal 54 (2): 519-58.

Noting the problems and inequities which characterize the plight of the
indigent tenant, this article asserts that the law governing landlord and
tenant relations has failed to adjust to the realities of the today's
predominantly urban society. The author contends that this failure is a
major obstacle in the way of efforts to secure decent housing for the
indigent. To remedy it, the author proposes several reforms which might be
effected by the judiciary, and he fashions theoretical bases on which the
judiciary might rely in the implementation of these reforms.@

0523.   Schwartz, Jeffrey B. 1972. Phase II Rent Stabilization. Urban Lawyer 4:

417-32.

Presently, a large portion of the 24 million rental units in the United States are exempt from rent controls. The remaining units are subject to rent control which limit permissible increases on all leases created after December 28, 1971. These controls have rightfully been the subject of much criticisms and controversy. The Phase II rent control program is too lenient in the increase permitted, too burdensome in implementation for both landlords and tenants, and perhaps, most importantly, too confusing in its entirety.*

0524. Selesnick, Herbert L. 1976. Rent Control. Lexington, Mass.: Lexington Books, D. C. Heath. 118 pp.

The title of this volume does not accurately reflect its contents. The unsuspecting reader must know that this book is not a general treatment of rent control in the United States as a whole. Rather, it is a report initially presented to the Massachusetts legislature in December 1974, supplemented with some new interview material. This book attempts to answer three questions: (1) Is there an emergency shortage of housing in Massachusetts? (2) Has rent control had any harmful economic effects on communities that have adopted the measure? And (3) has rent control been unfair to owners in failing to provide for rent increases and profit levels? From answers to these questions one draws the conclusion that rent control is a desirable measure. This book negates the alleged charge that rent controls had disastrous economic effects though eroding the tax base and by contributing to the low level of new housing construction starts and to housing deterioration. Its major point may be that increasing rents for lower income families is not likely to bring into the market more and better housing, then why should there be any rent increase.

0525. Shenkel, William M. 1974. Rent Control: A Critical Review. Journal of Property Management 39 (3): 101-10.

Rent control was initially introduced as war-time emergency measure to regulate rent during war-time housing shortages. This article examines the rationale offered in support of rent controls. But contrary to expectation, it finds that the measure harms tenants. It also assesses the rental market trends. The article suggests policy recommendations aimed at correcting the known deficiencies of administratively controlled housing rents.

0526. Shreiber, Chanoch, and Sirousse Tabriztchi. 1976. Rent Control in New York City: A Proposal to Improve Resource Allocation. Urban Affairs Quarterly 11 (4): 511-22.

This article examines rent control in New York City and makes three policy proposals: (1) To abolish rent control that will force all tenants whose "subjective rental value" is less than the market rent to vacate their units. This would perhaps solve the problem of inefficiency or the unproductive use of resources, but it would drastically change distribution of wealth, in the sense that landlords would become enriched at the expense of current and future tenants; (2) An alternative solution would be to make the right of statutory tenants marketable: all those tenants whose subjective rental

value is less than the market rent could sell their rights to others, and
inefficiency in housing allocation would be corrected; and (3) another
alternative, successfully adopted in Israel, is to allow a statutory tenant
to sell his tenancy right at any time, and proceeds be divided between the
outgoing tenant (two-thirds share) and the landlord (one-third), and
allowing the landlord to outbid any open-market offer.

0527.   Smith, Walter L. 1967. The Implementation of the Rent Supplement Program-
-A Staff View. Law and Contemporary Problems 32 (3): 482-89.

When the rent supplement program was signed into law in the fall of 1965, the
Federal Housing Administration (FHA) was plunged into a new field. The
shift in thrust from a moderate-income group to a low-income group demanded a
changed approach. A program designed primarily to serve families at the
public housing income level would of necessity have different imperatives
than would one intended to replace the below-market interest rate program.*

0528.   Starr, Roger. 1978. The Public Policy: Controlling Rents, Razing Cities.
American Spectator 11 (10): 21-24.

Starr examines the subject of rent control and finds that "it doesn't work."
Rent control is meaningless unless it forces landlords to maintain the
quality of their property. This article has two premises: (1) tenants are
the victims of a monopoly pricing system which rent control corrects; (2)
that without rent control, large number of units that do meet housing
standards would be financially out of reach of low income people. The major
conclusion of this article is "cities that consider imposing rent control as
a cheap way to insure low rents will get a better idea of its real costs by
studying New York--not only its towering housing, but its towering debts."

0529.   Vaughan, Ted R. 1968. The Landlord-Tenant Relations in a Low-Income Area.
Social Problems 16 (Fall): 208-18.

This paper examines a dimension of the housing conditions for the poor that
has been largely ignored--namely, the nature of the relationship between
landlords and tenants. By its very nature, a conflict of interest exists
within this relationship. But various strategies initiated primarily by
landlords minimize overt conflict. If the landlord is not immediately
dependent on a given tenant, the relationship tends to be marked by
impersonality and consequent disinterest in the housing situation. When
owners are less independent of their tenants, personalization of the
relationship occasions non-economic reliance of the tenant upon the
landlord. In attempting to prevent or minimize conflict, the conditions
that underlie conflict of interest are not relieved. Such efforts tend,
rather, to contribute to the situation that we find problematic.*

0530.   Weisbrod, Glen, and Avis Vidal. 1981. Housing Search Barriers for Low-
Income Renters. Urban Affairs Quaterly 16 (4): 465-82.

The success of rent or income subsidy programs in helping low-income
households obtain better housing depends on the ability of such households
to move. For some households, the desire to move is frustrated by problems
that constrain their search or housing choice. This article examines the
incidence of various search problems, and the effect of these problems and

household characteristics on the moving rate of those who have searched.
While evidence is found that searchers in certain demographic groups faced
barriers to mobility, those reporting search problems and those less likely
to move were often not the same. Receipt of housing allowance payments was
found to have no net effect on increasing their residential mobility.*

0531.   Welfeld, Irving H.   1967.   Rent Supplements and the Subsidy Dilemma: The
Equity of a Selective Subsidy System.   Law and Contemporary Problems 32 (3):
465-81.

The fate of the rent supplement program illustrates that the inability to
fulfill the nation's pledge to millions of low income families living in
substandard housing rests on something more than the failure to enlist
private enterprise in the task. Rent supplements were proposed and were
necessary because public housing could not produce the necessary volume.
However, the introduction of new players did not change the rules of the
game. The limitations imposed by Congress assure that private enterprise,
even though subsidized, will also fail to produce the necessary volume to
achieve the nation's housing goal. Both the thirty-year history of the
public housing program and the brief history of the rent supplement program
illustrate the paradoxical effect of the subsidy dilemma--the creation of
powerful instruments whose use has to be restricted because of their
capacity to achieve the very goal for which they were designed. The most
promising solution to the dilemma may be the elimination of the need for a
subsidy either by lowering development costs or by raising income levels of
the   poor.@

••••••••••••••••••••••••••••••◆◆◆◆◆◆◆◆◆◆◆••••••••••••••••••••••••••••

6
MINORITY STATUS, HOME OWNERSHIP AND HOME VALUE

0532. Anonymous. 1974. Federal Compensation for Victims of "Homeownership for the Poor" Program. Yale Law Journal 84 (2): 294-323.

Section 235 of the 1968 National Housing Act purported to promote home ownership for low-income families. Usually all participants in a program do not benefit equally. But, the federal "Homeownership for the poor" program has been unusual in the sense that 1000s of participants actually were left in a far worse condition than before they took part in the Section 235 program. To date, many suits for damages by the participants filed against the federal government have been unsuccessful. Also, the remedial legislation enacted has been ineffective. This article examines the plight of these participants and concludes that "many of these low-income homeownership victims should be held entitled to damages against the United States even under the present limited waiver of sovereign immunity represented by the Federal Tort Claims Act, but also that Congress should enact legislation to provide expeditious and full recompense to all such people and consider broader legislation to ensure that future hapless victims of government program will not go remediless."

0533. Bailey, Martin J. 1966. Effects of Race and of Other Demographic Factors on the Value of Single-Family Homes. Land Economics 42 (2): 215-220.

Does the arrival of blacks or other non-Caucasian residents in a neighborhood cause a decline in property values? The author points out that studies of this topic have produced mixed results. The present study examines the effects of race and other demographic factors on home values as well as contract monthly rent. On the question, "whether slum dwellers and non-Caucasians pay more than others for equivalent housing, these data not only fail to support this idea but on the contrary point to the opposite situation. This study also concludes that "values in slum and Negro areas in this instance, relating of course only to single-family dwellings, seem to have fallen below the values of comparable housing within the middle-income areas nearby." The impact of "blockbusting" on home values is also discussed.

0534.   Berry, Brian J. L.   1976.   Ghetto expansion and Single Family House Prices:
        Chicago, 1968-1972.   Journal of Urban Economics 3 (4): 397-423.

        Analysis of selling prices of single-family homes in the City of Chicago
        during the period 1968-1972 confirms that, controlling for structure and
        other characteristics, price levels and rates of price increase were lower
        in black than in white neighborhoods, and that blacks were willing to pay
        more to move into white neighborhoods but whites showed an aversion to living
        in changing neighborhoods or those contiguous to black areas. Differences
        in price changes at the white-Latino interface indicate that the most
        general influence on levels and changes is neighborhood filtering among
        submarkets segmented by income, race, and other characteristics, but that
        arbitrage mechanisms must be invoked in the case of the white-black
        interface.*

0535.   Better, Shirley. 1983. Black Women and Homeownership: The Financial
        Challenge of the '80s. Black Scholar 14 (5): 38-45.

        Women in general, and black women in particular, must now challenge the old
        male-dominancy and must engage in proprietorship of new and existing
        housing. Contending that social and economic force in the past 25 years
        have compelled women to assume new roles, this article examines the
        importance of home ownership for working black women and their
        socioeconomic stability in their new roles. This same article was
        originally published in 1979 in The Black Scholar 11 (2): 23-30.

0536.   Bianchi, Suzanne M., Reynolds Farley, and Daphne Spain. 1982. Racial
        Inequalities in Housing: An Examination of Recent Trends. Demography 19
        (1): 37-51. Also appears in: Race, Ethnicity, and Minority Housing in the
        United States. Jamshid A. Momeni (ed.). Westport, CT.: Greenwood Press.
        1986.

        Changes in racial differences in homeownership and objective indicators of
        housing quality are examined using 1960 Census data and 1977 Annual Housing
        Survey data. Blacks, net of differences in socioeconomic status, family
        composition, and regional-metropolitan location, remained less likely
        than whites to own homes and somewhat more likely to live in older, crowded
        and structurally inadequate units in 1977. In general, however, net
        effects for race were much smaller in 1977 than in 1960. Racial
        differences in homeownership and crowding were smaller among recent movers
        than among the total sample in 1977, suggesting continued but gradual
        improvement in housing conditions for blacks in the latter 1970s.

0537.   Birnbaum, Howard, and Rafael Weston. 1972. Home Ownership and the Wealth
        Position of Black and White Americans. Cambridge, Mass.: Harvard
        University, Program on Regional and Urban Economics. 34 pp.

        Most economic studies on black-white differentials have dealt with income,
        employment, and prices and their link to discrimination in the labor and
        housing markets. They have generally ignored wealth consideration.
        Wealth, the total material resources, is much less evenly distributed than
        annual income among both blacks and whites. Studies have shown that twice
        as much black wealth is invested in home equity as whites. Yet, only 39
        percent of blacks own their homes, as compared to 59 percent of whites.

This study shows that at every income level, blacks consistently invest a larger percentage of wealth in home and car equity than do whites. It concludes that investment differences are perhaps not solely due to the income and wealth position of blacks, but may be due to a smaller set of investment options available to them.

0538. Birnbaum, Howard, and Rafael Weston. 1974. Home Ownership and the Wealth Position of Black and White Americans. Review of Economic and Wealth 20 (March): 103-118.

This paper examines the wealth position of blacks relative to whites, on the basis of data in the Survey of Economic Opportunity. The analysis indicates that at the same levels of both income and wealth blacks consistently invest more in consumer durables, especially housing, than do whites. The paper then explores possible explanations for this finding, suggesting that these investment differences are not solely due to the income and wealth position of blacks, but may be due to a smaller set of investment opportunities institutionally fostered by discriminatory forces.*

0539. Boles, Alen. 1969. Black Homeowning. New Republic 161 (24): 7-9.

This article explains two civil rights cases that are lumbering toward trial in Chicago. The cases are filed by a community organization called the Contract Buyers League. These class action suits are filed on behalf of some 3500 home purchasers against some 250 speculators, banks, savings and loan associations, insurance companies and builders. The suits claim that "Chicago's Jim Crow housing market impelled them to pay exorbitant prices for their homes. They ask the court to put the differences between what they paid and what the homes were actually worth at the time of purchase back into the black pocket." The author asserts that a victory may mark the awakening of black home buyers and may signal long-term relief from their predicament.

0540. Bradford, Calvin. 1979. Financing Home Ownership: The Federal Role in Neighborhood Decline. Urban Affairs Quarterly 14 (3): 313-35.

This article argues that the federal government in its attempt to cure the problem of redlining in inner city housing has actually made the problem worse. From its early days in 1930s, the policies of the Federal Housing Administration and the Federal Home Loan Bank Board were based on policies that discriminated against minorities and discouraged lending to minority and/or racially mixed neighborhoods. The result was minority neighborhood decline, foreclosures, and abandonment.

0541. Bullard, Robert D. 1986. Blacks and the American Dream of Housing. In: Race, Ethnicity, and Minority Housing in the United States. Jamshid A. Momeni (ed.). Westport, Connecticut: Greenwood Press. Chapter IV.

The goal of a "decent" home for all Americans has not been achieved. Federal housing policies have improved the quality of housing and have stimulated home ownership for millions of Americans. However, many of the federal policies and programs that were implemented after World War II had a differential impact on the housing markets for black and white families. White families have been the primary benefactors of federal efforts to promote home ownership. Many of the federal housing policies have subsidized the growth and development of the suburbs which remain largely white. These policies, at the same times, have accelerated the decline of America's inner cities, which are becoming increasingly black.@

0542.   Burstein, Joseph. 1983. Housing Ownership by Low-Income Families: Elderly Could Pave the Way. Journal of Housing 40 (4): 104-107.

Some home ownership forms are available that create incentives for the occupants to conserve and minimize the destructive antagonism of the landlord-tenant relationships. These forms allow the low-income and elderly tenants to achieve ownership with monthly payments close to rental costs. This essay examines the potential use of lease-purchase and cooperative arrangements, both of which have been used on experimental basis. The author contends that the use of these methods, may help the low-income and the elderly to meet the traditional American dream of home ownership.

0543.   Dlugosch, James F., and Mark Korell. 1978. Home Ownership Opportunities Provided for Low-Income Families via State Assistance in Minnesota. Journal of Housing 35 (3): 131-33.

In an attempt to provide housing for low-income families, the 1977 Minnesota legislature appropriated $7.5 million to the Minnesota Housing Finance Agency to develop a program which would aid low-income families in purchasing a home, structure loan payments consistent with changes in income, and and provide assistance in meeting down payment requirements. This article examines these and other features of the program relative to the level of assistance it offers and how it was implemented.

0544.   Follain, James R., Jr., and Raymond J. Struyk. 1979. Is the American Dream Really Threatened? Real Estate Review 8 (4): 65-70.

This is an examination of affordability crisis for American homeowners. This article suggests that some estimates of the problem overstate the case. Examining trends in home ownership and house prices, the article proposes alternative measures of affordability that give more weight to the value of equity and suggests alternative mortgages that would start out with lower payments, thus making home ownership more affordable by eliminating the capital component as a cost factor. These mortgages can be an alternative to government subsidies.

0545.   Franklin, Scott B. 1981. Housing Cooperatives: A Viable Means of Home Ownership for Low-Income Families. Journal of Housing 38 (7): 392-398.

The 1949 National Housing Act announced the goal of "a decent home and suitable living environment for every American family." Even today, nearly 30 years later, the nation is experiencing a national crisis in low-income housing market. This article examines the cooperative concept and concludes that "cooperative housing projects generally have not been understood by public and traditionally have been treated as 'orphan children' by HUD. It is time to adopt this misunderstood orphan and recognize the cooperative concept as a viable means of providing home ownership for low-income people."

0546.   Haney, Richard L., Jr. 1977. Race and Housing Value: A Review of their
         Relationship. Appraisal Journal 45 (3): 356-65.

         This article reviews the relationship between ethnic composition of the
         neighborhood to the value of the neighborhood's housing. The author first
         summarizes the "relationship that economic theory suggests exists between
         changes in the neighborhood's racial composition and the corresponding
         changes in the value of the neighborhood's housing." The last section of
         this article offers some concluding comments on the interrelationship
         between race and housing value. It concludes that "it appears as if race can
         have a significant impact on housing values, but that the nature of the
         relationship varies from city to city."

0547.   Henretta, John C. 1979. Race Differences in Middle Class lifestyles:
         The Role of Home Ownership. Social Science Research 8 (1): 63-78.

         This paper examines race differences in two aspects of "middle class"
         lifestyle: home ownership and net worth. Home ownership indicates
         stability; and for older persons net worth is an important part of
         economic status. Data from the NLS [National Longitudinal Studies]
         studies of older men are analyzed. The major findings are: (a) while whites
         at any earnings level are very likely to own homes by ages 50-64, only at
         relatively high earning levels do blacks begin to approach home ownership
         rates of whites; (b) the net worth of blacks is substantially lower than
         that of whites after adjusting for variables in a standard status attainment
         model; and (c) however, among home owners the race difference as well as
         effects of other variables are much smaller than for renters. This is
         attributed to forced saving through home ownership. The paper concludes
         with a discussion of possible sources of low home ownership rates and low net
         worth of blacks and the implication of these findings for the study of middle
         class status.*

0548.   Henretta, John C., and Richard T. Campbell. 1978. Net Worth as an Aspect
         of Status. American Journal of Sociology 83 (5): 1204-1223.

         While Sociologists have recognized the importance of wealth for analysis of
         political power, they have given little attention to wealth as a measure of
         economic status. Yet from both a sociological and an economic point of
         view, wealth is an important determinant of status and life chances,
         especially at the end of the life cycle. In this paper we discuss the role of
         net worth as a component of status, and using data from the National
         Longitudinal Studies of Labor Force Participation, estimate a status-
         attainment model for net worth. Net Worth includes savings, home equity,
         business assets, and real estate holdings. We find that (a) the effects of
         family background are transmitted via education; (b) the effect of
         education is asymptotic rather than linear; (c) single and divorced
         persons possess substantially fewer assets, net of other characteristics,
         than married persons; and (d) net of all other variables, earnings have a
         substantial effect on net worth. The effects of family background and
         socioeconomic attainments on net worth suggest that expanded definitions of
         status may yield more understanding of the stratification system.*

0549.   Jackman, Mary R., and Robert W. Jackman. 1980. Racial Inequalities in

Home Ownership. Social Forces 58 (4): 1221-1234. Also appears in: Race, Ethnicity, and Minority Housing in the United States. Jamshid A. Momeni (ed.). Westport, CT: Greenwood Press, 1986.

This paper examines black-white differences in patterns of home ownership, using data from a recent national survey. Race differences are estimated net of household characteristics, family composition, and location. Results indicate, first, that the probability of home ownership is considerably lower for blacks than it is for comparable whites, throughout the United States. Second, outside the South (but not in the South), black owner-occupied homes are worth considerably less than the homes of comparable whites. The paper concludes by discussing the implications of these results.*

0550. Krivo, Lauren J. 1982. Housing Price Inequalities: A Comparison of Anglos, Blacks, and Spanish-Origin Populations. **Urban Affairs Quarterly** 17 (4): 445-462.

This article analyzes data from the Annual Housing Survey on the black and Spanish-origin populations in a sample of United States SMSAs to determine whether these minorities pay more than Anglos for comparable housing. These data demonstrate that both blacks and Spanish-origin populations as a whole pay more than Anglos for the same quality housing in the rental market while no group pays significantly more than Anglos in the owners' market.@

0551. Krivo, Lauren J. 1985. **Home Ownership Differentials Among the Spanish Origin and Anglo Populations.** A paper presented at the 80th Annual Meetings of the American Sociological Association, August 26-30, 1985, Washington, D.C. 13 pp.

This study compares home ownership rates of Spanish origin population with those of blacks and Anglo households. Results show that the Spanish origin population experiences significant limitations to home ownership as compared to the Anglo households, and that the limitations among some Spanish subgroups are more severe than those experienced by blacks.

0552. Ladenson, Mark L. 1978. Race and Sex Discrimination in Housing: The Evidence from Probabilities of Homeownership. **Southern Economic Journal** 45 (2): 559-575.

Previous studies of the relationship between race and home ownership have indicated a large gap in the probability of home ownerships by race. This study estimates probability of home purchase equation for the years 1969 through 1974. The author finds that the difference in probability of home purchase due to being black fell in the years after the passage in 1968 of the National Fair Housing Act and the Section 235 program, but rose upon the suspension of 235 in early 1973. The paper also investigates the matter of sex and home ownership, the question of tax implications, and the matter of the role of assets in the probability of home ownership equation. The findings indicate that 10-25 percent of the difference in black-white home ownership can be explained by black-white differentials in assets.

0553. Lake, Robert W. 1979. Racial Transition and Black Home Ownership in American Suburbs. **Annals of the American Academy of Political and Social**

Science 441 (January): 142-167.

Home ownership has traditionally served as an efficient wealth generating mechanism for the American middle class. Recent data indicating an increase in the metropolitan area black population living in the suburbs raise two questions: is black suburbanization equivalent to home-ownership, and does black suburban homeownership lead to equity accumulation and the generation of wealth? These questions are addressed through analysis of a national sample of suburban housing units surveyed in 1974, and again in 1975, as part of the census Bureau's Annual Housing Survey. As of the mid-1970s, black suburbanization has not been entirely synonymous with home ownership nor has home ownership automatically served the wealth generating function for blacks that it has provided for earlier suburbanizing aspirants to the middle class.*

0554. Lake, Robert W. 1981. The New Suburbanites: Race and Housing in the Suburbs. New Brunswick, N. J.: Rutgers University for Urban Policy research. 303 pp.

In addition to national trends in black suburbanization, and black suburban experiences, this book's major purpose is to explores the topic of black suburban home ownership. The discussions includes such issues as possible limitations to the housing submarket open to blacks, barriers to housing information, relative ease and efficiency of housing search, relative equity accumulation, home values, and the role of the real estate broker in perpetuating conditions of discrimination.

0555. Lapham, Victoria Cannon. 1970. Price Differences for Black and White Housing. Unpublished Ph.D. Dissertation. Southern Methodist University. 120 pp.

This study tests the hypothesis that the price of housing bought by blacks is equal to price of housing bought by whites using housing transactions in Dallas in 1960. Two comparisons are made. The first is based on a black unit with the average of all black characteristics. The price of this unit is calculated first assuming that the prices of the characteristics are those found in the black sample and then assuming that the prices are those found in the white sample. This produces the conclusion that the price of black housing is 4 to 6 percent less than the price of white housing. The second comparison is based on a white unit with the average of all white characteristics. The price of this unit is calculated assuming that the prices of its characteristics are those found in the white sample and then those found in the black sample. This produces the conclusion that the price of white housing is .3 to .8 percent less than the price of black housing.@

0556. Laurenti, Luigi. 1960. Property Values and Race: Studies in Seven Cities. Berkeley: University of California Press. 256 pp.

This is a detailed study of price trends in 20 neighborhoods in seven cities--San Francisco and Oakland, California; Philadelphia, Pennsylvania; Chicago, Kansas City, Detroit, and Portland, Oregon--where nonwhite entry occurred in all-white areas. But the bulk of the study is based on original studies made in the two California cities. This study finds that nonwhite entry most often was associated with price improvement or stability. The author detects no single or uniform pattern of nonwhite influence on property values.

0557.   Marcus, Matityahu. 1968. Racial Composition and Home Price Changes: A Case Study. **Journal of the American Institute of Planners** 34 (5): 334-38.

This case study of Plainfield, New Jersey, examines the hypothesis that black entry into a suburban community, surrounded by municipalities without black population, brings about a decline in property values. Examination of price changes since 1955 turns up no evidence of either an absolute or relative adverse racial effect on home values. That is, the hypothesis is not supported.

0558.   Marcuse, Peter. 1972. Homeownership for Low Income Families: Financial Implications. **Land Economics** 48 (2): 134-143.

This study examines financial assumptions which underlie the advocacy of home ownership for the poor. That is, it explores the pros and cons of home ownership by the poor. Assumptions analyzed are: investment advantages of home ownership, consequences of combining ownership with occupancy, tax advantages, settlement costs of buying a house and protection against changes in housing costs. The author concludes that "the stance that public policy should take towards homeownership for low-income families lies in the possibilities of institutional changes in existing tenure arrangements, and in the social or political, not the financial characteristics of homeownership."

0559.   Meer, Bernard, and Edward Freedman. 1966. The Impact of Negro Neighbors on White Home Owners. **Social Forces** 45 (1): 11-19.

The purpose of this study was to test the hypothesis that equal-status residential contact between Negroes and whites in a predominantly white middle- to upper-middle-class neighborhood would lead to a reduction of prejudice. The results suggest that equal-status contact in one area (in this case residential) does lead to a reduction of prejudice in that area (Negroes were more accepted as neighbor), but this change does not necessarily generalize to other areas of interpersonal contact. However, when residential contact leads to more intimate types of interactions, a more extensive reduction in prejudice may follow.*

0560.   Mingche, M. Li. 1977. A Logit Model of Homeownership. **Econometrica** 45 (5): 1081-97.

"This paper estimates all possible multidimensional interaction effects in a logit model of homeownership, assesses the relative importance of these interactions, and interprets the results in light of existing theories of housing consumption." Race, income, and age of head of household are among variables included in the model. The findings indicate that the interaction between race variable and other "explanatory variables, attributable to racial discrimination, are found to be secondary to the income-[family]size and the age-[family]size interaction."

0561.   Parcel, Toby L. 1982. Wealth Accumulation of Black and White Men: The Case of Housing Equity. **Social Problems** 30 (2): 199-211.

This paper looks at racial differences in how male workers accumulate housing equity. Findings from a national sample suggest major differences favoring whites in the payoff to such characteristics as earnings, age, marital status, and area of current residence. Blacks and whites also differ in the form of the relationship between years of schooling and housing equity. When the analysis is confined to homeowners only, many of these racial differences remain. The findings provide evidence concerning racial inequality in the United States housing markets and thus allow inferences concerning discrimination in housing. The findings also dramatize racial differences in a key form of wealth accumulation as a complement to other reports of racial differences in socio-economic outcomes.*

562. Parente, Frank. 1980. The Fading Dream of Home Ownership. AFL-CIO **American Federationist** 87 (11): 18-23.

The author sums up the housing crisis in the U.S. by stating that three-fourth of the people are only able to buy one-fourth of the housing; from this observation it is inferred that a growing number of families are effectively priced out of the housing market, that includes most families headed by a minority group member, a female, or an elderly person. To help meet this crisis, during the 1970-79 period, housing production begun on an estimated 2.8 million HUD- and FMHA-assisted housing units nationally. Another important program is HUD's direct loan program for the elderly and handicapped, which provides rental housing at reduced prices to lower-income tenants. In the 1980s, the top priorities include: regulating credit to produce reasonable interest rates for housing and keeping production up under cash housing subsidy programs like Section 8 leasing, low rent public housing, and home ownership assistance for the low-income groups.

563. Pearce, Diana M. 1979. Gatekeepers and Homeseekers: Institutional Patterns in Racial Steering. **Social Problems** 26 (3): 338-342.

Racial Patterns in housing are a paradox of continued segregation in spite of apparent liberalization of white attitudes. This paper explores the problem of examining the role of real estate agents, acting as community gatekeepers, in the perpetuation of racial segregation. An experimental field study was conducted ascertaining real estate agents' behavior toward matched black and white couples seeking to buy homes were shown, and where they were located. The conclusion was drawn that while the locus of actions was individual, the context is institutional.*

564. Phares, Donald. 1971. Racial Change and Housing Values: Transition in an Inner Suburb. **Social Science Quarterly** 52 (3): 560-73.

The major objective of this study is to examine empirically racial transition and the value of property in an inner suburbs of the St. Louis metropolitan area, University City, Missouri. "The main point to be derived from this analysis is that there is no unequivocal relationship between racial transition and the value of single family residential property."

0565. Piovia, Esther. 1976. Housing Conditions of Black Southern Homeowners.
       Urban League Review 2 (1): 30-36.

       Both the 1949 and 1968 Housing Acts mandate "a decent home and a suitable
       living environment for every American family." Asserting that these
       mandates have fallen short of fulfilling their promises, this article
       examines the housing conditions of black homeowners in the South. The topics
       examined are: where southern blacks live, extent of black home ownership in
       the south, age of housing, inadequacy and overcrowding, income and housing
       values, neighborhood conditions and services, black elderly home owners,
       housing and neighborhood conditions inside and outside the south, and a
       discussion of policy implications.

0566. Robinson, David, Jr. 1973. Homeownership for the Poor Jeopardized by
       Mortgage Problems. **Journal of Housing** 30 (6): 284-85.

       This article outlines the homeownership goals and problems of the poor and
       suggests some ways to meet these problems. It is suggested that a
       continuing financial counseling program be available to low-income
       families; that this program should include recertification assistance;
       that mortgage company policies consider increasing escrow accounts for
       contingencies and that mortgage companies and counseling agent cooperate
       with one another in helping the poor.

0567. Roistacher, Elizabeth. 1975. Housing and Homeownership. In: **Five
       Thousand American Families: Patterns of Economic Progress, Volume II.**
       James N. Morgan (ed.). Ann Arbor, Michigan: Institute for Social Research,
       University of Michigan. Chapter 1, pp. 1-40.

       The overall objective of this article (and others in this book) is to examine
       the factors determining the fortune of families, particularly the poor. In
       this chapter the author examines who owns homes, and analyzes the recent
       trends in the pattern of homeownership. In particular, the author is
       "concerned with the position of lower income and black households in the
       housing market."

0568. Roistacher, Elizabeth A., and John L. Goodman, Jr. 1976. Race and Home
       Ownership: Is Discrimination Disappearing? **Economic Inquiry** 14 (1):
       59-70.

       Racial differentials in home ownership rates are examined using data on
       households in the twenty-four largest metropolitan areas. Considerable
       recent reduction in racial discrimination is indicated, in contrast to the
       findings of a previous analysis of the St. Louis housing market. The
       results are maintained under a number of modifications of the model and
       estimation technique.*

0569. Schietinger, E. Frederick. 1964. Racial Succession and Changing Property
       Values in Residential Chicago. In: **Contributions to Urban Sociology.** E.
       W. Burgess, and D. J. Bogue (eds.). Chicago: University of Chicago Press.
       Pp. 86-99.

       The central purpose of this article is to determine relationships between stages of racial succession and price of residential property under conditions which prevailed on the South Side of Chicago during the 1940-1951 period. The implications of price movements are also discussed. "The most general conclusion of the study is that the 'effect of race on property values' varied with the type of property, community, and stage of succession."

570. Schnare, Ann B.   1976.   Racial and Ethnic Price Differentials in an Urban Housing Market.   **Urban Studies** 13 (2): 107-120.

This study: (1) examines the role of racial and ethnic preferences in an urban housing market;   (2) develops a simple, long-run equilibrium model of household behavior and location that examines the relationship between demographic externalities, housing market segregation, and housing prices; and (4) attempts to verify some of the implications of this model. "In particular, it examines the relationship in Boston between housing rents and values and neighborhood's concentration of blacks, Italian, Puerto Rican, and Chinese households."

571. Sengstock, Frank S., and Mary C. Sengstock. 1969. Home Ownership: A Goal for All Americans. **Journal of Urban Law** 46 (3): 317-602.

This entire issue of **Journal of Urban Law** is devoted to a detailed examination of home ownership as a goal for all Americans. Among the major topics discussed are current efforts to provide homeownership to low and moderate income families, low-income housing and tax exemptions, and welfare as an impediment to homeownership.

572. Stegman, Michael A. 1973. Low-Income Ownership: Exploitation and Opportunity. **Journal of Urban Law** 50 (2): 371-402.

Despite the fact that home ownership is a dream shared by all Americans, until 1968, no serious governmental efforts were made to extend home ownership opportunities to families in the low-income range. Indicating that as a result of the creation of Section 235 program in the 1968 Housing Act, home ownership by the low-income families was given a vigorous shot in the arm, this article attempts to determine whether the failures of Section 235 were "inherent in its concept or in its application, and whether subsidized home ownerships should be abandoned or be encouraged to continue." Some modifications in the program are recommended.

573. Sternlieb, George, and Robert W. Burchell. 1973. Those Who Remain: The New Minority Owners. In: Residential Abandonment: **The Tenement** Landlord Revisited. New Brunswick, N.J.: Center for Urban Policy Research, Rutgers University. Pp. 97-133.

This is a study of three areas of Newark, New Jersey. It shows that about 58 percent of black home owners for whom data were available were resident owners, as compared to only 10.4 percent of the white owners. The study also shows that more than 80 percent of black owned parcels, as compared to about 56 percent of whites, were in the hands of individuals. Corporate holdings made up about a quarter of white-owned parcels as opposed to under 10 percent of black-owned parcels. More than 9 percent of black-owned parcels, as against about 82 percent whites, had no commercial occupancy. Less than 1 in 10 of the black-owned properties had outside professional managers, compared to 4 out of 10 in the case of white-owned buildings. This study shows that as the housing market degenerates in Newark, the role of professional managers decline. The owner, however, is often locked into his property by the inability to refinance for improvements. Or, faced with the possibility that his property will be included in the urban renewal program, and thus he is not disposed to make long-term investments.

0574. Sternlieb, George, and Robert W. Lake. 1975. Aging Suburbs and Black Homeownership. Annals of the American Academy of Political and Social Science 422 (November): 105-17.

Restrictions on black homeownership in the past, and continued discriminatory practices, significantly contribute to limit blacks' suburbanization. The impacts of these restrictions on housing demands in the inner suburbs are analyzed. "The primary source of demand for these units in the inner suburbs appears to be the upwardly mobile black middle class seeking to leave the central city. While black suburbanization is increasing in some localities, however, black [purchase] demand appears to be below the level expected based on income. In suburban home purchase, the availability of equity associated with previous homeownership may be a better index of buying power than current income." The authors conclude that historical restrictions on black homeownership continues to limit black suburban home purchase. It is suggested that new public policy initiatives are needed to remedy the problem.

0575. Stewart, John K. 1983. Subsidy Housing: The Ownership Alternative. Journal of Property Management 48 (3): 48-51.

Due to the dismal performance of the Section 235 home ownership subsidy program, it is being debated if the proper place for low- and moderate-income families is the well subsidized rental housing. This essay provides some insight into the debate relative to transition from subsidized ownership to rental housing. In addition to discussing some successful projects (e.g., Marines Village, San Francisco) within the program, the author reviews the historical problems of Section 235 program that caused its virtual extinction.

0576. Struyk, Raymond J. 1975. Determinants of the Rate of Home Ownership of Black Relative to White Households. Journal of Urban Economics 2 (4): 291-306.

This paper investigates the reasons for the lower rate of home ownership of black households compared to white households in urban areas. A model of the demand for owner-occupancy by blacks relative to the demand by whites is formulated and econometrically estimated. The principal finding is that a percentage increase in the mean level of black household income produces a larger increase in the relative rate of blacks' home ownership than an equivalent reduction in the price of owner-occupied housing which they face. Although significant effects of within market discrimination against blacks as reflected in higher prices of owner-occupied housing to blacks are found, attempts to associate this price premium with measures of residential segregation were unsuccessful.*

0577. Terrell, Henry S. 1971. Wealth Accumulation of Black and White Families:

The Empirical Evidence. *Journal of Finance* 26 (2): 363-377.

The information on the relative wealth position of blacks is very scarce. This study, utilizing the 1967 Survey of Economic Opportunity (SEO) data, attempts to examine the size, composition, and concentration of net wealth accumulation of blacks as compared to whites. The major conclusion drawn from this study is that "the net wealth position of black families is substantially poorer than that of white families of similar characteristics."

578.   U.S. Commission on Civil Rights. 1971. Homeownership for Lower Income Families: A Report on the Racial and Ethnic Impact of the Section 235 Program. Washington, D.C.: GPO.

As a part of the 1968 National Housing Act, Congress established a program of homeownership for lower-income families. This program, called Section 235, is the first large scale attempt to bring both material and psychological benefits of homeownership within the reach of the less privileged families. Indicating that Section 235 has the potential value of enabling low-income families, especially minority families, become homeowners, this report investigates the "operation of the program in four metropolitan areas, Philadelphia, Little Rock, St. Louis, and Denver. It [also seeks] to determine the extent of participation by lower-income minority families and the program's impact in opening up housing opportunities for minority families outside areas of existing minority concentration."

579.   Van Houten, Beth. 1972. Cooperative Housing. *Journal of Housing* 29 (7): 335-8.

This article examines the cooperative housing services provided by the nonprofit Foundation for Cooperative Housing (FCH), whose objective is to make ownership available to families of all income ranges. This analysis concludes that cooperative housing is gaining growing acceptance in low and middle income neighborhoods. The FCH offers technical assistance for developing this type of home ownership.

580.   Wieand, Ken. 1975. Housing Price Determination in Urban Ghettos. *Urban Studies* 12: 193-204.

"This paper develops and presents some tentative empirical support for a model of housing price determination in urban ghettos."

581.   Winston, Ronald. 1979. The Challenge to Future Homeowners: Note of a Student Research Aide. *Black Scholar* 11 (2): 31-34.

This essay discusses the influence of discrimination on black home ownership in general, and black females in particular. It concludes that the area of "housing financing is opening more for women, with less chance of being denied a home loan. Many women, with an adequate credit background are in a better position today, than ever before, to become homeowners."

582.   Yinger, John. 1978. The Black-White Price Differential in Housing: Some Further Evidence. *Land Economics* 54 (2): 187-206.

Studies regarding black-white price differential in housing have not been conclusive. One reason has to do with the complexity of the problem. This article discusses theories about the black-white price differential in housing, and using data from St. Louis, presents and tests two econometric models for testing these theories. Overall, it tries to clarify several issues surrounding the estimation of the black-white price differential in housing by showing how "the various theories about this differential can be reflected in the econometric specification used to estimate it."

··◆◆◆◆◆◆◆◆◆◆··

7
MINORITY STATUS
AND HOUSING SUBSIDY

0583. Ahlbrandt, Roger S., Jr., Paul C. Brophy, and William Farkas. 1974.
Should the Number of Families in a Community Living Below the Poverty Line
Become the Criterion for Allocating Federal Funds for Housing? **Journal of
Housing** 31 (1): 11-14.

This article examines housing issues under current national debate.
Indicating that the traditional definitions of housing needs are
inadequate, it shows that the neighborhood environment has been excluded
from the analysis of housing needs and housing programs have been
inadequately defined. Programs are not funded to cope with the
neighborhood effects. The housing problem should not be conceptualized in
terms of substandard units. Rather, it must be seen as an economic problem
of ineffective consumer demand. This article highlights the limitations of
aggregate data, and stresses the importance of environment in determining
the quality of housing services. It indicates that states, counties, and
local governments are best suited to identify local housing problems.

0584. Ahlbrandt, Roger S., Jr. 1976. Governmentally assisted Housing:
Institutions and incentives. In: The **Delivery of Urban Services: Outcome
of Change.** Volume 10, Urban Affairs Annual Review. Elinor Ostrom (ed.).
Beverly Hills, California: Sage Publications. Pp. 15-47.

HUD's policy has emphasized private-sector participation, and has uprooted
the autonomy of local government in providing housing services for the poor.
Federal regulations usually contribute to higher costs, and often restrict
choice. Federally assisted programs generally attach the subsidy directly
to a particular physical unit, and the decision concerning the location is
made by the producer. The consumers have very little input. But new rules
may be implemented to give tenants greater voice over management decisions
and the transfer of ownership to the tenants. This article recommends that
the local government's approach must be directed toward preventing
neighborhood decline; and, declining neighborhoods must be targeted for
home improvement loan funds.

0585. Akre, M. Jan. 1974. Urban Homesteading: Once More Down the Yellow Brick

Road. **Environmental Affairs** 3 (3): 563-594.

This study presents the successes and failures of federal efforts at urban
renewal; and, in that context examines the homesteading program as an
effective solution to the national environmental problem of deteriorating
urban and low-income group housing. The last section in this study analyzes
the mechanics of homesteading ordinance as passed by the city councils of
Boston, Philadelphia, and Wilmington. The author concludes that if
properly executed, homesteading has a bright future provided that
politicians and planners recognize its strengths and try to minimize its
weaknesses.

0586. Anonymous. 1972. Housing Money that Goes to the People. **Business Week**
(2210): 51-52.

George Romney, the HUD Secretary, announces a $10 billion housing allowance
pilot project. The aim is to encourage builders and landlords to compete
for the low-income dollars and to avoid some of the shortcomings of the
existing housing subsidy programs, characterized by massive bureaucracy and
runaway building costs. The article presents the points of views of housing
experts, economists, landlords, builders, and politicians on the new
allowance scheme.

0587. Anonymous. 1972. Romney Hits Hard at Subsidy Scandals. **Business Week**
(2216): 28, 30.

This article examines the evidence for alleged wide-spread corruption
graft, kick backs using subsidy programs. And, how thousands of the
families these programs were designed to help have been victimized by
unscrupulous operators.

0588. Anonymous. 1972. The Bankruptcy of Subsidized Housing. **Business Week**
(2230): 42-45, 48.

According to this article, "in the past 30 years, the U.S. has spent some $11-
billion on housing subsidies, urban renewal, and related efforts to help the
cities. Yet, as Romney [HUD Secretary] says: 'The central cities are still
going downhill.' If nothing else, this means some better ways should be
found to spend the next $11-billion." The failure of federal government
housing subsidy program to solve the inner city housing problems are
discussed; potential new directions for federal housing subsidies for
assisting the low-income families are examined. It is concluded that new
programs are needed but "no one is sure what form they should take."

0589. Anonymous. 1972. Housing: How Ed Logue Does It. **Newsweek** 80 (19): 88, 91-
92.

This article describes the success of New York State's Urban Development
Corporation (UDC) and its master builder/director, Edward J. Logue. The
article concludes that as Logue sees it one out of every five housing units in
New York State is substandard, and about two million persons live in blighted
neighborhoods; and the only way to change all this is through a "massive
combination of Federal subsidies, statewide authority and private
investment." Political limitations to UDC's success are also enumerated.

0590. Anonymous. 1973. Procedural Due Process in Government-Subsidized
       Housing. **Harvard Law Review** 86 (5): 880-913.

       The Housing and Urban Development Act of 1968 established the Section 236
       program. And, Congress reaffirmed the national goal of "a decent home and
       living environment for every American family. The Congress also declared
       that in carrying out the programs "the fullest practicable utilization of
       the resource and capabilities of private enterprise" should be utilized.
       However, private enterprises receiving federal funds are subject to
       constitutional restrictions on the manner in which they can operate. Given
       the failure of the FHA to provide procedures to protect the constitutional
       interests of tenants, responsibility has fallen upon the courts to protect
       these interests by defining constitutional standards under which publicly
       subsidized landlords must operate. Problems arise because courts do not
       have continuing contacts with subsidized housing projects; the article
       suggests that landlords, tenants, and taxpayers would benefit if the FHA
       defined model procedures to govern applications, rent increases, evictions,
       and related matters of mutual interests. Because of its continuous contact
       with subsidized housing, the FHA is in a position to define all procedures
       that provide constitutionally required protection for the tenants.

0591. Atkinson, Reilly, William Hamilton, and Dowel Myers. 1980. Economic and
       Racial/Ethnic Concentration in the Housing Allowance Demand Experiment.
       Washington, D.C.: HUD, Office of Policy Development and Research.

       This is a study of the effect of Experimental Housing Allowance Programs on
       the residential location of households enrolled in the Housing Allowance
       Demand Experiment. The specific neighborhood characteristics considered
       are concentration of low-income and minority residents census tracts.
       Other factors considered are crime rates and a neighborhood hedonic index.
       The study concludes that the housing allowance did not induce households to
       choose neighborhoods with significantly different economic , racial, and
       ethnic compositions from those that households would have chosen without the
       program. It is found that the lack of any substantial effect from the
       allowance programs on racial composition is consistent with the general lack
       of any strong relationship between racial segregation and household income.
       Similarly, cross sectional analysis suggests that changes in housing
       expenditures engendered by the allowance cannot normally be expected to
       result in any substantial change in the low-income concentration of census
       tracts selected by the recipients.

0592. Austin, David M. 1974. The Design of a Housing Allowance: Lessons from
       Public Assistance. **Public Welfare** 32 (1): 24-34.

       In 1974 President Nixon endorsed the national program of housing allowances
       as an alternative to the existing low-income housing subsidy programs with
       priority given to the elderly. The endorsement was made because of the
       alleged charges that the current housing programs were inefficient,
       ineffective, and not equitable--that is, they had failed to meet the needs of
       families in the most desperate housing conditions, and the failure of the
       programs to prevent housing deterioration and abandonment in large cities.
       This study is an examination of the U.S. experience with the administration

public assistance, with special emphasis on the experience with shelter component policy. The study concludes that "the proposal for housing allowances offers an opportunity for a fresh approach to the closely linked problems of poverty and bad housing, problems that are also linked to institutionalized patterns of discrimination, on one hand, and to the steady deterioration of central city neighborhoods on the other."

0593. Barnett, C. Lance. 1979. Expected and Actual Effects of Housing Allowances on Housing Prices. **Journal of American Real Estate and Urban Economics Review** 7 (3): 277-297.

Most analysts and policy makers expected full scale housing allowance programs to substantially disturb local housing markets, causing housing prices to increase sharply. This paper reviews conjectures about expected price effects, summarizes evidence from the Housing Assistance Supply Experiment, and explains why the program did not engender the expected price inflation.*

0594. Beckham, Robert. 1973. The Experimental Housing Allowance Program. **Journal of Housing** 30 (1): 12-17.

A provision of the 1970 Housing and Urban Development Act (Section 501) stated the Secretary of the Department of Housing and Urban Development "shall undertake on an experimental basis a program to demonstrate the feasibility of providing families with low-income with housing allowances to assist them in obtaining rental housing of their choice in existing standard housing." In this study, the author attempts to describe the experimental housing allowance program from which HUD hoped to discover whether it was desirable to add a new element to the range of housing subsidy available to the low-income groups, or to simply adjust the existing programs.

0595. Berry, Mary F. 1974. Homesteading: New Prescription for Urban Ills. **HUD Challenge** 5 (1): 2-5.

By the idea of homesteading it is meant to give an abandoned, foreclosed house to a homesteader to fix it up to municipal code standards and live in it for some specified period of time. Homesteader will be exempt from real estate taxes, and a low interest loan would be made available to a poor family to pay for the rehabilitation costs. Based on homesteading data from Wilmington (Delaware), Baltimore (Maryland), and Philadelphia (Pennsylvania) the article concludes that homesteading is doomed to failure if it is seen just as a way to transfer the burden of abandonment and foreclosure from government to homesteader. The author also indicates that the project will also fail if it continues to be implemented on a large scale basis as seen in some cities. It is suggested that the government should accept the major responsibility of rehabilitating the declining neighborhoods and create new and viable communities in former slums. This may cost money, but its long-term public benefits will outweigh the costs.

0596. Boyer, Brian D. 1973. The $70 Billion Slum. In: **Cities Destroyed for Cash: The FHA Scandal at HUD.** Chicago: Follett. Pp. 3-23.

This study attempts to show that the FHA scandal was a deliberate program of urban ruin for profit, under the cover of a government housing law. The author contends that the general pattern and evidence in almost every large city pointed to a widespread conspiracy between the real estate and the mortgage interests, with the help/approval of the government officials. The problem of HUD's ownership of about 390,000 housing units was compounded by the decision to end FHA mortgages for the inner city. By September 1972 HUD's offices in New York, Chicago, Detroit, and Los Angeles had again red-lined the core cities. The end of subsidized housing in 1973 effectively ended the FHA's resale of its repossessed units. Home owners could not afford to resell their houses, and had to abandon them if they wanted to move, which added units to the FHA inventory.

0597.   Bratt, Rachel G. 1983. The Housing Payment Program: Its Possible Effects on Minorities, Poor. Journal of Housing 40 (4): 108-110.

Should a housing policy be aimed at producing subsidized housing or provide the lower-income families with more buying power to enable them to compete better in the private market? This is a question that has been debated for several years. In this article the author examines this question and critiques the President's Commission's Housing Payments Program (HPP) findings. The author concludes that: "first, a voucher or housing payment could be a useful component of a housing policy if it is accompanied by appropriate supports, and if it includes nonexclusionary eligibility criteria. Second, this type of subsidy could be important as one tool among an array of housing programs, with each program tailored to specific needs of particular housing markets. Finally, there is a continued need in this country for employment and income assistance programs that guarantee each family a minimum but adequate income." According to Bratt, a housing policy alone may provide housing. But, a jobs/income/housing policy would provide the low-income families with the money to pay for housing.

0598.   Breckenfeld, Gurney. 1972. Housing Subsidies are a Grand Delusion. Fortune 96 (February): 136-139, 163-164, 166, 171.

The 235 and 236 housing subsidy programs, aimed at ameliorating the housing conditions of the poor, have been self defeating. Runaway costs, and unwieldy federal machinery, patched over legislation and various other abuses plague the program. The author maintains that the current subsidy system has played a great role in the rise of a permanently dependent, resentful, and rebellious group of housing occupants. He recommends that the U.S. Congress should scrap the subsidy program, change tax laws that subsidize the misuse of land, and attack the runaway building costs that makes subsidies seem necessary. Breckenfeld favors housing allowance and any guaranteed annual income program over the existing subsidy program. However, he indicates that no reform or program is likely to reach the gritty problem that underlies the present trouble with housing subsidies: inherited poverty and dependency.

0599.   Breckenfeld, Gurney. 1983. "Robinhood" Subsidies: A Dubious New Fad. Fortune 107 (6):148-51.

As the Reagan Administration shuts the spigot on most federal housing subsidies, a scramble is on for other ways to produce "affordable" homes for low- and moderate-income families. One provocative new idea is for localities to force builders to erect a quota of cut-price homes or contribute to their construction nearby. The disappointing results of this attempt to substitute private for public subsidy—or, more often, to blend the two—show that smarter techniques are needed.*

0600. Carlson, James E. 1973. Our National Housing Goal: Where Do They Stand Now? Architectural Record 153 (5): 62.

The 1968 Housing and Urban Development Act set the goal of building 26-million housing units, six million of which were expected to be subsidized units for low-income families. This meant to acknowledge the fact that the free market had to be supplemented by public aid. The author asserts that in terms of total units the tremendous number of housing starts in the past few years has put the nation above the trend needed to achieve the 26-million goal by 1978. This edge on the trend line gave the Administration impetus to suspend the public subsidy program. In the final section of this article, the question of attaining versus sustaining is dealt with. Carlson asks: "Will the spirit of the 1968 Housing Act really be achieved by 1978?" He concludes that "At this point there's room for doubt."

0601. Carlton, Dennis W., and Joseph Ferreira, Jr. 1975. The Market Effects of Housing Allowance Payment Formulas. Cambridge, Mass.: Joint Center of Urban Studies of the Massachusetts Institute of Technology and Harvard University. Working Paper No. 32. 81 pp.

Improving the housing conditions of the low-income groups is possible, but it is expensive. The impact of an average $20 allowance per household per month on increases in rents are assessed. It is concluded that price increases in the lower-quality housing submarkets will be accompanied by increases in housing consumption, because higher prices are needed to maintain the units at a higher quality level.

0602. Carlton, Dennis W., and Joseph Ferreira, Jr. 1977. Selecting Subsidy Strategies for Housing Allowance Programs. Journal of Urban Economics 4 (2): 221-247.

The market effects of alternative housing payment formulas are analyzed and compared for a metropolitan housing market using measures of efficiency and distributional equity. The effects of "earmarking" allowance payments are considered. Estimated market effects are based on a model of housing market behavior over a 10-year period. The results differ significantly from what one might anticipate based on demand analyses of individual behavior. "Housing gap" formulas perform better than percent-of-rent formulas. Certain characteristics of the housing market together with particular income redistribution effects of the allowances appear to explain the market behavior.*

0603. Casey, Timothy J., and Henry A. Freedman. 1979. The Case Against Direct Vendor Payment. Public Welfare 37 (1): 37-40.

There are two schools of thought regarding the method of paying the rent for AFDC clients: (1) payment to the recipient; (b) direct vendor payments to the landlord. In this article the authors discuss the disadvantages of a direct vendor payment. They argue that direct vendor payments would diminish

recipient freedom and will lower the quality of housing available to
recipients. And, "the freedom to control one's benefit is important
because of its tremendous pragmatic value, nowhere better exemplified than
in the housing area."

0604.   Conyers, John, Jr. 1976. The Real Problem is Poverty. **Nation** 222 (3):
83-85.

In the 1930s the housing programs allowed home buyers to write mortgage
interests off their income taxes. The mortgage interest write off from
income taxes along with the capital gains arrangement, resulted in a $9
billion annual federal subsidy by 1972. By 1971 Congress was providing
about $2.5 billion in housing subsidies for low-income families; however,
a disproportionately small number of housing units were produced for the sum
paid. The government failed to realize that home ownership was not an
economically sound program for low-income groups for they cannot easily
afford the necessary maintenance. It is concluded that only a system of
full employment at equitable wages can provide home ownership for low-income
families.

0605.   Courter, Eileen M. 1979. Michigan Favors Direct Vendor Payments. **Public
Welfare** 37 (1): 31-35.

In this article the author presents the advantages and disadvantages of
paying the rent for AFDC clients directly to the landlord. Courter points
out that landlords in Michigan have been adamant about receiving direct
payments from social services if they were to continue renting to AFDC
recipients. Existing government policy favors payments to be made to the
recipients. But, Department of Social Services (DSS) in Michigan, while
pushing for changes in federal policy, has attempted to work with landlords
as much as possible within the existing law. The Michigan's DDS support for
changes in federal law governing protective and vendor payments based on the
belief that such change will encourage more landlords to consider renting to
AFDC recipients, thus broadening the housing options available to such
clients.

0606.   Cozzens, William Oxford. 1976. **The Formation and Implementation of
Federal Urban Policy: The Department of Housing and Urban Development and
the Project Selection Criteria for Subsidized Housing.** Unpublished Ph.D.
Dissertation. University of Pennsylvania. 440 pp.

In this dissertation the author seeks to explain the policy responses of HUD
in the early 1970s to the question of subsidized housing location and
residential segregation in metropolitan areas. To be more specific, this
research examines the development and implementation of HUD's Project
Selection Criteria (PSC) for subsidized housing. The published PSC and
their earlier drafts are used as indicator of policy development outcome.
The examination of the project processing files for all Section 236 and low-
rent public housing applications processed between Spring 1971 and Fall 1974
in Philadelphia Area Office of HUD constitutes data regarding
implementation outcomes. Findings indicate that generally, at the
Philadelphia Area Office of HUD, "the PSC were not implemented as intended.
A very few applications in Philadelphia County were rejected because of poor
ratings on Criterion 2, Minority Housing Opportunities. Otherwise, the PSC

were not used to make decisions on project applications. The priority ranking system was ignored completely. For the most part, only those projects that had already been approved received PSC rating. For most projects, PSC became, in effect, a pro forma part of the application process." Factors limiting the rigorous implementation of PSC are discussed in details. It is concluded that the case of HUD and the PSC illustrate many problems facing large public organizations.

0607.   Dean, Andrea O. 1977. Evaluation: A Subsidized Housing Development Designed to Turn Inward upon Itself. AIA Journal 66 (2): 20-25.

The Charlesview housing project for low- and moderate-income families is located in Allston, Massachusetts. Despite of being surrounded by streets with heavy traffics, industrial and commercial buildings, Harvard stadium and playing fields, the study shows that the residents have formed a feeling of community spirit. This is attributed to the architecture design of the development that lends itself to an inward orientation. Designer comments, factors affecting the construction of the development, and residents views on their life style are discussed. It is concluded that only few residents felt the stigma of living in a subsidized housing.

0608.   Demkovich, Linda E. 1975. Housing Report/Administration Weighing Plans for Low Income Allowances. National Journal Reports 7 (7): 243-248.

An experimental program to test the policy of giving low income families monthly cash grants so that they can buy or rent housing of their own choice is well underway, and early returns have been described as satisfactory by officials in the HUD Department's Office of Policy Development and Research. Soon the Administration will have to decide whether to begin phasing in the housing allowance program on a permanent basis. The verdict is likely to be no, or at best on a limited, scaled down basis.*

0609.   DeSalvo, Joseph S. 1976. Housing Subsidies: Do We Know What We Are Doing? Policy Analysis 2 (1): 39-60.

Under what conditions should the government subsidize housing? Do current subsidy programs meet these criteria? Is there a better way of subsidizing housing? In examining these questions the author focuses on the merit-good rationale for government intervention interpreted in terms of consumption externalities, discusses a theory of transfers incorporating this merit-good idea, and surveys relevant theoretical and empirical work. After comparing the efficacy of cash vs. in-kind subsidies, he suggests a new policy alternative, rent certificates: if housing is a merit-good, it should be subsidized via rent certificates; if not, then it should not be specifically subsidized, and whatever transfers are justified should be in cash. Which case fits the U.S. today is an empirical question yet to be answered.*

0610.   Dolbeare, Cushing N. 1974. Nixon's Nonprogram for Housing. Dissent 21 (1): 12-14.

President Nixon suspended all federal housing subsidy programs in 1973. He called for reliance on the private sector for housing construction, and suggested housing allowances for low-income families. Dolbeare contends that an income solution, even a complete equality in income, will not necessarily solve the housing problem, because the housing provided by the private sector is beyond the economic reach of about 80 percent of American families. The author provides statistics in favor of the argument that only a fraction of housing subsidies in fact do go to the low-income families. If the nation is to achieve the 1968 goal adopted by the Congress calling for the production of 26 million new (or rehabilitated) housing units in ten years, about 25 percent of all new housing units should be affordable by households with an annual income less than $4,000.

0611. Downs, Anthony. 1972. Are Subsidies the Best Answer for Housing Low and Moderate Income Households? **Urban Lawyer** 4 3): 405-416.

In this article the author examines the issues relative to housing subsidy program, including the extent of direct housing subsidies, the nature and need for direct housing subsidies, the nation's unwillingness to meet this need fully, possible objectives of housing subsidies, and the need for a mixture of different subsidy programs. The author concludes that housing "subsidies are the only way to help low and moderate income households who live in poor quality housing, or pay abnormally high fractions of their income for housing, to upgrade their housing to the standards we define as 'minimal' in quality and 'normal' in cost as a fraction of income." The author's main contention regarding the nation's unwillingness to meet the need fully is epitomized in the statement that: "In short, we do not want to provide equality of opportunity to our fellow citizens if that requires us to share our every day lives with them. Apparently, we believe that would be pushing the concept of 'human brotherhood' too far. Until we alter that attitude, I must agree with that native American philosopher, Pogo, that, concerning the ultimate issue of housing for the urban poor, 'we have met the enemy, and he is us.'"

0612. Ellickson, Robert. 1967. Government Housing Assistance to the Poor. **Yale Law Review** 76 (3): 508-544.

The low-income families have a special claim to government housing assistance. But the critiques have argued that some thirty years of federal intervention in the housing market has not been a bonanza for the poor. In this paper, the author considers four approaches that are part of the federal housing program: The Public Housing Program, Section 221 (d)(3) Below Market Interest Rate (BMIR) mortgages, the Widnall "leased units" plan, and Rent Supplements. Alternative criteria for low-income housing assistance are discussed. Regarding the public housing program, the author concludes that it suffers from "archaic system for project financing and sponsorship. At present it is both a very expensive and slow means of increasing the housing stock and a contributor to residential segregation." The capacity to integrate neighborhoods is regarded as the only positive aspect of the Widnall Plan. Relative to Section 221(d)(3) BMIR program, it is believed that it could be the most efficient way of increasing housing production, promote integration, and prevent governmental interference in the lives of its tenants. According to Ellickson, "the critical flaw of this program is that it fails to provide housing for the poor, and to correlate subsidy with need." As to the rent supplements program, the author believes it is the best of the four programs, for it could be the best tool for integrating neighborhoods, and it can be an excellent means "for getting the government out of the business of managing low-cost housing projects."

0613. Feldman, Saul J. 1977. Rescuing Subsidized Housing Projects. **Real Estate Review** 7 (1): 44-47.

The area that stands out as being most in serious trouble in housing industry is usually that of federally subsidized housing developments. That is, the units insured under Section 221(d)(3), Section 236, or one of the other subsidized programs under the National Housing Act. This article discusses different approaches for rescuing subsidized housing projects, including direct assistance from lenders, investors, and limited partners, the federally insured operating loss loan, and transfer of assets to the general contractor.

0614. Franklin, Herbert M. 1973. Land Use and Litigation. **Urban Land** 32 (5): 3-8.

This study examines some recent court decisions in the housing area which may shed light on the administration's decision to terminate federal subsidies for low-income housing construction. The author points out that these decisions may also prove instructive for state authorities who may be required to assume the burden of decision making if there was to be public subsidy of housing construction for the low-income families in the U.S. The author shows how the federal courts have construed federal civil rights laws and constitutional guarantee of equal protection of the law to prohibit federal housing programs from reinforcing residential racial concentration; and, how state courts are beginning to interpret state land use control laws in a way that will place curbs on the rights of a locality to exclude unwanted groups.

0615. Fried, Joseph P. 1973. Housing Allowances: The Latest Panacea. **Nation** 216 (10): 304-308.

A new "panacea is abroad in the land. It is the 'housing allowance' and it is being trumpeted as the long sought answer to the nation's slum-housing problem." The "housing allowance" concept is described; and advantages of the system are enumerated. The author cautions, however, that the allowance system will be threatened by the same abuses and failures that have afflicted other subsidized programs such as 1937 public housing, 1949 urban renewal, 1965 rent supplements, 1966 model cities, and 1968 mortgage-interest subsidies. The author indicates that the proposed program offers a remedy to "stigma-bearing" housing projects, but many unknowns cloaking a housing allowance approach block full fledge support. The Kansas City experience with housing allowance experiment is reported on.

0616. Frieden, Bernard J. 1980. Housing Allowances: An Experiment that Worked. **Public Interest** (59): 15-35.

The Department of Housing and Urban Development's experimental housing allowance program, one of the largest social experiments ever undertaken by the government that began with a great fanfare in 1973 ended quietly in 1980. The housing allowance experiment was designed as another approach to deal with the problem of improving the housing conditions of low-income families. The article examines the housing allowance program and indicates that six years later there is no clear-cut answer to all the questions this experiment purported to investigate. The experiment produced unexpected results that challenged the designers' assumptions and the traditional conception of low-income housing problems. It revealed a sharp conflict between the government's priorities and those of the poor families. The article concludes that at a minimum the housing allowance project "calls into question those housing goals that are based mainly on the weight of tradition or on the organizational mission of an established federal agency." It provided the rare opportunity to recognize the changing needs of the beneficiaries.

0617.   Fuerst, J. S. 1977. Subsidized Housing: Amateurs Need Not Apply. Journal of Property Management 42 (5): 261-64.

This article details the factors that are important in producing successful housing developments for low and moderate income families. The study is based on 33 housing projects in the Chicago area, which show that developments can become successful provided that a number of complex and interrelated conditions are met. According to Fuerst, the strongest factors that determine success or failure are location, design, management, size, number of rooms per unit, number of children per project, type of tenants selected, and local tax assessments.

0618.   Gainer, William. 1983. Subsidized Housing Production: Profiting From Past Errors. Journal of Housing 40 (3): 77-79.

This article examines various past problems with different subsidy programs, and provides some lessons for policy makers. According to Gainer, any new program will have some unanticipated consequences, but careful design should screen-out potential problems and eliminate the need to repeat errors.

0619.   Gleeson, Michael E. 1980. Budgeting for Federal Housing Programs: A Problem and What to Do About It. Public Administration Review 40 (4): 321-330.

This article deals with the question whether the federal government has budgeted too much, too little, or about the right amount to meet contractual commitments for Section 8--the nation's largest housing construction subsidy program. In this paper, the author argues that the authorized budget is not sufficient to meet the full terms of commitments. He analyzes alternative means of addressing the problem. The study concludes with a discussion of ways to prevent the problem from arising in the future.

0620.   Goedert, Jeanne E. 1979. Earmarking Housing Allowances: The Trade-Off Between Housing Consumption and Program Participation. Washington,D.C.: Urban Institute. 117 pp.

This report examines the impact of housing requirements on the housing consumption choices of housing allowance recipients. It also explores the effect of housing requirements on the ability of enrollees to qualify as recipients and the implication of trade-off between housing requirements and number and types of participants for the aggregate consumption change induced by housing allowances. This report is based on the two years of program data from the completed Experimental Allowance Program Demand Experiment. Results imply that a housing program with specific physical and occupancy standards provides a more effective and cost-efficient means of increasing the aggregate level of housing consumption than a program with minimum rent requirements or a program of unconstrained grants. Housing authorities face the difficult task of developing a set of housing requirements that balance the trade- off between upgrading the quality of housing consumption and increasing allowance participation among low-income, minority, and large households. This study also suggests that there are limits on the extent to which allowance programs can upgrade the housing conditions of those living in seriously deficient units.

0621.   Golde, Madeleine. 1980. Federal Programs Provide Housing Assistance for Battered Women. **Journal of Housing** 37 (8): 443-446.

According to this article a 1976 national survey on wife beating showed that about 1.8 million wives are beaten by their husbands each year and the number is growing. Thus, the shelter needs of battered women are receiving increasing attention by some local officials for the use of housing and community development funds. The article describes the magnitude of the problem, and the attempts by many battered women's groups who have approached local public housing authorities requesting priority status in securing Section 8 certificates. The article elaborates on Federal response to the housing needs of this group, and points out that community development and housing resources exist to help battered women, but local administrators must be willing to use them.

0622.   Halperin, Jerome Y., and Michael J. Brenner. 1976. Opportunities Under the New Section 8 Housing Program. **Real Estate Review** 6 (1): 67-71.

The Section 8 Housing Program of the 1974 Housing and Community Development Act was authorized to generate privately financed and constructed housing. The program was designed to subsidize both new and rehabilitated housing units. The main thrust of the Section 8 Program, unlike other subsidy programs, is that the subsidy goes to the tenant rather than to the agency financing the project. This article examines Section 8 Program and highlights the problems for the builder-developer in development, processing, financing and management. It also examines the opportunities in an equity syndication of a newly constructed project. The study concludes that the overall success of the program is dependent upon several factors. The use of innovative financing techniques, coupled with equity syndication, and the allocation of Section 8 funds to the filed office could provide a significant "carrot" to encourage housing development and new construction starts.

0623.   Hartman, Chester. 1975. Good Homes. **Working Papers for a New Society** 3 (1): 18-27.

"The administration's housing allowance program, like past federal housing programs, will fail in its goal 'to make a decent housing available for all low income families.' A different sort of housing allowance could do the job, and not just for the poor."

0624.   Hartman, Chester. 1983. Housing Allowances: A Critical Look. **Journal of**

Urban Affairs 5 (1): 41-55.

The Reagan Administration would like to introduce housing allowances as the federal government's principal low-income housing program. The results of HUD's 10-year Experimental Housing Allowance Program suggest important structural limitation to this approach. Only a small portion of the housing allowance is spent on housing. An allowance is likely to least serve those who most need housing assistance. The stock of vacant units is inadequate to meet the demands of voucher recipients. Landlords are not likely to repair substandard units to meet this limited added buying power. And housing market discrimination inhibits mobility that might capture existing standard units. Additional evidence from the Section 8 existing housing and public assistance programs suggest the limitations of the housing allowance approach. The true motivation for introducing housing allowances would appear to be a desire to withdraw the federal government from its traditional role as housing provider.*

0625.   Hartman, Chester, and Dennis Keating. 1974. The Housing Allowance Delusion. Social Policy 4 (4): 31-37.

As presently conceived, the housing allowances are bound to fail those who need help in getting a decent place to live, just as they are bound to bring windfall profits to those who control the housing market. Further, the housing allowance approach does not touch the larger issue of eradicating slum neighborhoods and environments and municipal services. Until we are willing to deal with the question of how and by whom housing resources—in particular, land and mortgage money—are controlled; until we face the conflict between the profit instincts of those who control the housing market and the human right to live decently; until we are willing to pay the necessary costs to make up for the decades of neglect of our existing housing stock and our failure to build a sufficient number [of] units for low- and moderate income households, we will not even come close to meeting the national goal (first promulgated by Congress in 1949 and reiterated in 1968) of "a decent home and suitable living environment for every American family."*

0626.   Havemann, J., and Rochelle Stanfield. 1977. Housing a Part of Welfare: An Agency Battles for Its Turf. National Journal 9 (31):1190-1192.

HUD does not like Carter Administration's proposed welfare reform package. HUD fears that the package could threaten existing housing policy and at the same time cut heavy into HUD's budget. HUD's officials also feel that they have been left out of the debate. However, the authors conclude that "as Carter said in Yazoo City, the Administration will not 'do away with the housing subsidy program,' but he indicated he will look carefully at its costs and the extent of its benefits. The substantive debate that HUD says is missing from the current furor is bound to come soon."

0627.   Herbers, John. 1974. Subsidized Housing. In: Suburbia in Transition. Louis H. Masotti and Jeffrey K. Hadden (eds.). New York: New Viewpoints. Pp. 125-128.

Investors and builders in the subsidized housing field are increasingly sponsoring projects in the suburbs and avoid the troubled inner cities.

There are two basic view points on the site selection for subsidized housing construction: (1) that the construction of subsidized suburban housing may at last provide an escape to stable neighborhoods and job opportunities for families with marginal means who have been confined to the decaying areas of center cities for too long; (2) Mayors and other urban officials express alarm at the subsidized suburban housing trend, and point out that they are left with holding of vast areas of cleared land for housing that may never be built. This article discusses pros and cons regarding the suburban trend and site selection for subsidized housing.

0628.   HUD (Department of Housing and Urban Development). 1975. Eight Facts About Section 8: A Better Way to Aid Lower Income Families in Obtaining Standard Housing from the Existing Housing Stock. **HUD Challenge** 6 (7): 28-29.

The Section 8 housing program , established by the Housing and Community Development Act in 1974, is the federal government's major operating program for helping lower income families in securing decent, safe, and sanitary housing. This program emphasizes the competitive forces of the private market while leaving to the public housing agency responsibility for providing lower income families with necessary financial and other assistance. Eight facts concerning this program, including the scope of Section 8 and the landlord's role, are described.

0629.   HUD (Jacksonville, Florida Office). 1975. **Experimental Housing Allowance Program of the Department of Housing and Urban Development, Jacksonville, Florida.** Jacksonville, Florida: HUD. 125 pp.

The Housing Allowance Program provides direct cash payments to low income families to obtain adequate housing through the general (private) housing market. This report provides a description of the experimental site, successes, and impact of the Jacksonville, Florida, Experimental Housing Allowance Program. Findings indicate that some families could operate very effectively in the private housing market, despite their low-income and minority group membership. However, many families needed extensive support and guidance in dealing with the private market. This report recommends increased anonymity in the Housing Allowance Program in order to reduce discrimination against minorities and low-income families by sellers and renters.

0630.   Jacobs, Scott. 1973. The Housing Allowance Program in Kansas City Turns into a Notable Failure. **Planning** 39 (9): 10-13.

The Environmental Research and Development Foundation Survey in Kansas City reveals that the Kansas City Model Cities housing allowance program has had a "notable failure" rate of 32 percent. After a 15-month period, the major problems encountered by the recipients were studied. They included: Rents paid late; never notified anyone of moving; left area; kicked out for obvious fraud; encountered financial problems; encountered moving problems; recipient damaged property; had problems with landlords; and, rented substandard housing. It is believed that low-income families have multiple problems and that housing allowance program alone is not the answer, suggesting that housing allowance must be part of a larger package for assisting lower income families.

0631. Kaplan, Edward H.   1985.   Tenant Assignments: How PHAs Fill Their Units.
Journal of Housing 42 (1): 13-20.

At the heart of public housing management and operation lies the question:
What is the method used and which household is the most eligible household to
occupy the next available unit.   In this article, Kaplan examines the
procedures used in selecting public housing occupants.

0632. Khadduri, Jill, Katharine Lyall, and Raymond Struyk.   1978.   Welfare
Reform and Housing Assistance: A National Policy Debate.   AIP Journal   44
(1): 2-12.

Early in the Carter administration the Department of Health, Education, and
Welfare was directed to develop a welfare reform plan that would reduce
inequities in treatment among individuals, provide an incentive to work, and
entail no net additional cost to the federal budget beyond sums spent for
existing programs.   One suggestion to provide funding was to reduce
expenditures on current housing programs and use these resources to help
support a general program of cash transfers to poor families.   This article
argues that exclusive reliance on cash transfers to provide decent housing
for the poor would be both unsuccessful and inefficient.*

0633. Khadduri, Jill, and Raymond J. Struyk.   1982.   Housing Voucher for the
Poor.   Journal of Policy Analysis and Management 1 (2); 196-208.

Can the nation's social programs survive the push toward leaner
appropriations, a greater use of the market, and a narrower definition of the
needy? A program to provide housing assistance for the poor is proposed that
fills all these requirements.   Housing vouchers are found to be cheaper than
other housing programs and more satisfactory for participants.   Moreover,
the political climate augers well for the new approach.*

0634. Kleinman, Alan H.   1978.   Tenants' Rights in Federally-Subsidized Housing
Acquired by HUD.   Urban Lawyer 110 (2); 289-317.

Thousands of tenants currently are subject to a HUD disposition policy for
acquired subsidized projects which attempts to achieve the highest possible
financial return by sale of the projects.   After a detail examination of the
history and operation of the subsidized rental housing, this article argues
that HUD's present disposition policy for acquired projects, aimed at
achieving the highest financial return, misconstrues the congressional
mandate contained in the housing legislation.   The author contends that the
Congress has not granted HUD unlimited discretionary power in project
disposition, because it is HUD's obligation to provide decent and low-cost
housing for the needy.   From his analyses and the applicability of the due
process clause to the property disposition scheme, the author concludes that
tenants should be "afforded a right to be heard before HUD makes property
disposition decisions."

0635. Lazin, Frederick A.   1976.   Federal Low Income Housing Assistance Programs
and Racial Segregation: Leased Public Housing.   Public Policy 24 (3): 337-
360.

Section 23 of the Housing and Urban Development Act of 1965 authorized the Federal Public Housing Authority to make funds available to local housing authorities to lease privately owned units for 1-3 years. In doing this, advocates of Section 23 expected to avoid many drawbacks of regular public housing program. The first part of this article presents a case study of the local operation of a Section 23 program. The second part examines the provisions of the legislation that contributed to furthering segregation. Despite its advantages, it is indicated that Section 23 had a propensity to further racial segregation. The study attempts to explain how Section 23 enabled and facilitated housing authorities to pursue policies of segregating racial minorities. In the third part, the federal role in the administration of the program is discussed. In the concluding part the author makes recommendations on how new federal housing programs might break the cycle of support for policies of racial segregation.

0636.   Lewis, Cynthia D. 1972. Tenant Selection in Federal-Subsidized Housing. Journal of Property Management 37 (3): 102-105.

This article describes tenant eligibility for federally subsidized housing. This includes a review of recent judicial decisions in the area of tenant assisted housing. Conflicts between policies of HUD's Office of Equal Opportunity, HUD's new Office of Housing Management, and private sponsors are examined. Two specific cases are reviewed to illustrate placement of government restrictions on private owners of federally subsidized housing. It Examines the dilemma facing private owners of subsidized housing.

0637.   Lowry, Ira S. 1974. The Housing Assistance Supply Experiment: Tensions in Design and Implementation. Santa Monica, California: Rand Corporation. 6 pp.

According to Lowry, the Housing Assistance Supply Experiment is designed to assess the effects of a full-scale housing allowance program on the housing market. This paper discusses several unusual features of the program, and concludes that this experiment should provide housing researchers with data far-better than any other existing data file.

0638.   MacMillan, Jean. 1980. Mobility in the Housing Allowance Demand Experiment. Cambridge, Mass.: Abt Associates, Inc.

This is one in a series of technical reports on the results of programs tested in the Housing Allowance Demand Experiment. It analyzes residential mobility of households enrolled in the experiment. Mobility process is divided into four stages: (1) becoming dissatisfied with current housing or neighborhood; (2) planning to move; (3) searching for new housing, and (4) actually moving. The report is based on data from experiments conducted in Pittsburgh, Pennsylvania, and Phoenix, Arizona. Results show that, even without housing allowance, most low- income renters would move over the course of several years; but a substantial number would not move for a long time. Allowance offers did lead to increased mobility; some groups were less likely to move; minority households in Pittsburgh were less likely to remain in the program after they moved than those in Phoenix, Arizona. This study also shows that households in crowded dwellings lacking basic facilities were more likely to move.

0639. Mandelker, Daniel R. 1973. **Housing Subsidies in the United States and England.** New York: Bobbs-Merrill. 246 pp.

Housing subsidy programs are being reviewed both in the United States and England. Significant legislative reforms could be in the making. In this book, the author examines the "debate over the future of housing subsidies, with a special emphasis on subsidized housing that is both publicly owned and rented and which serves the lowest income groups" in the population. From his analyses, the author concludes that no one alternative will solve all the problems, or satisfy all of the social and economic interests involved in housing subsidy programs.

0640. Marcuse, Peter. 1969. Comparative Analysis of Federally Aided Low- and Moderate-Income Housing Programs. **Journal of Housing** 26 (10): 536-539.

In this article Marcuse presents, in a chart form, a comparative analysis of federally subsidized low- and moderate income housing programs.

0641. Marr, John A. 1979. Financing Subsidized Housing with Municipal Bonds. **Real Estate Review** 9 (2): 23-30.

The 1974 Housing Act permitted the issuance of tax-exempt municipal bonds to finance housing projects that have Section 8 subsidy from HUD, and also allowed a private developer to use this tax-exempt financing method for specific projects. This article explains how an underwriter finances a Section 8 housing project with municipal bonds; it also describes the rationale for the safeguard that bond buyers require, and notes the advantages that this method of financing has for real estate developers.

0642. Mayo, Stephen. 1977. **Housing Expenditures and Quality. Part 1: Report on Housing Expenditures Under a Percent Rent Housing Allowance. Housing Allowance Demand Experiment.** Cambridge, Mass.: Abt Associates, Inc. 196 pp.

One type of housing allowance payment formula tested in the Housing Allowance Demand Experiment is a percent rent subsidy. Under this experiment, households receive a rebate equal to a certain proportion of their monthly rent. This report is based on a study of 764 (426 receiving allowances and 338 controls) households in Pittsburgh, Pennsylvania, and 657 households (342 receiving allowances and 315 controls) in Phoenix, Arizona. These households are divided into five groups, each receiving 20, 30, 40, 50, or 60 percent of their monthly rent as subsidy. Amount of subsidies paid was tied to the household's own contribution. Findings based on the first year data indicate that: (1) rent subsidies significantly increased housing consumption; (2) the relative degree of this consumption was greater in Phoenix than in Pittsburgh; (3) many households did not perceive rent subsidies as permanent, and thus, they were very slow to respond to subsidy payments; and (4) minority households adjusted their housing more readily than the non-minority families. As a whole, it is concluded that the program does have a beneficial long-term effect.

0643. McFarland, M. Carter. 1972. The Rising Tide of Housing Allowances. **AIA Journal** 58 (4): 26-28.

Recent housing programs for low and moderate income families have encountered increasing social and financial difficulties. Experimentation is now taking place with a plan which would provide federal monthly cash payment subsidies to families directly for the rental or purchase of decent housing units on the private market. It is expedient that the architect know what's good and bad about the concept which is gaining rapid acceptance.*

0644.   Meyer, Mary Helen. 1980. HUD-Assisted Housing for Indians and Alaska Natives: An Overview. HUD Challenge 12 (6): 5-6.

Department of Housing and Urban Development (HUD) provides for both development and management of housing for Indians and Alaska Natives under the Public Housing Program, in accordance with the U.S. Housing Act of 1937. However, it was not until 1961 that the determination was made that American Indians had legal authority under Indian law to establish tribal housing authorities to operate low-income public housing projects under the Housing Act. The Public Housing Program provides most of the housing assistance in Indian Areas. HUD assistance can be either in the form of rental or Mutual Help Homeownership Opportunity housing. These options are briefly explained.

0645.   Meyer, Paul A., and Neil M. Singer. 1976. Local Fiscal Effects of Subsidized Housing. Public Finance Quarterly 4: 409-430.

Local governments are sometimes reluctant to allow the operation of subsidized housing programs in their jurisdictions, for the fear of adverse impacts on property taxes, population characteristics, and demands for public services. This study examines the validity of the local government's reluctance by estimating nonproperty tax and transfer receipt as a function of population characteristics of residents of subsidized housing in a sample of Maryland counties.

0646.   Mixon, John. 1973. Housing Subsidies, Impoundment, and Equal Protection. Houston Law Review 10 (4): 793-855.

The equal protection ideal is not protected under the current system of housing subsidies. This is due to the fact that upper-income groups can obtain large amounts of housing subsidies with a relative ease. On the contrary, for the low- and moderate-income groups, subsidies are often small, unavailable at the local level, and difficult to obtain. This paper examines the legal and judicial aspects of this inequity in details, and raises the fundamental question that when inequities such as this prevail, does the U.S. constitutional system empower the executives to impound such congressionally appropriated subsidy funds.

0647.   Moorstein, Mark A. 1981. A New Equity Model Decreases Dependence on Housing Subsidies. Journal of Housing 38 (7): 382-387.

The rise in interest rates has caused a sharp fall in the production of low- and moderate-income housing units. Heavily federal subsidy has also become unavailable. In this article the author explains a method of equity-building that will reduce dependence on housing subsidies, and concludes that "in short, equity can provide a path out of the inflationary maze. It is little wonder that debt financing suffers during inflation when the dollar erodes quickly. But the equity counterpart can restore an equilibrium vital to finance, and especially to the financing of housing projects."

0648. Murray, Michael P. 1977. A Potential Hazard of Housing Allowances for Public Housing. Journal of Urban Economics 4 (2): 119-134.

Benefit estimates indicate a large number of small households would emigrate from public housing if faced with an either-or choice between public housing and a housing allowance. Moreover, waiting lists are not sufficiently long to replace the emigres, so vacancy rates for small apartments might run as high as 55% under such a scheme. Raising public housing rents and making public housing tenants eligible for housing allowances seems a viable way to reduce emigration, although the scheme tried here, which sets rents equal to operating costs, does not eliminate emigration or vacancies entirely.*

0649. Murray, Michael P. 1978. Methodologies for Estimating Housing Subsidy Benefits. Public Finance Quarterly 6 (2): 161-192.

The traditional subsidy program benefit measurement techniques for a composite commodity ("housing services") model are reviewed and extended for use in the increasingly popular hedonic price framework in which housing is decomposed into vector of characteristics. Since recent work has suggested that observed hedonic prices may not reflect market phenomena, a generalized approach is suggested which uses housing characteristics but is free of hedonic prices.*

0650. Myers, Dowell. 1975. Housing Allowances, Submarket Relationships and the Filtering Process. Urban Affairs Quarterly 11 (2): 215-240.

The desire for a novel and simple solution to our nation's housing problems presses legislators and citizens alike to embrace eagerly the housing allowance concept of family assistance. The numerous difficulties experienced with publicly subsidized housing programs have been well publicized. Briefly, these include financial scandals involving developers and administrators, ghettoization of the tenants combined with deteriorating social and physical conditions in public housing projects, and extreme difficulties in locating new projects outside areas of present minority concentration. In addition, many public housing authorities are unable even to maintain projects on present subsidies. Both public and private programs are charged with being too costly, even though they serve only a fraction of the needy.*

0651. NAHRO. 1972. Comparison of Major Elements in Federally Assisted Housing Programs. Journal of Housing 29 (5): 220-221.

In a chart-form, major elements of federally subsidized housing programs under the proposed Housing and Urban Development Act of 1972 (Bill reported by the Housing Subcommittee on Housing May 11, 1972), are compared to the housing provisions of the omnibus bill passed by the Senate on March 2, 1972 (S3248). Income limits and definition of low-income housing (Sections 235 and 236), public housing occupancy, cross-section of income occupancy for new low-income units and housing projects, operating subsidies, rent payments and fiscal feasibility, and new production-home ownership provisions constitute the major dimensions for comparison.

0652.   Nenno, Mary K. 1972. 1972: A Year of Truth for the Future Course of Urban Affairs. Journal of Housing 29 (2); 61-68.

This is an analysis of the administrative changes and regulations during the Nixon administration which shifted the federal housing programs. The analyses include: changing concepts of federal assistance programs, administrative initiatives in housing and community development, organization of the Washington office of HUD, decentralization of HUD into area offices, equal opportunity housing and the project selection criteria, as well as HUD budget for FY 1973.

0653.   Newman, Sandra J., and Ann B. Schnare. 1986. HUD and HHS Shelter Assistance: America's Two Approaches to Housing the Poor. Journal of Housing 43 (1): 22, 27-31.

In 1984, the federal government spent about $18.9 billion for housing assistance for low income households. About $9.9 billion was spent by HUD and the remaining $9.0 billion was spent through the Department of Health and Human Services (HHS)welfare programs. Contending that these programs operate in a fragmental, inequitable, and inefficient method at best, the authors emphasize that there is very little information regarding the ways in which HUD and housing assistance programs interact with HHS welfare assistance; or more fundamentally, what is the best way to spend the scarce federal dollars to provide maximum housing opportunities for low income families. This article analyzes different ways federal dollars are spend and concludes that needy households who receive HUD housing assistance fare considerably better than those who are assisted only through payments they receive under HHS welfare program.

0654.   Newman, Sandra J., and Raymond Struyk. 1984. An Alternative Targeting Strategy for Housing Assistance. Gerontologist 24 (6): 584-92.

This paper examines the consequences for housing assistance to the elderly of shifting from current income eligibility criteria to a permanence of poverty standard. A multivariate model of the probability of being permanently poor shows the elderly to have disproportionately high probabilities of persistent need. A comparison of the short- and long-term housing situation of these permanently poor households with the housing status of other households strengthens the position of the elderly as a group that would command a large proportion of housing assistance benefits under a permanent poverty need standard.*

0655.   Nolon, John R. 1982. Reexamining Federal Housing Programs in a Time of Fiscal Austerity: The Trend Toward Block Grants and Housing Allowances. Urban Lawyer 14 (2): 249-282.

Some recent actions at the federal level represent a fundamental shift in the government's role in pressing for "a decent home and suitable living environment for all Americans." The 1981 congressional act reducing federal spending for housing by fifty percent, and the emphasis placed on federal programs to subsidize the existing housing rather than providing for new constructions are two examples of such shifts in the federal policy. This article examines these changes and concludes that federal housing initiatives during the past four decades were built on the belief that "achieving decent housing for the poor required highly prescriptive federal programs to increase the supply of newly constructed and substantially rehabilitated housing." The shift in emphasis to subsidize existing housing, and providing housing allowances directly to the poor may mark the end of federal spending for low-income housing.

0656.   North Dakota State Social Service Board. 1976. **North Dakota Experimental Housing Allowance Project.** Bismark, North Dakota: State Social Service Board. 187 pp.

The main objective of the North Dakota Experimental Housing Allowance Project was to provide housing assistance to some 400 eligible renter households in four Counties: Stark, Morton, Burleigh, and Stutsman. The report outlines the philosophy relative to applicants' self-declaration of income and assets, self-inspection reports on housing quality, and minimal reliance on the staff for assistance in services other than those specified in the housing allowance program; the project authorities assume that recipients were capable of handling their own affairs. The data collected showed a total of 9,072 clients, the majority of whom were female-headed households, households of low-income, and those in younger age groups. Special effort was made to reach minority households. As a result, a desirable ratio of minority enrollment was achieved. Results showed that clients responded positively towards the housing allowance program, because it allowed them to enjoy a higher standards of living. Benefits of direct cash assistance payment made the program very attractive.

0657.   Olsen, Edgar O., and William J. Reeder. 1983. Misdirected Rental Subsidies. Journal of Policy Analysis and Management 2 (4): 614-620.

The Section 8 Existing Housing Program provides housing assistance to low income families in privately owned rental units. Currently, it is the second largest subsidy program, surpassed only by the low-income public housing program. The main objective of Section 8 is to help families to occupy housing that meets certain space and quality standards. This article examines the rental subsidies and concludes that: "Subsidies under Section 8 housing programs are much larger than necessary to induce families to occupy housing that meets the program's space and quality standards. Reducing the maximum subsidy available at each income level would remove from the program the least needy eligible families and insure that more of the neediest families are served." The authors suggest that the goals of the Section 8 program would be better served by adopting this proposal.

0658.   Peabody, Malcolm E., Jr. 1974. A New Way to House the Poor: Housing Allowances. **New Republic** 170 (10): 20-23.

The 1968 Housing Act produced financial, social, and political monsters. Therefore, the U.S. may be at the end of an era of subsidized housing construction, and at the beginning of a new era of direct cash payment to low-income families. This was the conclusion reached at the end of two housing allowance experiments conducted in Kansas City and Wilmington during 1971 and 1972. According to Peabody, housing allowances are no panacea, however. Although it may be regarded as superior to subsidized construction program, allowances cannot be used in tight markets where vacancy rates are less than 5-6 percent, if there is no parallel program to expand housing production for the middle income families. Thus, a program may be needed that would use federal subsidies and loan guarantees to build new housing for the middle-income families. Using this double-barreled approach may work much faster than the current approach of building for the poor only.

0659.   Phillips, James G.   1973.   Housing Report: HUD Proposes Cash Allowance System as Link to Broad Plan for Welfare Reform.   **National Journal Reports** 5 (34): 1255-1261.

Disenchanted with policies inherited from past Democratic Administrations, the HUD Department is proposing sweeping new initiatives in the housing field, highlighted by a program of cash housing allowances to supplement and eventually replace, public housing and other HUD housing subsidies for the poor.   HUD also is proposing a package of housing assistance for "Middle America," including tax incentives to home builders, an increase in the $33,000 limit on FHA loan insurance and lower payments for young homeowners over the first five years of FHA-insured loans.*

0660.   Pratter, Jerome.   1972.   Gateway to Frustration: Housing in St. Louis. **Urban Lawyer** 4 (4): 746-756.

Using five different events, this article illustrates why, even with federal subsidies, providing housing for anyone but the elderly and middle upper income families is a struggle in St. Louis, Missouri, or any other American city.

0661.   Pulley, Rodmar H.   1979.   Section 8 Plus Money-Saving Incentives Spur a New Construction Program in Santa Cruz County, California.   **Journal of Housing** 36 (3): 139-141.

In 1978, when voters in Santa Cruz County, California, approved Measure J (a growth management ballot proposition), they also voted for a 15 percent low- and moderate income housing factor as a percentage of all new constructions. However, the state's Proposition 13 was also mandated, making the realization of constructing low-income housing almost impossible. Faced with opposing signals from the voters, by providing several options under Section 8 program to developers and investors, the Santa Cruz County housing authority has discovered an innovative method to build new housing for its low-income residents. This article elaborates on the success and the method employed by the County in satisfying both Measure J and Proposition 13.

0662.   Rosenbaum, Elizabeth B., and Rosemarie Noonan. 1979. Welfare Housing. **Journal of Housing** 36 (6): 314-316.

One of the major housing policy issues is whether housing allowances can be used to purchase quality housing for the poor. And if so, what incentives can be used to encourage landlords and tenants to maintain and live in quality housing. This article explains an example of a program that thrives in Westchester County, New York, as a result of multi-agency coordination. The article concludes that if the "Westchester County program continues on its successful path," the challenge of maintaining the momentum will turn on the ability of HUD and HEW officials to coordinate policies at the national level.

0663.   Rubinowitz, Leonard S.   1973.   A Question of Choice: Access of the Poor and the Black to Suburban Housing. In: The Urbanization of the Suburbs. Louis H. Masotti, and Jeffrey K. Hadden (eds.). Beverly Hills/London: Sage Publications. Pp. 329-66.

The author asserts that public policies and subsidies have in the past provided an option for the white and the affluent families to live any where they want in the metropolitan areas. The question raised in this article is whether this nation is prepared to provide the same choice to the poor and the blacks. This analysis concludes that "for the future, we must assume that federal subsidy programs will continue to exist, in some form. This is not a safe assumption but it is a necessary one if housing opportunities for poor are to be expanded."

0664.   Rydell, C. Peter. 1976. Measuring the Supply Response to Housing Allowances.   Santa Monica, California: Rand Corporation Paper P-5564.   35 pp.

In this paper the author presents a model studying the impact of housing allowances on housing production, and whether low-income home-owners and renters can obtain adequate housing through the allowances; or, whether landlords get a windfall.

0665.   Sadacca, Robert, Morton Isler, and David Carlson. 1976. Effective Subsidized Housing Management Practices. Journal of Property Management 41 (5): 210-15.

In an attempt to develop a better understanding of housing management for low-income families, the Urban institute undertook an intensive analysis of all aspects of housing management processes. The findings indicate that management practices prove to be an invaluable guide to effective management operations.

0666.   Schechter, Henry B.   1973.   Federally Subsidized Housing Program Benefits. In: Government Spending and Land Values: Public Money and Private Gain. C. Lowell Harris (ed.). Madison: University of Wisconsin Press. pp. 31-63.

The data on home ownership suggest that low-income owners of subsidized new homes receive a higher proportion of the subsidy benefits than do renters. Thus, it is concluded that, in the long run, low-income housing needs can be met at a lower subsidy cost by subsidizing home ownership than rental projects.

0667.   Schechter, Henry B.   1976.   The Depth of the Housing Crisis. American Federationist 83 (1): 8-11.

Projections indicate that five million households may need subsidized housing within the decade. Currently, more than 11 million households

reside under overcrowded and deficient housing conditions;   or, have a high
rent burden. The majority of those in the 25-34 are priced out of the new
housing market, whether for rent or purchase. According to the U.S. Bureau
of the Census figures, 1.5 million occupied units need rehabilitation;
another 2.5 million occupied units lack complete plumbing facilities;   and
800,000 households have been doubled-up with others. It is concluded that
if housing production does not meet the anticipated needs of about 26.5
million housing units in the following decade, mortgage and rent costs will
further escalate in such a tight housing market.

0668.   Seiders, David F. 1982. The President's Commission on Housing:
Perspectives on Mortgage Finance. **Housing Finance Review** 1 (4): 323-48.

The President's Commission on Housing developed a wide-range and, in some
cases, revolutionary set of recommendations on the mortgage finance
systems. This paper provides an insider's view of the Commission's
perspective and approach, incorporating information not available in the
Report. Discussion of the process by which major decisions were reached
provides a richer understanding of positions finally adopted. Comparisons
drawn with other major packages of recommendations on housing finance show
the extent to which the Housing Commission departed from the philosophies
and techniques reflected in earlier commission, congressional, or
interagency reports. And a review of progress made toward implementation
provides clues concerning the commitment of the Administration to place
greater reliance on a deregulated and more broadly based private mortgage
delivery system.[*] The report has implication for the housing of low- and
moderate-income families.

0669.   Siegan, Bernard H. 1974. Best Housing Hope. **Freeman** 24 (4): 221-23.

The Housing Act of 1968 called for the construction or rehabilitation of 6
million housing units for low- and moderate-income families during the
following 10 years. The Act also established a supporting subsidy program
to accomplish this goal. Siegan asserts that under this program, the
average cost of a successful subsidized unit will be about the cost of
housing in Beverly Hills but hardly with the same resale value. A close
scrutiny of the operation of real estate market provides the answer to
meeting the housing needs of the less fortunate in society: if builders are
enabled or allowed to build more private housing, the less fortunate
families will benefit as much as the affluent families through the filtering
process.

0670.   Solomon, Arthur P., and Chester G. Fenton. 1974. The Nation's First
Experience with Housing Allowances: The Kansas City Demonstration. **Land
Economics** 50 (3): 213-23.

Indicating that federal housing subsidy programs have come under increasing
political fire, this article presents a report on the findings to date of the
small housing allowance experiment in Kansas City, Missouri. Initiated as
part of the local Model Cities program, the experiment has been in operation
for more than two year. Areas reported on include: cost of subsidized
housing, expenditures for housing, housing and neighborhood conditions,
residential desegregation and work response. The study concludes that "in
spite of its shortcomings, the nation's first experience with housing

allowances indicates that the concept of directly providing low- and moderate income families with income earmarked for housing appears to be a viable strategy." The authors recommend that if similar results are obtained in other experiments, then housing allowance program must become an integral component of the national social welfare system.

0671. Solomon, Arthur P., and Chester G. Fenton. 1975. The Nation's First Experience with Housing Allowances: The Kansas City Demonstration. **Urban and Social Change Review** 8 (1): 3-8.

What lessons can be learned from the Kansas City experience for the implementation of a large-scale housing allowance program? This is an up-dated version of an earlier article (see previous item) published in 1974. The final conclusions in both articles are the same.

0672. Springer, Michael. 1978. Enforcing Housing Quality Standards: Some Findings From the Experimental Housing Allowance Program. Washington, D.C.: Urban Institute. 23 pp.

This report reviews some of the salient findings from the Experimental Housing Allowance program with particular attention paid to the enforcement of housing standards and general implications for programs involving the maintenance, rehabilitation, or leasing of existing housing units. Results show that rent levels were not reliable indicators of quality of specific units, and that actual inspection of each unit was necessary. Findings also indicated that application of housing quality standards were shown to result in reduced participation in a program, especially among the nonelderly, minorities, larger households, and those who had to move in order to qualify for benefits.

0673. Stanfield, Rochelle L. 1980. HUD Gets Money for Housing: But Is It Enough for the Poor? **National Journal** 12 (9): 360-64.

President Carter asked for $32.5 billion in long-term federal housing aid commitments for fiscal 1981 budget--an increase of $6 billion in HUD's long term budget. The article indicates that even if the $6 billion increase is approved by the Congress, the HUD's housing programs appear headed for financial troubles. Due to budgetary limits, aid can be made available to only one tenth of eligible families.

0674. Struyk, Raymond J., and Marc Bendick, Jr. (eds.). 1981. **Housing Voucher for the Poor: Lessons from a National Experiment.** Washington, D.C.: Urban Institute Press. 424 pp.

Generally, housing programs to assist poor families in the U.S. have been primarily supply oriented programs that have provided housing by encouraging new construction. The 1970 Housing and Urban Development Act mandated that HUD conduct a program, on an experimental basis, to test the feasibility of an alternative approach, a housing allowance (or voucher) program. The Experimental Housing Allowance Program (EHAP) provided housing assistance to more than 30,000 low income households in twelve metropolitan areas and tested a variety of alternative program designs. This book attempts to provide a comprehensive overview of the EHAP findings, and what they would reveal about the feasibility of being implemented on a national level.

0675.   Struyk, Raymond, and Jill Khadduri. 1980. Saving the Housing Assistance
Plan. Journal of the American Planning Association 46 (4): 387-97.

The Housing Assistance Plan (HAP), created by the landmark Housing and
Community Development Act of 1974, was designed to improve the coordination
between housing and community development activities and to cause local
governments to develop genuine housing strategies in the context of their
market conditions to assist low-income, poorly housed residents obtain
adequate housing. During the 1979 budget preparation and legislative
process considerable skepticism was voiced about the quality of the locally
prepared HAPs and hence about the utility of the mix of assisted housing
among new constructions, rehabilitation, and leasing existing units
proposed by HUD. This paper very briefly reviews the relevant sections of
the 1974 Act and its intent, and then describes the HAP process, as designed
and implemented by HUD. The final section of the paper outlines a series of
steps that could be taken to improve the incentives to local communities and
to improve the actual Housing Assistance Plan process.**

0676.   Tobe, Brenda H. 1985. The Relationship of Housing Assistance to the
Social and Economic Conditions of Low and Moderate Income Households.
Unpublished Ph.D. Dissertation. George Washington University. 166 pp.

This dissertation analyzes the effects of housing assistance upon recipient
households to determine whether housing assistance helps families realize
benefits in areas other than physical improvements in the dwelling unit.
The analysis is based on data from the Experimental Housing Allowance
Program Study. Findings show: (1) on an aggregate basis, the social and
economic gains achieved by housing assistance recipients are not as apparent
as when data are analyzed in the disaggregate; (2) the disaggregate
analysis of data shows that families who benefited from housing assistance
were those headed by persons with less than a high school education and
nonworking persons, regardless of race.; and (3) "the continued emphasis
of the federal government in divestiture of its involvement with housing for
low and moderate income families forces the economic dimension of housing to
become primary in the lives of assisted families and treats the social and
physical dimensions as incidental. The data presented within this study
and analysis of the housing directives of the Reagan administration are the
bases for concluding that the abandonment of social goals in the interest of
narrow economic objectives forces the focus of housing policy to be reduced
to the need for physical shelter."

0677.   Varady, David P. 1982. Indirect Benefits of Subsidized Housing Programs.
APA Journal 48 (4): 432-40.

This article's review of the social science literature provides little
support for the widely accepted belief that government subsidized housing
programs have neighborhood spillover effects and that the programs produce
indirect benefits over large areas. In particular, the evidence on the
relationship between housing programs and property values is contradictory
and confusing. Of the recent HUD funded studies reviewed in this article,
only one supports the existence of neighborhood spillover effects. In the
Urban Homesteading Demonstration, higher investments and property values

radiated out from homesteading sites during the 1970s. This program is, however, relatively unique in terms of the magnitude and visibility of improvements to individual dwellings. The preceding indicates that government subsidized housing programs will have to be justified on the basis of the direct benefits provided to participants rather than on any possible indirect effects.*

0678. Wallace, James E. 1978. Preliminary Findings From the Housing Allowance Demand Experiment. Cambridge, Mass.: Abt Associates, Inc. 25 pp.

This report is based on first-year data from the Housing Allowance Demand Experiment, conducted in Pittsburgh, Pennsylvania, and Phoenix, Arizona. Findings indicate that a housing allowance can make housing more affordable for those already in adequate homes; and it facilitates housing improvements for those not already in adequate units. The rent rebate program showed that this type of subsidy resulted in a greater increase in housing expenditure than a pure income transfer plan. None of the plans had any effect on the desegregation of the poor and minorities.

0679. Walsh, Albert A. 1977. Financing for Section 8 Will be Easier as a Result of New Regulations. Journal of Housing 34 (9) 447-50.

During the past several years NAHRO (National Association of Housing and Redevelopment Officials) members and housing developers have complained that, though an excellent tenant subsidy, Section 8 cannot produce housing without a companion debt financing mechanism. As a result of a new set of regulations intended to facilitate the issuance of tax-exempt bonds by local housing authorities and public housing agencies to finance Section 8, the problem may be solved. This article discusses the provision of the new regulations, including eligible organizations, tax exemption, procedures, and restrictions.

0680. Warren, Elizabeth C. 1986. Measuring the Dispersal of Subsidized Housing in Three Cities. Journal of Urban Affairs 8 (1): 19-55.

This paper uses the Index of Dissimilarity to measure the degree of dispersal of subsidized housing between 1970 and 1980 in three cities-- Chicago, Baltimore, and St. Louis. The data show that subsidized housing has been dispersed in each of the cities, in accordance with federal housing policies of the late 1960s and 1970s. There are differences among the cities, however, in the degree of dispersal and the size of the subsidized housing inventories. The data also show that subsidized housing has been extended to predominantly white census tracts and tracts with incomes higher than the city-wide median incomes. These white, higher-income tracts have lower densities of subsidized housing than poorer tracts with large black populations.*

0681. Weaver, Robert C. 1975. Housing Allowances. Land Economics 51 (3): 247-57.

The concept of housing allowances and advocacy of utilizing existing units as shelter for the low-income families are not new. This article chronicles the development and evolution of the housing allowances programs for the poor. It concludes that "while it is difficult to anticipate what HUD's housing allowance experiments will demonstrate, there is fragmentary evidence that results so far are not conclusive. One of the experiments in Jackson, Florida, designed to analyze administrative issues inherent in housing allowances, is in difficulty. There are problems of securing participants. Even among those involved, some, despite HUD's ground rules to the contrary, were in substandard housing. The director of the experiment reported a lack of an adequate volume of vacant standard dwelling units."

0682. Weinberg, Daniel H. 1982. Housing Benefits from the Section 8 Housing Program. **Evaluation Review** 6 (1): 5-24.

The Section 8 housing program is the largest U.S. housing assistance program. This article presents the first systematic analysis of the benefits participating households receive and compares those benefits with federal government costs. Section 8 New Construction projects provide acceptable housing at an affordable price to those low-income households fortunate enough to be accepted by the developers. However, about 20% of the total project rents goes to program-related costs rather than to tenant benefits. A major advantage of the section 8 Existing Housing Program is that tenant benefits are provided without excessive rent increases. But, most units in that program do not meet Section 8 Acceptability Criteria. A shift in emphasis from the New Construction to the Existing Housing program can save the government significant amount of money yet maintain the number of households assisted.*

0683. Weinstein, Jerome I. 1974. Housing Subsidies: An Overview. **Journal of Urban Law** 51 (4):723-50.

The main objective of this study is to "identify and explain the magnitude of housing subsidies existing beyond the common programatic nomenclature." In doing this, this study attempts to provide both clarification and insight into the complex system of federal housing subsidy programs--public housing, below-market interest rates, direct cash payments, loan-related subsidies, and taxation.

0684. Whitman, Dale A. 1977. Federal Housing Assistance for the Poor: Old Problems and New Directions. **Urban Lawyer** 9 (1): 1-60.

This article attempts to show that universally-available housing assistance can become a practical reality, and that "it is preferable to more traditional methods in terms of fairness and efficiency."

0685. Williams, Roger M. 1977. The New Urban Pioneers: Homesteading in the Slums. **Saturday Review** 4 (21): 9-14.

In New York South Bronx slums, the Peoples's Development Corporation (PDC), is transforming tenements into decent and livable apartment buildings. Its approach, urban homesteading or sweat equity, involves investing work instead of money in real estate. The approach has caught on other cities across the country. The PDC, known for its strong leadership and little money, is made up of Hispanics, blacks, women and college students. This articles describes a project on Washington Avenue and assesses the PDC's success and prospect for the future.

································◆◆◆◆◆◆◆◆◆◆································

8
MINORITIES AND
PUBLIC HOUSING

0686. Aiken, Michael, and Robert R. Alford. 1970. Community Structure and Innovation: The Case of Public Housing. **American Political Science Review** 64 (3): 843-64.

Defining innovation as an activity, process, service, or idea that is new to an American city, this study is concerned with the characteristics of cities that have successfully implemented innovations in federally financed public housing. The study focuses on three points: first, the presence/absence of federally financed housing program in the city; second, the speed of innovation of such a program; and third, the level of output or performance of such innovative activity. This study concludes that three properties of communities namely, structural differentiation, the accumulation of experience and information, and the stability and extensiveness of interorganizational network in the city may contribute to the capacity of the city to generate the kind of social resources necessary for innovations in federally financed public housing.

0687. Amick, Daniel J., and Frederick J. Kviz. 1975. Social Alienation in Public Housing. **Ekistics** 39 (231): 118-20.

Overcrowding is measured by the number of persons per room. High density is measured by the number of families or persons per acre. Utilizing data from the 1970 Annual Statistical Report of the Chicago Housing Authority, this study calculates an index of interaction restriction for each of the six Chicago Housing Authority public housing sites for the nonelderly. Alienation scale is developed using data based on personal interviews. Findings indicate that residents of low-income public housing show differing levels of integration with regards to their social environment. The degree of integration is found to depend on the amount and nature of physical restraints exerted upon interpersonal contacts—high social integration is found to be associated with a low ratio of dwelling density to site density, and low-rise as opposed to high-rise residency. It is suggested that ground coverage should be increased relative to dwelling density by constructing low-rise units. Finally, based on this study physical isolation among residents is found to be an important factor determining the prevailing level of alienation.

0688.   Anonymous. 1972. Senate Adopts HUD Bill by a Vote of 80 to 1. Journal of Housing 29 (3): 113-15.

By a vote of 80 to 1, the Senate on March 2, passed the Housing and Urban Development Act of 1972 (S3248). This article discusses major revisions and new authorization provisions of this Act. Reform provisions requiring an income cross-section in public housing and FHA rental housing assistance are among the topics discussed. A comparative chart of some of the basic elements in the assisted housing program is presented.

0689.   Anonymous. 1973. Myths/Realities of Public Housing. Journal of Housing 30 (4): 179-91.

On April 12, NAHRO made its second appearance of the month before the subcommittee on housing and urban affairs of the Senate Committee on Banking, Housing and Urban Affairs—this time to present an evaluation of the public housing program. This article is a transcript of the statements made by a 9-member delegation of NAHRO. NAHRO states that there is a continuing and critical need for federal housing assistance, and that the public housing program, despite its present fiscal dilemma, is a strong and flexible program that has the capacity to continue as a major contributor in relieving the nation's housing needs of the low-income families.

0690.   Anonymous. 1973. Money Cuts, New Rules—Hard Times for Public Housing. U.S. News & World Report (March 26): 87-88.

"One problem after another is piling up for housing for the poor. If the experience in Norfolk is typical, programs all over the U.S. are in peril."

0691.   Anonymous. 1975. Performance Funding System. Journal of Housing 32 (4): 180-85.

Director of the Office of Management Information and Field Support at HUD, explains the new system of payment of public housing operating subsidies to local housing authorities. This explanation is given to the subcommittee on housing and urban affairs of the Senate Committee on Banking, Housing, and Urban Affairs. This article also includes NAHRO's position on the system and some critical commentary on it.

0692.   Anonymous. 1979. How to Avoid Public Housing Blight. American City and County 94 (9): 87-88.

This article shows that scattered site low-income public housing in Evanston, Illinois, has gained acceptance. Twenty-six rental family units were located in all types of neighborhoods, and were designed to fit in with the mostly detached homes. Residents were involved in all phases of planning and the design of the project and generally approved of it, with the fear of drop in property values never occurring after the pre-screened tenants moved in. Rents were kept low due to the Cook County's Housing Authority involvement with many public housing projects, enabling direct costs to be spread over the entire budget. The basic finding of this study is that home values do not have to drop when low-income families move in.

0693. Anonymous. 1981. Improving Public Housing: An Interview with Clyde McHenry. Journal of Property Management 46 (4): 192-96.

This article consists of an interview with Clyde McHenry, a former HUD official who talks about a new federal program designed to make millions of dollars available to public housing authorities to improve the physical conditions of public housing; he also discusses public housing past, present and future. He expresses pessimism over the administration's willingness to provide additional assistance for low income people in need of housing. He also indicates that "I am not sure what alternative poor people have, because, by and large, the public housing in this country is filled, and other forms of subsidized housing are filled. And there are very few vacancies around the country." This means that the needs cannot be met, and this is somewhat disturbing.

0694. Anonymous. 1982. The President's Housing Commission: Public Housing. Housing Law Bulletin 12 (3): 3-6.

The Commission on Housing established in 1981 produced its final report in April 1982. This document, **The Report of the President's Commission on Housing**, among many other things has a chapter on public housing. The present article analyzes this particular chapter of the Commission's report. The discussion is highly critical of the Commission's public housing recommendations. "The weaknesses in some of the Commission's reasoning and public judgments have already led Congress to consider legislation restraining HUD's implementation of some of the recommendations. Nonetheless, public housing tenants and those who represent them must be vigilant to prevent implementation of those radical recommendations that would deny poor people the benefits of the public housing program."

0695. Anonymous. 1983. Public Housing and Section 8 Statute Amended: Income Eligibility, Preferences and Priorities for Displacees, Occupants of Substandard Housing and Economic Mix, and Full Utilization of Section 8. **Housing Law Bulletin** 13 (2): 1-7.

In 1981, Congress amended the public housing and Section 8 statute to establish a uniform definition of eligible families. Based on the amendments, public housing and Section 8 units must only be rented to lower-income families, defined as families whose income did not exceed 80 percent of the median income for the area. Congress has ordered that for both public housing and Section 8, displacees and families living in substandard housing be given first priority, but HUD has yet to publish supporting regulations to the 1979 congressional priorities. In the area of economic mix, Congress has been less decisive in fully accepting the idea; in 1981, Congress acted to target 90-95 percent of the units to very-low-income families—those whose income did not exceed 50 percent of the area median income; but again, HUD has been slow to publish supporting regulations; instead HUD proposed regulations that do not wholly comport with congressional design. Finally, relative to the issue of full utilization of available units, Congress, in the Section 8 has provided that there must be full utilization of the units; proposed regulations on this statutory amendment are still pending. Thus, HUD's reluctance to act has jeopardized low-income families most in need and has increased the cost of low-income housing by spawning litigation and forcing some public housing authorities and Section 8 project owners to duplicate efforts in an attempt to comply with the statute.

0696. Astorino, Robert L. 1981. Public Housing Authorities Should be Less Dependent on HUD Subsidies for Operations. **Journal of Housing** 38 (4): 203-204.

With changing trends in government that has resulted in inadequate funding, public housing authorities have become obsolete.   That is, the traditional methods of public housing are failing. This article examines two alternatives for the future and survival of the public housing program. These are: (1) do nothing and hope for possible federal relief;   (2) become new entities capable of shaping their own future without being dependent on federal subsidies. The author suggests that the selection of the first alternative may be a wishful thinking, given the current political climate in Washington, D.C. This leaves the communities with only one choice, the second alternative.

0697. Beckham, Robert. 1972. GAO Attacks Creating Public Housing Through Direct Acquisition. **Journal of Housing** 29 (9): 453-54.

This article reviews the United States General Accounting Office's (GAO's) report on HUD's direct acquisition program which assisted local housing authorities to acquire 16,400 housing units at a total cost of $235 million. As indicated by Bekham, the report reviews the impact of the program on the national housing goal, the needs of low-income families, prior occupants of acquired units and community loss of potential property tax revenues.   A brief account of HUD's comments on the GAO's report and recommendation are also provided.

0698. Beckham, Robert. 1973. Innovative Tenant Services is Heart of Jersey City's Public Housing Program. **Journal of Housing** 30 (3): 134-40.

Based on this study, the future of Jersey City's housing authority is severely jeopardized by pending cutbacks in federal health, education, and welfare (HEW) assistance programs. Four years earlier, this became the first public housing authority in the country to provide children with breakfast, hot lunches, and after-school supplements through the USDA program, administered by the New Jersey department of HEW. This article chronicles and describes those programs facing forced cutbacks and/or termination. They are: Operation Feed Need, Parole Resource Office and Orientation Facility, Neighborhood Youth Corps and its senior citizens equivalent Operation Service, tutoring, art education, consumer protection, and Housing News.

0699. Bellin, Seymour S., and Louis Kriesberg. 1967. Relationship Among Attitudes, and Behavior: The Case of Applying for Public Housing. **Sociology and Social Research** 51 (4): 453-469.

Attitudes about public housing were found to be related to interest in public housing. Circumstances, however, were better predictors of actually applying for public housing. After deciding to apply, some attitudes apparently were modified to conform with the decision. The

data are from interviews with a sample of households eligible for public
housing.*

0700.   Bingham, Richard D. 1975. Public Housing and Urban Renewal: An Analysis
         of Federal-Local Relations. New York: Praeger Publishers. 255 pp.

This book is a study of federal grant programs with two questions in mind: (1)
why federal grants are extensively utilized by some cities, while others
virtually ignore them; and (2) what impacts these federal grants have on
cities that use them. The study covers all incorporated U.S. cities with a
population of 50,000 or more in 1960. Results indicate that the local
politics and population characteristics of the city had significant
intervening influence. Housing and urban renewal grants were found not to
be related to the short-term economic health of the community; but some
evidence was found that construction of public housing had some effect on
employment. It is concluded that if it has any impact at all, it takes a long
time for urban renewal and housing grants to promote economic vigor in the
city.

0701.   Birch, Eugenie Ladner. 1978. Woman-Made America: The Case of Early
         Public Housing Policy.   Journal of the American Institute of Planners   44
         (1): 130-144.

The 1937 Wagner-Steagall Act provided for the first permanent public housing
program subsidized by the federal government. Although immediate economic
conditions caused by the Depression provided the direct impetus for its
passage, a painstakingly constructed intellectual background and grass
roots political support created the climate for its acceptance. This
atmosphere was the product of the work of many housing reformers. However,
two women, Edith Elmer Wood and Catherine Bauer, stand out as leaders having
the most significant impact on the formulation of the new policy. As women,
they contributed two major facets to it: the recognition of the need for
government construction   of dwellings when the private sector did not
build;   the demand that publicly constructed homes be positively supportive
of family life.*

0702.   Bollinger, Stephen J. 1981. Public Housing Today and Tomorrow: A
         Director's Perspective. Journal of Property Management 46 (4): 188-90.

The director of a public housing authority explains how present public
housing problems may be solved.

0703.   Bratt, Rachel G. 1985. Controversies and Contributions: A Public Housing
         Critique. Journal of Housing 42 (5): 165-73

In this article, Bratt examines problems and successes of public housing and
assesses its value in America. It is concluded that: "Public ownership,
tenant ownership, and community ownership are critical strategies for
providing decent low-rent housing. By placing control and ownership
squarely in the hands of public or other nonprofit entities, a new housing
agenda would be formulated on the assumption that decent housing is a
'right'--a matter of public concern, not private exploitation or political
whim."

0704.   Burstein, Joseph. 1967. New Techniques in Public Housing. **Law and Contemporary Problems.** 32 (3, Part II): 528-549.

Creative new programs have been devised to implement goals of public housing and to provide homes--and sometimes homeownership--for low income families. Fortunately, the legal profession has used its tools and skills to make these programs a reality, rather than merely a dream. The extent of the lawyers' contribution in this regard serves to corroborate the writer's conclusion several years ago that: "We are approaching a period where the country will again be calling upon the talents of lawyers to lead, if possible, but at least to guide the policy makers in a major effort to implement the vision of the 'Great Society' and to make that vision a reality for every American family."*

0705.   Burstein, Joseph. 1979. Local Agencies Can be the Catalysts that Pull Together Public and Private Resources. **Journal of Housing** 36 (10): 513-18.

Public housing and redevelopment authorities are in a unique position to pull together the forces of federal and state laws and financial assistance to revitalize the cities, suburban, and rural areas. They can provide a range of ownership and renting opportunities for low- and moderate income families. The secret of this task lies in understanding the history of the enabling legislation for public housing authorities and in closely scrutinizing public housing laws now on the books. This understanding will enhance the ability to take full advantage of all legal options open to public housing and redevelopment authorities. The authorities must also learn to work in cooperation with the private sector. By enhancing their roles, the public housing and redevelopment authorities can become a more active force in influencing federal, state, and local programs.

0706.   Cagle, Laurence T. 1973. Interracial Housing: A Reassessment of the Equal-Status Contact Hypothesis. **Sociology and Social Research** 57 (3): 342-55.

With a view toward a viable applied sociology, two pioneering studies in interracial public housing are reexamined. Findings suggest that, however much prejudice was reduced, interracial (and intraracial) contacts were not very intimate. Adding to the complexity of testing the equal-status contact hypothesis are considerations such as inadequate behavioral measures, selectivity, changes within the black community, and the character of neighborhood in urban society.*

0707.   Carrigan, Dennis. 1973. West Virginia Housing Fund Experience Demonstrates Need for Rural Housing Program. **Journal of Housing** 30 (3): 125-30.

According to Carrigan the HUD subsidized housing programs, with the exclusion of public housing, are not relevant to the needs of rural residents in America. Public housing offers the greatest hope of producing shelter at costs realistic for the truly poor. A profile of Logan County, with particular emphasis on income and housing needs, is presented. A look at the future of housing finance agencies (HFA) is provided; the author suggests that HFAs with their public purpose, grass roots orientation, and growth in number and experience, are ideally suited to the implementation and feedback phases.

0708. Cassttevens, Thomas W. 1968. The Defeat of Berkeley's Fair-Housing Ordinance. In : The Politics of Fair-Housing Legislation: State and Local Case Studies. Lynn W. Eley, and Thomas W. Casstevens (eds.). San Francisco, CA: Chandler Publishing Company. Pp. 187-236.

Racial discrimination in housing became an issue in Berkeley politics in the 1950's, and after local liberals captured a majority on the city council, a fair-housing ordinance was enacted in 1963. Local conservatives counterattacked with a referendum, and in a campaign that attracted nationwide attention, the ordinance was defeated before going into effect.*

0709. Casstevens, Thomas W. 1968. California's Rumford Act and Proposition 14. In: The Politics of Fair-Housing Legislation: State and Local Case Studies. Lynn W. Eley, and Thomas W. Casstevens (eds.). San Francisco, CA: Chandler Publishing Company. Pp. 237-284.

California's fair-housing legislation, culminating in the 1963 Rumford act, was suspended by the electorate's 1964 adoption of Proposition 14, an initiative constitutional amendment precluding state and local fair-housing legislation. After the state supreme court ruled in 1966 that Proposition 14 violated the constitution of the United States, the Rumford act was again enforced.*

0710. Catlin, Robert. 1982. An Assessment of the Public Housing Initiatives Program. Urban League Review 6 (2): 34-38.

Is the Carter administration's Public Housing Urban Initiative Program (PHUIP) an exercise in frustration and futility or a legitimate housing policy experiment to modernize and better manage and maintain the nation's many public housing projects? Not an easy question to answer, an examination of the Carter administration program selection process, its implementation and early results as well as a look at the current administration's position on PHUIP should help us assess the significance of this program relative to future initiatives designed to upgrade and modernize public housing.*

0711. Corcoran, Joseph E. 1980. King's Lynne: Public Housing Becomes Private Housing. Urban Land 39 (3): 7-12.

In 1970, America Park was among the worst public housing projects in the Boston metropolitan area. Built in the late 1940s, it had deteriorated to the point where many units were uninhabitable. But, a determined tenant group was able to conceive and implement a plan to replace the public project with privately owned, mixed-income housing. Through the tenants' efforts, special legislation allocating full state funding for many items involved in the conversion was passed. A partnership between tenants' organization and a private developer was formed, and political and citizen support was garnered. Interim private management of the existing public housing was implemented, and supporting social services for relocating tenant was provided. Professional advertising techniques were used for marketing to a mixed-income community. Nine years later, America Park was transformed into King's Lynne, and the same tenants were coowner-developers and residents of a private $21 million mixed-income rental housing complex.

0712.   Daniel, Edwin C. 1978. Evanston, Illinois, Builds Its First Public Housing. **Journal of Housing** 35 (10): 527-28.

This article examines the ten year effort to supply scattered site public housing in Evanston--an affluent Chicago suburb. The difficulty in providing units for low-income families was overcome by combining those units with lower cost high rise units for the elderly, bringing down the average cost per unit in the final proposal. The 26-family units are on ten sites scattered throughout the city, with no one site having more than four units.

0713.   Demerath, Nicholas J. 1962. St. Louis Public Housing Study. **Journal of Housing** 19 (8):   472-478.

Worldwide, urbanization has been associated with slums, blight, broken families, poverty, discrimination, alcoholism, drug addiction, delinquency, crime, loneliness, ghettos, and despair, to mention a few. With these problems and frustrations, the city of St. Louis is well acquainted.   The city has tried a major surgery by bulldozers and brickmasons and is taking "the urban medicines in large and costly doses." Accordingly, the city has began a novel course of treatment relative to its housing problem for its lower-income groups. This article consists of a summary of the St. Louis Plan from the report of the Mayor's committee on public housing and Social Services--a committee the author of this article had served on as its chairman. The author indicates that St. Louis has set off community development program in an attempt to meet its social needs.

0714.   DeSalvo, Joseph S. 1976. Housing Subsidies: Do We Know What We Are Doing? **Policy Analysis** 2 (1): 39-60.

Under what conditions should the government subsidize housing? DO current subsidy programs meet these criteria? Is there a better way of subsidizing housing? In examining these questions the author focuses on the merit-good rationale for government intervention interpreted in terms of consumption externalities, discusses a theory of transfers incorporating this merit-good idea, and surveys relevant theoretical and empirical work. After comparing the efficacy of cash vs. in-kind subsidies, he suggests a new policy alternative, rent certificates: if housing is a merit good, it should be subsidized, and whatever transfers are justified should be in cash. Which case fits the U.S. today is an empirical question yet to be answered.*

0715.   Deutsch, Morton, and Mary Evans Collins. 1951. **Interracial Housing: A Psychological Evaluation of a Social Experiment.** Minneapolis: University of Minnesota Press.   173 pp.

This book consists of a study of four public housing projects--two in Newark, New Jersey, and two in New York City. All four projects housed black and white families. In two of them blacks and whites were segregated within the project. The remaining two were interracial--that is, there was no segregation and/or discrimination. The main objective of the book is to investigate the influence of the two patterns on the social attitudes of the occupants. The study indicated that in those projects where blacks and whites lived side by side, there was less prejudice, more harmony, and democratic intergroup relations; but in projects where blacks and whites occupied separate wings or buildings higher levels of prejudice prevailed.

0716.   Dolbeare, Cushing N. 1976. How to Develop Creative Public Housing Communities for Low-Income People Through Conventional and Leased Programs. In: Housing Costs and Housing Needs. Alexander Greendale, and Stanley F. Krock, Jr. (eds.). New York: Praeger. Pp. 47-85.

There is no sharp distinction between public and private housing in this country. The use of either term must be accompanied with qualifications. The most widely used federal housing program is the housing subsidy for single-family home ownership through tax deduction. For example, in 1973, 25 million American families took advantage of this subsidy program. But, only one out of every four had incomes below $15,000. In contrast, less than three million families received the more publicized housing subsidies of HUD and FHA. The nature of housing market in the U.S. is such that it is impossible for anyone to provide adequate housing without subsidy at costs that low- and moderate income families can afford it. Public housing and Section 8 (housing assistance payment) currently provide adequate housing for many needy families. This is the only means now available to meet low-income housing needs.

0717.   Downs, Anthony. 1972. Are Subsidies the Best Answer for Housing Low and Moderate Income Households? The Urban Lawyer 4: 405-416.

In summary, housing subsidies are the only way to help low and moderate income households who live in poor quality housing, or pay abnormally   high fraction of their income for housing, to upgrade their housing to the standards we define as "minimal" in quality and "normal" in cost as a fraction of income. However, Americans as a whole are almost certainly not willing to achieve these objectives completely. Middle income and upper income groups would have to pay a much bigger total housing subsidy to the poor than they are now willing to bear. Even the particular forms of housing subsidies we choose will depend in part upon how fully the middle and upper income majority in America wishes to confront and deal effectively with the causes of urban poverty. It appears to me that any effective attack on those causes must involve the sharing by many middle and upper income suburban households of their job opportunities, their schools, and their neighborhoods with significant number of those poor households who are now excluded from these benefits. At present, I believe most Americans do not want to live near or share their schools or neighborhoods with the poor, regardless of race. In short, we do not want to provide equality of opportunity to our fellow citizens if that requires us to share our everyday lives with them. Apparently, we believe that would be pushing the concept of "human brotherhood" too far. Until we alter that attitude, I must agree with that native American philosopher, Pogo, that concerning the ultimate issue of housing for the urban poor, "we have met the enemy, and he is us."*

0718.   Farley, John E. 1982. Has Public Housing Gotten a Boom Rap? The Incidence of Crime in St. Louis Public Housing Developments. Environment and Behavior 14 (4): 443-77.

This study examines patterns of crime in multiblock areas containing ten public housing developments in the city of St. Louis during a 7-year period. This study concludes that "the crime rates per 100,000 population in and near the public housing developments are not significantly higher than in the city as a whole, nor are they higher than would be expected based on citywide relationships of crime to demographic and locational predictors."

0719.   Fielding, Byron. 1972. NAHRO Rallies "To Save Public Housing." Journal of Housing 29 (10): 491-93.

In 1972 it appeared that the public housing program had weathered its worst financial crisis in its 35 years history. Some housing authorities threatened to shut down all or a major portion of their operations, and others indicated that they will go to court to prevent the cut off of financial support needed for their operation. This article chronicles the NAHRO's efforts to persuade the federal government to release $100 million for housing subsidies, needed to continue local programs through the end of fiscal year. NAHRO alerted Local Housing Authorities and others to the shortage of funds through a series of action bulletins, mustered support for additional money in Congress, and convinced HUD and the Administration of the urgent need for funds. NAHRO also kept up pressure by filing a law suit against HUD on behalf of the housing authorities and tenants in order to save public housing.

0720.   Forman, E. M. S. 1976. Ethnic and Income Housing Occupancy Patterns of Federal Moderate-Income Housing and Federal Public Housing in Low- and Moderate-Income Neighborhoods in New York City. Environment and Planning A 8 (6): 707-14.

Economic and racial-ethnic housing patterns of FHA Section 236 moderate income and federally aided low-income public housing projects were examined in order to determine the relationships between the tenant-selection process, neighborhood racial-ethnic mix, and housing occupancy patterns. The overall results show that in moderate-income neighborhoods federal income-admissions and integration regulations were successfully implemented regardless of the economic type of the project. In low-income neighborhoods federal income admissions and integration regulation were unsuccessfully implemented for projects of both economic types.

0721.   Fox, Clara. 1974. Public Programs for Housing in New York. City Almanac 8 (5): 1-11.

New York City has a long record of helping its low- and middle-income residents to meet their housing needs. Currently, much of the city's housing is in need of rehabilitation or replacement. As a result, a number of programs were initiated in the late 1950s--e.g., the Mitchell-Lama program, Neighborhood Conservation, and Municipal Loan Programs. In addition, there are the federal Model Cities and Urban Renewal. But the most enduring program of all is public housing, which houses one of every thirteen New Yorkers. To deal with the problem of increasing construction and maintenance costs and pathologies facing the public housing, new programs have been introduced: Urban Development Corporation, which is a cooperative conversion effort, and a new approach at neighborhood preservation. The New York City's administration most serious challenge is to respond to the recent moratorium on federal housing assistance. Fox suggests that on an interim basis, both the city and state can substitute capital funds for the federal inputs, but it is essential that federal funds be reinstated to preserve the city's ability to continue to provide housing for its low- and middle-income residents.

0722.   Fox, Clara. 1984. Public Housing's Future: A Look Ahead. Journal of Housing 41 (6): 192-195.

The author points out that public housing construction programs have all but become things of the past, mainly as a result of changes in the local and federal public policies. This article examines changes in these policies and concludes that "it is axiomatic to state that the private sector will not, and in fact cannot, build or maintain housing for the poor and, with the end of the Section 8 program, only public housing can fill that need." It is, therefore, suggested that various financial resources be explored to support the restoration of public housing to its rightful place as the most effective program for low-income individuals and families.

0723.   Freedman, Leonard. 1969. Public Housing: The Politics of Poverty. New York: Holt, Rinehart and Winston, Inc. 217 pp.

This book is a legal description and evaluation of the United States public housing. That is, it describes the evolution and development of public housing. There are chapters on public attitudes toward the poor, the racial overtones of the public housing controversies, and the ideological conflicts over questions of public ownership. The problem of public housing is treated as a case study of the powerlessness of the poor in the American political system. In short, the author has two major objectives: (1) to describe public housing policy in the U.S.; (2) to interpret the conditions giving rise to the problems confronted in providing public housing; the second half of the book highlights the factors responsible for popular opposition to public housing; the author explains how each of these factors has cost public housing support in the U.S. Congress. As a whole, the book attempts to illustrate that the government and political system in the U.S. work against the interest of the poor.

0724.   Friedman, Lawrence M. 1966. Public Housing and the Poor: An Overview. California Law Review 54 (2): 642-669.

Public housing became a reality in the U.S. only in the days of the New Deal. This article provides a critically important overview of the federal public housing programs. It concludes that the programs have generally failed to provide housing for the poor. This is because these programs never really intended to serve the poor. The author asserts that "public housing is meaningless or hypocritical if it is not an effective vehicle to make better the life of the poor. That is the object, or ought to be; management is only an instrument. Bureaucratic convenience and paternalism are not the point of public housing; they are perversions. Much of the fault for present ills can be found in the long shadow of history, as this paper has attempted to show. But the program is not incurable. What is needed, quite simply, is more subtle flexibility, in fitting the means to the ends."

0725.   Friedman, Lawrence M.   1971.   Public Housing and the Poor.   In: **Problems in**
Political   Economy: An   Urban   Perspective.   David   M.   Gordon   (ed.).
Lexington, Mass.: D.C. Heath and Company.   Pp. 395-400.

This article provides a critically important historical perspective on the
federal public housing program.   According to Friedman, the program "has
been generally abandoned and has failed to provide very much housing for the
poor," for it was never intended for the purpose of serving the needs of the
poor.   Given this history, it seems much more difficult to argue that public
housing has failed to meet an objective it never intended to achieve.   This
article is a shorter version of the article by the author cited above
(previous item).

0726.   Fuerst, J. S.   1973.   Public Housing: Promise and Despair in Chicago.
Planning 39 (9): 14-18.

Chicago exemplifies the promise and despair of public housing, for not only
Chicago's public housing has fallen to such a low estate, but because in 1953
Chicago had a creative program which might have truly revitalized the city.
Chicago's experience with public housing began in 1935.   The Chicago
Housing Authority (CHA) directed these efforts and recognized that the
problem of public housing in Chicago was in large measure a problem of race.
Since 1953 the authority built housing for families in black areas only.   It
was for this discrimination against blacks in site selection that it was
finally enjoined in the federal courts in 1968.   The **Gautreaux v. CHA**
decision   forbade   the   CHA   from   building   exclusively   in   black   areas.
Reaction to this decision stopped all public housing in Chicago.

0727.   Fuerst, J. S.   1973.   Hidden Successes of Public Housing.   **Nation** 217 (16):
493-96.

This article provides a brief history of public housing in the United States.
It highlights the difficulties in creating a successful public housing
project.   Examines some of the successful public housing projects;   the
common criteria found in these projects are noted.   Whether such strengths
in public housing can win over the forces that seem determined to pull public
housing down is a question that remains to be answered.   The article
concludes: "Are the successful projects and the effective administrators
mentioned above persuasive enough to overcome the image of failure, or has
the dominant character of the public-housing program been   so crystallized
by its enemies that no amount of success can save it?"

0728.   Fuerst, J. S.   1974.   Class, Family, and Housing.   Society 12 (1): 48-53.

The author asserts that we have the human and financial resources to achieve
a continuously rising standard of living and eliminate extremes of poverty.
That is, if we had the will, we can build and rehabilitate enough housing for
all those in need of housing.   The author suggests that in order to preserve
projects from becoming "leper colonies" for the poor, public housing
authorities must have the same degree of latitude that private housing
managers have.   Present public housing authorities provide no answer to
many families in need of housing.

0729.   Glazer, Nathan.   1967.   Housing Problems and Housing Policies.   **Public**

Interest 7: 21-51.

Examining housing problems and policies the author concludes that housing policy in the U.S. has permitted the majority of Americans to improve their housing conditions, and to gain family settings that were superior to those of their parents. However, the policies have done little for a substantial minority of poor households who have not had the resources to achieve the minimally desired housing conditions. For this group, the author suggests to devise income maintenance policies that would permit them to achieve such housing;   or, they must be provided with housing subsidies that would produce the same results.

0730.   Hamilton, Raymond Warren. 1971. **The Public Housing Program in the United States: An Analysis and Evaluation.** Unpublished Ph.D. Dissertation. University of Maryland. 181 pp.

The nation's inadequate progress in realizing the goal of "a decent home and a suitable living environment for every American family" led to enactment of the Housing Act of 1968, which called for the development of twenty-six million housing units, six million of these for low- and moderate-income families, within a decade. The public housing program, the oldest federal program providing financial assistance for the provision of decent housing for low-income families, is expected to provide a fifth of the six million assisted units during the housing goal decade. This study examines the basic economic aspects of public housing program. Under this program, the federal government provides financial and technical assistance to local housing authorities for the development of public housing units. This study concludes that public housing should continue to be the primary subsidy program because it has important and distinctive features which enables it to provide decent shelter for the low-income and most disadvantaged families.*

0731.   Hamlar, Portia Trenholm. 1972. Hud's Authority to Mandate Effective Management of Public Housing. **Journal of Urban Law** 50 (1); 79-128.

This article comments on the public housing tenants' right to effective management and maintenance of public housing. It asserts that the ultimate responsibility for effective management is vested in HUD, and that recent legislative history and judicial decisions have placed upon HUD the responsibility of requiring compliance with HUD policies by local housing authorities in management of public housing.

0732.   Hartman, Chester. 1963. The Limitations of Public Housing: Relocation Choices in a Working-Class Community. **Journal of the American Institute of Planners** 29 (November): 283-96.

Public housing is regarded as a major resource for rehousing families displaced by the urban renewal and highway programs. Yet a study of some 500 families relocated from Boston's West End reveals that the overwhelming majority refused to consider the possibility of living in a housing project, for reasons consistent with their performance for the residential patterns and life-styles prevalent in their former neighborhood. Those who do relocate in projects are not typical of the stable working class, and most frequently are characterized by some personal situation that limits their housing choice. Planners are confronted with the alternative of allowing public housing to become a care-taking institution for the disabled elements of the society, or of creating new forms for the public housing subsidy to encourage mobility, to provide satisfactory living environments consistent with the values of the inhabitants, and to permit the kinds of heterogeneity which prevail in existing neighborhoods.*

0733. Hartman, Chester, and Margaret Levi. 1973. Public Housing Managers: An Appraisal. Journal of the American Institute of Planners 39 (2): 125-37.

This article presents an overview of the characteristics and attitudes of public housing project managers, as drawn from a mailed questionnaire sent to managers in public housing projects in the nation. Findings indicated that demographically managers differed sharply from the residents of public housing; that managers' positions were ill-defined; that managers did not admit to much tenant-management conflict; nor there was much sentiments favoring increased tenants' participation in project management. The authors assert that the fundamental problem must be faced with respect to the inadequate subsidies for the low-rent housing programs; and, the underlying issue of race and income distribution which are at the root of housing problem must be solved. It is concluded that public housing programs, have never been universally popular, and continue to be the targets of attacks and abuse. These must be corrected, and adjustments should be made to meet the needs of the current clientele--lower class, nonwhite, and elderly--of public housing.

0734. Hays, R. Allen. 1982. Public Sector Housing Rehabilitation: A Survey of Program Impact. Urban Interest 4 (1): 70-86.

This article reports and analyzes data from a national survey of public sector housing rehabilitation programs, to which 154 local housing and community development agencies responded. Four central aspects of rehabilitation programs are examined: (1) funding sources; (2) the populations which these programs are designed to serve, especially their impact on low and moderate-income persons; (3) the scope of their rehabilitation efforts; and (4) the relationship of these efforts to the overall need for upgrading the nation's existing housing stock. The survey found that the major funding sources for these programs are Section 312 loans, loans and grants from Community Development Block Grants, subsidized loans from local lending institutions, and loans from states housing finance agencies. As to the population served, it was found that most programs use income limits to target their programs to families below the median income, but that a restricted segment of low to moderate income persons are served; namely, those who are homeowners in neighborhoods with only moderate degree of deterioration. As to the scope of rehabilitation, it was found that the volume of loans and grants is very low (less than 50 units per year) in almost all communities and that it does not increase with size of the community.

0735. Hirshen, Al, and Vivian Brown. 1972. Public Housing's Neglected Resources: The Tenants. City 6 (4): 14-21.

The authors review the positive rewards of tenants' involvement in policy making in St. Louis, Philadelphia, and other cities. In St. Louis a Tenant Affairs Board had convinced authorities to expand employment opportunities for tenants within its own operations. And, Philadelphia's advisory board had attempted to educate tenants to the necessity of paying rent on time. The authors suggest the establishment of formal mechanism for insuring recognition to tenants' rights.

0736. Hirshen, Al, and Vivian N. Brown. 1972.   Too Poor for Public Housing: Roger Starr's Poverty Preference. Social Policy 3 (1): 28-32.

In an outspoken article published in the Spring 1971 issue of Public Interest, Mr. Roger Starr offered some provocative theories to explain the current crisis in public housing. Hirshen and Brown point out that Mr. Starr predicts disaster, accelerated deterioration, and the consequent reluctance of the federal government to build more low cost housing if public housing is made available to all those for whom it was intended. The present article attempts to show that to the contrary, disaster will result if Mr. Starr's ostrichlike approach—shifting the blame on destructive behavior to its ultimate victims rather than alleviating the pressures that contribute to its cause—is accepted as a solution.@

0737. Hirshen, Al, and Richard LeGates. 1973. Dreary Deadlock Revisited. Architectural Forum 138 (2): 66-70.

Public housing (PH), it may be acknowledged, will never become a popular and accepted program unless it is made indistinguishable from private housing. This is the main theme of the comments made by the authors of the "dreary deadlock," a group of eleven nationally known housing reformers who wrote in the Forum sixteen years ago. Techniques to make public housing less distinguishable from private housing are discussed. They include a housing policy favoring scattered units, a home ownership program, purchase of existing private units, and leasing of units by a local authority in existing private housing. The "dreary deadlock" authors also included management reforms of the public housing program to make it more acceptable to tenants and Turnkey units. They concluded that a housing allowance program may be a viable way to make sure that PH remains indistinguishable from private housing. It is the conclusion of the present article that "without a new national commitment, the next generation of housing reformers will surely be as vexed as we are. Without it, the poor will continue to be victimized."

0738. Hojnacki, W. P., and F. Steggert. 1982. Impact and Equity in the Distribution of Municipal Housing Services. In: Analyzing Urban Service Distributions. R. Rich (ed.). Lexington, Mass.: Lexington Books. Pp. 135-51.

This study applies research techniques to the task of evaluating the delivery of municipally administered housing services. More specifically, it attempts to answer questions regarding the effectiveness and equity in the distribution of such services in South Bend, Indiana. Findings point at the existence of two problems: (1) the substantive difficulty cities face in attempting to deliver housing services; (2) the methodological difficulty researchers face when trying to measure the impact of such urban service distribution. In this regard, the study identifies a service that was equitably distributed in geographic terms, but had no equity in its class or demographic distribution. From a methodological point of view, findings show that it is crucial to explore service distributions by population and geographic areas.

0739.   Hoshino, George, and Mary Lynch.   1975.   Public Housing: A Case Study in
Administrative Justice.   **Public Welfare** 33 (3): 41-47.

This is a case study of the Housing and Redevelopment Authority study in a
city of about 550,000, with a relatively small racial and minority
population in comparison with other cities of this size. Applicants were
interviewed when applying for housing. If application was approved, it was
placed on a waiting list; if not approved, applicant was given the
opportunity to appeal. As a whole, the housing authorities acted as judges,
and families were judged on the basis of how closely they matched the
authorities standards of behavior. Some projects had long waiting list
because of their desirability of location, racial composition, and type,
while in some other projects there were surplus public housing. The
findings suggest that the applicant's need and interest in obtaining public
housing was not necessarily given a high priority; rather, the interest of
the present tenants, the larger community, and the staff of housing
authorities came first.

0740.   Huth, Mary Jo.   1981.   An Examination of Public Housing in the United States
After Forty Years.   **Journal of Sociology and Social Welfare** 8 (3): 471-88.

This article first reviews the history of public housing (PH) in the U.S.
since its inception in 1937, noting that growing obsolescence of PH units,
the deterioration of inner-city neighborhoods surrounding PH projects,
racial tensions, and inflation have aggravated PH problems in recent years.
Moreover, PH tenants are no longer predominantly white, upwardly-mobile,
two-parent, working-class families, but predominantly non-white, non-
mobile, female-headed, lower-class families. The second part of this
article presents the findings of a 1978 field survey of PH in the U.S.
conducted by HUD in preparation for its Public Housing Urban Initiatives
Programs. This survey revealed the number of "troubled" projects and their
major characteristics, identified and explained the principal variables
causing these projects to be labeled "troubled," and, finally assessed the
impact of a variety of remedial intervention strategies proposed by HUD
field office personnel. The author concludes that, in the balance, the
positive aspects of PH program in the U.S. outweigh its negative features.
There are problems with inconsistent regulations at the federal level, with
site selection, with fraud and crime, with management-tenant relations, and
with underfinancing, but the system has also responded fairly well over the
past forty years to the demand for low-income housing and to changing tenant
expectations in terms of the structure of PH units and their amenities,
besides incorporating new housing technologies and architectural styles.@

0741.   Huth, Mary Jo.   1981.   Strategies for Crime Reduction in Public Housing.
Journal of Sociology and Social Welfare 8 (3): 587-600.

Many recent studies have revealed that not only are residents of public
housing the most vulnerable segment of the American population in terms of
criminal victimization, but that even in projects where the actual incidence
of crime is not high, a great fear of crime prevails, especially among the
elderly tenants. There is general consensus among crime prevention experts
that crime reduction programs in public housing must utilize an integrated
set of measures, including: (1) physical design, security hardware, and

maintenance improvements by management; (2) increased organization of
tenants around crime prevention issues; (3) employment of unemployed
tenants--both youths and adults--on the rehabilitation of their projects;
(4) establishment of on-site crisis intervention and other social service
programs; (5) better cooperation between public housing security
personnel and the local police; and (6) more public-private agency
investment in the upgrading of public housing projects and their surrounding
neighborhoods. The Department of Housing and Urban Development's two-
year, $40 million Anti-Crime Demonstration in Public Housing launched in
1979 is the first attempt by the Federal government to wage such a
comprehensive attack on crime and its attendant problems in our nation's
most neglected residential areas.*

0742. Huttman, Elizabeth Dickerson. 1969. **Stigma and Public Housing: A
Comparison of British and American Policies and Experience.** Unpublished
Ph.D. Dissertation. University of California, Berkeley. 964 pp.

This dissertation consists of a comparative study of policies that lead to
negative labeling or stigma in public housing. The author asserts that in
the U.S., public housing is a highly stigmatized service, and many potential
applicants refuse to use it because of its bad reputation; and most non-
users severely negatively label the program. In contrast, in Great
Britain, public (council) housing is a much larger and much more acceptable
program; and most working class people desire to use the service and most
middle class non-users give it only very mild negative label. This
dissertation compares the policies of these two countries with a focus on
policy aspects that makes public housing more acceptable in Britain than in
the United States. The study shows that tenant selection criteria play a
major role in causing a low or high degree of stigma for the program. Tenant
selection criteria in both countries are discussed. Site selection is
another factor. Differences in site selection procedures and its impacts
on acceptability of public housing in the two nations are explained.

0743. Jackson, Hubert M. 1958. Public Housing and Minority Groups. Phylon 19
(1): 21-30.

The growth of America since World War I has been phenomenal. One such growth
and development is the problem of housing, a problem recognized by the
federal government. Asserting that great inequality in housing exists,
this article reviews the federal government's attempt to remedy the problem.
The author calls upon the government to wage a total war against the slums of
the nation. As the last word the author points out that "public housing
program will continue to complement the private housing industry in the
attainment of our national housing objective--the realization as soon as
feasible of the goal of a decent home and suitable living environment for
every American family."

0744. Jahoda, Marie, and Patricia Salter West. 1951. Race Relations in Public
Housing. Journal of Social Issues 7 (1 & 2): 132-39.

Race relations have become matters of concern for housing planners and
administrators in recent years. The problem of segregated housing is
perhaps the most important aspect of race relation; and it is in the public
housing projects that the problem is faced most squarely. This article

reports some of the findings from two studies of black-white relations in
public housing projects: (1) a project of about 800 families, half black and
half white in an eastern industrial city; (2) a research conducted by
Research Center for Human Relations of New York University of two Newark and
two New York housing projects with different patterns of racial occupancy.
Findings indicate greater intimacy between black and white housewives in the
integrated projects than in the segregated projects. According to this
article, "approximately 70 percent of the white women in the integrated
projects disagreed with the statement that 'generally speaking, colored
people are lazy and ignorant,' as compared with 50 percent in the segregated
projects." The implications and value of such findings for public housing
planners administrators are discussed.

0745. Kanner, Stephen Barrett. 1977. The Future of Public Housing. **Real
Estate Law Journal** 6 (1): 34-45.

The Supreme Court decision in Hills v. Gautreaux suggests the possibility of
locating public housing in the suburbs under programs not requiring local
approval. At the same time, suggests this author, the decision puts strong
pressure on Congress to limit such programs. The author examines Gautreaux
in the context of a series of recent cases affecting public housing policy,
and considers ways the federal government--strongly committed under the
present Administration to take new initiatives--may successfully meet
housing goals in the face of the constraints created by these decisions.*

0746. Klutznick, Philip M. 1985. Poverty and Politics: The Challenge of Public
Housing. **Journal of Housing** 42 (1): 9-12.

If anything can be learned since the inception of public housing program, it
is that housing and the peoples' need of it are primarily a matter of income
and family size, and not a lack of the desire for good housing. This article
provides a review of the perceptions and policies that effect the provisions
of public housing.

0747. Knox, Michael D., Marilyn S. Kolton, and Louis Dwarshuis. 1974. Community
Development in Housing: Increased Tenant Participation. **Public Welfare** 32
(3): 48-53.

In 1971, HUD sent out requests to Housing Authorities around the country to
submit proposals for providing increased tenant services on a cost-
effective basis. The proposal included these suggestions: (1) increasing
tenant responsibility for decision-making; (2) accelerating upward
mobility of tenants; and (3) training and employment of tenants. The main
objective of the proposal was to foster community development and to
forestall alienation and anomie in public housing projects. A framework
for implementation of the project was developed by 1973. The framework
provided information about tenant needs and concerns, data about goods and
services, guidelines for decision-making and policy requirements, and
information on home ownership. These activities had the effect of
facilitating the authorities to reach the goal of increasing resident
participation in public housing projects.

0748. Kriesberg, Louis. 1968. Neighborhood Setting and the Isolation of Public
Housing Tenants. **Journal of the American Institute of Planners** 34

(January): 43-49.

Underlying many controversies about desirable location of lower-income public housing projects are differentials in beliefs about the consequences of placing low-income families in middle-income neighborhoods. The kinds of people living in low-income public housing projects vary greatly. The physical features of the projects and the surrounding areas, and the processes of self-selection by tenants and of admission by the housing authorities all affect the social composition of each project. In view of such variability, it is possible to study how certain conditions affect the social isolation of project tenants from residents in the surrounding area. This article analyzes the extent to which social isolation between project tenants and residents in the surrounding area exists and is affected by the socioeconomic differences between them. In doing this the author chooses projects that vary in neighborhood characteristics and socio-economic conditions. The study is based upon a survey of families in four low-income public housing projects called Park, Grant, Evans, and Stern, all located in Syracuse, New York. The author concludes: "In the beginning of this paper, I listed a variety of ways in which low-income families living in middle-income neighborhoods might learn, develop, and express the life styles of middle-income families. The social isolation of project tenants would impede some of the processes by which such changes occur. The evidence of this analysis indicates that socioeconomic status differences are not a particularly important barrier to social interaction between project tenants and neighborhood residents. I believe that the resolution of such factual controversies will contribute to the reasoned discussion of policy alternatives."

0749.   Kunze, Carr. 1981. Public Housing Cooperatives Reduce Dependence on Operating Subsidies, Modernization Funding. **Journal of Housing** 38 (9): 489-p3.

In the face of severe budgetary cutbacks, when housing authorities may lose operating subsidies and modernization funds, the development or conversion of public housing units to a cooperative model may offer an alternative to bankruptcy or to returning units to the government. This article elaborates on the advantages of the cooperative alternative. As its major advantage, the author emphasizes that "cooperatives develop a peer pressure environment that encourages leadership and the will to move ahead."

0750.   Kviz, Frederick James. 1975. **Response to** Environment: The Case of Public **Housing in an American City.** Unpublished Ph.D. Dissertation. University of Illinois at Chicago Circle.. 120 pp.

Despite a large number of studies concerning man and his social environment, the topic of the relationship between the physical environment and his contacts with items of non-personal nature has been relatively neglected. This research attempts to fill this gap by exploring the relationship between aspects of physical environment--building type and floor level--and non-personal contacts such as awareness and utilization of local facilities and services, among residents of a low-income public housing project. The analysis is based on an interview sample of 915 residents, of whom 87 percent were females, 92 percent were black and 79 percent in the 19-50 age group, all of whom resided in six public housing projects for non-elderly in the city of

Chicago. Findings indicate that residents in low rise buildings and on the lower floors of high rise buildings displayed greater awareness and utilization of local facilities and services than those on the upper floors of high-rise buildings. This study also indicates that "the influence of the physical environment observed is not independent of the social environment. Social factors, especially the number and age of children in the household and length of residence in the development, interact with the physical factors to influence behavior patterns."

0751.   Lazin, Frederick Aaron. 1973. The Failure of Federal Enforcement of Civil Rights Regulations in Public Housing, 1963-1971: The Cooperation of a Federal Agency by its Local Constituency. Policy Science 4 (3): 263-73.

This paper reports on research regarding the federal role with respect to racially discriminatory practices in public housing. It is a case study of federal efforts to deal with inadequate housing for low-income Americans, based on Public Housing in Chicago from 1963 through June 1971.*

0752.   Ledbetter, William, Jr. 1967. Public Housing: A Social Experiment Seeks Acceptance. Law and Contemporary Problems 32 (3): 490-527.

The large number of projects designed to improve the living conditions of the less privileged in the U.S. has become known as social welfare. One such project is the public housing program. This article describes the origin and history of public housing; it offers a brief summary of how the program works; it surveys and evaluates the most common criticisms of the program, and finally studies "new approaches to public housing in an effort to see whether the program can rise to acceptance from the present nadir of its fortunes." The author concludes that public housing cannot be replaced by any program thus far developed, but it can be supplemented and improved.

0753.   Lefcoe, George. 1971. HUD's Authority to Mandate Tenants' Rights in Public Housing. Yale Law Journal 80 (3): 463-514.

HUD's Secretary has recently mandated more favorable lease terms and grievance procedures for the 2.5 million tenants who reside in public housing. These actions grew out of a series of meetings with representatives of tenants and local agencies that manage public housing. "This essay presents the case that there are sensible statutory limits on the discretion of the Secretary, even when it comes to an act so clearly decent as trying to protect poor people in public housing from harsh treatment." The author asserts that these limitations derive from the congressional design of the public housing program with its strong preference for local control of management. That is, the essay elaborates on the problem areas where HUD cannot impose the terms of these leases and grievance procedures on local authorities.

0754.   Leigh, Wilhelmina A., and Mildred O. Mitchell. 1980. Public Housing and the Black Community. Review of Black Political Economy 11 (1): 53- 74.

This paper focuses upon public housing and blacks. According to the authors nearly 31 percent of black Americans have poverty level incomes; thus, many blacks are in need of assistance through public housing. This article enumerates five major goals of federal housing policy; public housing has operated to provide adequate and affordable housing. But, recent financial problems triggered by increased costs in the face of decreasing revenues have often been adjusted by decrease in housing maintenance, and thus lowering the adequacy of public housing. This article asserts that as long as income of about one third of blacks is at the poverty level, they remain in need of public housing; it also suggests that the proposed maximum 30 % of income tenants should pay as rent, if put into effect, will make public housing less affordable.

0755.   Lempert, Richard, and Kiyoshi Ikeda. 1970. Eviction from Public Housing: Effects of Independent Review. **American** Sociological Review 35 (5): 852-60.

This paper examines the change in eviction decisions within a local housing authority which occurred when the power to make those decisions was transferred from a board of authority officials to a board of citizen volunteers. Accountability to tenant interests, as measured by the percentage of favorable decisions, increased; accountability to project managers decreased. This is reflected by a percentage change in the kinds of actions brought before the board and by efforts to evade the formal system. The direction of change is seen as likely but not inexorable result of independent review. Role theory elaborates this idea. The process by which citizens were incorporated into the decision making theory is viewed as a form of co-operation*

0756.   Lilley, William III, and Timothy B. Clark. 1972. Immense Costs, Scandals, Social Ills Plague Low-Income Housing Programs. **National Journal** 4 (27): 1075-83.

The gap between expectation and realization characteristic of many federal programs is best portrayed by the demolition of an 11-story apartment building in the Pruitt-Igoe housing complex in St. Louis, Missouri. This article describes major federal low cost and public housing programs designed to provide decent housing for the poor. The demolition of the Pruitt-Igoe project is attributed to the government's inability to make the project viable. The authors point out that the St. Louis project is only one of the many trouble spots in federal housing. They assert that "scandals, insolvencies and lack of municipal services have combined to make the future of low-income housing as bleak as the ruins of Pruitt-Igoe."

0757.   Luttrell, Jordan D. 1966. The Public Housing Administration and Discrimination in Federally Assisted Low-Rent Housing. **Michigan** Law Review 64 (5): 871-89.

The Failure of PHA to achieve more than token desegregation of the nation's public housing program seems traceable to its reluctance to undertake action which would effectively offset its own past discriminatory site- and tenant-selection practices as well as those of local authorities. If PHA is to remove the discrimination which now taints the nation's low-rent housing programs, and present federal antidiscrimination policies strongly suggest that it must, then it seems that PHA should consider implementing the following suggestion. First, it should ensure that future low-rent housing projects are placed in racially mixed neighborhoods or are dispersed in smaller units throughout the community. The adoption of such an approach, however, will not affect the bulk of low-rent housing already constructed in homogeneous neighborhoods. Second, since the free choice plan now extolled by PHA has proved inadequate in removing the stigma of past discrimination, PHA should discard it, and demand that local authorities institute a first-come-first-served plan. Through these methods PHA should be able to guarantee open access to all public housing projects, not merely to those labeled "Negro" or "white."*

0758.   Lym, Glen Robert. 1967. Effect of a Public Housing Project on a Neighborhood: Case Study of Oakland, California. **Land Economics** 43 (4): 461-66.

Land use zoning and existing laws are two effective methods of controlling the size and the type of a city's growth. Concentrating on the existing land use laws, this article attempts to study the impacts of a low-income public housing project named Campbell Village, in Oakland, California.

0759.   Maloney, Lawrence, et al. 1980. Public Housing: Some Old Sad Tale. U.S. **News and World Report** 89 (17): 89-90.

"For millions of nation's poor, home is often a shabby apartment in a building rife with crime, drugs and vandalism." This article asserts that thousands of poor families in the U.S., who have no alternatives, continue to line up for the nation's supply of deteriorating, crime-ridden public housing. The article cites examples of the poor quality of living in public housing in several cities. Despite federal subsidies of $742 million this year, maintenance costs have outdistanced the available funds. Management officials complain that tenants abuse their units, making maintenance more costly. Solutions to problems facing public housing are difficult to find, but some experts recommend the expansion of Section 8 program that allows tenants to find their own housing and the government pays them a subsidy. Others believe that inspiring local housing authorities to do a better job may turn out to be more effective and less expensive.

0760.   McCue, George. 1973. $57,000,000 Later. **Architectural Forum** 138 (4): 42-45.

The disgrace associated with Pruitt-Igoe, an internationally known public housing project, may yet be redeemed if a proposed development plan survives the federal purge of housing programs. The failure of Pruitt-Igoe as a public housing project could not be attributed to the architecture alone, to the community or to the tenants, but must be recognized to be the result of a series of social events and social conflicts. This article is a summary of one of a series of reports by a task force commissioned to analyze what happened to Pruitt-Igoe, and to see what can be retrieved from its ruins.

0761.   McGrew, Jane Lang. 1981. Resistance to Change Continues to Restrict Public Housing Choices. **Journal of Housing** 38 (7): 375-81.

When 120 townhouses for low-income families were built in Whitman Park, a Philadelphia community, the neighbors draped their doors with black crepe in protest. The housing officials in the country struggle with site selection decision for public housing. Housing discrimination is prohibited by law—Title VIII of the Civil Rights Act of 1968, the rationale for which lie in the

13th and 14th amendments of the U.S. constitution. The law also mandates federal agencies to promote fair housing in the nation. The author discusses opposition to public housing in the central city as opposed to scattered suburban site location decisions. The author asserts that more effective Title VIII enforcement is needed. It is indicated that deconcentration of low-income families is not a realistic objective; instead, expansion of housing choices must be the objective.

0762.   McGuire, Marie C. 1962. 25 Years Ahead: A Look at the Future of Public Housing. Journal of Housing 19 (8): 430-45.

This article consists of legislative history of public housing traced through 25 years. Headings are: Before the turn of the century; basic public policy at issue; federal government builds; first of three bills goes in; the 1937 Act passes; war reorganization; new look, new law needed; the 1949 Act; the Eisenhower era; the 1954 Act; the 1956 Act; the 1959 Act; the Kennedy administration; the 1961 Act; and, hope ahead. For anyone interested in a complete history of public housing development up to 1962, this is an excellent source to turn to.

0763.   Meehan, Eugene J. 1975. Looking the Gift Horse in the Mouth--The Conventional Public Housing Program in St. Louis. Urban Affairs Quarterly 10 (4): 423-63.

Prior to 1950 the conventional public housing program was regarded as reasonably successful. By the end of 1969, there were about 750,000 public housing units in the country, and almost every major city in the U.S. was involved in the program. By the same year the St. Louis public housing has produced an internationally famous disaster. The results in St. Louis may not have been completely typical, but it was consistent with results in many other cities. The program turned into a failure because policy was ambiguous with respect to both purposes: site selection, and target population; and, it failed to take into account the changing social and economic conditions. The most disappointing aspect of the public housing program is that the institutions responsible for it failed to improve their performance with time. Consumers of these services face a genuine dilemma. What if even the established institutions cannot learn from experience? However, the author asserts that there is no evidence to support the contention that the program would have been a success if it were locally controlled.

0764.   Meehan, Eugene J. 1983. Is There a Future for Public Housing? Journal of Housing 40 (3): 73-76.

In this article Meehan examines the implications of past and present public housing policies, and concludes that "the most likely future for housing assistance, given the society's track record, will be to provide a limited subsidy to the low-income family, paid to the tenant by voucher or transfer directly to the owner. Since those subsidies will result from producer pressures, rather than assessment of individual need, the subsidy can be expected to take a form that will maximize benefits to the producer--not the tenants. That should leave society as a whole reasonably content, for it will allow a gesture of support for the "sparrows" without seriously inconveniencing the "horses.""

0765.   Meyerson, Martin, and Edward C. Banfield. 1955. **Politics, Planning, and the Public Interest.** Glencoe, Illinois: Free Press. 353 pp.

This book consists of an analysis of how decisions were reached on site-selection for low-rent public housing in Chicago after the passage of Federal Public Housing Act of 1949; it also deals with the topics of how black groups react on public issues, and the impossibility of separating housing problem from racial and political issues.

0766.   Miller, Ted R., and Mildred DePallo. 1986. Desegregating Public Housing: Effective Strategies. **Journal of Housing** 43 (1): 11-21.

This article discusses how legal barriers have prevented us to come up with the development of a workable desegregation plan. It considers alternative approaches that may result in successfully integrated housing projects.

0767.   Morrall, John F., III, and Edgar O. Olsen. 1980. The Cost-effectiveness of Leased Public Housing. **Policy Analysis** 6 (2); 151-69.

This paper discusses the methods and findings of a study that examined the cost-effectiveness of various ways of providing leased public housing services to low-income families. The study found little difference in the cost-effectiveness of new, existing, and rehabilitated leased-housing programs, and little difference depending upon the way in which each is operated, except that renting dwellings subsidized under FHA programs and using single-family dwellings are not cost-effective.*

0768.   Murray, Michael P. 1975. The Distribution of Tenant Benefits in Public Housing. **Econometrica** 43 (4): 771-88.

In this paper we estimate the Hicksian equivalent variation of consumer's surplus for a sample of public housing tenants and examine the distribution of these surpluses by household characteristics. To do this we estimate the parameters of a generalized CES utility function (imposing second order constraints as needed) and of a Cobb-Douglas utility function. The Cobb-Douglas specification is rejected statistically and benefit estimates based on it follow a significantly different distributional pattern than those estimated with the generalized CES, although there is not much difference in average benefits.*

0769.   Nourse, Hugh O. 1963. The Effect of Public Housing on Property Values in St. Louis. **Land Economics** 39 (4): 433-41.

This study provides no support for the view that public housing projects increase the value of surrounding properties. Property values in area A and B had the same general trend as those in their control neighborhoods. Property values in area C rose somewhat more than those in its control neighborhood although there is some evidence that the increase in prices in area C was at least partly due to truckers demand. In only one year was there a statistically significant difference between the real estate price indexes of a public housing neighborhood and its control area and in this instance the index for the public housing neighborhood was below that of its control neighborhood. The author asserts that this is the first research of

its kind; it is suggested that further research on the effect of public
housing on property values in other parts of the country be pursued.@

0770.   Ostrowski, Elaine T. 1984. Managing Public Housing: The Impact of the
80s. Journal of Housing 41 (2): 40-42.

This article discusses priorities for public housing managers. These
priorities are a matter of commitment by the federal government to solve the
outstanding public housing problems, and commitment by the local housing
authorities to improve the management of their programs. Through the
development of standards, improvement of funding mechanisms, a concerted
effort to upgrade and modernize existing public housing stock, the
commitment can be attained. The need for a better funding program for PHAs
is examined in the context of federal subsidies which are based on
performance.

0771.   Pozen, Robert. 19873. The Financing of Local Housing Authorities: A
Contract Approach for Public Corporation. Yale Law Journal 82 (6): 1208-
27.

Since the program began in 1937, the public housing program has been run by
Local Housing Authorities (LHAs). Presently, many LHAs are faced with
bankruptcy because of limitations on rentals coupled with rising operating
costs. This article examines the fiscal problems of LHAs as a case study in
the financing of public corporations. The author traces the legislative
and executive roots of the fiscal crisis facing the LHAs. Barriers to
resolving these crises through administrative law are discussed. The
author suggests a contract approach, supplemented by a funding formula, as a
means to solve these financial problems.

0772.   Queely, Mary, et al. 1981. Tenant Management: Findings from a Three-Year
Experiment in Public Housing. Cambridge, Mass.: Ballinger Publishing
Company. 269 pp.

This is a book produced by the Manpower Demonstration Research Corporation.
It is based on a three-year study designed to test the feasibility of turning
the management of public housing to tenants. The experiment involves seven
public housing projects consisting of about 4,800 housing units and 19,000
residents; eighteen matched sites constitute the control group.
Residents in all, except two, projects are largely low income blacks with a
large number of families headed by women. Some of the findings include: (1)
tenant-managed projects did not do any better, or worse than the
conventionally-managed projects with regard to average rent collections,
vacancy rates, and speed of response to maintenance requests; (2)
residents perceived tenant managers as stricter than conventional managers;
(3) however, tenant management was associated with substantial increase in
resident employment, a sense of personal accomplishment, and a greater
overall satisfaction with management; (4) but, tenant management was found
to be a costly enterprise, likely to become viable only within a relatively
narrow parameters—tenant management meant 13 to 62 percent increase in
management cost, which raises the question regarding the future of tenant
management of public housing. Factors necessary to make tenant-management
successful are discussed. As a whole, this study casts serious doubts on
the ability of tenants to manage public housing in any more efficient fashion

than the conventional managers.

0773.   Reene, David. 1979. Proposal for Moderate Rehabilitation: An Early Analysis of the Program and What it Portend for PHAs. **Journal of Housing** 36 (5): 264-66.

The moderate rehabilitation program offers Public Housing Authorities a good opportunity to upgrade public housing and assist low-income families to improve their housing conditions and rent-paying abilities. This article discusses the major elements of the moderate rehabilitation program that enables the PHAs to achieve these objectives.

0774.   Roncek, Dennis W., and Gail E. Weinberger. 1981. Neighborhoods of Leased Public Housing. **Evaluation Review** 5 (2): 231-44.

A major problem in the operation of housing programs is finding suitable locations for public housing. We examine the characteristics of the locations used by the Section 23 Leased Housing Program in San Diego. Our concern is whether or not this program, which uses privately owned dwellings, is able to provide low-income households with "suitable living environment." We compare the characteristics of city blocks that became Section 23 locations with blocks that did not on safety, population concentration, and social composition. The results are that the program is only partially successful. Section 23 housing was relatively dispersed throughout the city, but refined analysis techniques show that Section 23 housing is concentrated in more disadvantaged areas than those that did not become Section 23 locations.*

0775.   Rubenstein, James M., and Robert F. Ferguson. 1978. Baltimore Relocation Study. **Journal of Housing** 35 (10): 534-38.

This article investigates the effects of public housing projects such as urban renewal and interstate highways, on racially changing neighborhoods. More specifically, it first provides a summary of the historical migration of blacks into Baltimore, and the characteristics of blacks' recent displacement; then it examines the effects of displacement of racially changing neighborhoods. The study concludes that "government-induced relocation of inner-city families has not played a significant role in changing patterns of residential location in Baltimore. The patterns of relocation provide evidence of a stronger sense of community in the black inner-city neighborhoods than is frequently thought likely. Families seek out housing as close as possible to their former homes. Their method of securing replacement housing gives further testimony to the strength of community."

0776.   Sanoff, Henry. 1975. User Assessment of a Low-Income Residential Environment: Chapel Hill, North Carolina, USA. **Ekistics** 39 (235): 390-93.

This is a study based on interviews conducted with 90 percent of households of a black public housing project in Chapel Hill, North Carolina. The main objective of the study is to evaluate the residents' satisfaction with both the dwelling and the neighborhood. The sample consists of 80 black respondents, 32 of whom are female, with an average family size of 5.6 persons. Inconvenience to shopping center, safety, lack of playground for

children, and shortage of nice neighbors constituted least satisfactory
items. With respect to dwelling dissatisfaction, street noise, front
porch, outdoor privacy, and lack of storage space were mentioned. However,
two thirds of the sample reported the neighborhood as satisfactory.

0777.   Schuler, Gregory. 1983. Financing Section 8 Pipeline Projects: A Section
11 (b) Funding Guide. Journal of Housing 40(2); 44-46.

Until recently, municipal Public Housing Authorities (PHAs) have not been
involved in the financial aspects of construction low-income housing
developments. This matter was left exclusively to HUD. But this is
changing rapidly as Section 8 developers rely more and more on municipal PHAs
to provide financing via the sale of tax-exempt notes and bonds under Section
11 (b) of the Housing Act. This article explains the reasons for the change
and concludes that: successful Section 11 (b) financing in Chicago and in
cities nationwide demonstrate the ability of Municipal PHAs to administer
housing finance programs. With across-the-board cutbacks in federal
housing assistance program, PHAs' continued assumption of this role will be
crucial. Unless regulatory changes disengage the Section 11 (b) process
from the uncertain future of the Section 8 program, this role may well be
shortlived." The author asserts that the present situation calls for
seeking new sources of funds and ideas to substitute the dying ones, and
based on what has been learned in Chicago, any change in the rules that would
ensure the expanded role of PHAs will be useful.

0778.   Scobie, Richard S. 1973. "Problem Families" and Public Housing. Public
Interest (31): 126-29.

Roger Starr, in an article entitled: "Which of the Poor Shall Live in Public
Housing" (Public Interest, No. 23, Spring 1971; also cited in this chapter)
argued that there is some degree of incompatibility between the "working
poor" and "dependent poor" families living in the same public housing
project, and unless the "dependent poor" families are excluded, the conflict
between these two types of families will mean that the "dependent poor"
families will drive out the less problematic "working poor" families from
public housing. This thesis became a subject of great controversy.
"Dependent poor" families were defined as usually black, female headed
families who depended on AFDC welfare payments as the only source of income.
In the present article, Scobie attempts to test Roger Starr's hypothesis by
studying four developments in Boston, housing almost 4,000 low income
families. Scobie attempts to get answers to the following questions: How
many problem tenants do housing managers really have to contend with? Just
what is it that makes managers consider them to be problems? Of those so
identified, how many fit the classical description of the "problem family"?
Do the problem tenants differ in any special ways from the general project
population? How do Starr's "working poor" and "dependent poor" really get
along with one another? And when conflict does occur, who complains about
whom? Scobie concludes that his data did not provide evidence in support of
Roger Starr's hypothesis. However, following Scobie's article, Roger
Starr presents a five-page long reply to Scobie. In his reply to Scobie,
Roger Starr without questioning the validity of Scobie's statistics,
provides a powerful argument contending that Scobie failed to interpret his
statistics properly, and thus failed to refute the central thesis of his
(Roger Starr) article.

0779. Silver, Hilary, Judith McDonald, and Ronald J. Ortiz. 1985. Selling Public Housing: The Methods and Motivations. Journal of Housing 42 (6): 213-15.

The sale of public housing to low-income tenants is one of many proposals currently under study in an attempt to "privatize" public housing. This article examines the origins and the ideology behind attempts to privatize public housing; it also discusses the implication of this ideology/policy on the entire housing industry.

0780. Smith, Mary E. H. 1983. Public Housing Priorities: Lessons from Britain. Journal of Housing 40 (2): 40-43.

This article examines similarities and dissimilarities between the U.S. and British public housing programs. The author finds a striking similarity in the programs in the two countries; but there are also differences. In contrast to the U.S. where public housing is for the poor, the British do not refer to public housing as "low income" or "welfare" housing. That is, public housing in England is not provided according to any type of income criteria--the program is committed to the ideal of providing adequate housing for all. Its allocation is based on the widest interpretation of both social and housing need. This article also reviews problems facing public housing projects in both countries.

0781. Smolensky, Eugene. 1968. Public Housing or Income Supplements: The Economics of Housing for the Poor. Journal of the American Institute of Planners 34 (2): 94-101.

The notion that income supplements ought to be given to the poor to exploit cost savings available from private sector is at least as old as public housing; only permitting the poor to "keep the change" if any may be novel. That structural improvement of existing buildings is preferable to new construction is also an old idea, but that its prime advantage may be in maximizing the number of families living in safe and sanitary housing has not been generally perceived. A planner has vigorously espoused subsidizing the poor as a means to get the housing stock rehabilitated and the largest number of families in decent housing, and he was opposed a decade and half ago. Why has this obvious and simple scheme been avoided in most planning discussions? Part of the explanation undoubtedly lies in the enthusiasm of real estate dealers and builders for some aspects of the idea. The author's criticisms reflect earlier characteristics of the housing market. Low levels of construction for two decades accompanied by a massive spatial redistribution of the population preceded the 1949 Act. There has also been confusion about the administrative costs of such programs. However, despite the many existing problems, public housing must continue to be what it has been. But the way is open for vigorous debate and extensive field testing. Even if the results prove the existing programs to be the best, the exercise will have been significant for future housing policy.@

0782. Stafford, Walter William. 1973. An Analysis of Grants and Public Housing Units Approved for Municipalities by the Department of Housing and Urban Development 1965-1970 and their Relationships to the Black Population. Unpublished Ph.D. Dissertation. University of Pittsburgh. 383 pp.

The establishment of HUD in 1965 was a significant step in providing
institutional leadership and guidance for channeling the federal assistance
for urban areas. This study analyzes grants and public housing units
approved for municipalities by HUD from 1965 to 1970. More specifically, it
attempts to: (1) determine patterns of approval by size of localities and
whether size was a significant variable; (2) if percent black population in
the locality was linked to approval; (3) to what extent approvals were made
for areas where racial and socio-economic heterogeneity do not exist; and
(4) the relationship of approvals of seniority or assignment by the
appropriations or Banking and Currency Committees of the House of
Representatives. Findings indicate that the most significant variables were
population size of localities and committee assignments of Congressional
Representatives. The percentage of blacks within localities had little
relationship to approval patterns, except for immediate assistance
programs, particularly Model Cities and Neighborhood Facilities Programs.
The study found that Civil Rights organizations historically were not
particularly effective in influencing legislation of the programs
analyzed or subsequent agency implementation in local communities.
Localities which received the greatest benefits in terms of public housing
units were those with populations of 50,000 - 500,000 people. Larger cities
benefited basically from immediate assistance programs and smaller cities
from area-wide grant programs.@

0783.   Starr, Roger. 1971.   Which of the Poor Shall Live in Public Housing.
        Public Interest (23): 116-24.

        The author argues that public housing has been relatively successful in New
        York City as contrasted with other cities, because New York City Housing
        Authority provides homes acceptable to the "working poor".   It is further
        argued that the willingness of the working poor to reside in the New York City
        public housing is explained by the vigilance of the Authority "to keep its
        non-working population within limits that would be acceptable to the
        working-class population....".   Still further, Starr argues that most
        problem families are members of the non-working population, and that the
        presence of these families in the same projects threatens the continued
        willingness of working poor to live in New York City public housing.   In this
        article the author argues that there is some degree of incompatibility
        between the "working poor" and "dependent poor" families living in the same
        public housing project, and unless the "dependent poor" families" are
        excluded, the conflict between these two types of families will mean that the
        "dependent poor" families will drive out the less problematic "working poor"
        families from public housing.   "Dependent poor" families are defined as
        usually black, female headed families who depended on Aid to Families with
        Dependent Children (AFDC) welfare payments as the only source of income.
        For a criticism of this thesis see Richard S. Scobie's article cited above.

0784.   Stegman, Michael A. 1968. Comment on "Public Housing or Income
        Supplements: The Economics of Housing for the Poor." Journal of the
        American Institute of Planners 34 (3): 195-198.

        Stegman reviews and comments on the article by Eugene Smolensky, cited
        above.   Stegman asserts that Smolensky's article supports a statement made
        more than two decades ago by Charles Abrams that "relationship between

housing and the subsidy has been permitted to grow without benefit of maximum
or definition [and that] formulation of principles on the subsidy was never
more critical than it is today." Not only that, Smolensky's article "serves
to hammer another nail into the coffin of one of the oldest and most
controversial housing programs yet devised; namely, the public housing
program." According to Smolensky's calculations, private sector can
provide housing more cheaply than the public sector. Thus, a combined
private rehabilitation-income supplement program is a more efficient means
of providing decent housing for the poor who are living in substandard units.

0785.   Stegman, Michael A. 1972. Private Investment and Public Housing. Urban
Affairs Quarterly 8 (2): 161-79.

This article presents a review of the progress of subsidized housing program
since the turn of the decade; examines the relationship between inflation,
tight money, residential construction activity and subsidized housing
production, and stresses the importance of the continuation of low- and
moderate income subsidized housing; it also describes the abuses by
private investors in this endeavor.

0786.   Struyk, Raymond J. 1980. Public Housing Modernization: An Analysis of
Problems and Prospects. Journal of Housing 37 (9): 492-96.

Modernization of public housing projects means upgrading. Thus, a lot
depends on the definition of upgrading. It could be defined narrowly to
mean alterations, additions, replacement, or a major repair; or, a more
comprehensive definition could be employed to mean a general capital
improvement and include the fundamental management changes as part of
upgrading and/or modernization. Current regulation uses the narrow
definition of upgrading; in practice, this definition has proved to be
ineffective. "A discouraging picture of poor structure and multiple
disincentives emerges from a review of the modernization program's current
funding needs and use of resources." Recently, the U.S. Congress and HUD
have taken the initiative to apply the broader definition of upgrading-
capital improvement- to existing public housing projects. This article
examines problems and prospects of this new initiative. Topics covered
are: modernization funding, allocation process, incentives and
disincentives, and needed improvements. It is concluded that "the
comprehensive assistance program has the correct thrust."

0787.   Struyk, Raymond J., and John A. Tuccillo. 1983. Defining the Federal Role
in Housing: Back to Basics. Journal of Urban Economics 14 (2): 206-23.

The several objectives of government intervention in the housing sector and
the economic rationale for them are briefly reviewed. The case for and
efficiency of this intervention is then examined pursuant to two objectives-
-ensuring the availability of adequate and affordable housing to low-income
households and encouraging homeownership. Present approaches are found
wanting in both cases. The paper concludes with suggested modifications
that appear to be reasonable on budgeting efficiency, and political
grounds.*

0788.   Weicher, John C. 1980. Housing: Federal Policies and Programs.
Washington, D. C.: American Enterprise Institute for Policy Research. 161

pp.

Among many other topics, this book examines the historical development of subsidy programs including public housing, Section 8 new construction, Section 8 rehabilitation, Section 8 existing housing, and Section 8 loan management and property disposition. federal policy regarding the subsidy programs since 1974 is also discussed.

0789.   Weidemann, Sue, and James R. Anderson. 1982. Residents' Perceptions of Satisfaction and Safety: A Basis for Change in Multifamily Housing. Environment and Behavior 4 (6): 695-724.

This article reports on the use of the concepts of residential satisfaction and safety in the evaluation of a specific multifamily public housing site and illustrates the potential of these concepts for providing critical information for the future planning and design of that site. The evaluation was primarily based on structured self-reports from residents about perceptions of their housing environment and their expressed satisfaction with that housing. Issues such as privacy, appearance, management, maintenance, safety from crime, resident similarity, and economic value of the residence were among those examined. The results clearly show the interdependence between the physical environment and the residents and managers of that environment. The study concludes with some recommendations for change.@

••••••••••••••••••••••••••◆◆◆◆◆◆◆◆◆◆••••••••••••••••••••••••••

9
MINORITY HOUSING, REGULATORY ACTION, THE LAWS, AND THE COURTS

0790. Ackerman, Bruce. 1971. Regulating Slum Housing Markets on Behalf of the Poor: Of Housing Codes, Housing Subsidies and Income Distribution Policy. Yale Law Journal 80 (6): 1093-1197.

This article consists of a detail examination of laws governing housing codes, housing subsidy programs, and income redistribution policies, as they relate to the poor. It assesses the conditions under which the government's investment of a dollar in code enforcement would benefit the poor more than a dollar of public money invested in a negative income tax; the fairness of these two programs to the poor are studied. In a more general terms, this essay attempts to trace the relationship between property law problems--revolving around tenants' organization, tenants' private remedies, code enforcement and housing subsidies--with more general considerations of income redistribution.

0791. Anonymous. 1968. The Impact of Title VI on Housing. The Goerge Washington Law Review 36 (4): 994-1006.

The 1964 Civil Rights Act imposed on federal agencies the responsibility of assuring that no discrimination would be countenanced in programs paid for by the federal funds. This paper attempts to ascertain the manner in which the government has implemented its mandate relative housing and what effects that mandate has had on the federal programs. The essay concludes that HUD "has been exceedingly cautious and painfully slow in implementing Title VI objectives. To date, HUD has directed its energies toward improving the quality and expanding the quantity of available housing, sacrificing civil rights goals where necessary to meet this end. The recurrent tension in HUD programs over the order of priority of various policy objectives has relegated civil rights and Title VI to a secondary status in every major HUD program. While HUD administrators feel that they are making their contribution to the solution of the housing problem by increasing the housing supply, they are doing so in open contradiction of the mandate of Congress, which was to provide not maximum housing units, but maximum desegregated housing units."

0792. Anonymous. 1968. Owner of Private Subdivision May Refuse to Sell to
       Negroes. Vanderbilt Law Review 21 (2): 271-77.

       The owners of a private subdivision built without state or federal aid or
       financing, refused to sell a home to a plaintiff because the plaintiff-
       husband was a black. The denial was based on the argument that the existing
       zoning laws and ordinances did allow private owners to refuse to sell to
       Negroes. "Plaintiffs brought an action in federal district court alleging
       that defendants' refusal to sell was a denial of their rights guaranteed
       under the thirteenth and fourteenth amendments. Plaintiffs further
       alleged a violation of their right to buy property as declared in 42 U.S.C.
       Section 1982. The district court dismissed the action and on appeal to the
       United States Court of Appeals for the Eight Circuit, held, affirmed. Any
       owner of a private subdivision who refuses to sell to a Negro solely on the
       basis of race does not deny rights guaranteed under the thirteenth or
       fourteenth amendments and does not violate section 1982." Section 1982,
       derived from the Civil Rights Act of 1866 and 1870, guarantees to all
       citizens the same rights to purchase and hold property. This article
       examines the constitutionality of the Eighth Circuit's opinion and
       concludes that "in view of the trend in recent cases involving racial
       discrimination and in light of the previously mentioned political and social
       implications of segregated urban housing, it is submitted that the Supreme
       Court should reverse the instant decision."

0793. Anonymous. 1969. The "New" Thirteenth Amendment: A Preliminary Analysis.
       Harvard Law Review 82 (6): 1294-1321.

       In Jones v. Alfred H. Mayer Co. the Court re-examined the thirteenth
       amendment and found that it supports an extraordinarily broad protection of
       civil rights. "The petitioners in Jones had allegedly been denied housing
       in a private development because Mr. Jones was a Negro. The Court held this
       denial to be in violation of a provision of the 1866 Civil Rights Act,"
       granting to all citizens of the United States equal protection. This
       article examines the origins of the "new" thirteenth amendment, evaluates
       the basic components of judicial analysis offered in the Jones case, and
       raises the more fundamental issues that are likely to emerge as the scope of
       the amendment is explored.

0794. Anonymous. 1982. 1982 Developments in Housing Law. Housing Law Bulletin
       12 (6): 1-12.

       The focus of housing for low-income families shifted in 1982 from Congress to
       the agencies and the courts. This article reviews the most salient
       developments divided by agency and issue. In some instances interim or
       proposed regulations are also discussed.

0795. Aurbach, Herbert A., John R. Coleman, and Bernard Mausner. 1960.
       Restrictive and Protective Viewpoints of Fair Housing Legislation: A
       Comparative Study of Attitudes. Social Problems 8 (2): 118-125.

       This study tests two forms of a questionnaires intended to elicit opinions on
       a proposed fair housing legislation: (1) questionnaire developed by a public
       relations firm under contract for the Greater Pittsburgh Board of Realtors
       publicly opposing the proposed state fair housing laws; (2) one developed

by a group of social scientists interested in the promotion of fair housing laws and better intergroup relations. The Board of Realtor's questionnaire presented the law as a coercive device intended to enforce integrated housing. The Social Scientists form presented the laws as a protective device intended to assure individual rights in seeking housing in a free market regardless of race or color. Questionnaires were administered to equal size samples of residents in three widely differing areas in Pittsburgh. According the authors, "the result of this study lead to only one conclusion: Expressed attitudes toward an emotion-laden issue such as integrated housing depend heavily upon the way in which the questions are posed; it is possible to illicit pro-'fair housing law' sentiments if the question is worded in terms of basic equal protection of the law, it is still easier to get an overwhelming anti-'fair housing law' expression if the question is couched in terms of compulsory integration."

0796. Berger, Curtis. 1969. Slum Area Rehabilitation by Private Enterprise. Columbia Law Review 69 (5): 739-69.

Until recently only lawyers in city halls and in neighborhood law practices have had much professional concern with legal problems arising out of the operation, neglect and rehabilitation of the nation's present housing stock.

0797. Constantino, Mark A., and Vito A. Cannavo. 1979. Housing Site Selection Litigation: The House that Brown Built. New York Law School Law Review 25 (1): 21-39.

Housing remains a fundamental area of concern in antidiscrimination efforts in this country. The evolution of case law and statutory authority poses a viable solution to the problem. Burdensome, costly and evasive goals lose favor against more direct and simple ad hoc solutions. Challenges that are narrowly drawn to alleviate conditions in the immediate area raise the greatest likelihood of success. This approach and choice of remedies are wise, since the probability of the granting of multi-district or multi-country remedies is minimal in light of recent case law. Moreover, the practicality of large scale enforcement efforts is questionable, in light of the immediate results achieved through ad hoc remedies on a neighborhood level. As the chances for individual successes improve, policy-making bodies will scrutinize their procedures to direct funding for housing in the most equitable way. Hopefully, the general goal of providing decent housing will be achieved without the use of misdirected bulldozers.*

0798. Duncan, John B., and Albert Mindlin. 1964. Municipal Fair Housing Legislation: Community Beliefs and Facts. Phylon 25 (3): 217-37.

The current movement toward racial equality and democracy, especially in the North, is the effort to eliminate discrimination in housing. By December 1961 some 18 states and 12 cities had enacted laws prohibiting racial discrimination in housing. This article has two objectives: (1) to present a summary of the opinions and line of reasoning that ordinary citizens tend to hold on the subject, as expressed in an extended public hearing held to determine whether a fair housing ordinance should be issued in the District of Columbia; and, (2) to present some statistical study of some of the issues. The study concludes that based on its findings, the Board of

Commissioners, under its police powers, in 1963 issued a comprehensive fair housing ordinance for the District of Columbia, the third large city in the nation, to have a comprehensive statutes.

0799.   Fisher, Robert S. 1958. The New Jersey Housing Anti-Bias Law: Applicability to Non-State-Aided Development. **Rutgers Law Review** 12 (4): 557- 81.

The New Jersey law prohibiting discrimination in the sale or rental of FHA aided housing is the most recent restriction on one's power to freely dispose of his/her private property. The law was passed in the spring of 1957. This law evoked considerable momentum. But the law has not undergone a court test to determine its validity. This article attempts to determine the constitutional validity of the restrictions the ordinance will impose upon the vendors and lessors. It also examines the possible alternative sources of protection available to minorities in the FHA housing field. The last part of the article deals with an investigation of the anticipated problems in enforcing the New Jersey statutes. As his final statement, the author provides three rationales for need to protect minorities from discrimination in FHA-aid housing, and concludes: "the contention that the New Jersey statute is incompatible with FHA policy must be rejected if there is to be an ultimate realization of the government's plan to eliminate 'slumlords' from American society."

0800.   Friedman, Lawrence M., and James E. Krier. 1968. A New Lease on Life: Section 23 Housing and the Poor. **University of Pennsylvania Law Review** 116 (4): 611-47.

American efforts in public housing began during the early 1930s. At first there were high hopes for the program's success. But since the end of World War II, the program has lost its image. The purpose of this article is to attempt a preliminary assessment of Section 23 housing, and to explore whether it can succeed in attaining its objectives. Topics discussed are: the legislative background, leased housing, prerogative of choice, the leasing program and the housing supply, and the dilemma of decentralization. The study concludes: "The leasing program has helped the public housing movement revive from the lethargy of a decade or more." The author notes that the program (Section 23, leasing program) will mark a genuine advance over conventional public housing and will make possible "a real betterment of life for many of the poor."

0801.   Gettle, Donald W. 1962. Racially Restrictive Covenants in Deeds. **Georgia Bar Journal** 25 (2): 232-38.

For centuries, discrimination by race, color, creed, or national origin has been a grave social problem. Governments have often been seen to exploit minority groups by means of various discriminatory practices. In the U.S., the first step to correct the problem was the 14th amendment, which guarantees to all men the equal protection of the laws. This article examines the meaning/practice and the implication of fourteenth amendments as they apply to private property and minority housing.

0802.   Gregg, Gail. 1980. Congress Approves Cutbacks in U.S. Housing Programs, Boosts Urban Grant Funding. **Congressional Quarterly** 38 (2): 71-5.

The 1979 revision of the housing laws limited many government—subsidized housing programs while providing more funds for President Carter's key urban grant program. The omnibus housing authorization bill (HR 3875—PL96-153) also made a sweeping revision of regulations regulating the sale of land across state borders. Congress increased the authorization for the Urban Development Action Grant (UDAG) program to $675 million in fiscal year 1980; this program is designed to encourage private investment in projects in financially ailing urban areas. Provisions of the bill authorized $1.14 billion in additional contract authority for low—income housing assistance, increased funding for homes for the elderly and the handicapped, and required developers who provided federally subsidized low—income units to maintain that property for poor residents for the full terms of their governmental contracts. This essay outlines the provisions of the Housing and Community Development Amendments of 1979, and details the political compromises involved in its passage by the Congress.

0803.   Hager, Don J.   1960.   Housing Discrimination, Social Conflict, and the New Law.   **Social Problems** 8 (1): 80-87.

Violation of laws against discrimination in housing is currently a critical civil rights issue in the North. This article reports on the deliberations of a national conference on housing problems and the difficulty of promoting equal opportunity in housing. It reviews all the stubborn and irreducible factors related to discriminatory housing practices. Topics discussed are: Law, housing, and social conflict; legislative purpose and limitations; the "quota" problem; and, strategy and federal responsibility. It concludes that: "On occasion, laws and programs designed to promote public welfare can be used to thwart that end. It is a most serious development, therefore, that Title I of the Federal Housing Act of 1949, enacted to assist local communities in managing the problems of slums and blight, is being used as an instrumentality for creating segregated housing in areas where it did not exist." According to Hager, as the laws stand now, there is no major obstacle in the way of various communities to develop segregated housing with the use of Federal funds and governmental authority. The author calls for changes in the laws to prevent communities from such practices.

0804.   Hellerstein, William E.   1963.   The Benign Quota, Equal Protection, and "the Rule in Shelley's Case".   **Rutgers Law Review** 17 (3): 531-61.

This article has been to a great extent result-oriented. It has assumed that integration is desirable and that efforts to achieve integration should be encouraged. Hence, a considerable amount of space and effort has been devoted to a specific refutation of arguments that have been advanced against the Benign Quota. An ancillary purpose of this attempted refutation has been to demonstrate the uniqueness of a plan which requires "partial discrimination in an area in order to ameliorate the consequences of our heritage of racial discrimination. While our democratic ideals are focused primarily on personal liberty, it seems doubtful whether prior to Shelley a court would have brought a private plan for integration within the concept of state action. The final objection to the Quota has been its propensity for abuse. Yet the Quota is assumed to be a transitional device, and it must follow that its use will ease when it is no longer necessary for the achievement of its goal. If a developer should seek enforcement of an agreement that is designed to be exclusionary, there seems little reason to believe a court could not discern that design in light of past judicial experience with changing conditions.@

0805. Henkin, Louis. 1962. Shelley v. Kramer: Notes for a Revised Opinion. University of Pennsylvania Law Review 110 (4): 473-505.

What is Shelley v. Kramer? "Briefly, property subject to a restrictive covenant had been conveyed to Shelley, a Negro. Owners of nearby property, parties to the restrictive covenant, brought suit to restrain Shelley from taking possession and to have his title divested and revested in the grantor. The state courts granted relief requested. The Supreme Court reversed unanimously, three justices not participating." The Supreme Court's opinion was that "the right to acquire, enjoy, or dispose of property is clearly protected by the fourteenth amendment from discriminatory state action." This decision by the Supreme Court was hailed as the promise of another new deal for the individual, particularly the Negro individual. However, the author asserts that many constitutional lawyers were troubled by it. This article examines various points of views regarding this landmark Supreme Court decision, particularly with respect to the broader interpretation given to the fourteenth amendment. It is concluded that "the creative character of the Constitution cannot be denied from fear that wise judges may not be available to keep it alive."

0806. Jorgensen, Paul V. 1981. Tearing Down the Walls: The Federal Challenge to Exclusionary Land Use Laws. Urban Lawyer 13 (2): 201-20.

The exercise of control through land use regulation provides an excellent opportunity to deter some groups from moving into a community. In the past this practice has been blatantly discriminatory, such as the covenants against blacks popularly recorded in the land titles until the early sixties. The more modern devices talk about the exclusion of the "undesirables," such as racial minorities, children, and low-income classes from the housing market by high pricing and similar techniques, that can have the effect of inhibiting movement into new areas by middle- and low-income families. Although modern exclusionary land use control do not expressly use race, color, religion, national origin, or sex as criteria, it is readily apparent that the systematic exclusion of low-income groups through land use controls disproportionately affects certain minorities. This article examines the guiding principles behind numerous zoning ordinances, growth plans, and other similar devices. It concludes that the mere existence of federal law designed to provide protection against exclusionary action does not necessarily assure a remedy to discrimination. Title VIII only provides a somewhat toothless administrative enforcement mechanism. Some specific cases are discussed.

0807. Komesar, Neil K. 1973. Return to Slumville: A Critique of the Ackerman Analysis of Housing Code Enforcement and the Poor.

This article is a critical evaluation of Akerman's (1971) paper cited above. According to Komesar, the problems of low-income housing are both important and complex. The Ackerman's analysis, may make significant contributions to the legal literature, but the complexity of the analysis and its unfamiliarity to many readers of legal journals require additional care on the part of the analyst. The major Komesar's criticism of Ackerman's paper may best be summarized in this statement: "The process of achieving the correct policy solution in this highly complex area is incremental at best. Small, frustratingly slow steps are the reality; sweeping pronouncements are illusion."

0808.   Kozol, Lee H.   1962.   The Massachusetts Fair Housing Practices Law. Massachusetts Law Quarterly 47 (3): 295-305.

In May 1962, the Supreme Judicial Court upheld the constitutionality of the Fair Housing Practices Law in the state of Massachusetts. The law, originally enacted in 1957 applied only to publicly assisted housing. In 1959 the statute was amended to apply to nonpublicly assisted multiple dwelling and continuously located housing. The Massachusetts Commission Against Discrimination had found racial discrimination against a Negro in the renting of a privately owned and financed apartment development. The Commission entered an order which required the respondent to comply with the fair housing law. "The respondent argued that the statute deprived him, without due process of law, of his liberty of contract and his rights to administer and develop his property." The Court rejected the respondent's contention. This article details the judicial argument about this case and whether the Massachusetts fair housing law should/shouldn't be extended to include private housing.

0809.   Krooth, David L.   1971.   Court Decisions.   Journal of Housing 28 (11): 606-608.

In this article the author highlights various court decisions affecting minority housing—rent control, restrictive zoning, low-income quotas, and relocation violations.

0810.   Lefcoe, George.   1972.   From Capital Hill: The Impact of Civil Rights Litigation on HUD Policy.   Urban Lawyer 4 (1): 112-28.

This article analyzes the racial and economic impacts of four leading cases that bear on project and site selection for federally assisted housing—Gautreaux, Shannon, Valtierra, and Lackawanna. HUD's new criteria for project and site selection and the government's position on fair housing and local zoning prerogatives are also discussed.

0811.   McGraw, B. T.   1955.   The Housing Act of 1954 and Implications for Minorities.   Phylon 16 (Spring): 171-82.

The 1954 Housing Act amends existing housing laws and enacts new legislation designed to facilitate the flow of home mortgage credit to meet the neglected needs of racial and ethnic minorities. This article examines the potential of the 1954 Housing Act and its basic implications for minorities, and concludes that despite of several encouraging trends and progress, most of the new private housing units have been generally restricted or have excluded non-whites, and the market demand among racial minorities for decent housing has been less than adequately served by the private housing and home financed markets than has the comparable demand among other groups. The author states that minorities don't want anything special--they are only

asking for a fair treatment. It is also asserted that all actions to free
the operation of housing and home finance markets of racial differentials or
exclusion would be in line with the President's statement that "there should
be no discrimination based upon any reason that was not recognized by our
constitution."

0812. McNeill, Thomas B. 1958. Is There a Civil Right to Housing
Accommodations? **Notre Dame Lawyer** 33 (3): 463-88.

On the heels of a World War and an unprecedented economic boom, and while this
nation tried to adjust itself both externally and internally as one of the
powers of the world, the internal problem of the second-class citizenship of
the Negro loomed large—on social, political, and economic levels. In 1954
and 1955 the Supreme Court forthrightly dealt with it in one of its most
critical aspects, public education, when the Court decided **Brown v. Board of
Education**. Subsequent years have shown that something more is needed; the
Negro problem still exists. Conspicuously, the Negro ghetto remains—
hence this investigation of the nature of that phase of the problem.
Assuming that the causes of this situation is discrimination on the part of
landlords, it must be determined whether this activity offends our
Constitution and reflects a glaring hypocrisy in American conduct, or
whether such behavior is merely the cultural result of permissible personal
choice. Judicially considered the problem focuses on the fifth and
fourteenth amendments to the Constitution. The question is whether they
impose any duty upon landlords when dealing with prospective tenants to act
other than indiscriminately. The answer seems to be that there is such a
duty—to regard all persons equally—only when the landlord acts by, for or
as the state. The determination of when a landlord is so acting is the
socio-legal problem to which this Note is addressed.ℓ

0813. Morris, Arval A., and L. A. Powe, Jr. 1968. Constitutional and Statutory
Rights to Open Housing. **Washington Law Review** 44 (October): 1-84.

This article discusses presently available laws seeking an end to racial
discrimination in housing. The authors restrict themselves to an
examination of three areas of discrimination: (1) black buyer and
discriminating seller; (2) black buyer, seller and discriminating
realtor; and, (3) black buyer and discriminating tract developer. The
authors analyze the interests which may be asserted by the participants in
these transactions, and discuss the constitutional remedies afforded the
black buyer through application of alternative state action concepts under
the fourteenth amendment. In Part II, the authors comment upon the Supreme
Court's recent decision in Jones v. Alfred H. Mayer Co. (1968), and compare
statutory remedies under Title 42, Section 1982 (Civil Rights Act of 1866)
with relief provided by the Civil Rights Act of 1968.ℓ

0814. National Committee Against Discrimination in Housing. 1974. **Fair Housing
and Exclusionary Land Use**. Washington, D. C.: Urban Land Institute.
Research Report 23. 72 pp.

Exclusionary land use litigation is an integral part of fair housing efforts
that began more about ten years ago. That litigation has assumed central
importance in the attack on exclusionary barriers. It is more a reflection
of the failure of efforts to develop techniques of any innate superior

effectiveness. Lawsuits over several years have challenged the use of a number of well-established discretionary prerogatives of local governments and have had the salutary effect of focusing public attention on exclusionary land-use practices as a major factor in the continuing racial housing problem and economic stratification in the metropolitan areas. Furthermore, a number of court challenges have been successful. However, the exact elements of a successful court challenge to such practices are still uncertain, and are only dimly defined.

0815.   Navasky, Victor S. 1960. The Benevolent Housing Quota. **Howard Law Journal** 6 (1): 30-60.

"Can you discriminate to achieve integration? This is the perplexing problem of the Benevolent Quota. It is a legal problem, a moral problem, and a tactical problem." This article discusses this question on a hypothetical basis, and concludes that those interested in housing integration should work for passage of effective enforcement of nondiscriminatory laws and also must increase the housing supply. In the opinion of the author, these are better remedies than the quota approach.

0816.   Nourse, Hugh O., and Donald Phares. 1975. The Impact of FHA Insurance Practices on Urban Housing Markets in Transition: The St. Louis Case. **Urban Law Annual** 9: 111-128.

In 1966 Congress passed a law changing the Federal Housing Administration (FHA) insurance practices. This paper formulates and tests several hypotheses regarding housing markets in transition from higher to lower income levels and from one race to another. The article examines the expected impact of the law that brought about changes in FHA insurance practices on prices, income, and racial transition. The authors also develop actual price and income data for St. Louis housing markets in transition, and assess the impact of the shift in FHA policy on housing in transition in St. Louis.

0817.   Palmer, Robert G. 1970. Section 23 Housing: Low-Rent Housing in Private Accommodations. **Journal of Urban Law** 48 (1): 255-78.

In 1965 Congress first authorized the local Housing Authority to lease standard existing privately owned housing units for use by low-income families. Such leasing or Section 23 housing was designed to supplement other public housing, but differs significantly from conventional programs. This article enumerates the advantages of this new ordinance, and concludes that leasing offers a flexible approach to solving the low-income housing problems.

0818.   Robinson, Joseph B. 1968. Fair Housing Legislation in the City and State of New York. In: **The Politics of Fair-Housing Legislation.** Lynn W. Eley, and Thomas W. Casstevens (eds.). San Francisco, California: Chandler Publishing Company. Pp. 27-64.

Legislation to ban discrimination in housing began in New York City. Attempts commenced in the late 1930's, and proved successful in the late 1940's, to obtain a local policy banning racial or religious discrimination in public and publicly assisted housing. Spearheaded by the New York State

Committee on Discrimination in Housing, the nation's first law prohibiting discrimination in parts of the private housing market was enacted in New York City on December 30, 1957. Thereafter, efforts were transferred to the state government and culminated in the passage of a state law in 1961. Since then the fair-housing forces have moved back and forth between the city and state political arenas and have secured important strengthening amendments to both laws.*

0819.   Rosenblum, Michael F. 1967. Equal Protection: Constitutional Amendment Prohibiting State Fair Housing Laws Is State Action Denying Equal Protection of the Laws. Villanova Law Review 13 (1): 199-205.

A review of Supreme Court's opinion in Reitman v. Mulkey [a black couple] in terms of guidelines for future development must take into account two significant points. The first is that the Supreme Court is reluctant, at the present time, to apply the public function theory to the field of urban housing and thereby establish affirmative governmental responsibility in that area. This is evident by its strained finding of state action in this case through the characterization of Proposition Fourteen as a positive assertion of state power directly contributing to private discriminatory activity [in housing]. However, it should also be noted that in its desire to limit the basis of its decision, the Supreme Court has left room for a much more radical inference, that is, that the state action requirement has been effectively eliminated, not only in the area of housing, but in other fields as well.*

0820.   Sager, Lawrence Gene. 1969. Tight Little Islands: Exclusionary Zoning, Equal Protection, and the Indigent. Stanford Law Review 21 (4): 767-800.

This article examines the application of the "energized equal protection doctrine to what will be called 'exclusionary zoning'; that is, zoning that raises the price of residential access to a particular area, and thereby denies that access to members of low income groups." In extending its scope to a problem that has been ignored by the Supreme Court, the author also examines the emerging doctrine and its antecedents.

0821.   Sax, Joseph L., and Fred J. Hiestand. 1967. Slumlord as a Tort. Michigan Law Review 65 (5): 869-922.

It may appear to some as odd that as we pass more laws, we get more lawlessness. Others may feel the need for adopting additional laws as far reaching as required to solve the problem designed to alleviate. This article addresses this issue. Indicating that as social issues nothing surpasses the problem of slum housing, the author states that "today, half a century after slum dwelling laws were widely enacted in response to public outrage, and a generation since the principles of public housing became operative, there remains vast number of urban housing units in which the most appalling conditions continue to exist. Yet, it would be difficult to find a social wrong that has been more thoroughly and elaborately attacked in law." To show the lack of effect of the current laws, the authors cite the example of New York City that has at least five major legal devices designed to eliminate substandard housing. Yet New York City ranks number one in the quantity and detestability of its slum dwellings. Despite these strong, and some may say draconian measures, the authors contend that abominable slum conditions prevail in New York City in great quantity. The authors failing to find any connection between laws and the existing quantity of slums, attribute the failure of these laws to four common weaknesses. The authors elaborate on the weaknesses of the existing laws and present a new proposal for the courts to consider in the hope it may help to eliminate the appalling slum housing conditions some minorities are condemned to.

0822. Schier, Carl. 1966. Protecting the Interest of Indigent Tenant. California Law Review 54 (2): 670-93.

The person with inadequate means, seeking a suitable family dwelling in the city, is often a hapless figure. Space can be had only on a short-term basis, and most available housing is run-down, dirty, and without adequate services. The law of landlord and tenant is not so lacking in conceptual development that the indigent tenant must necessarily be denied redress in court. The heart of the matter is not entirely the shortcomings of the substantive law, rather it is a combination of related problems: the procedural anomaly of a statute which grants the right to regain possession but excludes otherwise acceptable defenses, the lack of tenant-plaintiffs and counsel to represent them, and hard-headed or recalcitrant judges whose sympathies lie with the landlords upon whom the poor descend to run their buildings into slum. Current attempts to achieve satisfaction in the courts are meeting with some success, but success at the bar should be supplemented by a program of progressive legislation designed to overcome many of the seemingly insurmountable problems such as too-short duration and discrimination in tenant selection based on race and economic status. The suggested legislative approach of creating a uniform statutory lease proceeds on the theory that the legal incidents of leaseholding would be of benefit to indigent persons. Should a wide ranging effort fail, one can adopt a piecemeal approach. This method seems to be favored by legislators, since the smaller the steps by which one proceeds the fewer persons will take notice and complain. A legislative program, plus renewed efforts in the courts, should make an appreciable difference in the landlord- tenant relationship of the urban poor.@

0823. Semer, Milton P., and Martin E. Sloane. 1964. Equal Housing Opportunity and Individual Property Rights. Federal Bar Journal 24 (1): 47-75.

In the area of housing in recent years, the law has become an important force for equality, for the Courts have given broader meaning to the constitutional term "equal protection of the law." In the area of housing, the principal objection to the legal measures taken to assure equality of housing opportunity has been that they "constitute an unwarranted interference with individual property rights. And, the all too glib answer is that the law quite properly favors 'human rights' over 'property rights'." It is the purpose of this article to analyze the legal developments pertaining to the prevention of racial discrimination in housing in terms of their effect on individual property rights.

0824. Sloane, Martin E. 1984. The 1983 Housing Act: A Leap Backward. Journal of Housing 41 (4): 112-13.

The Housing and Urban-Rural Recovery Act of 1983 makes significant changes in federal housing and community development programs, by revamping the traditional approach to housing assistance. The Act eliminates almost all new constructions under existing subsidized housing programs, such as public housing and Section 8. In their place the 1983 Housing Act establishes a new rental rehabilitation and a demonstration program of housing vouchers. This article assesses the impacts of this Act on low-income housing and indicates that the effect of this new approach "will be to exacerbate problems of inadequate housing for the poor and to inhibit further the ability of the poor to exercise free housing choice." The article concludes that the new approach is a "regressive, even oppressive, piece of legislation."

0825.   Sparkman, John. 1964. Civil Rights and Property Rights. Federal Bar Journal 24 (1): 31-46.

This is an article written by a lawyer and United States Senator from Alabama, and Chairman, Senate Subcommittee on Housing. According to Sparkman: The present "Civil Rights Bill" involves numerous questions of legislative policy, many of which are beclouded because the term "civil rights" is a misnomer and conceals the basic issue which is the thrust of federal power. The protection of property rights against this proposed extension of federal power constitutes the main purpose of this paper. The gist of this article is best expressed in the statement that: "Equality under our Constitution does not demand the abrogation of the rights of 168 million people in order to give 20 million Negroes the doubtful benefits of forced integration--accomplished at least on paper, but hardly in actual practice. Attempts to legislate this end are, and will prove to be, as foolish as the Prohibition Amendment and the Volstead Act [National Prohibition Act of 1919], which proved beyond any shadow of a doubt that law in and of itself cannot change social customs and personal habits, even under attempted rigid enforcement. These changes must spring from the thinking and the personal lives of those who are involved."

0826.   St. Thomas More Institute for Legal Research. 1969. Law and the Demise of the Urban Ghetto. Catholic Lawyer 15 (1): 39-55.

This is the first of a two part article examining the impact of recent developments in the law upon the urban ghetto. More specifically, Part I, discusses the interpretation of the thirteenth amendment adopted by the Supreme Court in Jones v. Alfred H. Mayer Company case.

0827.   St. Thomas More Institute for Legal Research. 1969. Law and the Demise of Urban Ghetto: Part II. Catholic Lawyer 15 (2): 143-57.

This is the second of a two part article examining the impact of recent developments in the law upon the urban ghetto. Part II focuses its attention on the scope of the open-housing section of the Civil Rights Act of 1968, as well as the constitutional obstacles confronting the Act.

0828.   Stegman, Michael A. 1981. Housing Block Grants: Legislation is Unlikely This Year. Journal of Housing 38 (6): 317-24.

The Housing Assistance Block Grant (HABG) program is a funds distribution program based on a formula that HUD would use to link an area's relative housing needs with a share of available federal money. Based on the view

expressed by the proponents of HABG , they can be turned into a flexible
responsive housing assistance system that will provide opportunities for
innovation at the local level, reduce the present tendency to depend on new
construction to house the poor, and reduce the direct federal role in
development loan processing and program administration. A recent Senate
hearing on the subject raised and clarified several important issues in
establishing HABGs, which are discussed in this article.

0829.   Van Alstyne, William W. 1962. The O'Meara Case and Constitutional
Requirements of State Anti-Discrimination Housing Laws. **Howard Law
Journal** 8 (2): 158-68.

In 1957, Washington joined several other states that had resolved to
eliminate racial discrimination in publicly-assisted housing. Based on
the determination that demonstration of discrimination menaced the
legitimate aspiration of black citizens to secure shelter adequate to their
needs and ability to pay, the legislature declared it to be unlawful for the
owner of publicly-assisted housing to discriminate on the basis of race,
creed, color, or national origin. Publicly assisted housing was defined as
any housing financed, in whole or in part, by the federal government. The
first case to reach the Superior Court under the 1957 statute (**O'Meara v.
Washington State Board Against Discrimination**), Washington's effort to
prevent discrimination was declared unconstitutional. This article
compares the O'Meara case with two similar cases in New York and New Jersey,
and explains the reasons for the resolution.

0830.   Vose, Clement E. 1955. NAACP Strategy in the Covenant Cases. **Western
Reserve Law Review** 6: 101-45.

Scrutiny of the NAACP's part in the successful litigation which ended the
court enforcement of racial restrictive covenants indicates techniques used
by a pressure group dealing mainly with the judiciary. The NAACP carefully
planned its test cases and encouraged publication of articles for use in its
legal briefs. The Association showed adeptness in bringing the Court's
attention to its political strength in the Executive Branch and in the nation
at large by winning the support of the justice Department and the
organization which filed amici curiae briefs. Other interest groups in
controversies before state and federal courts need to be studied. In
numerous instances today organized pressure groups are seeking favorable
decisions from the United States Supreme Court. The power and techniques of
these groups need be understood if the movement of constitutional
interpretation is to be comprehended. It is hoped that analysis of the role
of organizations and their attorneys in Supreme Court cases will become as
common as interest in judicial biography. Doctrinal evolution does not
take place in a vacuum.*

0831.   Walsh, Robert E. 1971. The Constitutionality of a Length-of-Time
Residency Test for Admission to Public Housing. **Journal of Urban Law** 49
(1): 121-129.

Residents who have lived in a community for a substantial period of time may
not, as applicants for public housing, be preferred to those who have been
domiciled in the community for a shorter period, and perhaps not even be
preferred to those who have not been domiciled in the community but who would

like to be. But on an individual decision basis, the fact that an applicant has roots, valuable economic or social relations which will be preserved or strengthened by admitting him to public housing, may be considered along with other applicable criteria in determining who should be awarded a vacant public housing unit when a shortage of such units exists.*

0832. Weil, Joseph H. 1958. Racial Restrictions in Leaseholds. **University of Florida Law Review** 11 (3): 344-51.

Prior to 1948 there was no proved constitutional basis upon which to sustain an attack on restrictive covenants, the primary means by which blacks and other minorities were excluded from the purchase or use of real property. Some recent Court's decisions in the civil rights area indicate that federal courts have withdrawn many constitutional sanctions upon which racial discriminations rested. This article examines some of these cases and concludes that the question of racial restrictions in leaseholds is the problem involving the conflict between civil rights and property rights. The author points out that the courts have not yet declared restrictive covenants unlawful per se, but merely unforceable. That is, by implication, the owner may still discriminate, and thus, segregation in private housing is not at an end yet.

⟡⟡⟡⟡⟡⟡⟡⟡⟡

10
ELDERLY HOUSING

0833. Anderson, Elaine A. 1984. Housing Strategies for the Elderly: Beyond the Ecological Model. Journal of Housing for the Elderly 2 (3): 55-60.

Gerontologists often speak of a need to create a continuum of alternative housing environments to increase the number of housing options between those with no services and those with a high level of complementary services. By expanding the number of alternatives, it is expected that the elderly will select an environment consistent with their needs and at least implicitly maximize life satisfaction. This paper examines a set of assumptions and values implicit in calls for such a continuum. The analysis identifies a number of issues not generally recognized in the literature which may hinder or facilitate the development and implementation of housing programs for the elderly.*

0834. Anderson, Peggye Dilworth. 1975. The Black Aged: Dispositions Toward Seeking Age Concentrated Housing in a Small Town. Unpublished Ph.D. Dissertation. Northwestern University. 189 pp.

This dissertation explores elderly blacks' attitudes toward seeking aged concentrated housing. It examines factors that influence their desire to seek this style of life. The study is based on a sample of 208 black elderly age 65 and over, conducted in Tuskegee, Alabama. The findings show that the majority of the respondents favored age concentrated housing for the elderly, but not for themselves. Only less than 25 percent of the sample indicated they would personally seek retirement home living. Morale, employment status, income, and health status of the respondents were found to influence their desire to seek age-concentrated housing in the order presented. The impacts of variables such as family relations, sex, age and age identification are also examined.

0835. Bernstein, Judith. 1982. Housing for the Elderly Requires Thoughtful Management. **Journal of Property Management** 47 (3): 18-20.

About 800,000 persons over age 62 currently live in apartments built with federal assistance. Many others live in privately funded units, or in specially planned housing units built with state assistance, local tax incentives, and block grant allocations. This article examines the management aspects of elderly housing and concludes that the managers who work with housing for the elderly face unique problems.

0836. Birenbaum, Arnold. 1984. Aging and Housing: A Note on How Housing Expresses Social Status. **Journal of Housing for the Elderly** 2 (1): 33-40.

Housing is conceptualized as a source of positive or negative status. Some environmentally related indicators of status are generated to open new line of inquiry. The social class limits of new housing as a source of accorded status are discussed.*

0837. Brown, David S. 1980. Housing for the Elderly: Federal Subsidy Policy and its Effect on Age-Group Isolation. **University of Detroit Journal of Urban Law** 57 (2): 257-93.

The overall effect of different federal housing programs for the elderly has been to encourage their segregation or residential concentration. The segregation of the elderly from the young has impacted the family ties. It is also acting as a role model preparation for the young. Contending that the long-term economic and social benefits of age-segregation are formidable, this article first reviews the position and function of the older people in the society, and then tries to examine the substantial role the federal housing subsidy programs play in the age-group segregation.

0838. Chellis, Roberto D., James F. Seagle, and Barbara M. Seagle. 1982. **Congregate Housing for Older People: A Solution for the 1980s.** Lexington, Mass.: Lexington Books. 226 pp.

This book focuses on congregate housing. Its main themes pertain to general concerns and needs for elderly housing in terms of new construction and rehabilitation, continued aging and its implications on environmental, health, economic, and psychological services. It also discusses community and management issues concerning elderly housing.

0839. Clark, Alex Rees. 1979. **Low-Income Housing for the Elderly in Baltimore: A Spatial Analysis of a Social Policy.** Unpublished Ph.D. Dissertation. Pennsylvania State University. 264 pp.

This dissertation adopts a holistic framework for analyzing the locations of housing projects for the low income elderly in Baltimore, Maryland. It points out that the extensive literature on the subject is nonspatially based, and theories of aging and urban income distribution also have weak spatial components as applied to elderly housing. This study reviews nonspatial theories and suggests possible extensions. The study concludes that "in most cases the addition of [elderly housing] projects moved the locality toward lower status, higher density, and increased age segregation."

0840. DeLaski-Smith, Deborah L. 1984. Housing the Elderly: Intergenerational
       Family Settings. **Journal of Housing for the Elderly** 2 (3): 61-70.

       This paper explores the intergenerational housing option as a viable and
       frequently necessary housing option for elderly individuals. The
       advantages and disadvantages are presented both for the elderly individuals
       as well as the affected family members; along with cultural and religious
       affiliations   that   influence   filial   intergenerational   housing
       responsibilities. The following topics are also discussed: federal and
       local support systems, housing style options and future research
       recommendations for intergenerational housing.*

0841. Devlin, Ann Sloan. 1980. Housing for the Elderly: Cognitive
       Considerations. **Environment and Behavior** 12 (4): 451-66.

       "Criticism of highrise housing for low-income families abounds, yet
       highrise structures have been deemed suitable for those nearing the end of
       life cycle." This article examines the effects of several cognitive
       variables such as building legibility, attentional demands imposed by the
       housing design, and feelings of safety and security among 77 residents, 73
       women and 4 men, in four public housing developments for the elderly in New
       London, Connecticut. The study points at a number of important concerns for
       designers of housing for the elderly.

0842. Donahue, Wilma T., Marie McGuire Thompson, and D. J. Curren. 1977.
       Congregate Housing for Older People: An Urgent Need, A Growing Demand.
       Washington, D.C.: U.S. Department of Health, Education and Welfare, Office
       of Human Development, Administration on Aging. 221 pp.

       This publication consists of a collection of papers presented at a 1975
       conference sponsored jointly by the Administration on Aging and HUD.
       Articles included cover basic research topics, design problems, project
       planning, and management of elderly housing. The coverage includes a
       discussion of levels of housing care, the need for supplementary federal
       housing legislation to provide integrated housing, methodologies for
       estimating future housing needs, and future policy considerations.

0843. Engler, Nick. 1979. Appalachian New York Finds a Successful Housing
       Formula. **Appalachia** 12 (5): 15-25.

       The 1975 amendments to the Appalachian Regional Development Act allowed each
       Appalachian state to create its own program of low and moderate income
       housing with funding from the Appalachian Regional Commission. The NY
       State Urban Development Corporation (UDC) is chosen by that state to
       coordinate and administer the program. This article examines some of the
       projects, such as housing for the elderly, UDC has been involved in. The
       examination of the UDC's activities illustrate the positive results that can
       be achieved from the cooperation between the public and private sectors.

0844. Fields, Clavin. 1982. Housing Programs and Outreach Strategies for the
       Elderly. **Urban League Review** 6 (2): 50-55.

       The availability of adequate, low-cost housing for the elderly is very

limited. About 20 percent of older adults in the U.S. live in inadequate
housing, and the proportion is twice as great for older blacks. "Housing
facilities for the elderly should be developed in an environment that is not
only safe but offers autonomy, personalization, independence, community
integration, and social integration."

0845.   Frankel, Fred. 1979. Life Care Communities: Housing for Both the Active
and Infirm Elderly. Journal of Property Management 44 (2): 82-84.

The size of the elderly population has reached a level to have created a
totally new and unique market for housing industry. This article examines
the demand for specially designed housing units for the elderly. Among
topics discussed are: traditional housing for the elderly, life care
communities, and need for special housing.

0846.   Golant, Stephen M. 1982. Individual Differences Underlying the Dwelling
Satisfaction of the Elderly. Journal of Social Issues 38 (3): 121-133.

Dwelling satisfaction is identified often as a subjective indicator of a
population's quality of life and as a predictor of residential relocation
plans and preferences. In old age, the dwelling is an especially important
part of the individual's total life situation. Because objective
indicators of housing quality incompletely and misleadingly explain the
variations in older person's reported dwelling satisfaction, a set of
individual characteristics are proposed as antecedents. Structured
interview data were collected from a random sample of 400 persons aged 60 and
over living in a midwestern, middle class community. It was found that old
people who were more satisfied with their dwellings were less favorably
disposed toward stimulating or novel environments, were happier with their
lives, traveled less frequently outside their dwellings, lived longer in
their present residences, were home owners, and were less likely to report
financial difficulties. The findings emphasize the difficulties of
interpreting subjective indicators of housing quality for policy and
planning purposes.*

0847.   Grittani, Joseph J. 1980. Chicago Boosts Options for Senior Citizens
Housing. HUD Challenge 11 (2); 26-30.

The Chicago Housing Authority (CHA) has recognized that in providing
adequate housing for the elderly, the mere provision of housing is not
enough. Therefore, CHA has been searching for ways to respond to the needs
created by increases in life expectancy and at the same time improve the
lives of its residents. In order to allow elderly residents an
alternative to nursing homes, CHA decides to consider congregate housing.
This study examines how CHA has developed a congregate housing program to
meet the needs of its elderly population.

0848.   Gutowski, M. F. 1979. Integrating Housing and Social Services for the
Elderly Household. Thrust: The Journal for Employment and Training
Professionals 1 (2): 205-19.

"The housing needs and decisions of elderly households differ markedly from
younger households. Proximity to children who set up their own households,
hospitals, churches and senior citizen centers affect decisions which in

turn are shaped by actual or anticipated declines in health and income."
According to Gutowski, "improvement of existing housing programs and
development of new and innovative housing programs and policies to serve the
elderly can be made more effective by attempting to integrate these services
[home health care, home delivered meals, housing maintenance, and
transportation] with housing."

0849. Hackman, Helen. 1978. Day Care for the Frail Elderly: An Alternative.
       Public Welfare 36 (4): 36-44.

       By 1976 there were 15,700 people age 65 and over in Arlington, Virginia.
       This essay, drawing on the author's experience from the European countries
       in general, and England in particular, argues for the desirability of
       establishing day care for the elderly so that they can remain with their
       families as long as possible, before they are committed to housing
       institutions. It also describes how the day care was established in
       Arlington using James Madison Elementary School that became available in
       1975.

0850. Heller, Tamar, Thomas O. Byerts, and David E. Drehmer. 1984. Impact of
       Environment on Social and Activity Behavior in Public Housing for the
       Elderly. Journal of Housing for the Elderly 2 (2): 17-25.

       The study examines the inter-relationships of physical design and service
       environment on the social and activity behaviors of residents in public
       housing for the elderly. It compares the observed behavior patterns found
       in the common spaces of 11 apartment buildings administered by a midwest
       housing authority. The findings indicate that building height, number of
       apartment doors ajar and provision of meal service can facilitate increased
       resident sociability in the public spaces of senior housing buildings.*

0851. Heumann, Leonard F. 1984. Rent Subsidies and the Elderly. Journal of
       Housing for the Elderly 2 (3): 71-87.

       This paper brings together the relatively meager and widely dispersed
       findings that apply to how the elderly would fair if rent voucher program
       were to become the single government housing subsidy to households of low and
       moderate income. The paper begins by reviewing the findings that apply to
       the elderly from the recent Experimental Housing Allowance Program (EHAP),
       and then relates these EHAP findings to findings on housing needs of
       various types of elderly such as low income elderly, racial minority elderly
       and elderly with functional impairments. [It is concluded that] at best the
       housing voucher concept would make sense as one among several housing
       subsidy options open to elderly recipients. If it became the only option
       many of the poorest, most disenfranchised elderly would find themselves
       without a housing subsidy.@

0852. Hoover, Sally L. 1978. Black and Spanish Elderly: Their Housing
       Characteristics and Housing Quality. Journal of Minority Aging 5 (3): 249-
       272.

       Available 1970 and 1975 housing data were used to compare the
       characteristics and quality of housing of black, white and Spanish
       households where the heads were over 65 years of age. Based upon an

examination of such indicators as value of the housing unit, gross rent, condition of plumbing and heating equipment, older white owners lived in relatively better structures than blacks or Spanish, and the Spanish tended to have better housing than blacks. The most problematic housing occurred among older black renters. Problems associated with the neighborhood tended to cut across racial and ethnic lines, suggesting that federal programs for home improvement cannot be divorced feasibly from neighborhood rejuvenation. The housing situation of older Americans needs greater attention than it has presently received, and overhousing is not an historical accident.*

0853. Hoover, Sally. 1981. Black and Spanish Elderly: Their Housing Characteristics and Housing Quality. In M. Powell Lawton, and Sally L. Hoover (eds.). Community Housing Choices for Older Americans. New York: Springer Publishing Company.

This is a comparative analysis of housing characteristics of elderly blacks, whites, and persons of Spanish origin. According to this study, blacks are more likely to remain in a home once it is purchased, and thus as a group black elderly may experience the problems of overhousing. Older Spanish persons are less likely to be either property owners or long-term residents if the property is owned. Thus, their social service needs are different from those of older whites; like older blacks, Spanish persons may be disproportionately excluded from programs that only apply to home owners; older whites seem to have a greater interest in moving into mobile homes or large apartment complexes which offer lower maintenance levels. Older whites live in relatively better structure; older black home owners live in units that have the most structural deficiencies; older black renters are also more likely to live in problematic housing.

0854. Hoyt, Charles K. 1977. Housing the Aging. Architectural Record 161 (5): 123-25.

"The living conditions suffered by many people over 65 urgently point toward the need for both construction of better physical facilities and more positive attitudes about a national problem. The fast-growing portion of the population that will be pressing their needs on us demands radical change—and better answers. For the design professions, this will mean a re-examination of everything that has been built for the elderly—and it will mean hard work coupled with a search for knowledge." The author also discusses some examples of the best forms of housing that are now being built and what the elderly people think about them.

0855. Hubbard, Linda, and Tom Beck (eds.). 1984. Housing Options for Older Americans. Washington, D.C.: American Association of Retired Persons. 43 pp.

This publication explains some of the housing and living options available for the elderly—both for those who want to stay put and for those who plan to move. Examples of the options examined are: Accessory Apartments, Boarding Homes, Cooperatives, Congregate Housing, Conventional Rental Housing, ECHO Housing, Federally Assisted Public Housing, Shared Housing, Foster Care Homes, Mobile Homes, and so forth. This is a very useful handbook for all people 65 years of age and older.

0856.   Jirovec, Ronald, Mary M. Jirovec, and Raymond Bosse. 1984. Architectural
        Predictors of Housing Satisfaction Among Urban Elderly Men. Journal of
        Housing for the Elderly 2 (1): 21-32.

        The purpose of this study was to identify in a comprehensive manner the
        architectural predictors of housing satisfaction among urban elderly men.
        Four architectural characteristics (i.e., modernness, familiarity, sense
        of community, safety) emerged as predictors of housing satisfaction but
        their combined predictive power was overshadowed by that of neighborhood
        satisfaction which explained over four-fifth of the variance accounted for
        in housing satisfaction.@

0857.   Lane, Terry Saunders, and Judith D. Feins. 1985. Are the Elderly
        Overhoused? Definitions of Space Utilization and Policy Implications.
        The Gerontologist 25 (3): 243-250.

        This paper explores the widely-held belief that elderly-headed households
        live in dwellings too large for their needs and more suitable for larger
        families. Using data from recent Annual Housing Surveys, the article
        demonstrates that most elderly households do not underutilize their housing
        space. In addition, few of their units become available for reoccupancy
        each year, because mobility rates among the elderly, especially those in
        underutilized dwellings, are very low. When the elderly do release their
        homes into the market, the new occupants include a wide range of household
        types, not just younger, larger families.*

0858.   Lauber, Daniel. 1980. Condominium Conversion: The Number Prompts
        Controls to Protect the Poor and Elderly. Journal of Housing 37 (4): 201-
        09.

        Condominium conversion has hit the tight housing markets in most U.S. cities
        because of the opportunity for the investors to generate huge, instant
        profits and the chance for the buyers to become homeowners. Conversion
        projects, however, cause significant problems for a number of poor and
        elderly tenants. This article examines some of the problems these
        conversions cause for the poor and the elderly housing.

0859.   Lawton, M. Powell. 1980. Housing the Elderly: Residential Quality and
        Residential Satisfaction. Research on Aging 2 (3): 309-328.

        Data from over 12,000 elderly-headed households interviewed for the Annual
        Housing Survey are analyzed in terms of (a) identifying subgroups of the
        elderly in need of housing-related services, (b) specifying the elements of
        housing quality and neighborhood attributes most salient to residential
        satisfaction, and (c) exploring more general questions in the study of
        person-environment relationships. Results indicated that the black aged,
        rural-area residents, and renters had greatest housing needs. While
        subjective housing quality was related to objective quality indicators, the
        two aspects of environment were quite disparate. Evidence was found that
        residential satisfaction is incremental, depending on a large number of
        possible contributors to perceived quality, few of which are overwhelmingly
        stronger than others. Adequacy of heating was somewhat more important than
        other housing indicators and fear of crime somewhat more important than

other neighborhood attributes (particularly in high-risk subgroups).*

0860. Lawton, M. Powell. 1985. The Relevance of Impairments to Age Targeting of
Housing Assistance. **The Gerontologist** 25 (1): 31-34.

This study is based on the theme that there is a need for rethinking housing
policy for the elderly, by expanding the definition of housing and housing-
related services to forge stronger linkage to health and long term care;
or, by a more efficient and creative use of available resources. More
specifically, Lawton considers the broad definition of need for housing
assistance, and the corresponding definition of the population to be served.
He also examines the feasibility of targeting the disabled population.

0861. Lawton, M. Powell, Miriam Moss, and Miriam Grimes. 1985. The Changing
Service Needs of Older Tenants in Planned Housing. **The Gerontologist** 25
(3): 258-264.

The health and well-being of 494 residents living in five federal assisted
housing projects for the elderly were assessed 12 to 14 years after a similar
sample of original occupants of the five projects were studied. A decl_ne
in functioning was more notable in psychological than in health domains.
All five environments had accommodated such declines by developing
different clusters of services delivered by community agencies, and this
"patchwork of services" was working reasonably well.*

0862. Malozemoff, I. K., J. G. Anderson, and L. V. Rosenbaum. 1978. **Housing for
the Elderly: Evaluation of the Effectiveness of Congregate Residences.**
Boulder, Colorado: Westview Press. 320 pp.

Congregate housing refers to specially planned,designed and managed multi-
unit rental housing, usually with self-contained apartments. Supportive
services such as meals, transportation, and so forth are usually provided.
This book describes and discusses a study of twenty-seven congregate housing
facilities throughout the U.S., ranging from federally supported projects
for low-income elderly to privately owned and operated luxury facilities.
The outcomes show that congregate housing is a relatively desirable means of
housing the elderly.

0863. Malpezzi, Stephen. 1985. Urban Revitalization and the Elderly: Evidence
From Three Neighborhoods. **Journal of Housing for the Elderly** 2 (4): 27-
50.

Since the mid-1970s some evidence exists that some American cities are being
"revitalized". This paper presents empirical evidence on the effects of
revitalization on the elderly in three neighborhoods in Washington, D.C.,
Boston, and St. Paul. Changes in people, and changes in safety and
security, are the most commonly perceived neighborhood changes. The
housing consumption of many of the elderly, particularly homeowners, is not
related to their current income. Public or private programs which increase
their mobility and enable them to augment their current income by obtaining
annuities backed by housing could increase their welfare at little or no cost
to government.@

0864. Markstrom, Wilbur J., and John Clymer. 1979. Barrier to the Development of Community-Based Residential Facilities for the Elderly. **Urban Lawyer** 11 (3): 461-80.

Policy makers in the areas of housing, health care, aging, mental health and vocational rehabilitation, are now paying more attention to the need for nonmedical issues supportive of elderly and handicapped. "Personal care housing" is defined as living in an environment with resident staff members providing assistance with daily living activities to persons too mentally ill or physically disabled or too frail to live independently. The Congress has estimated the potential need for 1.5 to 1.9 million such housing units, while less than 800,000 are actually in existence. This essay identifies the main barriers to the development of this supportive housing; it also discusses the legal dimensions of the problem, and recommends solutions for overcoming these barriers.

0865. Mayer, Neil S. 1980. Helping the Elderly Repair Their Homes. HUD **Challenge** 11 (9): 13-16.

Housing repair and maintenance are expensive propositions with serious implications for elderly households in general, and the low- and fixed-income elderly in particular. In this article Mayer offers some theories addressing this problem. Among his suggestions is that federal assistance to elderly homeowners must concentrate heavily among the lower-income households.

0866. Mayer, Neil S. 1981. Grants, Loans, and Housing Repair for the Elderly. **APA Journal** 47 (1): 25-34.

Many elderly homeowners need assistance in repairing and improving their homes. They receive less of the overall federally funded aid for home repairs than their share of total homeowner needs might warrant. But individual programs differ greatly in serving the elderly. Using detailed data on past program recipients, this article demonstrates that providing assistance in the form of grants rather than loan is critical to gaining elderly households' participation. It also shows that inability to qualify for or repay loans because of low incomes, more than unwillingness to borrow, limits participation by the elderly in repair loan programs. The paper considers various options for obtaining improved housing quality for elderly people and concludes that providing and expanding grant assistance for home repair and rehabilitation is a necessary major component of successful policy.*

0867. Nasar, Jack L., and Mitra Farokhpay. 1985. Assessment of Activity Priorities and Design Preferences of Elderly Residents in Public Housing: A Case Study. **The Gerontologist** 25 (3): 251-257.

A technique for assessing priorities of and the desired environmental characteristics for in-unit activities of elderly residents is presented. Design priority for activities was considered as having three components: time spent, importance, and unit adequacy. Residents were questioned, and a composite of these measures revealed the high priority activities as sleeping, watching television, preparing food, resting/relaxing and eating. Through additional interviews, the desired environmental characteristics for these activities were gleaned. The utility of the instrument is discussed.*

0868. Newman, Sandra J. 1981. Exploring Housing Adjustments of Older People: The HUD-HEW Longitudinal Study. Research on Aging 3 (4): 417-427.

"The most wide-scale attack on the housing problems suffered by elder Americans was declared by Congress in 1974 with passage of the Housing and Community Development Act." These strategies are: (a) to produce new housing units; and (b) to provide home owners and renters with cash assistance. This paper provides a background discussion and description of a major new longitudinal study of the housing adjustment of older Americans supported jointly by HUD and the Department of Health, Education, and Welfare. Research and policy issues are also addressed.

0869. Newman, Sandra J. 1984. The Availability of Adequate Housing for Older People: Issue Areas for Advocates. Journal of Housing for the Elderly 2 (3): 3-13.

Part of the strength of the arguments posed by housing advocates for the elderly rests on why the elderly merit special attention. Using two indicators of housing need, physical adequacy and affordability, the elderly are shown to be relatively less well-off than the nonelderly both at a point in time and persistently over time. A review of the federal government's response to the elderly's housing needs suggests that the number of households in need will continue to outdistance the number of households who actually receive assistance.*

0870. Newman, Sandra J. 1985. Housing and Long-Term Care: The Suitability of the Elderly's Housing on the Provision of In-Home Services. The Gerontologist 25 (1): 35-40.

This is an initial exploration of the long-term housing needs of the dependent elderly. Two conclusions emerge: (1) a significant proportion of the elderly population who are the most likely targets of long-term care services delivered in the home are living in housing units and environment that either impede the efficiency of these services or preclude their delivery altogether; and (2) as the policy debate over the future course of long-term care evolves in the U.S., the importance of three factors that largely determine the effectiveness of in-home-long-term care services must be recognized: the individual, the service provider, and the housing environment.

0871. Niebanck, Paul L. 1975. Rehab Grants for Elderly Housing Funded Through $100,000 of City Funds in Santa Cruz, California. Journal of Housing 32 (5):237-39.

A recently initiated rehabilitation program in Santa Cruz, California, could become a model for other small cities. Elderly persons living in inferior housing, who are financially unable to make the necessary repairs, are provided with grants for the purpose of improving their housing. The essential ingredient of the program and the eligibility criteria for funding are summarized.

0872. O'Bryant, Shirley L., and Susan M. Wolf. 1983. Explanation of Housing

Satisfaction of Older Homeowners and Renters. **Research on Aging** 5 (2): 217–233.

The purposes of this study are: (1) to investigate the usefulness of three types of variables in predicting the housing satisfaction of older homeowners and older renters; and (2) to determine whether these types of variables would function in similar ways in explaining the housing satisfaction of these two tenure groups. Personal-demographic variables, housing characteristics, and a group of subjective factors measuring "attachment to home" are examined. Participants were 464 older persons who completed a survey. Data analyses indicate that the attachment to home factors are more useful in understanding homeowners' housing satisfaction than the other two sets of variables, whereas physical housing characteristics are more relevant to renters' satisfaction. These findings suggest the importance of considering a wide variety of variables, including subjective ones, when assessing older persons' housing.*

0873.   Parker, Rosetta E. 1984. **Housing for the Elderly: The Handbook for Managers.** Chicago: Institute of Real Estate Management of the National Association of Realtors. 135 pp.

This book primarily offers a guide for managers of elderly housing. But it also contains substantial background information on aging process, and the resulting special housing needs of the aged. In the last section the author takes a look at the future housing needs of the elderly, and calls for more and better-trained managers.

0874.   Pastalan, Leon A. 1984. Manufactured Housing for the Elderly: A Viable Alternative. **Journal of Housing for the Elderly** 2 (3): 89–91.

In this brief article, the author chronicles the history of mobile homes, and argues that mobile homes are viable alternative housing for the elderly. The author concludes: "Clearly, the manufactured housing industry can play a significant role in providing adequate, affordable housing to the elderly population. In this day and age viable alternatives to traditional solutions are more important than ever and manufactured housing can certainly play an important role."

0875.   Pringle, Bruce M. 1979. Housing Living Arrangements for the Elderly: Some Ideas from Northern Europe. **Journal of Property Management** 44 (2): 74–78.

"Should older people live scattered among people of various ages, or are they better off in housing that is only for the elderly?" This is the question that this article attempts to answer. Based on his experience of visiting some northern European countries, the author indicates that Europeans do not have the answer to the above question. However, the European experience in housing the elderly seem to emphasize extended family care of the elderly, family ties, personal choice, integration, and involvement.

0876.   Pynoos, Jon. 1984. Setting the Elderly Housing Agenda. **Policy Studies Journal** 13 (1): 173–184.

In this study, Pynoos explores how the broad economic and political

situations in the society define the nature of the housing problems that are
dealt with, and the extent to which input from various organized groups will
influence the housing decisions affecting the elderly. The paper discusses
the importance of housing for the elderly; it describes the major actors in
the policy arena, and analyzes the influence of elderly interest-groups on
policy. Furthermore, it identifies agenda items yet to be addressed, and
highlights the emerging directions in housing policy. The author suggests
how the current policy developments may influence the future of elderly
housing.

0877. Radosevich, Julianne. 1980. Housing Hispanic Elderly: A Profile of the
Lower Rio Grande Valley. HUD Challenge 11 (10): 11-15.

The burden of housing varies by group membership. Among Hispanic elderly,
the burden is overwhelming because adversities encountered over the years
continue to influence the lives of Hispanics. This article examines the
housing conditions of Hispanic elderly in the lower Rio Grande Valley and the
involvement of private organizations in the matter. It concludes that the
interests of the private organizations in helping the Hispanic elderly
reflect the genuine need that something must be done to improve the housing
conditions of the elderly in the Valley.

0878. Reddick, Josephine. 1985. The Interdependence of Health and Housing for
the Elderly. Journal of Housing for the Elderly 2 (4): 77-82.

A survey was done of the environmental conditions in five senior citizen
housing apartment buildings over a period of five years. It was found that
the health problems of the residents had to be considered in association with
the details of design and environmental conditions.*

0879. Salzman, Michael H. 1975. Converted Building Redeemed, Converted to
Leased Housing for the Elderly. Journal of Housing 32 (7): 327-29.

This article explains how through the efforts and ingenuity of Los Angeles
Housing Authority, a foreclosed plush 204-unit building was redeemed and
converted to a leased housing for the elderly.

0880. Schuler, Greg. 1980. Hitting the Hardcore: Housing for the Neediest
Elderly. HUD Challenge 11 (15): 4-8.

Sometimes the bureaucratic process necessary to secure housing for the
elderly excludes a certain segment of elderly population--usually those who
lack information, mobility, bureaucratic resourcefulness, and who are
destitute. These elderly people need a comprehensive program which
provides an initial outreach effort to find them, provide personal
counseling and help in filing application. This article describes a
program adopted by the Little Brothers of the poor, a social service agency
in Chicago to help the neediest elderly to secure adequate housing. The
article concludes that "a comprehensive assistance program is needed to
develop access to subsidized housing for the elderly in greatest need."

0881. Smart, Eric. 1983. With a Maturing Population, Age is Only Part of the
Picture. Urban Land 42 (5): 32-33.

This article examines the impact of increasing elderly population on real estate industry and housing. The impacts of the expanded wealth of retirees is just beginning to be noted by developers since fewer adults depend on the family unit and are seeking to maintain more independent lives. The different types of housing accommodation for the elderly population in local communities, along with the key factors influencing such developments in the real estate market, are discussed.

0882.   Struyk, Raymond J. 1985. Housing-Related Needs of Elderly Americans and Possible Federal Responses. Journal of Housing for the Elderly 2 (4): 3-26.

Meeting the housing-related needs of the elderly is complex and challenging, both because of the diversity of the needs themselves and because of the way in which the provision of housing assistance and aid for support services have been organized. It will be essential for the Congress to rise above narrow committee jurisdictional issues to formulate an overall strategy for dealing with these problems. The challenge is to design a strategy that is cost-effective by closely matching the assistance provided with the unmet needs of the elderly. Likewise, more explicit attention should be given to focusing on those groups in greatest need. In this regard the higher incidence of both dwelling-specific and dwelling-use problems of blacks and those in rural, non-farm areas is specially striking.*

0883.   Struyk, Raymond J. 1985. Future Housing Assistance Policy for the Elderly. The Gerontologist 25 (1): 41-46.

Contending that the policy on elderly housing in the U.S. is changing very rapidly, this article looks into the future of government housing policy, programs and choices for the elderly Americans. It concludes that "the choices ahead are difficult. Each produces losers as well as beneficiaries. Above all, the overriding goal must be greater equity in the treatment of similar households and a greater use of housing assistance to expand the choices available to elderly Americans."

0884.   Struyk, Raymond J., and Beth Soldo. 1980. Improving the Elderly's Housing: A Key to Preserving the Nation's Housing Stock and Neighborhoods. Cambridge, Mass.: Ballinger Publishing Company. 325 pp.

This book consists of nine chapters (and several technical appendixes) dealing with such topics as: the elderly and their housing, the elderly in the housing market, who are the elderly, the existing housing situation, determinants of housing maintenance, social services and housing quality, location and neighborhood conditions of the elderly, neighborhood preservation, the scope of elderly housing problem, and a discussion of current policy proposals and new initiatives in housing services for the elderly.

0885.   Struyk, Raymond J., and Margery Austin Turner. 1984. Changes in the Housing Situation of the Elderly: 1974-79. Journal of Housing for the Elderly 2 (1): 3-19.

This paper presents results of a careful examination of the changes in the housing circumstances of the elderly over the 1974-79 period, using data from the Annual Housing Survey. The focus is on both the quality of housing occupied and the level of income devoted to housing. The outcomes show that among elderly households there has been substantial and widespread improvement in housing quality especially the incidence of serious structural defects. Improvements in housing quality appear to be achieved by the elderly expending more of their incomes for housing. This however may be a temporary problem due to several factors. Stabilized energy prices, reduced inflation, and a rental building surge fostered by the provisions of the Economic Tax Recovery Act of 1981 may offer some relief.*

0886.   Stephens, Joyce. 1976. **Loners, Losers, and Lovers: Elderly Tenants in a Slum Hotel.** Seattle: University of Washington Press. 118 pp.

In recent years, social scientists have turned their attention to the housing problem of aged Americans. But, they are still overlooking those who live in old and deteriorating hotels in large urban centers. These single-room-occupancy hotels provide little in the way of recreational services, and health care for their aged tenants. However, they do provide a shelter, autonomy, and some degree of privacy for their urban poor elderly clients. These tenants are primarily male, single, and in extreme poverty, some of whom suffer from mental and physical handicaps. These are the truly loners who could use some help.

0887.   Sweaney, Anne L., Joe F. Pittman, Jr., and James E. Montgomery. 1984. The Influence of Marital Status and Age on the Housing Behavior of Older Southern Women. **Journal of Housing for the Elderly** 2 (3): 25-36.

"Age and marital status are frequently cited as predictors of the housing and living arrangements of individuals and facilities." This study investigates the influence of these two variables on the housing behavior of older Southern women. The study is based on a sample of 227 widowed female householders and the same number of married women, with husband present. The outcomes show that both widowhood and age are "relatively important determinants of housing behavior and attitudes."

0888.   Turner, Margery Austin. 1985. Building Housing for the Low-Income Elderly: Cost Containment in the Section 202 Program. **The Gerontologist** 25 (3): 271-277.

This paper presents an assessment of recent cost containment and modest design requirements for the Section 202 direct loan program. Findings are based on case study analysis of Section 202 projects in five HUD field offices. Analysis suggests that cost savings are being achieved but that changes in project design and amenities may be undermining the rationale for maintaining Section 202 as a housing production program. An alternative approach to improving the cost effectiveness of Section 202 is advanced.*

0889.   U.S. Bureau of the Census. 1973. **Housing of Senior Citizens.** 1970 Census of Housing. Subject Reports, HC(7)-2. Washington, D.C.: GPO. 963 pp., appendixes.

This report from the 1970 Census of Housing presents data on senior citizens cross-classified by various housing and household characteristics. The data relate to population age 60 and over and the housings they occupy. Data are presented for the U.S., inside and outside SMSAs, States, and selected places. Data are also presented separately for all races combined, blacks, and Spanish-Origin population.

0890.   Varady, David P. 1980. Housing Problems and Mobility Plans Among the Elderly. Journal of the American Planning Association 46 (3): 301-314.

This paper seeks to determine the ways in which the residential mobility process among the elderly is different from that of the non-elderly. A mobility model consisting of three sets of variables is presented: (1) background characteristics (related to individual, dwelling units, and neighborhood) and housing and neighborhood problems, (2) housing and neighborhood satisfaction, and (3) intra-metropolitan moving plans. Regression analysis utilized to explain variations in the likelihood of formulating intra-metropolitan moving plans among a sample of elderly residents of Cincinnati , Ohio. Residential problems (i.e., rising costs, physical deterioration, and crime) and failing health are shown to be important determinants of moving plans. Several background characteristics contribute to plans to remain, as does participation in governmental housing programs for the elderly. These results imply that an expansion in these programs could enable many elderly to remain in their homes who otherwise would have to move.*

0891.   Varady, David P. 1984. Determinants of Interest in Senior Citizen Housing Among the Community Resident Elderly. The Gerontologist 24 (4): 392-395.

Multiple regression analysis was applied to Cincinnati, Ohio data set to identify the determinants of interest in senior citizen housing. Mixed support was found for the notion that demand for this type of housing comes chiefly from the least needy segments of the elderly population. The importance of improved outreach activities and more flexible rental cost subsidy programs is discussed.*

0892.   Wallace, Edward C. 1981. Housing for the Black Elderly: The Need Remains. In: Community Housing Choices for Older Americans. M. Powell Lawton, and Sally L. Hoover (eds.). New York: Springer Publishing Company. Pp. 59-64.

"One thing is known, however, on the basis of partial data that are available from limited surveys, except for public housing, elderly blacks have been virtually excluded from federally financed elderly housing, that is, Section 202, 236, and 231 housing. The irony of the situation is that they are the ones who need that help most, now and in the future." This article attempts to substantiate this contention regarding the neglect of the minority elderly housing problem.

0893.   Wilner, Mary Ann, and Janet L. Witkin. 1980. Shared Living for Elders: A Viable Alternative. HUD Challenge 11 (9): 5-11.

From a socio-economic standpoint, housing for the elderly must be tailored to special needs of this growing segment of the population in the U.S. Among different approaches is the implementation of the concept of shared housing, an arrangement in which a small number (usually 3 or more) of unrelated persons share a house or an apartment. This article describes some local experiences with shared housing concept.

0894. Zais, James P., Raymond Struyk, and Thomas Thibodeau. 1982. **Housing Assistance for Older Americans: The Reagan Prescription.** Washington, D.C.: Urban Institute Press. 125 pp.

This book addresses the impact of Reagan Administration housing policies on the elderly. In eight chapters, the book reviews and analyzes housing programs and policies of previous administrations and provides an assessment of the impact of the legislative changes in the system of housing assistance enacted into law in 1981.

0895. Zais, James, and Thomas G. Thibodeau. 1983. **The Elderly and Urban Housing.** Washington, D.C.: Urban Institute Press. 107 pp.

This research monograph consists of an evaluation of the impacts of urban revitalization on housing units occupied by the elderly. The analysis is based on data from the 1974-1979 Annual Housing Survey relative to Washington, D.C., Boston, and St. Paul. The authors conclude that contrary to popular belief, the elderly "often appeared to benefit from revitalization" program.

································◆◆◆◆◆◆◆◆◆◆································

11
MINORITIES, HOUSING POLICY, AND HOUSING POLITICS

0896.   Agnew, John Alexander. 1976. **Public Policy and the Spatial Form of the City: The Case of Public Housing Location.** Unpublished Ph.D. Dissertation. The Ohio State University. 353 pp.

The impact of public policy on the spatial form of cities is a relatively neglected subject. This study attempts to examine the impact of public housing policy program on one aspect of residential form namely, residential segregation by social class. Five American and five English cities constitute the sample of cities in which the pattern of public housing are studied. "The major finding of this research is that patterns of public housing location can reinforce patterns of residential segregation by social class. This happens when there are opponents of specific public housing sites who can successfully resist the proposals of public housing agencies. However, this research also shows that given an appropriate institutional and various ameliorative public policies, negative attitudes can be reduced in number and impact." That is, public attitudes toward public housing are conditioned by policy and institutional environment. This study also shows that the more favorable public attitude and institutional policy in England have served to diminish public housing segregation in that country.

0897.   Auger, Deborah A. 1979. The Politics of Revitalization in Gentrifying Neighborhoods: The Case of Boston's South End. **Journal of the American Planning Association** 45 (4): 515-22.

Federal and local officials have in recent years enacted programs to escalate the middle-class resettlement of city neighborhoods. Enamoured with the physical and economic benefits promised by the back-to-the-city movement, they have underestimated the shortcomings of this neighborhood revitalization strategy. The experience of Boston's South End with publicly supported middle-class resettlement illustrates the severe social and political strains that can develop between incumbents and more affluent "pioneers"—strains which can ultimately inflict damage on the neighborhood's poor. Officials must direct current resources to aid the cities' poorer residents and avoid stimulating gentrification until its adverse side effects can be controlled.*

0898. Bell, Robert Kenneth. 1980. Constructing the Public Interest: A Sociological Analysis of Administrative Deliberation and the Interpretation of Federal Subsidized Housing Policy. Unpublished Ph.D. Dissertation. University of California, Berkeley. 312 pp.

This dissertation examines the "process by which government organizations interpret their responsibilities and some social factors that affect how well they do so. Neither a legislature nor an elected executive can supply policy guidance that obviates the necessity for organization to think. Agencies must mold disparate sources of legal authority into coherent and defensible version of their mandates." The focus of this particular study is on the government organization that formulated and reviewed federal subsidized housing policies between 1968 and 1977. Major topics discussed are: delegation and discretion, the economic approach to policy, the interplay of politics and principle, and the costs of activism and liberalism. It is concluded that "activism and liberalism deter administrators from adopting a common law approach to decision-making and developing principled statements of public goals inductively. Yet a common law approach would seem to accord well with the institutional responsibility of administration to rationalize the disparate sources of law into coherent public policy."

0899. Berman, Richard A. 1982. The Housing Crisis: Responses to New Federalism. Journal of Housing 39 (6): 173-76.

Despite the worsening housing situation, stemming from changes in economic and demographic forces, the Reagan Administration has significantly reduced federal support for housing programs insisting that "state and local governments and the private sector must carry the major responsibility for creating an adequate supply of decent affordable housing." This article examines this policy, the New Federalism, with respect to the national picture, local, state and private sector roles. It concludes that "the housing problems of the 1980s include many of those of the 1970s, worsened by high interest rates, a sluggish economy, and the retreat of the federal government from its previous support. Low-income families and individuals, the elderly, and other special populations can not find safe, decent, and affordable housing." The author asserts that given the federal blue print for withdrawal from housing policy, the local governments must develop new strategies to deal with the problem of providing affordable housing in central cities and rural areas where the difficulties are very acute.

0900. Braid, Ralph M. 1984. The Effects of Government Housing Policies in a Vintage Filtering Model. Journal of Urban Economics 16 (3): 272-96.

Long-run (and short-run) effects of low-income governmental housing policies are examined, in a model that treats housing as a durable good which declines in quality over time. Short-run and long-run market equilibria are characterized, rent subsidies are analyzed in detail, and results for other policies are presented.*

0901.   Clapp, John M. 1976. The Formation of Housing Policy in New York City, 1960-1970. **Policy Sciences** 7 (1): 77-91.

The 1964 and 1965 defeat of state bond issues significantly reduced the number of public housing units that could be started during the 1966-1970 period. The opposition of local communities to new starts in public housing resulted in further reductions in the number of units that could be built. The strong political power of tenants was able to retain rent control in the city. However, rent stabilization measure was adopted in 1969 as an alternative to rent control. And, in 1971 the state legislature approved a bill which decontrols apartments upon vacancy. The factors associated with abandonment and its impact on public policy and public opinion are also discussed.

0902.   Dagodag, William Tim. 1972. **Public Policy and the Housing Patterns of Urban Mexican-Americans in Selected Cities of the Central Valley.** Unpublished Ph.D. Dissertation. University of Oregon. 292 pp.

"This study suggests a hypothesis linking the spatial control of Mexican-Americans and public policies. Where Mexican-Americans live in the city, and the conditions under which they live are seen to be determined by public policies. Residential space and the quality of that space have been interpreted as being synonymous with housing, while public policies are defined as legal or quasi-legal courses of action adopted by any level or agency of government." The author contents that often inconsistent and contradictory policies such as urban renewal, public housing, subsidized housing, and so forth, have produced changes in the pattern of Mexican American housing. Cities of Sacramento, Stockton, Fresno, and Bakersfield in California's Central Valley are chosen for description and analysis. This study arrives at several conclusions: (1) The urban areas of the Central Valley are unprepared for the in-migration and settlement of low-income Mexican Americans; (2) Mexican-Americans have no choice in selecting where they will settle in the city; (3) the reaction of governmental agencies is colored by a persistent ideology strongly rooted in environmental determinism; (4) economic factors outweigh all other factors in devising of housing and related policies; and (5) Mexican Americans have no voice in the formulation of policies which controls their movements in the urban space.

0903.   Darden, Joe T. 1983. Demographic Changes 1970-1980: Implications for Federal Fair Housing. In: **Shelter Crisis: The State of Fair Housing.** U.S. Commission on Civil Rights (ed.). Washington, D.C. Pp. 5-30.

This paper analyzes demographic developments during the 1970-1980 decade and assesses their impacts on racial/ethnic residential discrimination and segregation. "It has been 15 years since the Federal Fair Housing Act was passed. The act was supposed to eliminate housing discrimination in both the public and private housing markets. However, it is clear from the demographic data that blacks, whites, and Hispanics have different patterns of population distribution which have resulted from different patterns of buying and renting homes. Since these differences cannot be totally explained by differences in buying power, the patterns suggest that discrimination against blacks and Hispanics continues to be a problem in need of a solution. Clearly, the role played by the Federal government has not been effective in counteracting racial residential segregation, presently so deeply ingrained in American residential structures that the mere elimination of existing discriminatory practices may not be sufficient to eradicate it. Just as 'affirmative' segregationist policies and practices created racial residential segregation, so it would take 'affirmative' integrationist policies and practices to end it."

0904.   Downs, Anthony. 1974. The Successes and Failures of Federal Housing Policy. **Public Interest** (34): 124-145.

This article examines the effectiveness of federal urban housing-related policies along several dimensions. The outcomes of the analysis show that federal urban housing policies for the period 1960-1972 were very effective in generating high-level housing production, providing adequate housing finance, attracting private investors, and creating good quality new neighborhoods; these policies were moderately effective in promoting overall economic stabilization, providing housing assistance to low and moderate income families, and encouraging home ownership; they were moderately ineffective in stabilizing housing production, and very ineffective in reducing housing costs and improving conditions in deteriorating inner-city neighborhoods.

0905.   Downs, Anthony. 1978. Public Policy and the Rising Cost of Housing. **Real Estate Review** 8 (1): 27-38.

Since 1970, the median price of homes in the U.S. has risen much faster than median family income and the overall cost of living index. This had led to a widespread concern over the fact that many American families are being "priced out of the market" for new and existing homes. This article examines the extent to which increase in housing costs during the 1970-1976 period have adversely affected American households. It also discusses the more recent trends in housing costs, and explores their impacts upon different groups of households. The striking conclusion of this study is that "most American households actually experienced some reduction [emphasis mine] in the relative burden of their total housing occupancy costs from 1970 to 1976. One reason for this paradoxical result is that one-third of American households are renters, and rents have been rising far more slowly than household incomes, on the average. A second reason is that two-thirds of American households are owner/occupants, whose equity investments have benefited mightily from he rapid increases in home prices since 1970." As a matter of policy, the author suggests that any "massive" federal action intended to reduce housing costs through "direct financial subsidies or regulations are probably neither desirable nor feasible."

0906.   Frieden, Bernard J. 1971. Urban Housing: Old Policies and New Realities. In: **Problems in Political Economy: An Urban Perspective.** David M. Gordon (ed.). Lexington, Mass.: D.C. Heath and Company. Pp. 380-85.

This article provides a general perspective on the performance of private housing. The author first summarizes the essential dynamics of the turnover process in the housing market, and then questions the market's capacity to provide enough suitable low-cost housing for the poor.

0907.   Glazer, Nathan. 1967. Housing Policy and the Family. **Journal of**

Marriage and the Family 29 (February): 140-63.

This article examines the effects of housing policy on family in the United States. Asserting that establishing such a direct link is not an easy task, this study concludes "that our housing policy has permitted the majority of American families to improve their living conditions and to gain family settings for themselves that are superior to those they left. We have done little for a substantial minority of poor families who have not had the resources to achieve what the society considers (and they, too) minimally desirable housing; for them, we must achieve income maintenance policies or housing subsidies that permit them to achieve such housing."

0908.   Glazer, Nathan.   1967.   Housing Problems and Policies. Public Interest (7): 21-51.

The author concludes that housing policy in this country has permitted the majority of American families to improve their living conditions, and to gain family settings for themselves that were superior to those they left. It has done little for a substantial minority of poor families who have not had the resources to achieve what the society considers (and they do, too) minimally desirable housing; for them, we must devise income maintenance policies that permit them to achieve such housing, or housing subsidies that work to the same effect.@

0909.   Glazer, Nathan.   1970.   Dilemmas of Housing Policy.   In: Toward a National Urban Policy.   Daniel P. Moynihan (ed.).   New York: Basic Books, Inc., Publishers.   Pp. 50-65.

This article examines the variety of American housing conditions (e. g., New York City vs. Berkeley California) and then poses the questions that given this variety of American housing conditions: (1) just what are our housing problems? (2) how serious they are? and (3) what policies should we devise to improve them? In response to these questions the author concludes: (a) there is no one massive housing problem in this country; (b) "At a cost of adding a billion or a billion and a half dollars a year to the federal budget, we would have a situation in which no poor family in our big cities would need to live in substandard housing. I do not underestimate the difficulties of getting Congress to appropriate even such a sum—but we are not now talking of tens of billions. A billion or two would not loom very large in our federal budget, and would permit us to face the world and ourselves with less embarrassment."

0910.   Goering, John M.   1982.   Race, Housing, and Public Policies: A Strategy for Social Science Research.   Urban Affairs Quarterly   17 (4): 463-89.

This article proposes some of the components for a social science strategy for conducting policy-relevant research on fair housing issues. Three components are proposed for the development of a more comprehensive strategy aimed at racial discrimination and integration. Included in this analysis is a discussion of major conceptual, methodological, and analysis issues related to race, housing, and public policies.*

0911.   Grier, George C.   1967.   The Negro Ghettos and Federal Housing Policy. Law and Contemporary Problems 32 (3): 550-60.

"The summer racial disturbances which have recently become epidemic have focused attention upon the United States' most important and perplexing domestic problem--rampant racial ghettoization of its major cities." Contending that the ghettos are by and large the result of American housing policies, this article analyzes the policies that have led to the creation of ghettos and in turn the summer racial violence. The author concludes that "federal housing policies encouraged the growth of the ghettos in two main ways. First, during the major part of the postwar housing boom, federal benefits were largely restricted to whites for both economic and racial reasons; as we have indicated, the economic selectivity is by far the more important. Second, the geographic location of new federally-stimulated construction was such as to enhance segregation by drawing whites out of the central cities toward the suburbs, and permitting the areas they left behind to be occupied by Negroes." To remedy the problem, the author calls for a fundamental change in values and policies--the majority must learn to accept and live with the minorities in an integrated community.

1912. Grigsby, William G., and Louis Rosenburg. 1975. **Urban Housing Policy.** New Brunswick, N. J.: Rutgers University Press. 341 pp.

Many studies have associated substandard housing conditions to socio-demographic factors such as income, race, age, tenure, sex of householder, family size, and so forth. It appears that the associations between housing deprivations and the employment and health history of family members is not as clear. More detail client history is essential to the establishment of priorities among deprived groups. The inner city real estate market is presently raising the cost and lowering the quality of housing which lower income families occupy. The policy recommendations to remedy these problems include giving high priority to housing for the poor.

1913. Hartman, Chester. 1972. The Politics of Housing: Displaced Persons. Society 9 (9): 53-65.

In sum, one would do well not to be optimistic about the prospects of relocatees getting decent housing and neighborhoods at rents they can afford. The cards simply are too heavily stacked against them. Short of major redistribution of power and resources in our society, it appears that the most that can be done is to describe fully the costs and benefits involved in relocation, analyze the way the system operates and prevent official deception from becoming the accepted truth.*

1914. Hartman, Chester. 1975. **Housing and Social Policy.** Englewood Cliffs, N. J.: Prentice Hall. 184 pp.

The basic theme of this book is that all Americans are **entitled** to or have the **right** to decent housing in decent environment of their own choice at rents or prices they can afford. The author asserts that this **right** is not currently upheld; nor, it is ever likely that it would be upheld unless some fundamental policy changes occur in how housing is built and distributed.

1915. Hays, R. Allen. 1982. Housing Rehabilitation as an Urban Policy Alternative. Journal of Urban Affairs 4 (2): 39-54.

Economic and social changes in central cities have made physical decay widespread, and housing rehabilitation has become an increasingly important strategy for reversing this decay. The principal factor which affects the design and impact of housing rehabilitation programs is the income group at which they are targeted. Programs directed at housing the poor face a series of problems related to the lack of resources of these groups, while the principal problem of program aimed at middle-income groups is reversing the pattern of neighborhood disinvestment. All types of rehabilitation programs share problems of slow productivity due to the complexity of the rehabilitation process and to the overall lack of resources committed to them. As a part of a larger community development process, housing rehabilitations must embrace and reconcile the sometimes conflicting goals of maximum physical revitalization and the provision of improved housing services for the poor.@

0916.   Headey, Bruce. 1978. **Housing Policy in the Developed Economy.** New York: St. Martins Press. 276 pp.

This book provides an analytic evaluation of twentieth century governmental housing policies in three countries: Sweden, Britain, and the United States, as examples of developed economies (societies). The basic purpose of this book is to see whether the policies implemented by these countries do actually help to equalize the availability of housing services to all income groups in these countries. The findings indicate that in Sweden the government has succeeded to change the housing conditions and costs in accordance with its stated objective and priorities. But, in the other two countries the answer is in the negative, because in Britain and the United States the price and cost depend as much on market fluctuations as on public policies and priorities.

0917.   Heinberg, John D. 1978. Housing Policy—Federal Objectives and the Local Role for Analysis. **Urban Analysis** 5 (2): 237-49.

Recent changes in federal legislation—Titles I and II of the 1974 Housing Act—increase the demand for local policy analysis in housing. Title I, designed to insure greater flexibility in local government use of federal assistance by providing block grants for community development, includes a specific requirement for the local preparation of a Housing Assistance Plan. Yet housing remains a substantive area where federal objectives will heavily influence local actions. This paper discusses some major issues that the federal-local relationship poses for housing policy analysis and development at the local level and presents implications relevant to these issues drawn from a major research effort—the Experimental Housing Allowance Program (EHAP). Overall findings indicate the likelihood of extensive federal involvement to achieve national objectives. They support a somewhat limited scope for local policy analysis in housing, directed principally at planning, coordination and implementation tasks.*

0918.   Holden, Stephen Michael. 1975. **Ideology and Social Policy: Citizen Participation and the Omnibus Housing Act of 1954.** Unpublished Ph.D. Dissertation. Bryn Mawr College, The Graduate School of Social Work and Social Research. 310 pp.

"This study has focused on the effect of ideology on the development of social policy by discussing the ideological underpinnings of the 'workable program' of the Omnibus Housing Act of 1954." It examines six federal legislative acts which have included citizen participation (the 1954 Omnibus Housing Act being one of them), along the liberal and conservative ideological positions. Overall findings indicate that with respect to the role of citizens, debates reflected a conservative bias. But, the view of change embodied in the debates reflected a liberal bias. "The study suggests that within this context, the 'workable program' could be expected to support a definition of citizen participation that was either therapeutic or program enhancing, but not power redistributive."

0919. Houseman, Gerald L. 1981. Access of Minorities to the Suburbs: An Inventory of Policy Approaches. **Urban and Social Change Review** 14 (1): 11-20.

This article provides a detail analysis of policies regarding the access of minorities to suburban housing. Topics examined are: minority access to the suburbs, policy approaches to the issue of minority access to the suburbs (direct and indirect policies), compliance with nondiscriminatory laws, the government's involvement in housing and mobility policy making, and private and voluntary policies. The overall review of the policy approaches in the inventory leads the author to these conclusions: "1. There are very few programs actually in existence which promote minority access to the suburbs in a direct and affirmative way. 2. The compliance provisions found in HUD laws and regulations, while positive in their overall effects, are neither as direct nor as useful as the affirmative programs and provisions which are in effect. 3. Greater government involvement in housing and development policy-making will tend to yield greater opportunities for minority access to the suburbs. 4. Private and voluntary efforts in this field have yielded little overall impact, but HUD funding of local fair housing groups could help effect a change in this situation."

0920. Ingram, Helen Moyer. 1967. **Congress and Housing Policy.** Unpublished Ph.D. Dissertation. Columbia University. 368 pp.

"This dissertation challenges the doctrine that the President rather than Congress is the initiator and innovator in legislation affecting urban areas. It also questions the supposed connection of Congress from urban constituencies and high level activities on housing legislation thought to be important to cities and metropolitan areas." To substantiate his argument, the author analyzes seven major housing bills passed between 1934 and 1964.

0921. Kain, John F. 1973. **What Should America's Housing Policy Be?** Cambridge, Mass.: Harvard University. 42 pp.

Recently, many economic analyses of housing problems have pointed out that housing is primarily a private good, that substandard housing conditions are largely the result of poverty, and that existing housing policies are inefficient and inequitable, in the sense that a low proportion of benefits actually reach the real needy people. Economists recommend that the existing housing assistance program be substituted with a general income transfer or a housing allowance. Federal housing policies and programs must be designed to encourage minority households to consider housing outside the established minority neighborhoods, in order to integrate and to ensure that subsidized developers pursue active open occupancy policy and equal opportunity in housing. The author suggests that federal polices and programs must be evaluated to insure that they do not support and maintain the existing patterns of racial segregation.

0922.   Kain, John F.   1979.   Failure in Diagnosis: A Critique of the National Urban Policy.   Urban Lawyer 11 (2): 247-69.

President Carter, on 28 March, 1978, presented his proposals for a comprehensive national urban policy to Congress. The proposal, however, fell far short of providing a coherent policy to deal with a host of housing, economic, and social problems referred to as "urban distress," for it failed to identify the underlying causes of urban distress. This article "discusses these underlying causes and recommends policies appropriate to its diagnosis." The article begins with first summarizing the President's proposals.

0923.   Kain, John F.   1983.   America's Persistent Housing Crises: Errors in Analysis and Policy.   Annals of the American Academy of Political and Social Science 465 (January): 136-48.

During the 1970s, the nation witnessed a housing abandonment crisis. Almost all studies and academic evaluation of the problem and policies came up with identical recommendations about the change in the direction of housing policy—that the housing problems of poor persons were increasingly recognized to be associated with poverty. Thus, studies argued in favor of reduction in housing subsidies for the middle and low income families and a greater reliance on cash payments that would provide assistance to lower income families in acquiring standard housing. This article concludes that "in spite of this near unanimity of findings and policy recommendations, the nation's housing policy has consistently followed a different course."

0924.   Keating, Edward Lauren.   1978.   Subsidized Housing, Filtering and Housing Policy.   Unpublished Ph.D. Dissertation. University of Wisconsin—Madison. 382 pp.

"Filtering, or the notion that new construction for the wealthiest households will eventually lead to an improvement in housing conditions for the poor, has been the pillar of America's amalgam of housing policies and programs for decades." This dissertation examines various components and the underlying assumptions and premises of the filtering market theories and concludes: "The measurements showed that, under ideal market conditions, filtering was ineffective in assisting poor people to acquire better housing."

0925.   Khadduri, Jill, Katharine Lyall, and Raymond Struyk.   1978.   Welfare Reform and Housing Assistance: A National Policy Debate.   Journal of the American Institute of Planners 44 (1): 2-12.

Early in the Carter Administration the Department of Health, Education, and Welfare was directed to develop a welfare plan that would reduce inequities in treatment among individuals, provide an incentive to work, and entail no net additional cost to the federal budget beyond sums spent for existing programs. One suggestion to provide funding was to reduce expenditure on current housing programs and use these resources to help support a general program of cash transfers to poor families. This article argues that exclusive reliance on cash transfers to provide   decent housing for the poor would be both unsuccessful and inefficient.*

0926. Kirby, Michael Paul. 1973. **Correlates of Public Housing Policy in American Cities.** Unpublished Ph.D. Dissertation. University of Wisconsin-Milwaukee. 205 pp.

"The purpose of this study was to describe various aspects or dimensions of public housing policy and to analyze the impact of potential system characteristics and environmental factors on these dimensions of policy." The author formulates the hypothesis that both political system and environmental factors produce variation in public housing policy. The analyses are based on an examination of political and environmental correlates of public housing policy formulations. The data on public housing relate to all units built prior to 1969. A set of nine findings is enumerated.

0927. Kivisto, Peter. 1986. An Historical Review of Changes in Public Housing Policies and their Impacts on Minorities. In: **Race, Ethnicity, and Minority Housing in the United States.** Jamshid A. Momeni (ed.). Westport, Connecticut: Greenwood Press. Chapter I.

As this historical review of federal housing policies and practices indicate, the public housing program during the past 50 years has been an extremely important provider of affordable housing for low-income black citizens. At the same time, it is a program that has been incapable of eliciting wide-spread public support. This lack of support has been due largely to the power of the ideology of the unfettered market combined with the enduring problems of race prejudice and discrimination. Though the private sector has provided no evidence that, if left to its own devices, it would be capable or interested in providing decent and affordable housing for the poor, it traditionally has been unresponsive to the efforts of the public sector to take an active role in the delivery of housing to the general populace. The consequence of this is a segmented housing market in which the state has been permitted to play an overt role in the provision of housing for specifically targeted groups. This review indicates that the immediate future would seem to signal an increasingly leaner and meaner welfare state. Because of this, the goal of the U.S. Housing Act of 1949 will remain, for a sizable portion of the lower-class minority community, unrealized.@

0928. Kogan, Arnold B. 1982. Recent Changes in Housing Policies and Standards. **Urban Lawyer** 14 (4): 746-48.

This article, written by a member of the Committee on Housing and Urban Development, provides an overview of the recent changes in federal housing policies and standards. Topics discussed are the Section 8 housing program, and the Economic Recovery Tax Act of 1981. The author points at the virtual elimination of the Section 8 housing program for low- and moderate income families as one of the changes in housing policy.

0929. Kokus, John, Jr. 1971. **An Evaluation of Policies of Private Real Estate**

Management **in** **Low** **and** **Moderate** **Income** **Housing.** Unpublished Ph.D. Dissertation. The American University. 338 pp.

The major purpose of this "dissertation consists of the evaluation of low and moderate income housing management. The assumption is that Federal policies are so structured as to preclude the evaluation of the performance of private management in its delivery of housing services in low and moderate income housing."

0930.   Kristof, Frank S. 1972. Federal Housing Policies: Subsidized Production, Filtration and Objectives: Part I. **Land Economics** 48 (4): 309-20.

This article examines the history of federal influence on housing policy for three periods: 1934-1961, 1961-1968, and 1968 to date. The main objective is to explore the extent to which the national housing goal was realized between 1950 and 1970 when 96 percent of new housing was built by the private sector, in contrast to the experience of the 1969-1971 period when government played a larger role, through federally subsidized constructions in compliance with the 1968 Housing Act. The major conclusion derived from this study is that any observed improvement in housing could not be attributed to filtration process.

0931.   Kristof, Frank S. 1973. Federal Housing Policies: Subsidized Production, Filtration and Objectives: Part II. **Land Economics** 49 (2):163-74.

This is the second of the two part article by the author (see previous item). In this part topics discussed are: new construction, housing turnover and improvement; housing abandonment in the central cities; housing conditions in central cities, 1960-1970; a program for central cities; and, a program for areas outside central cities, suggesting that it is in the outlying growth areas that the housing programs outlined under the 1968 Housing Act and subsequently could realize their best potential. Overall, the author concludes that "if the forgoing proposals for meeting the housing problems of the 1970s are sound—and are implemented—it will mean that the filtration or turnover process will be supplemented by measures to make its effects more constructive than has been the experience of the 1960s."

0932.   Lazin, Frederick A. 1980. Policy, Perception, and Program Failure: The Politics of Public Housing in Chicago and New York City. **Urbanism: Past and Present** (9): 1-12.

"Public housing in major American cities has long been associated with badly designed, drab highrises for poor blacks, welfare clients and other racial minorities, as well as with social malaise and crime in adjacent neighborhoods. ...This article is concerned with the influence of governmental policies on the public's perception of an institution and how that perception may affect later governmental decisions to alter the character of the institutions." More specifically, the author examines the site selection and tenant assignment policies of Chicago and New York City's Housing Authorities, prior to and during the mayoral terms of Richard J. Daley, and John V. Lindsay as mayors of Chicago and New York, respectively. This article attempts to show how policies influenced the public's perception of public housing and "how that in turn affected the formulation and implementation of later decisions by both mayors in areas of public housing and racial integration."

0933. Leibsohn, Daniel. 1980. Expanding the Local Government Role in Housing:
Local Ownership, Capital and Risk. **Western City** 56 (8): 16-20.

Among the major housing policy goals in the present housing market are to
ensure an adequate supply of affordable housing particularly for low- and
moderate-income families, and ensuring the soundness of the housing stock
itself. An effective method to achieve these objectives is to generate
enough capital to low- and moderate-income households. The public must
provide the needed capital, and reduce the risk to private lenders. This
essay discusses different approaches of expanding the federal role in
housing, and reducing the burden of private enterprise.

0934. Lett, Monica Rhea. 1976. **Rent Control as an Instrument of Local Housing
Policy.** Unpublished Ph.D. Dissertation. Rutgers University. 535 pp.

Recent pattern of inflation has generated the rebirth of rent control in many
urban areas of the country. In the past rent control was used as a war time
measure to combat housing shortages. But the recent rebirth of rent
regulation represents a peacetime economic emergency as the overriding
justification for the enactment of the measure. In view of the fact that the
underlying assumptions of these peacetime rent control measures vis-a-vis
its legislative approach and methods of regulation are different from the
war-time emergency measures, this dissertation attempts to determine
"whether rent control is an appropriate instrument of local housing policy
with which to deal with current housing problems." As a result of her
analyses, the author reaches the conclusion that since "the essence of the
rent control dilemma is the widening gap between tenants' ability to pay and
the increased rental required to operate and maintain a housing unit, rent
control is not an appropriate instrument to deal with this problem but is
being utilized in the absence of a comprehensive national program."

0935. Lilley, William, III. 1972. Federal Programs Spur Abandonment of Housing
in Major Cities. **National Journal** 4 (1): 26-33.

The federal government is becoming the largest owner of residential property
in many major cities. This is due to abandonment which seems to result from
the very programs designed to allow the poor to own homes. Free enterprise
has been misused by real estate speculators who prey on the inexperience of
welfare mothers. Department of Housing and Urban Development is studying
the possibility of using allowances as an alternative policy approach to
the existing program structure. If implemented, these cash grants or
substitutes would provide a radical redirection of low-income housing
policy.

0936. Maisel, Louis, II. 1971. **Process and policy in the House of
Representatives: The Case of Housing Policy, 1961-1968.** Unpublished Ph.D.
Dissertation. Columbia University. 412 pp.

Employing a "systems" analysis framework, this dissertation examines
Congressional action on housing legislation during the Kennedy and Johnson
Administrations. The study begins with the assumption that demonstrable
differences in output exist between Congresses. "Using housing policy as a

case in point, it seeks to explain those differences." The findings indicate "that the complexity of the Congressional process permitted circumstances to arise in which well-placed Congressmen could have considerable impact. Though the Executive Branch normally provided the initiative, Congressional influence at this stage was not totally absent."

0937.   Marando, Vincent L. 1975. A Metropolitan Lower Income Housing Allocation Policy. **American Behavioral Scientist** 19 (1): 75-103.

One of the current problems facing metropolitan areas is centered around the "mismatch" of lower income housing distribution between the central cities and suburbs and employment opportunities in suburban areas. This article discusses the "formulation and impact of a national metropolitan housing allocation policy. Specifically, discussion centers around the Department of Housing and Urban Development (HUD) and its interaction with Councils of Government (COGs) in developing a metropolitan-wide lower income housing allocation plan: a fair share plan. The policy's impact is assessed both in terms of actually locating lower income housing on metropolitan-wide basis and its effects on metropolitan decision-making." From this analysis the author concludes that the development of a national lower income housing policy has been an evolutionary process of relating planning to decision-making, involving governmental officials at all levels. The author suggests that the future location of lower income housing will increasingly depend on COGs utilization of metropolitan-wide criteria.

0938.   Marcuse, Peter. 1971. Social Indicators and Housing Policy. **Urban Affairs Quarterly** 7 (2): 193-217.

The attraction for easily quantifying housing goals and policy, using social indicators, are found to be quite misleading or meaningless and often with adverse effects on the poor. Existing indicators of housing progress are seen as limited and/or faulty. This article describes the criteria which should be used as guides to housing policy goals, and outlines a way to the development of better housing indicators.

0939.   Marcuse, Peter. 1978. Housing Policy and the Myth of the Benevolent State. **Social Policy** 8 (4): 21-26.

"Much intellectual analysis of government policies is premised on the myth of the benevolent state. In brief the myth is that government acts out of a primary concern for the welfare of all of its citizens, that its policies represent an effort to find solutions to recognized social problems, and that government efforts fall short of complete success only because of lack of knowledge, countervailing selfish interest, incompetence, or lack of courage." This article analyzes government policies relative to housing regulations and the public provisions of housing and concludes that "any claim to benevolent intervention in the housing situation to bring about more rationally organized and improved housing for the poor is now abandoned altogether." The author further asserts that "housing policy as a category is not only artificial, it creates a bias from its very use."

0940.   Marrow-Jones, Hazel Ann. 1980. The Impact of Federal Housing Policy on Population Distribution in the United States. Unpublished Ph.D. Dissertation. Ohio State University. 238 pp.

The federal Housing Administration's (FHA's) housing activities in the U.S. date back to 1934. Section 203(b), better known as the mutual mortgage insurance program, has been one of the largest and longest lived component of the 1934 National Housing Act. Section 203(b) was not intended to have effects on the spatial distribution of households. However, it is alleged that the unstated and perhaps the unintended consequences of Section 203(b) has been to encourage the suburbanization of selected households, and contribute to the decline of inner city neighborhoods. The purpose of this study is to examine the said allegation. Making a comparative analysis of FHA insured properties with nonFHA insured sales of homes having values under the FHA's maximum in Columbus, Ohio, in 1976 and 1977, the author finds that a higher proportion of white male-headed families tend to purchase homes further away from the Central Business District than nonwhite or female-headed families.

0941. Meehan, E. J. 1975. Public Housing Policy: Convention Versus Reality. New Brunswick, N. J.: Center for Urban Policy Research. 181 pp.

Between 1939 and 1970, the St. Louis Housing Authority built nine conventional public housing projects and a building for the elderly added to one of them. From the beginning, these awkwardly positioned buildings were surrounded by abandoned and decaying residential and commercial properties. These public housing projects were poorly maintained. By 1970, these projects had produced a famous disaster, by then symbolized by Pruitt-Igoe. The characteristics of the tenants had gradually changed to be dominated by black welfare recipients, with a large proportion being female householders. In this book, the author argues that the St. Louis housing policy produced a disaster for the project remained the same while the conditions to which the policy was applied had changed significantly.

0942. Meehan, Eugene J. 1979. The Quality of Federal Policymaking: Programmed Failure in Public Housing. Columbia, Missouri: University of Missouri Press. 230 pp.

"The inadequacies in federal policymaking can be illustrated in many areas but are particularly conspicuous in the field of public housing." According Meehan, with the 1937 Housing Act, the federal government initiated a program in public housing intended to solve a variety of social ills at the same time. "Unfortunately for the public housing program, this multipurpose approach made for ambiguous policies and uncertain target populations, which in turn made it difficult if not impossible to criticize, evaluate, or improve the program." In this book the author analyzes all the central features of the public housing program from its origin in 1937 through the late 1970s. The analyses are based on public housing program in St. Louis as a case study. The major conclusion reached is that government policies are associated with no learning, no improvement, and indifference to consequences. The author asserts that the government even "tends to ignore the effects of policy on the general public when considering policy changes."

0943. Mitchell, Robert E., and Richard A. Smith. 1979. Race and Housing: A Review and Comments on the Content and Effects of Federal Policy. Annals of the American Academy of Political and Social Science 441 (January): 168-85.

Unlike school integration measure, housing and community development policies attack the causes rather than simply the symptoms of racial segregation in urban communities. Federal policies are examined with regard to two goals: protection of the individual's right to a decent home and a suitable living environment, and the social goal of achieving stable interracial environments. Although both supply and demand housing strategies have had some, but still unmeasured, success in realizing both goals, the public and private sector delivery systems have sustained the dual housing market. Future progress will depend on the mixture of demand and supply strategies adopted, changes in delivery systems, the success of federal enforcement efforts, the emphasis placed on broad strategy options, and socioeconomic trends not easily influenced by public policy.*

0944. NAHRO (National Association of Housing and Redevelopment Officials). 1984. 50 Years of Housing Policy. **Journal of Housing** 41 (1); 20-22.

In 1984 NAHRO celebrated its 50th anniversary, honoring its half century "struggle to make the goal of a decent home and a suitable living environment a reality for all Americans. In addition to reaffirm its commitment to this goal." NAHRO has found it fitting to use this benchmark year to write this article reviewing the policies and findings of the past 50 years of activities in housing. The article is an "historical perspective of the struggles and accomplishments" in the housing field. It also provides a one-page selected bibliography.

0945. Naylor, Thomas H. 1967. The Impact of Fiscal and Monetary Policy on the Housing Market. **Law and Contemporary Problems** 32 (3): 384-96.

This article outlines "a number of possible relationships between fiscal and monetary policy, as well as federal housing program, and the housing market. Although a large number of empirical studies of the housing market have been conducted, none of these studies has as its principal aim the delineation of relationships between fiscal and monetary policy (and governmental housing programs) and the housing market. The major conclusion of this study is, therefore, that there is considerable need for an econometric model of the housing market which includes as instrumental variables (1) fiscal policy instruments (2) monetary policy instruments, and (3) federal housing program instruments. Until such a model is constructed, generalizations about the relationship between these policy instruments and the behavior of the housing market can at best be termed 'speculative.'"

0946. Nenno, Mary K. 1983. The Reagan Housing, CD Record: A Negative Rating. **Journal of Housing** 40 (5): 135-41.

This article analyzes President Reagan's housing policies during the first two-thirds of his term in office and concludes that "the Reagan's record in housing and community development [CD] is that it is negative--many would say deliberately destructive. The administration has used executive powers--in particular, the budget process--to cut deeply the federal commitment to authorized programs; to reduce federal government involvement and responsibility; and to damage seriously the morale and capacity of the Department of Housing and Urban Development." The author contends that the Reagan's Administration policy has also been negative in the sense that it has taken no new initiative of its own to respond to the critical housing needs of the 1980s.

0947. Nourse, Hugh O. 1973. **The Effects of Public Policy on Housing Markets.** Lexington, Mass.: D. C. Heath and Company. 130 pp.

This book uses the techniques of regression and linear modeling to obtain empirical view of urban housing, evaluate public housing, community development, and alternative approaches to housing for the poor. The analysis is based on data gathered in St. Louis. The book concludes: (1) public housing does not increase the value of surrounding properties; (2) it results in gains for low-income families, construction workers, and local governments; (3) it means losses for slum landlords and taxpayers—e.g., two-thirds of tenants in St. Louis public housing project came from substandard units; (4) urban renewal may not mean an increase in property values; and, (5) urban renewal tends to shift the location of slums. The author suggests that a guaranteed income policy may have as much impact on housing quality as the existing housing policies, and the standard of housing quality that can be attained and maintained is contingent on the size of money that can be redistributed among the poor.

0948. Nugent, Anne E. 1980. **Toward a Housing Policy Proposal for the Elderly Homeowner.** Unpublished Ph.D. Dissertation. University of Idaho. 203 pp.

This dissertation analyzes housing policy for the elderly population, whose size has increased in recent years and who are mostly home owners. The focus of this study is on the spatial distribution of the elderly in the 95 census tracts in Omaha, Nebraska. The results of this study show that "the elderly population has increased by 61.9 percent over the 20 year period with the female elderly population increasing at a higher rate. Thus, the trends are indicating an increase in the spatial distribution in various parts of the city." From the increase in the proportion of elderly population, the author infers that there is an increase in the number of homes owned by the elderly in Omaha. It is pointed out, however, that the "elderly tend to own lower valued property, they tend to spend less on maintenance despite the greater age of their homes and hence, they are in greater need of repair and they spend a larger fraction of their incomes on housing costs. The deterioration of the existing housing stock in Omaha suggests that previous housing policies have not assisted the elderly homeowners because the policies emphasized the construction of housing and rental subsidies." The author proposes a plan that emphasizes the preservation, repair and maintenance, of the existing housing stocks that belong to the elderly population in the city.

0949. Ohls, James C. 1975. Public Policy Toward Low Income Housing and Filtering in Housing Market. **Journal of Urban Economics 2** (2): 144-71.

The article presents a model of a housing market in which dwelling units are constructed for relatively high income families and then gradually become available to lower income groups as they depreciate in quality and price. Assumptions are made concerning values for the parameters of the model, and the model is then solved using numerical methods. Alternative possible policies for increasing the housing consumption of the poor are simulated in the model.*

0950. Peters, James. 1981. House of Cards. **Planning** 47 (9): 19-22.

"Federal housing policy always has been a rather abstract notion. Argument still continues as to whether the 1949 goal of a 'decent home and suitable living environment for every American family' was actually directed at substandard housing or a sluggish homebuilding industry." This article discusses housing affordability, President Reagan's vouchers, the dramatic cuts in housing programs, rent control, and the allocation problem. It concludes that "for local governments, understanding current federal housing policy is a guessing game."

0951. Quigley, John M. 1974. Indirect Policies to Reduce Residential Segregation. In: Patterns of Racial Discrimination. George von Furstenberg, et al. (eds.). Lexington, Mass.: Lexington Books. Pp. 188-92.

Several studies have concluded that "residential segregation imposes heavy economic and noneconomic costs upon minority groups in urban areas." In the light of this assertion, this article examines different indirect policies that are said to be aimed at reducing racial segregation. It concludes that "none of these small changes in policy emphasis will eliminate the massive ghettos that have been erected as a result of generations of systematic discrimination."

0952. Quigley, John M. 1979. Policies for Low and Moderate Income Housing: Housing Allowances and Demand Oriented Housing Subsidies. **Policy Studies Journal** 8 (2): 300-06.

It is estimated that the Federal government will spend more than $170 million on the Experimental Housing Allowance Program (EHAP). So far more than 50 million has been spent on EHAP research alone. This paper indicates some of the analytical issues in evaluation and suggests that housing allowance policies have ample historical precedents.*

0953. Reed, Christine Mary Howells. 1983. **Political Dynamics in the Evolution of Federal Housing Policy: The Gautreaux Case, 1966-1982.** Unpublished Ph.D. Dissertation. Brown University. 167 pp.

This dissertation examines the lengthy **Gautreaux v. Chicago Housing Authority** court case in search for establishing links between the political actors in Chicago's political process, private housing development process, and the judicial process. The focus of this study is on the relationships that caused the failure of Gautreaux to have any significant impact on racial segregation is Chicago's public housing. The author concludes that the Gautreaux case demonstrates that interactions among interdependent political actors exist "only in theory and that the obstacles to its realization are only partially understood."

0954. Roistacher, Elizabeth A. 1984. A Tale of Two Conservatives: Housing Policy Under Reagan and Thatcher. **APA Journal** 50 (4): 485-92.

Low-income housing policies under Ronald Reagan in the United States and

Margaret Thatcher in Great Britain have emphasized increased reliance on the market, individual choice, and sharper means testing of the recipients of subsidies. Their housing agendas were justified on grounds of promoting greater efficiency and equity in low-income rental housing programs. An evaluation of those policies indicates, however, that gains in efficiency-- a given amount of spending producing greater benefits--are small compared to increases in equities between low-income renters and other households, especially when all housing policies are considered.*

0955.   Sands, Gary, and Lewis L. Bower. 1976. **Housing Turnover and Housing Policy: Case Studies of Vacancy Chains in New York State.** New York: Praeger. 169 pp.

One of the basic doctrines of the federal housing policy is that aid to new housing for middle-income families will indirectly benefit lower-income households through turnover. This filtering or trickledown theory is favored because it costs less than providing housing directly for lower income families. However, the critics argue that this filtering approach has not been effective in eliminating housing crises. This study, using the housing markets of Rochester, Buffalo, and New York City, attempts to examine turnover effects of new constructions. The outcomes show that natural turnover achieves public policy objectives to some extent, but it is impossible to meet the total community's housing needs for the poor without direct intervention by the public sector.

0956.   Solomon, Arthur P. 1972. Housing and Public Policy Analysis. **Public Policy** 22 (3): 443-71.

In recent years there has been an intensified interest in the debate over national housing policy. Various factors have generated interest in the formulation of more effective federal housing strategy. This article examines the performances of three major low income housing programs (conventional public housing, leased public housing, and rent supplements) in an attempt to measure the efficiency and equity effects of the national housing programs. Results "illustrate that opposite conclusions can be drawn from the use of different evaluative standards." The application and the outcome of using different evaluative standards are discussed.

0957.   Sorter, Bruce W. 1976. Economic Sanctions of a Military Open Housing Policy as a Force for Social Change. **Urban and Social Change Review** 9 (1): 18-22.

This article examines the significance of the Department of Defense's change in housing policy on social change. "The program, initiated in 1967, was designed to end housing discrimination against black military personnel by securing open-occupancy housing agreements from civilian landlords." The article asserts that in addition to the target population, this policy had far reaching consequences in other segments of the society. It concludes that "the military engaged in an open-occupancy housing program using economic leverage which was highly effective in removing housing discrimination for black military personnel. It also stimulated wide-range social change in the broader civilian community which was not directly planned or evaluated at the level of implementation."

0958.   Stanfield, Rochelle L.   1981.   Cashing Out Housing--A Free Market Approach that Might Also Cost Less.   **National Journal** 13 (38): 1660-64.

In concert with many other shifts in policy relative to poverty programs, Reagan Administration now wants to shift the emphasis of federal funding for housing projects--President Reagan wants to redirect funds directly to the needy families through housing vouchers   that can be directly applied to the rent.   This article examines this shift in policy that has 40 years of history using construction approach to expand the supply of low income housing to a voucher system.   The article offers comments from a number of experts regarding the nature of the nation's low income housing problems and the possibility that the voucher system might offer a cheaper solution to housing for the poor than subsidized construction approach.

0959.   Stegman, Michael A.   1969.   Kaiser, Douglas, and Kerner On Low-Income Housing Policy.   **Journal of the American Institute of Planners** 35 (6): 422-27.

In 1967, President Lyndon Johnson commissioned three blue-ribbon panels to inquire into major social and housing problems threatening American society.   These Commissions are known as the Douglas Commission, chaired by Senator Paul Douglas;   the Kaiser Commission, headed by Edgar E. Kaiser; and the Kerner Commission, chaired by Governor Otto Kerner.   This article reviews the findings and recommendations of these three blue-ribbon commissions relative to low-income housing and urban problems to the government.   The review focuses on such topics as reducing the cost of new construction, private participation in low-income housing, maintaining the quality of existing housing stock, intergovernmental relations, and housing delivery systems.

0960.   Stegman,   Michael   A.   1972.   National   Housing   and   Land-Use   Policy Conflicts.   **Journal of Urban Law** 49 (4): 629-66.

There is a conflict between the national housing policy calling for increased production of low- and moderate-income housing with exclusionary local zoning ordinances designed to maintain homogeneous community developments.   This paper examines these relationships and suggests that the socio-spatial characteristics of Operation Breakthrough requires community and site selection which permits implementation of social experiments regarding low income housing.   The author also discusses a range of social experiments which could be pursued by Operation Breakthrough.

0961.   Struyk, Raymond J.   1977.   The Need for Local Flexibility in U.S. Housing Policy.   **Policy Analysis** 3 (4): 471-83.

Invariability of program provisions is a traditional hallmark of federally sponsored housing programs for metropolitan areas in this country.   Such rigidity ignores the diversity of conditions among urban housing markets. While in some locales such programs have done well, in others they have produced significant undesirable side effects.   This paper outlines the different outcomes which national housing policies can produce under alternative market conditions and argues for greater local flexibility in future federal housing programs.*

0962. Struyk, Raymond J., Sue A. Marshall, and Larry J. Ozanne. 1978. **Housing Policy for the Urban Poor.** Washington, D.C.: The Urban Institute. 153 pp.

The lack of understanding and/or an appreciation for local housing market dynamics is a problem that has continually plague the federal low income housing policymaking. Human ecologists and theoreticians in the fields have explored housing filtration and have identified housing submarkets, and have discussed the links between them. However, the problem has been the difficulty in operationalizing and empirically testing these theories. This book, while contenting that policies must take market flexibility into account, develops a simulation model to illustrate the need for such flexibility. The model, under certain specified conditions shows how and why certain programs create the impact that they do. From this analysis the authors arrive at the following major conclusions: (a) the local conditions do have significant impact on the effectiveness of housing programs both in terms of improving the housing standards of low-income families and in preserving the housing stock; (b) mixed actions to stimulate supply and demand will usually be more effective than exclusive reliance on either supply or demand side; and (c) the best policy should incorporate programs fueling housing demand with those augmenting the supply of units in the critical quality range. Overall, the argument presented in this book attempts to underscore the fact that any housing policy without the understanding of local conditions is bound to fail.

0963. Thompson, Walter Bernard. 1974. **An Analysis of Economic Policy Toward Substandard Housing Occupancy.** Unpublished Ph.D. Dissertation. University of Georgia. 296 pp.

This study examines the constraints and market imperfections surrounding the production of low-cost housing. The study is important because previous researches have revealed that HUD's basic goal is not cost reduction and increased production. Rather, to achieve a reduction and/or elimination of substandard housing occupancy. Thus, this study was designed to examine constraints/market imperfections within the context of national housing policies and objectives. The author formulates and tests several hypotheses.

0964. Welfeld, Irving H. 1985. Policies or Programs: Legislative Origins of PHA Problems. **Journal of Housing** 42 (4): 140-41.

As early as 1937 the debates concerning the definition of "low-income" families have plagued Public Housing Authorities (PHA). In this article the author makes a new assessment of the causes of public housing's administrative problems.

0965. Wolman, Harold Louis. 1968. **Politics and Public Policy: A Study of the Housing Political System.** Unpublished Ph.D. Dissertation. University of Michigan. 347 pp.

"This study describes and analyzes the politics of public policy area at the national level. The process by which major redistribution of values is brought about—or is prevented from being brought about—in the area of [poverty and low income] housing is viewed through the framework of systems analysis. In addition, the characteristics and attitudes of the decision-makers involved are investigated."   The study concludes that, overall, the housing political system met the requisites of a pluralistic society. That is, access was not open to every group, but the elite held attitudes representative of views of those outside the elite.

0966. Wrightson, Margaret Tucker. 1983. Metropolitan Regional Council Performance in Housing Assistance Policy: A Test of Two Models of Organizational Perspectives. Unpublished Ph.D. Dissertation. American University. 166 pp.

The main objective of this study is "to evaluate which of the two competing models—one from political science, the other from public administration—more effectively predicts regional council performance redistributing multifamily housing assistance in metropolitan areas since the passage of the Housing and Community Development Act of 1974." The 1974 Act sets forth a national policy of deconcentrating assisted housing and provides regional councils with new opportunities to influence allocation policies. The models and their respective effectiveness are assessed.

................................♦♦♦♦♦♦♦♦♦................................

12
HOMELESSNESS

0967. Anonymous. 1985. Homelessness: What Can be Done. Housing Law Bulletin 15 (3): 1-6.

The problem of homelessness is one which is not confined to one area in the nation. And, it did not spring up overnight. Yet there is no centralized, organized method of administering aid to these millions of people. In an examination of the programs which exist now at federal, state, and local levels, this article shows that the dichotomy of services by different levels of government creates a good deal of confusion and inability of the country to cope with this growing national social problem.

0968. Arce, A. Anthony, et al. 1983. A Psychiatric Profile of Street People Ad Admitted to an Emergency Shelter. Hospital and Community Psychiatry 34 (9): 812-17.

During the winter 1981-82 the City of Philadelphia operated an adult emergency shelter for two months. After reviewing the available records, the authors compiled a Psychiatric profile of the 193 residents admitted to the shelter. They grouped the residents into three classes: habitual street people, the episodic homeless, and those who did not usually live on the street but were undergoing an acute crisis. Although a large number of the street people who suffered from diagnosable mental illness improved with adequate treatment, the authors found it was extremely difficult to relocate many of the shelter residents. They discuss other problems such as the need for psychiatric expertise in treating the homeless and the lack of a coordinated effort among several city governments.*

0969. Bachrach, Leona L. 1984. Interpreting Research on the Homeless Mentally Ill: Some Caveats. Hospital and Community Psychiatry 35 (9): 914-17.

Applied research that is conducted in an atmosphere of urgency carries an implied risk. In the near future, findings from a number of studies of the service needs of the homeless mentally ill will become available to planners and service providers. Users of data from these studies are cautioned to view the results with care. Specifically, they should be mindful of biases in studies and aware of the complexity of the homeless mentally ill population. They should also take care not to make a metaphor of mental illness among the homeless mentally ill. Finally, they should remember that each community that plans services for its homeless mentally ill population must take cognizance of its own unique needs and resources.*

0970. Bahr, Howard M. 1969. Family Size and Stability as Antecedents of Homelessness and Excessive Drinking. Journal of Marriage and the Family 31 (3): 477-83.

Men from large families and from broken families have been described as overrepresented in skidrow and alcoholic populations. A reassessment of the linkage between these variables based on (1) survey data from two skid-row populations and a control sample of lower-class men, and (2) a reinterpretation of some of the findings of previous investigators, leads to the conclusion that neither the broken home nor the large family size are, in themselves, significant factors in the etiology of homelessness and excessive drinking.*

0971. Ball, F. L. Jessica, and Barbara E. Havassy. 1984. A Survey of the Problems and Needs of Homeless Consumers of Acute Psychiatric Services. Hospital and Community Psychiatry 35 (9): 917-21.

Efforts to alter the repeated use of costly hospital-based psychiatric services and the underuse of community mental health services by some homeless adults have yielded few successes. To better understand these failed efforts, the authors interviewed 112 self-identified homeless recidivists in San Francisco on several demographic variables, the problems they face in living in the community, and the resources they feel they need to be able to remain in the community. Most striking among the findings was the low priority respondents accorded to the psychiatric and social services currently offered by community mental health agencies; instead the respondents often blamed their inability to avoid readmissions on their lack of basic resources for survival. The authors discuss the relevance of the findings for mental health research, funding policies, and programming.*

0972. Bassuk, Ellen L. 1984. The Homelessness Problem. Scientific American 25 (1): 40-46.

"Many of the homeless people wandering the streets of American cities and crowding into emergency shelters are mentally ill. They require adequate housing and appropriate psychiatric care."

0973. Baxter, Ellen, and Kim Hopper. 1981. Private Lives/Public Spaces: Homeless Adults on the Streets of New York City. New York: Community Service Society. 129 pp.

This report looks at the contemporary causes of homelessness in New York City, the conditions and the operating procedures of public and private shelters, and the strategies of surviving on the streets of New York City.

0974. Baxter, Ellen, and Kim Hopper. 1982. The New Mendicancy: Homeless in New York City. American Journal of Orthopsychiatry 52 (3): 393-408.

An ethnographic study of the homeless poor in New York City suggests that significant changes have taken place in the size and composition of that population during the past 15 years. Among the disenfranchised, the mentally disabled figure prominently, many of them casualties of state deinstitutionalization and restricted admission policies. This paper argues that in the absence of safe and accessible shelter, rehabilitation efforts are doomed to failure. It is suggested that clinicians could play a critical advocacy role for an approach that sees therapeutic and social needs as intimately linked.*

0975.   Carlson, Peter. 1986. Homeless: The Shanty Builders. **People Weekly** 25 (7): 94-100.

This is the third article in People's series on the homeless in America, "who now number two million by some estimates. We have looked at the plight of 95 percent of these men and women--the 'new homeless'--people suddenly out of work, out of housing they can afford or discharged from mental hospitals without a place to go. This concluding story describes the life of more familiar figures, the country's hoboes."

0976.   Cohen, Neal L., Jane F. Putnam, and Ann M. Sullivan. 1984. The Mentally Ill Homeless: Isolation and Adaptation. **Hospital and Community Psychiatry** 35 (9): 922-24.

Project HELP was established in New York City in 1982 as a mobile outreach unit providing crisis medical and psychiatric services to impaired homeless persons. The author describes the demographic characteristics of the population served, the disposition of patients accepting treatment or shelter services, and the adaptation of the homeless to weather extremes. They discuss the difficulties in providing services to a population whose members are distrustful of authority and are unwilling to provide information about themselves. They conclude that the more disaffiliated members of the homeless population, such as those served by Project HELP, need even more extensive services than the homeless who use some kind of existing sheltered care, and they suggest various kinds of services to meet their needs.*

0977.   Collin, Robert W. 1984. Homelessness: The Policy and the Law. **Urban Lawyer** 16 (2): 317-29.

Homeless men and women situated in our urban areas have recently become the center of attention for social workers, urban planners, and poverty lawyers. This is largely due to their numbers and to new legal precedent in the field. This article examines some causes and dimensions of homelessness, and discusses the impact of Callahan v. Carey and its progeny.@

0978.   Crystal, Stephen. 1984. Homeless Men and Homeless Women: The Gender Gap. **Urban and Social Change Review** 17 (2): 2-6.

In recent years there has been a remarkable upsurge in the problem of homelessness in America. Some studies have dealt with the causes and various factors in its etiology. The recent rapid increases in the number of the homeless population in various cities have spurred efforts to understand the reasons for homelessness and shelter dependency and service needs of this population. Current studies of homelessness have pointed at the heterogenous nature of the homeless population. Contending that the understanding of differences among subgroups of homeless population is vital, this article examines the differences between homeless men and homeless women. However, the analyses here concern individuals who seek lodging in public shelters—that is, a group which may differ significantly from those who do not come into shelters.

0979.   Fabricant, Michael, and Irwin Epstein. 1984. Legal and Welfare Right Advocacy: Complementary Approaches in Organizing on Behalf of the Homeless. **Urban and Social Change Review** 17 (1): 15-20.

Homelessness has become an increasingly visible problem in the United States in recent years. This visibility is primarily attributed to the increase in the number of those without permanent shelter. "It has been estimated that at least two million Americans were homeless during 1982. This number is likely to rise dramatically in the near future. Clearly as measured by any indicator, homelessness is a massive social problem that is affecting the quality of life in every American municipality." The author points out that the few beds available in each of these metropolitan areas are usually supported by private and church groups, for local and state governments have been unwilling, or unable, to extend even the minimum life sustaining support to the homeless. This raises the question of welfare rights for the homeless. This article provides "a case study of a welfare rights advocacy effort in behalf of the homeless in Elizabeth, New Jersey." On the basis of this and other organizing efforts, the author also examines the complementary aspects of legal and welfare rights advocacy. It is concluded that "the recent Elizabeth experience suggests that welfare rights advocacy in behalf of the homeless is an immediately effective and timely tool. It effectively complements the work of the legal advocate by attempting to assure immediate shelter and food while legal cases in behalf of the homeless are either pending or in earlier stages of development."

0980.   Fustero, Steven. 1984. Home on the Street. **Psychology Today** 18 (February): 56-63.

"It's winter and homelessness is a hot issue again, but solutions to the problem are as hard to find as a warm place to sleep." Regarding causes of homelessness, the author states that "the buying up and remodeling of inner-city houses and changing them from inexpensive rooming houses into single-family dwellings and expensive condos is also contributing to homelessness. New York, for instance, has lost thousands of such units in the past decade." This article also discusses the innovative approach in Phoenix, Arizona, and the private and voluntary organizations efforts in moving some off the homeless of the streets.

0981.   Garrett, Gerald R., and Howard M. Bahr. 1973. Women on Skid Row. **Quarterly Journal of Studies on Alcohol** 34 (4): 1228-43.

"The drinking patterns and practices of homeless women and men are compared. Homeless women alcoholics may well be the most isolated and disaffiliated residents of Skid Row." This finding is based on data gathered by personal interview with 52 of the 61 women admitted to the Women's Emergency Shelter in New York City's Bower District in 1969, and a random sample of 199 men at

Cam LaGuardia, referrals from the Men's Shelter on the Bowry. The authors also provide a socio-demographic profile of the men and women in their samples.

0982. Gebran, Gail. 1980. Community Housing for People with Chronic Mental Illness--A Federal Perspective: HUD. HUD Challenge 11 (11): 23-25.

This article describes the grand opening and dedication of a nine units apartment building in Crookston, Minnesota, for mentally ill homeless persons. The author points out that this is the first of its kind developed as a result of the HUD's demonstration program for homeless mentally ill.

0983. Goldman, Howard H., and Joseph P. Morrissey. 1985. The Alchemy of Mental Health Policy: Homelessness and the Fourth Cycle of Reform. American Journal of Public Health 75 (7): 727-31.

The history of public mental health policy is characterized by a cyclical pattern of institutional reforms. 'This paper examines a fourth cycle of reform emerging in the past decade in response to the failures of community mental health and deinstitutionalization."

0984. Hombs, Mary Ellen, and Mitch Snyder. 1983. Homelessness in America: A Forced March to Nowhere. Washington, D.C.: Community for Creative Non-Violence. 146 pp.

This is a monograph prepared by two advocates of the homeless who have spent time on the streets and who have extensive experience in working with the homeless on the streets and homeless shelters in Washington, D.C.   This publication examines the causes and dimensions of homelessness at the national level. It also discusses issues affecting its solution, and devastation of Reaganomics regarding homelessness. The most controversial aspect of this report is its estimate of the extent of homelessness in America (over 3 million homeless) which sharply differs from the 353,000 figure provided by HUD.

0985. Hope, Marjorie, and James Young. 1984. From Backwards to Back Alleys: Deinstitutionalization and the Homeless. Urban and Social Change Review 17 (2): 7-11.

This article discusses the relationship between deinstitutionalization and homelessness. It points out that "far more attention has been paid in the media to the 'new poor'--working or middle class victims of unemployment and displacement--than to the deinstitutionalized mentally disabled who form the hard core of the nation's homeless." The author maintains that many of the jobless with marketable skills will eventually return to work. But the hard core is expected to remain with us until some aggressive and innovative measure is developed to deal with groups of homeless population in the nation.

0986. Hopper, Kim, and Jill Hamberg. 1986. The Making of America's Homeless: From Skid Row to New poor, 1945-1984. In: Cricial Perspectives on Housing. Rachel G. Bratt, Chester Hartman, and Ann Meyerson (eds.). Philadelphia: Temple University Press. Pp. 12-40.

Given the nature of the housing problem and its increasing intensity, it is not surprising that substantial numbers of people are now facing the most extreme form of housing deprivation--not simply inadequate shelter but **homelessness.** The homelessness phenomenon stems not only from changes taking place in the housing market but also from changes in the labor market (occupational structure, general economic decline, and household demography), in the structure of our urban areas, and in public policies designed for "dependent" populations. What we are witnessing in the 1980s is the culmination of structural trends developing over the previous decade that will continue to intensify even during cyclical periods of economic discovery.*

0987.   Hopper, Kim. 1983. Homelessness: Reducing the Distance. **New England Journal of Human Services** 3 (4): 30-47.

"This article--a melange of impressions, observations and secondary data-- makes no pretense to comprehensiveness. Its primary aim is to reduce the distance between those of us still living lives of relative stability and those--some of them our neighbors until quite recently--living lives of uncertainty and precariousness." Relative to the cause of homelessness, the author asserts that loss of housing and shortage of low-income units, and unemployment can become immediate precipitating factors. He also points out that "no aspect of contemporary homelessness is more riddled with myths and misunderstandings than its perceived association with chronic mental disability." This lengthy sociological analysis of homelessness concludes with these words: "Our own capacity to care as a society is on trial. The burden of this article has been to recover the familiarity of the homeless poor, in the strict sense of the term, as extended family. There can be no excuse for ignoring the plea of kinsfolk."

0988.   Hopper, Kim. 1984. Whose Lives are These, Anyway? A Comment on the Recently Issues Report on the Homeless and Emergency Shelters by the Department of Housing and Urban Development. **Urban and Social Change Review** 17 (2): 12-13.

In May 1984 the U.S Department of Housing and Urban Development issued the study entitled: **A Report to the Secretary on the Homeless and Emergency Shelter** (cited below) that put the number of homeless population in the U.S. at not more than 353,000. The present article is a critical evaluation of this report by HUD. This critical analysis concludes that "the Reagan Administration has undertaken a policy of relentless dismantling of the federal housing programs that still exist. The annual amount of funds committed by HUD to assisted housing has declined by 78% since 1980. This administration places its trust, not in subsidy, but in 'the genius of the private market, freed of the distortions forced by government housing policies and regulations,' as the President' Commission on Housing put it in 1982. So long as the homeless must be counted among its multifarious spawn, questions will be raised about the providence of such genius. And as they are raised, they may be referred to the Circumlocation Office now ensconced on the Potomac."

0989.   Jones, Robert E. 1983. Street People and Psychiatry: An Introduction. **Hospital and Community Psychiatry** 34 (9): 807-11.

This article discusses the recent history of homelessness, causes of homelessness, media coverage of it, and the literature on the subject. It also provides a profile of the street people, and describes the role of the advocates for the homeless. The author concludes that homelessness is not a new problem in the United States, but during the current recession we have witnessed an unprecedented increase in the number of people who live on the streets of American cities.

0990. Kasinitz, Philip. 1984. Gentrification and Homelessness; The Single Room Occupant and their Inner City Revival. **Urban and Social Change Review** 17 (1): 9-14.

Many developers are buying up inner city land on which single room housing is built. Developers are turning these areas into high-priced condominiums, thus displacing the inner city dwellers with wealthier people. This process, called gentrification, is forcing poor people out into the streets because there is no longer sufficient low-income housing to be found in or out of the cities. The homeless cannot be absorbed into the new neighborhoods, they are not wanted there and they cannot afford to live there. Nor they are welcomed in the suburbs. Gentrification and inner city revival are processes that are harming society because nothing is being done to offset the adverse effects and widescale homelessness that they create.

0991. Kaufman, Nancy K. 1984. Homelessness: A Comprehensive Policy Approach. **Urban and Social Change Review** 17 (1): 21-26.

This article discusses different types (groups) of the homeless populations pointing out that a large number of them are those who have been evicted or ousted from their homes and neighborhoods because of condominium conversion and gentrification. It is pointed out that to deal with the dilemma, local solutions must be offered and the federal government must support the local efforts with policies and with funds. The article also discusses the costly homeless program in the State of Massachusetts. It argues the point that although such programs are costly, the alternatives are even more expensive and would allow the problem to continue to increase in scope.

0992. Kondratas, S. Anna. 1985. A Strategy for Helping America's Homeless. **Backgrounder--The Herritage Foundation.** (431): 1-13.

According to this article the most reliable estimate of the number of homeless population in the United States is between 25,000 and 350,000. This article disputes estimates that put the number of homeless between two and three million. The author asserts that the causes of homelessness are not unemployment and federal budget cuts. Rather, the chief causes of homelessness are ill conceived mental health and deinstitutionalization of the mentally ill and the loss of low-income housing stock due to urban development, gentrification, and rent control. "More federal funding is not the answer. States should face up to their obligations and bear a larger burden in assisting the homeless, including making better use of discretionary federal block grant funds. Most important, fundamental changes in mental health and housing policies at all levels of governments are essential if America is serious about eliminating homelessness."

0993. Lamb, H. Richard. 1984. Deinstitutionalization and the Homeless Mentally Ill. **Hospital and Community Psychiatry** 35 (9): 899-907.

In this article the author argues that mental illness, deinstitutionalization, and homelessness are closely linked. But, homelessness is not the result of deinstitutionalization per se. Rather, it is the product of the way deinstitutionalization has been carried out. The author points out that the lack of planning for structured living arrangements and for adequate treatment and rehabilitative services in the community has been responsible for much of homelessness in America.

0994. Lamb, H. Richard (ed.). 1984. **The Homeless Mentally Ill: A Task Force Report of the American Psychiatric Association.** Washington, D. C.: American Psychiatric Association. 320 pp.

This book consists of 14 chapters some of which have been previously published in one form or the other. As its title indicates, this book provides a psychiatric perspective of the homeless problem in the nation. However, some chapters deal with non-psychiatric issues such as developing better service delivery system, shelter and housing, the legal system and the homeless, and the politics of homelessness.

0995. Levinson, Boris M. 1957. The Socioeconomic Status, Intelligence, and Psychometric Patterns of Native-Born White Homeless Men. **Journal of Genetic Psychology** 91: 205-11.

A study made of native-born white homeless men showed that they have a much higher occupational status, better education, and are much older than the general homeless population. While some of differences may be due to the artifacts of the sample, other factors to be considered are that native-born Americans, as a whole, have more schooling, better employment, and more resources than foreign born. A study of the intelligence of native-born homeless men indicated that their WAIS [Wechsler Adult Intelligence Scale] verbal IQ is 101.3 with SD of 12.31, a performance IQ of 91.62 with DS of 10.90, a full scale IQ of 96.01 with an SD of 20.60.@

0996. Levinson, Boris M. 1963. The Homeless Man: A Psychological Enigma. **Mental Hygene** 47 (4): 590-601.

"In conclusion: To me, the homeless man is a symbol of what's wrong with our society, an indication of man's brutality to man. He is the beacon light warning us of the reefs ahead. It may be noted that when social conditions become worse, the number of homeless men increases. Finally, he is the Rosetta stone of social pathology and psychopathology. When the homeless man passes from the scene, it will be one of the major indices pointing out that a key to our major sociopsychopathological disorders has been found."

0997. Lipton, Frank R., Albert Sabastini, and Steven E. Katz. 1983. Down and Out in the City: The Homeless Mentally Ill. **Hospital and Community Psychiatry** 34 (9): 817-21.

This article discusses the plight of the homeless in New York City and other urban areas. It attempts to clarify and understand the problem of homelessness by examining the demographic characteristics, psychiatric diagnoses, histories and disposition of 100 homeless persons treated at Bellevue Psychiatric Hospital's emergency service. The major finding of this study is that 96.6 percent of the sample had had a previous psychiatric hospitalization.

0998.   Locke, Harvey J. 1935. Unemployed Men in Chicago Shelters. **Sociology and Social Research** 19: 421-28.

The Chicago Service Bureau for Men maintains 20 shelters for unemployed and unattached men in need of housing. Presently there are 16,725 men listed in the files using this service. Most of them receive both meals and lodging. This is an analysis of the social and personal characteristics of this group of homeless people.

0999.   Main, Thomas J. 1983. The Homeless of New York. **Public Interest** (72): 3-28.

This is a detailed study of various aspects of homelessness in New York City. The topics discussed include: legal advocacy, the involvement of courts, new improved shelters for the homeless, types of homelessness (psychiatric, alcoholic, economic, and physical disability), and guidelines for shelter policy.

1000.   Mapes, Lynda V. 1985. Faulty Food and Shelter Programs Draw Charges That Nobody's Home to Homeless. **National Journal** 17 (9): 474-76.

"In Reagan's first term, initiatives to convert military buildings to shelters and distribute surplus food barely got off the ground. This year, budget cuts loom." This article on housing the homeless points out that the number of homeless in America is on the rise. And, critiques say that the Reagan Administration is doing very little to relive their plight, because of the proposed new spending cuts.

1001.   McGerigle, Paul, Paul C. Hunt, and Susan White. 1979. **The Management of Family Housing Crisis in the City of Boston.** Boston: United Community Planning Corporation. 57 pp.

This report examines why dishoused and the homeless families seek shelter. It also reviews the systems that exist to relieve these problem. The authors suggest ways in which existing formal and informal response systems might be improved. They include providing additional shelter beds, locating temporary housing in the family's neighborhoods, looking for permanent housing, and providing counselling and legal assistance as well as emergency health care.

1002.   McGerigle, Paul, and Alison S. Lauriat. 1984. **More than Shelter: A Comunity Response to Homelessness.** Boston: United Community Planning and Massachusetts Association for Mental Health. 156 pp.

This study is the result of a year long investigation of the homeless. Its main finding is that the homeless are not merely victims of the housing shortage or street people by choice. Rather, the homeless constitute a diverse group of families and individuals often suffering from mental illness, poverty, and alcoholism who are trapped into homelessness. The

study concludes with a set of recommendations to improve the conditions of
the homeless, particularly with respect to financial and housing problems.

1003.   Segal, Steven P., Jim Baumohl, and Elsie Johnson.   1977.   Falling Through
the Cracks: Mental Disorder and Social Margin in a Young Vagrant Population.
Social Problems 24 (3): 387-400.

Twenty-two percent of a young vagrant population reported on in this study,
and believed to be representative of similar groups in many American cities,
have been hospitalized for psychological disorder. These young mentally
disordered vagrants are the most marginal members of the vagrant subculture,
lacking social margin (i.e. resources, relationships, and credible
identity) with their families, community services and their peers. Their
critical lack of social margin is due to an incongruence of expectations
between disordered vagrants and potential benefactors. This incongruence
generates a situation in which apparently eligible clients fall or slip
through cracks of a new chronically disordered and dependent population
housed, at best, in community-based sheltered living arrangements as they
grow older.*

1004.   Sloss, Michael. 1984. The Crisis of Homelessness: Its Dimensions and
Solutions. Urban and Social Change Review 17 (2): 18-20.

The lack of emergency shelters and housing for the thousands of homeless
people in the large cities is nothing less than a national crisis. This
article is a brief review of the problem with respect to the subculture of the
homeless and lack of shelter for the homeless. It concludes that "in the
absence of legal decisions establishing the rights of the homeless to decent
homes, all levels of government can turn their backs on the homeless as they
have done in the past. ...Ballot initiatives on the right to decent shelter
are potential organizing tools. Borough Councils in New York City have
already taken votes on establishment of shelters in their areas. Similar
actions can be taken by community-based religious and civic organizations to
help to create new shelters. Both legal and political efforts to improve
the plight of the homeless should take advantage of emphasizing the
diversity of the homeless population and the development of homelessness
as a vital political issue."

1005.   Stoner, Madeleine R. 1984. An Analysis of Public and Private Sector
Provisions for Homeless People. Urban and Social Change Review 17 (1): 3-8.

"This article reviews the types of programs that have emerged, or existed
prior to the public outcry against homelessness in 1981, to deal with the
problem. It offers a range of explanations about who the homeless are and
what appear to be the causes of their condition. The article recommends a
systematic approach to meet the needs of homeless people and offers an
assessment of recent government attempts at solution to the problem."

1006.   U.S. Department of Housing and Urban Development. 1984. A Report to the
Secretary on the Homeless and Emergency Shelters. Washington, D.C.: HUD,
Office of Policy Development and Development Research. 50 pp.
Appendixes.

"The purpose of this report is to provide the Secretary of the Department of

Housing and Urban Development (HUD) with data and information on homelessness and emergency shelter in America. While the topic of homelessness has received considerable public attention, there has been insufficient reliable data for assessing the extent of homelessness nationally, the characteristics of homeless persons, and the availability of emergency shelters across the country." This report attempts to provide answers to all of these questions. It estimates the total number of homeless population not to exceed 353,000. Because this estimate is sharply different from the estimates of 2.5 to 3.5 million homeless made by some advocates of the homeless population, this report has been the subject of much discussion and controversy.

1007. Winograd, Kenneth. 1983. **Street People and Other Homeless—A Pittsburgh Study.** Pittsburgh, Pennsylvania. Emergency Shelter Task Force, Allegheny County MH/MR/D&R Programs. 56 pp.

This report attempts to determine who are the homeless in Pittsburgh, where do they live, and what are their needs. Obviously, food, shelter, and health care were found to be among their basic needs. The report makes recommendations relative to short- and long-run solutions in dealing with the problem.

················◆◆◆◆◆◆◆◆◆◆················

AUTHOR INDEX

A

Abrams, Charles 1, 2, 215, 216
Ackerman, Bruce 790
Ackerman, Bruce L. 390
Agelasto, M. A., II 160
Agnew, John Alexander 896
Ahlbrandt, Roger S., Jr. 217, 583, 584
Aiken, Michael 686
Akre, M. Jan 585
Aldrich, Howard 3
Aleinkoff, A. 295
Alexander, Robert C. 4
Alford, Robert R. 686
Amick, Daniel J. 687
Anderson, Elaine A. 833
Anderson, J. G. 862
Anderson, James R. 789
Anderson, Martin 5
Anderson, Peggy Dilworth 834
Andrews, Judy 391
Anonymous 6-9, 218-222, 392, 393, 477, 532, 586-590, 688-695, 791-794, 967
Appelbaum, Richard P. 478
Arce, A. Anthony, et al. 968
Askwig, William James 479
Astorino, Robert L. 696
Atkinson, Reilly 10, 591
Auger, Deborah A. 897
Aurbach, H. A. 399
Aurbach, Herbert A. 795
Austin, David M. 592
Avins, Alfred 223, 394

B

Babcock, Richard 11
Bachrach, Leona L. 969
Bahr, Howard M. 296, 970, 981
Bailey, Martin J. 533
Bair, Frederick, Jr. 12
Bakerman, T. 399
Balk, Alfred 395
Ball, F. L. Jessica 971
Ball, William B. 13
Banfield, Edward C. 14, 765
Banks, Jerry 15
Barnes, Peter 480
Barnett, C. Lance 593
Bartell, Jeffrey B. 396
Barth, Ernest A. T. 444
Bassuk, Ellen L. 972
Bauman, Gus 16
Baumohl, Jim 1003
Baxter, Ellen 973, 974

Collins, Mary Evans 234, 715
Colton, Ken W. 94
Commission on Race and Housing 230
Constantino, Mark A. 797
Corcoran, Joseph E. 711
Courant, Paul N. 231
Connolly, Edward 48
Connolly, Harold X. 49
Conyers, John, Jr. 604
Cook, Christine C. 50
Cooper, James R. 51
Cooper, Mark N., et al. 52
Corl, Thomas C. 101
Cortese, Charles F. 302
Cottingham, Phoebe H. 406
Courter, Eileen M. 605
Cowger, Bob. 53
Cowgill, Donald O. 303-305
Cowgill, Mary S. 305
Coyne, Deirdre C. 54
Cozzens, William Oxford 606
Craig, Lois 407
Cramer, M. Richard 450
Cressey, Paul Frederick 55
Cromien, Florence 418
Crystal, Stephen 978
Cuomo, Mario Matthew 56
Curren, D. J. 842

D

Dagodag, William Tim 902
Dahmann, Donald C. 57, 58
Daniel, Edwin C. 232, 712
Daniels, Charles B. 306
Danielson, Michael N. 307
Darden, Joe T. 59, 308-315, 903
Darvish, Rokneddin 62
David, Harris 484
Davidoff, Paul 31
Davis, Tom L. 60
Davis, Otto A. 61
Dean, Andrea O. 607
Delaney, Paul 63
DeLaski-Smith, Deborah L. 840
DeLeeuw, Frank 64
Demerath, Nicholas J. 713
Demkowitch, Linda E. 233, 608
DePallo, Mildred 441, 766
DeSalvo, Joseph S. 609, 714
Deskins, Donald R. 65
Deutsch, Martin 234
Deutsch, Morton 715
Devlin, Ann Sloan 841

E

F

Ham, Andrew M.   105
Hamberg, Jill   986
Hamilton, Raymond Warren   730
Hamilton, William   591
Hamlar, Portia Trenholm   731
Hamm, Rita R.   338
Hancock, Paul Roger   497
Haney, J. B.   315
Haney, Richard L., Jr.   546
Hanna, Sherman   106
Hansen, Julia L.   107
Harris, Robert J.   412
Hartman, Chester   29, 108, 623-625, 732, 733, 913, 914
Havassy, Barbara E.   971
Havemann, J.   626
Harvey, D. Harvey   498
Haugen, Robert A.   499
Hauser, Philip M.   71
Hawkins, Homer C.   109
Hays, Charles   110
Hays, R. Allen   734, 915
Headey, Bruce   916
Heinberg, John D.   917
Heins, A. James   499
Heller, Tamar   850
Hellerstein, William E.   804
Helper, Rose 239
Henderson, Juanita   500
Hendon, William S.   240
Henkin, Louis   805
Hennelly, J.   335
Herbers, John   627
Henretta, John C.   547, 548
Heumann, Leonard F.   851
Hiestand, Fred J.   821
Hill, Herbert   111
Hirsch, Arnold R.   336
Hirshen, Al.   735-737
Hojnacki, W. P.   738
Hojnacki, William P.   112
Holbert, Kenneth 241
Holden, Stephen Michael   918
Holleb, Doris B.   113
Holmgren, Edward   425
Holshouser, William L.   426
Hombs, Mary Ellen   984
Hood, Edwin T.   242
Hoover, Sally   853
Hoover, Sally L.   852
Hope, Marjorie   985
Hopper, Kim   973, 974, 986-988
Hoshino, George   739
Houseman, Gerald L.   919
Howe, John   446

M

S

•••••••••

SUBJECT INDEX

···································◆◆◆◆◆◆◆◆◆◆···································

About the Author

JAMSHID A. MOMENI, Associate Professor of Sociology and Demography at Howard University, is the author of *Demography of the Black Population in the United States* (Greenwood Press, 1983), *Demography of Racial and Ethnic Minorities in the United States* (Greenwood Press, 1984), *Race, Ethnicity, and Minority Housing in the United States* (Greenwood Press, 1986) and other books, as well as several scholarly journal articles on housing, population, and related topics.